HIDDEN
WATERS
~ of ~
New York
City

HIDDEN
WATERS
~ of ~
New York City

A History and Guide to
101 Forgotten Lakes, Ponds,
Creeks, and Streams
in the Five Boroughs

Sergey Kadinsky

THE COUNTRYMAN PRESS

A division of W. W. Norton & Company

Independent Publishers Since 1923

Copyright © 2016 by Sergey Kadinsky

For information about permission to reproduce selections from this book,
write to Permissions, The Countryman Press,
500 Fifth Avenue, New York, NY 10110

For information about special discounts for bulk purchases, please
contact W. W. Norton Special Sales at specialsales@wwnorton.com
or 800-233-4830

Library of Congress Cataloging-in-Publication Data

Names: Kadinsky, Sergey, author.
Title: Hidden waters of New York City : a history and guide to 101
forgotten lakes, ponds, creeks, and streams in the five boroughs / Sergey Kadinsky.
Description: Woodstock, VT : The Countryman Press, [2016] |
Includes bibliographical references and index.
Identifiers: LCCN 2015041163 | ISBN 9781581573558 (paperback)
Subjects: LCSH: Bodies of water—New York (State)—New York—History. |
Bodies of water—New York (State)—New York—
Guidebooks. | New York (N.Y.)—Description and travel.
Classification: LCC GB705.N7 K33 2016 | DDC 551.4809747/1—dc23
LC record available at http://lccn.loc.gov/2015041163

The Countryman Press
www.countrymanpress.com

A division of W. W. Norton & Company, Inc.
500 Fifth Avenue, New York, N.Y. 10110
www.wwnorton.com

1 2 3 4 5 6 7 8 9 0

As they before these Rivers bounds did show,
Here I come after with my Pen and row.

—John Taylor ("The Water Poet"),
1578–1653

In memory of my grandfather, Zakhar Vaysbukh,
who encouraged me to inquire.

In memory of my father, Anatoliy Kadinsky,
who took me on roads not taken.

~ Contents

THE BRONX

QUEENS

BROOKLYN

STATEN ISLAND

~ *Introduction*

The city of New York is built around water. Its avenues run parallel to the shorelines of the East and Hudson Rivers, while streets once extended beyond the shores as piers. Now, at the turn of the 21st century, large swaths of the formerly industrial waterfront have been transformed into parks and ferry docks. The city's waterways have become a place where the public is reminded of nature's presence in the city. Examples of celebrated waterfront parks include Hudson River Park, Brooklyn Bridge Park, and Gantry Plaza State Park, with their postmodern landscaping, canoe launches, and naturalistic appearance that preserves relics of their industrial past.

Farther inland, however, waterways are not as visible, having been buried beneath streets and concealed behind buildings. If one searches carefully, one can hear sounds of hidden streams churning beneath manholes and see traces of them in street names that recall a watery past. These now-hidden urban streams provided the wampum shells used as currency by the native Lenape people, powered the gristmills of New York's colonial settlements, and served as freight transportation corridors during the Industrial Revolution.

As other international cities are reclaiming their hidden streams, New York, too, offers numerous examples of stream reclamation throughout its five boroughs. This book serves as a guide to the streams by tracing their historical development along their courses. Each entry follows the routes of the waterways—along the way documenting events, personalities, and structures associated with each stream.

Some of the hidden streams that avoided burial are now experiencing a new life as linear parks, storm water conduits, and cultural venues. Along the shores of the Gowanus Canal and Newtown Creek in Brooklyn, intrepid canoe enthusiasts now ply the waters—which are still reeking of waste but are no longer lifeless, as fish and mollusk species repopulate the channels. In Manhattan, appreciation of history is exemplified in Collect Pond Park, a one-acre green space in Manhattan's Civic Center whose name commemorates a pond where many pivotal events took place in the first two centuries of the city's history. In 2012, the city began a reconstruction project that included a reflecting pool to evoke the park's namesake pond. To the northwest, Canal Street had two new parks built in the first decade of the new century that recall the long-buried namesake of this busy roadway. On Staten Island, instead of sewers, an innovative Bluebelt program repurposed the borough's ponds and creeks as natural drainage corridors for runoff coming from nearby streets, reducing the burden for sewage treatment plants.

The city's revived streams are benefiting their surrounding communities— contributing to increased land values, improved quality of life, and greater environmental sustainability. As in New York's early years as a Dutch colonial outpost, when canals served as transportation routes and ponds provided drinking water, inland waterways today have resumed their role as vital elements of the city's identity; providers of a sense of place.

~ *Exploring the Streams*

Nearly all surface streams are within walking distance of public transportation, and many are located within public parks.

For streams that are buried beneath the surface, this book follows their former courses, from their sources to their mouths, describing neighborhoods and landmarks above the surface whose history is closely intertwined with the streams.

Landmarks and places of interest on or near the streams, including places no longer extant, are in bold lettering.

Manhattan

➤ **The island of Manhattan is as diverse in its geology** as in its human population. Prior to European settlement, its waterways included kettle ponds, salt marshes, freshwater swamps, and springs that satiated the Lenape natives.

As the most densely developed of New York City's five boroughs, Manhattan initially covered its inland streams, but as early as the 1850s revived them in the form of managed waterways—for example, in Central Park. Central Park's ponds, fed by the city's aqueduct, coexist with reservoirs that once quenched the growing city's thirst.

To the north of 125th Street, the island of Manhattan gradually narrows until it reaches its northernmost tip, at the confluence of the Harlem and Hudson Rivers. A series of ridges separate the watersheds of the East and Hudson Rivers.

1. Collect Pond

The best-documented hidden waterway in Lower Manhattan is **Collect Pond**, which supplied drinking water to colonial settlers in the 17th and 18th centuries. Its center and deepest point was at the present-day intersection of Leonard and Centre Streets. The pond occupied 48 acres in an outline that includes present-day **Foley Square**, New York City Criminal Court, New York City Department of Health, and the New

MANHATTAN

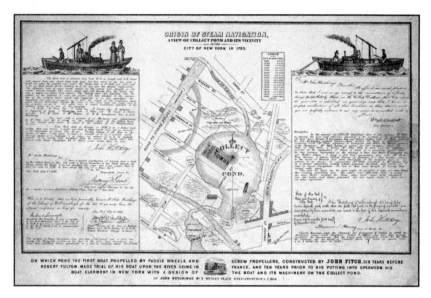

View of Collect Pond and its vicinity in the City of New York in 1793

York City Supreme Court. At Worth Street, a neck of land jutted into the pond, separating Little Collect from the larger section of the pond.

Following the pond's burial in 1825, its site continued to contribute to New York City's history as the location of the notorious Five Points slum district and **the Tombs** prison. In recent years, the pond has enjoyed a revival in the city's consciousness, with a reflecting pool as the centerpiece of a redesigned park that opened in 2014.

A kettle pond

When the Pleistocene period ice sheet gradually retreated north (nearly 15,000 years ago), chunks of ice that were detached from the ice cap melted on location, forming deep, kettle-shaped ponds. The 70-foot-deep Collect Pond had two outlets that drained into the Hudson River and the East River. In the event of a storm surge, these brooks would be swollen with seawater, severing Lower Manhattan from the rest of the island. Along the outflow brooks, beavers built dams to trap the alewives, sunfish, and perch that lived in the pond. **Old Wreck Brook** drained into the East River, winding through **Wolfert's Marsh**, where the Brooklyn Bridge was later constructed. The western outlet flowed through **Lispenard's Meadow** toward the Hudson River along a path that later became Canal Street.

On the southern side of the pond was **Werpoes**, the largest native

Lenape village in Lower Manhattan. Its location was chosen because the pond provided a steady supply of food and water. To the north of the pond, hills isolated the village from the surrounding landscape, in a natural amphitheater setting.

When the Dutch colonists arrived in 1625, they noted shells lining the shore and named the pond Kalck Hoek, or "lime point," as the shells resembled lime. Some say this name was later corrupted into the pond's English name, Collect Pond, though this theory is far from definitive.

The city's source of drinking water

When the Dutch settlers founded New Amsterdam at the southern tip of Manhattan, it quickly became a vital trading post because of its deep natural harbor and connections to major waterways. Settler Jacob Steendam penned a poem praising New Amsterdam's geography:

> *See: two streams my garden bind,*
> *From the East and North they wind,—*
> *Rivers pouring in the sea,*
> *Rich in fish, beyond degree.*

Steendam's poem was about Manhattan Island, but he failed to mention that with so much water in proximity, very little of it was pota-

Lithograph of the origin of steam navigation, a view of Collect Pond and its vicinity in the City of New York in 1796. The boat was piloted by inventor John Fitch and subsequently taken apart for scraps.

ble. Within New Amsterdam, the water provided by wells tended to be brackish, mixed with seawater that seeped into the groundwater. So the colonists looked north, and they found Collect Pond to serve as a source of freshwater for the young city.

In 1774, Christopher Colles proposed turning the pond into a reservoir, with wooden pipes to channel the water to the city, but work on this project was halted in April 1776, as hostilities developed between the colonists and the British authorities. Five months later, much of Lower Manhattan was engulfed in flames as the Revolutionary War raged around the metropolitan region. For much of the war, the city was a refuge for loyalists, and a formidable British garrison occupied Manhattan.

During this period, Prince William—the future King William IV—served as a midshipman on Admiral Robert Digby's fleet. According to Dutchess County resident Fitz-Greene Halleck, the royal heir was ice-skating atop Collect Pond in 1781 and fell through the ice. Halleck rescued the prince, but once the British authorities found out, he was no longer allowed to freely skate or stroll through New York unaccompanied.

To the east of the pond, at the present-day intersection of Baxter and Mulberry Streets, the **Tea Water Pump** supplied water used for brewing tea. This pump was popular enough to be used as a reference marker on 18th-century maps, and carts delivered the pump's water in barrels to eager customers. There were so many of these vendors that in 1757, the Common Council passed a law limiting their number. The same legislative body declared the pump a nuisance in 1797 and ordered it closed.

As the city expanded, the once-pristine pond became polluted. Local residents washed their linens in it and dumped their refuse into it, and fluids from nearby dyeing businesses drained into it. In 1799, Aaron Burr's Manhattan Company applied for the license to operate Colles Reservoir farther north, which would serve as a new source of drinking water. By then, Collect Pond was shrinking in size as development crept up around it, and Burr had plans to use his Manhattan Company to supply water from new sources. The company he founded to achieve this eventually became today's Chase Bank.

Slavery at the pond

Throughout the colonial period, New York had an uneasy relationship with its African American population, which included both slaves and freedmen. All had arrived in the city as slaves from western Africa, often stopping in the Caribbean to be "seasoned," or trained for a life of servitude. During the Dutch administration, many slaves were able to secure either complete or partial freedom, and they established a community of farms in present-day Greenwich Village.

The English were less tolerant, enacting laws that prohibited African Americans from being buried within the city or from owning land, and they levied a tax on owners who freed their slaves. A new cemetery was established on the city's northern outskirts, to the southeast of Collect Pond. This 6.6-acre site was known as the **African Burial Ground**. From 1697 to 1784, between 15,000 and 20,000 individuals were interred at this site.

Among those buried here were the 21 executed for taking part in the slave revolt of 1712. A second series of executions occurred in May 1741 following a wave of arsons and illegal gatherings of black individuals. In total, 17 blacks and 4 whites were executed outside a gunpowder storage magazine located on a peninsula in the pond, a spot called **Magazine Island**. The site of these executions is presently occupied by the Jacob K. Javits Federal Office Building, better known as **26 Federal Plaza**.

In 1794, the African Burial Ground was covered with 25 feet of landfill and developed. The cemetery didn't reemerge in the city's consciousness until 1991, when construction workers uncovered coffins on the block of Reade Street between Broadway and Elk Street. In total, 419 bodies were exhumed and then reburied, with full honors, following a historically charged procession. In 2003, the **African Burial Ground National Monument** officially opened to the public.

A block to the east, the southern tip of Foley Square, also known as **Thomas Paine Park**, was expanded to five acres in the 1990s, covering parts of the former cemetery's land. At the tip of the park is a monument, *Triumph of the Human Spirit* by Lorenzo Pace, which honors the city's early black residents. The abstract granite sculpture's design was inspired by the Chi Wara carved-antelope headdresses of the Bambara people in Mali. It sits atop an elongated boatlike structure that symbolizes canoes used by Native Americans as well as the Middle Passage of enslaved Africans crossing the Atlantic. The artist's own personal ancestry is referenced in the design with a replica of the inherited lock and key that held his great-great-grandfather in bondage.

On the pavement around the monument, medallions contain relief maps of Civic Center through the centuries. On these maps, one can see how Collect Pond shrank in size until its unceremonious burial in 1811.

The pond is buried

At the end of the 18th century, two competing proposals were envisioned for Collect Pond: its preservation and its demise. Under a 1788 plan by Pierre Charles L'Enfant, the pond would have been the centerpiece of a park that followed a canal between the East and Hudson Rivers. L'Enfant, a French-born civil engineer, went on to earn fame as the designer of the Washington, D.C., street grid.

New York's leaders had other plans for the pond, though. The eastern shore of Collect Pond became an industrial community of tanneries and slaughterhouses that polluted the pond, turning the city's first source of drinking water into an open-air sewer. City leaders feared that the pond was a health hazard and an impediment to the city's growth. In 1805, a 40-foot-wide canal was dug to the northeast of Collect Pond, taking its waters to the Hudson River. This canal became Canal Street, the extra-wide road that nearly traverses Manhattan from east to west.

Together with Canal Street, the pond was covered with fill from nearby **Bayard's Mount** and **Mount Pleasant**, two steep hilltops located north of the pond. In 1802, leveling began on the storied hill, revealing relics from the revolution. By 1811, Bayard's Mount was flattened, and so was the site of Collect Pond. A new neighborhood would rise atop the former pond, optimistically named Paradise Square.

The filthy and fearsome Five Points

The development of Collect Pond began on its eastern side, where the Bowery passed by the pond. This timeless route predates European settlement, connecting Lower Manhattan with points north. Around 1750, **Bull's Head Tavern** was established at what is now 50 Bowery. A popular stop for the cattle ranchers heading into the city, it was eventually surrounded by stockyards and became the city's first "meatpacking district." In 1813, the tavern relocated uptown to Third Avenue and East 24th Street, where it survived into the 1830s. With its location just north of the city's gates, the tavern served as a symbolic gateway into the city.

Although the pond was gone, poor drainage and landfill work resulted in soil that emitted methane gas and caused buildings' foundations to crumble. The gentry moved out, and a slum district developed. Paradise Square received a new moniker: **Five Points**, where Orange Street (now Baxter Street), Cross Street (now Mosco Street), Anthony Street (now Worth Street), and Little Water Street (no longer extant) all met.

The ground beneath this intersection gradually sunk in. Whenever there was rain, mosquitoes and disease followed. The neighborhood fell under the control of slumlords, organized crime groups, and corrupt politicians. While the living conditions were squalid, there was also an unprecedented level of social cohesion, as free blacks were living alongside poor whites.

The most notable building in Five Points was **Coulthard's Brewery**, built in 1792 near the southeast corner of Collect Pond. At the time, this part of the pond was called **Cow Bay** after the local livestock, who drank from this spot. The road extending into this neck of land was called **Little Water Street**. By the 1820s, the pond and the cows were gone, and the brewery was surrounded by tenements. In his 1842 visit to Five Points, British writer Charles Dickens very likely passed by Jacob's Ladder, a building accessible only by an exterior ladder. He wrote:

> *What place is this, to which the squalid street conducts us? A kind of square of leprous houses, some of which are attainable only by crazy wooden stairs without. What lies behind this tottering flight of steps? Let us go on again, and plunge into the Five Points. This is the place; these narrow ways diverging to the right and left, and reeking everywhere with dirt and filth.*

The brewery survived as a business until its bankruptcy in 1837. Hastily transformed and divided into apartments, it creaked on until 1852, when the Methodist Ladies of the Mission purchased it and had it demolished the following year. Establishing a mission in the heart of the notorious slum was a symbolic gesture, and it survives in the neighborhood to this day as the local nonprofit **Five Points Mission**.

Five Points to Civic Center

Throughout its quarter-century existence, Five Points had a reputation for averaging one murder per day. A block to the north of the Five Points intersection was another dangerous corner, the **Mulberry Bend**, a slight curve on Mulberry Street that enabled muggers to easily await their prey. Lined on both sides with firetrap tenements, this block was the site of numerous riots and shoot-outs. Its geography is a lasting legacy of the pond, as the street made its curve to avoid Collect Pond when it existed.

Recognizing the crowded conditions of Mulberry Bend, landscape architect Calvert Vaux proposed to raze the entire block and replace it with a park. The arrival of the country's leading park designer was a promising sign. Vaux's résumé included Central and Prospect Parks—sizable greenswards of preserved nature in the rapidly developing city.

Among the supporters of the proposed park was Jacob Riis, a Danish-born photographer whose book *How the Other Half Lives* documented the squalid conditions of Manhattan's immigrant slums.

Where Mulberry Street crooks like an elbow within hail of the old depravity of the Five Points, is "the Bend," foul core of New York's slums. Long years ago the cows coming home from the pasture trod a path over this hill. Echoes of tinkling bells linger there still, but they do not call up memories of green meadows and summer fields; they proclaim the home-coming of the rag-picker's cart.

The park opened in the summer of 1897, with bench-lined curved walkways and a lawn in its center. In 1911, it was renamed **Columbus Park**.

On the south side of Worth Street, the century-old Paradise Park triangle was replaced between 1913 and 1927 by the **New York County Courthouse**, a classical revival hexagonal structure that also wiped Little Water Street from the map. Within a half century, its new neighbors included the federal, state, and city courts. None of the Five Points tenements remain, and only three of the points are left in the old neighborhood's namesake intersection.

The pond returns to the surface

In the 1980s, Parks Commissioner Henry J. Stern restored Collect Pond to the map by renaming Civic Center Park as **Collect Pond Park**. In the aftermath of the September 11, 2001, terrorist bombing of the World Trade Center, the city and state founded the Lower Manhattan Development Corporation to coordinate rebuilding work in Lower Manhattan. Among its projects was a $4.9 million postmodern makeover for Collect Pond Park, which was expanded and given a **reflecting pool** that echoes the outlines of the original pond. At the pool's narrow waist, it is spanned by a metal bridge. Around the "pond," signs explain its long history and impact on the city's development.

The park was designed in-house by the Parks Department, with Nancy Owens Studio and Abel Bainnson Butz serving as outside historical and planning consultants. The introduction of a pond-shaped pool to the park lends a visual detail to its name, solidifying the connection to its storied namesake.

PLACES TO SEE:

✦ **Collect Pond Park** Bound by Centre Street, Franklin Street, Lafayette Street, and Leonard Street ✦ www.nycgovparks.org/parks/M242/history

✦ **Foley Square/Thomas Paine Park** Bound by Centre Street, Worth Street, Lafayette Street, and Duane Street ✦ www.nycgovparks.org/parks/thomaspainepark/history

✦ *Triumph of the Human Spirit* **sculpture** Foley Square Park at junction of Lafayette Street and Centre Street ✦ www.nycgovparks.org/parks/thomaspainepark/highlights/19692

✦ **African Burial Ground National Monument** Duane Street at Elk Street ✦ www.nps.gov/afbg/index.htm

✦ **Columbus Park** Bound by Baxter Street, Mulberry Street, Worth Street, and Bayard Street ✦ www.nycgovparks.org/parks/M015/history

✦ **New York County Courthouse** 60 Centre Street ✦ www.nycourts.gov/courts/1jd/supctmanh

✦ **Federal Plaza** Worth Street at Lafayette Street

GETTING THERE:

✦ **Bus**: M22 at Worth Street and Centre Street; M5 downtown at Broadway and Worth Street

✦ **Subway**: J, Z at Chambers Street; 4, 5, 6 at Brooklyn Bridge–City Hall

✦ **Bike**: There is a bike lane on Lafayette Street

2. Canal Street

The most traveled crosstown road in Manhattan below Midtown is **Canal Street**, which originates on the Lower East Side and runs westward through Little Italy, Chinatown, SoHo, and Tribeca toward the Hudson River. For much of its path, Canal Street is a link between the Manhattan Bridge and the Holland Tunnel, a through route for vehicles bypassing Manhattan. Along the way is America's largest Chinatown, a tight-knit ethnic community dating to 1858.

When standing on the corner of Broadway and Canal Street, looking north and south, one would notice a slight rise in elevation in both directions, indicating that Canal Street occupies the bottom of a valley.

Bridge at Broadway and Canal Street, 1811

Between 1807 and 1821, a canal ran down the middle of this street, draining the water of Collect Pond. During the namesake canal's short existence, it was lined with trees planted to shield local residents from the foul water. Although the pond and its canal were both buried by 1819, the stench lingered for decades, and Canal Street kept its name for eternity.

Prior to European settlement, land along present-day Canal Street was a salt meadow. In the 1670s, an influx of Huguenot refugees settled in New York. On the western shore of Manhattan, settler Anthony Lispenard was a prominent local leader, serving as an alderman, an assemblyman, and a treasurer of King's College (renamed Columbia University after the American Revolution). Until it was drained in the 1820s, the salt meadow around the future Canal Street was called **Lispenard's Meadow**. Lispenard Street in Tribeca also recalls this early settler.

Old Stone Bridge

During the canal's brief existence, a scenic stone bridge was constructed at Broadway, enabling the city's widest street to continue on its march northward. Prior to this bridge, the northward route out of the city was the precolonial **Weckquaesgeek Trail**, a route that made its way through Manhattan using present-day Park Row, Bowery, and Broadway north of Union Square. All three of these streets continue to defy the post-1811 grid. The extension of Broadway across the canal created a straight path between City Hall and Union Square, spurring the development of what would later become SoHo and Greenwich Village.

On the northeastern corner of Canal Street and Broadway stood **Stone Bridge Tavern**, a popular stop on the newly built route. With the burial of the canal, the bridge and tavern would have disappeared as well from public memory were it not for a woodcut depiction of them from 1800 that preserved the bucolic scene.

A century later, when the Nassau Street subway line was constructed, artist Jay Van Everen used the woodcut as a model for his mosaic tiles in the Canal Street station. The tiles, in color, perpetuate the memory of Canal Street's namesake. These tiles were relocated to the New York Transit Museum in the 1990s, with replicas on sale in the museum's gift shop.

Canal Park

When streets were laid out around Canal Street, colliding grids of opposing neighborhoods resulted in the formation of traffic triangles that later became public parks. Two of them, **Canal Park** and **Albert Capsouto Park**, today feature signage and landscaping that remind visitors of Canal Street's namesake.

Canal Park is the older of the two, located at a triangular intersection of Canal Street and West Street—the latter street perhaps better known as the West Side Highway. According to the plaque at the entrance of Canal Park, credit is given to King James II, who signed Governor Thomas Dongan's Charter of the City of New York on April 27, 1686. In this early city document, all "waste, vacant, unpatented and unappropriated lands" were assigned to the jurisdiction of the Common Council. Among the unused land was Lispenard's Meadow, which included the parcel that became Canal Park.

In 1833, this triangular city-owned plot at Canal Street and West Street was developed as **Clinton Market**, named after Governor DeWitt Clinton. The market arrived after nearly a decade of debates around its location—atop a buried sewer. "Your Committee cannot perceive why the presence of the Mammoth Sewer of Canal Street should not be as valid an objection against building a market," says a report submitted to the Common Council, arguing against building a market. The report cited the Fly Market on Maiden Lane as an example of another market that had to be removed because it was built atop a buried stream.

The committee's report was prescient. Clinton Market was built, but by 1860, it was described in the *New York Tribune* as "the old rotten building in the centre of the triangle." It was demolished less than 30 years after it opened and was replaced with a wagon parking area.

In 1871, the newly created Department of Public Parks planted trees and shrubs on the triangle, with a wrought-iron fence around its perimeter. This park existed until the neighborhood industrialized in 1921, and the city loaned the park's land to the New York/New Jersey Bridge and Tunnel Authority to use for construction of the **Holland Tunnel**. The tunnel opened to traffic on November 13, 1927.

The closing of the park for tunnel construction was only supposed to last four years, but as the area became more industrial, the city felt that a park was unnecessary for this location. Instead, the land served as a sanitation parking lot for the next eight decades.

While the Holland Tunnel passed below the former park, the elevated **Miller Highway** kept the site in its shadow between 1929 and 1973. Designed in conjunction with the High Line freight railway, this highway was intended to take traffic above West Street, speeding up commerce along the busy Hudson River piers.

The elevated highway was dismantled in the 1980s, and the boulevard-like West Street took its place as the **West Side Highway**. With the new highway's construction came the **Hudson River Park**, a thin green ribbon of shoreline land that stretches from Battery Park to Riverside Park.

While conducting research on the West Side Highway, resident Richard Barrett and the Tribeca Community Association discovered on old maps that the triangular parking lot was once a park and had been owned by the city since 1686. The civic group Canal West Coalition lobbied to restore Canal Park to its Victorian design and to improve traffic flow around the triangle. Thanks to their efforts, the park reopened in 2005.

The success of the park is reflected by the local businesses that have adopted its name. At 505 Canal Street is the **Canal Park Playhouse**, a neo-vaudeville performance space housed in an 1826 Federal-style brick structure, which opened to the public in 2010. At 508 Canal Street, the **Canal Park Inn** opened less than a year after the theater, offering country-style lodging in the big city. The four rooms of the hotel—Batby, Sinnot, Denot, and Kennedy—are named after the families that once occupied the building. Triple-glazed windows ensure that traffic noise from Canal Street does not disturb the inner serenity of this urban bed-and-breakfast.

Capsouto Park

In contrast to Canal Park, **Capsouto Park** has a much shorter history—but what it lacks in age, it makes up for with historical plaques and public artwork that reference the canal buried beneath. Located at the junction of Canal, Varick, and Laight Streets, this former parking lot was redesigned in 2008 by Parks Capital Designer Gail Wittwer-Laird and SoHo artist Elyn Zimmerman. Its winding paths pay tribute to the Victorian-period pocket parks such as the nearby Canal Park. At each of the three entrances to the triangular park are etched stainless-steel plaques with historical images from the New-York Historical Society, New York Public Library, and Library of Congress.

The park attraction that puts the canal back into Canal Street is a 114-foot-long sculptural fountain by Zimmerman. The water originates in a waterfall, which passes through locks and spills along a straight path framing the park's northern border. The location of this "spillway" separates the park's lawn from the traffic of Canal Street, replacing honking horns with the sound of rushing water.

Initially, the park was named CaVaLa Park, a pun on the three streets on its border: Canal, Varick, and Laight. Seeking to inject history in place of humor and tired of acronym toponyms inspired by gentrification (think SoHo, Tribeca, Nolita), local civic organizations and Community Board 2 proposed renaming the park after Albert Capsouto. Capsouto was a founder of the Tribeca Organization and a member of Community Board 1. He died of a brain tumor in January 2009 at age 53. In October 2010, CaVaLa Park became Capsouto Park.

Along the length of Canal Street west of Broadway, surging land values and availability of funds for park expansion have resulted in the dedication of many more new parks along Canal Street that recall its namesake canal.

PLACES TO SEE:

✦ **Canal Park** Bound by Canal Street, West Street, and Washington Street
✦ **Capsouto Park** Bound by Canal Street, Varick Street, and Laight Street

GETTING THERE:

✦ **Bus**: M20 uptown at Hudson Street and Laight Street; M20 downtown at Varick Street and Watts Street
✦ **Subway**: 1 at Canal Street (at Varick Street); A, C, E at Canal Street (at Sixth Avenue)
✦ **Bike**: There are bike lanes on Grand Street and Lafayette Street in proximity to Canal Street; the Hudson River Greenway also intersects with Canal Street

3. Minetta Brook

Greenwich Village is perhaps the most storied of all the residential neighborhoods in Lower Manhattan. Through the heart of this urban village flows an underground stream—one that occasionally reappears in flooded basements, flowing beneath alleys that carry its name.

Minetta Brook originated from two tributaries, the main one having its source near what is now Fifth Avenue and 21st Street, and a secondary one at Sixth Avenue and 16th Street. The streams merged at a point just west of the intersection of Fifth Avenue and 11th Street.

The stream continued into what became **Washington Square Park**, turning southwest toward the Hudson River. One of the curves in the stream was immortalized in the form of **Minetta Street**, a one-block alley in the heart of Greenwich Village. At its northern end, this street intersects with **Minetta Lane**.

The stream's name is a variation of a commonly used Algonquin term: *manitou* or "spirit," a toponym that appears throughout the northeastern states and as far west as the Canadian province of Manitoba. Local historians believed that Minetta translated as "evil spirit" or "snake water."

According to the Lenape religion, Minetta was an evil snake spirit who tormented humanity from the dawn of time until the heroic Nanabush forced him underground. In 1609, the natives observed the arrival of Europeans aboard tall sailing ships and wondered whether they represented this heroic spirit.

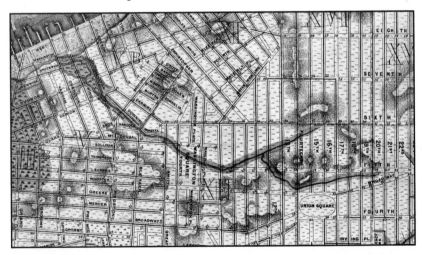

Approximate course of Minetta Creek, overlayed with street grid as of 1865

Natives and Africans along the creek

Where the present-day Meatpacking District is located was once an Unami-speaking Lenape village and trading post, **Sapokanikan**, which translates to "tobacco field." For the native residents of Manhattan, tobacco served as currency, alongside wampum belts made from shells. When the Dutch colonized the island, they established tobacco farms on the site of the former Lenape village. It was a dangerous location, outside of the protective palisade of Wall Street, and the Dutch farms were subject to attacks by the displaced natives.

In Washington Square

Among Manhattan's numbered avenues, Fifth Avenue has the strongest identity and status. Its 137-block route features iconic skyscrapers, upscale shopping, Museum Mile, and Central Park. Its southern terminus is marked by the **Washington Square Arch**, a monument completed in 1889 on the centennial of George Washington's inauguration as president.

The 9.75-acre **Washington Square Park** is the historic meeting space in the heart of Greenwich Village—a space for street performances, outdoor chess, graduation celebrations, and political protests. The park is sprinkled with monuments and markers attesting to its history as a cultural hub. But prior to the park's development, Minetta Brook ran across this land, from Fifth Avenue toward the park's southwest corner. Along its banks, tobacco fields fueled the native and early colonial economies.

It was along this section of the stream that freed slaves Big Manuel and Paul Angola established their farms in 1643, after being granted "half freedom" by the Dutch West India Company. Along with nine other former slaves, they founded New York's first African American community. At the time, this "Little Africa" was on the northern outskirts of New Amsterdam, a swampy expanse that acted as a buffer between the town and hostile natives farther north. Early mapmakers dubbed a path along Minetta Brook, which connected their farms, Negroes Causeway.

In 1797, the farms were repurposed as cemeteries, shared between a city-run potter's field and local churches. Over the following 30 years, more than 20,000 dead were interred here. Near the northwest corner of Washington Square Park, the **Hanging Elm** is a reminder of a time when convicts were publicly executed and then buried in this potter's field.

The number of dead increased dramatically in the series of yellow fever epidemics that swept across the city between 1797 and 1803. The graveyard filled up, and the city purchased land for a second cemetery on the site of the future Bryant Park. As the city expanded north, the potter's field was forced to island-hop, relocating to Wards Island and finally to Hart Island in 1869.

When the potter's field was rezoned as parkland in 1826, most of the bodies were removed; but on occasion, during construction in Washington Square Park, coffins may still be found. This happened most recently in 2009—a tombstone dating to 1799 and attributed to 28-year-old Irish immigrant James Jackson, a victim of yellow fever.

In the 1820s, what remained of Minetta Brook on the surface was buried by leveling the Sand Hills to its east.

Since 1827, Washington Square Park has served as an open public space. In its most recent redesign, the central fountain was aligned to stand in the park's center, facing Fifth Avenue. There are no plans, however, to daylight or recreate the buried portion of Minetta Brook that ran through the park.

Little Africa

After African American farms gave way to a potter's field, the center of the black community was Minetta Street, a one-block street to the south of Washington Square Park, with an elbow-like bend that once followed a turn in the stream.

Atop the buried stream, tenements were built and settled with successive generations of African American newcomers. As older residents moved uptown, former slaves from Virginia replaced them.

The alleys and tight turns along Minetta Street made it a haven for crime—an uptown version of Five Points. When local residents weren't dodging fists and bullets, they drank and danced in "black-and-tan saloons," given this name because of their mixed clientele, a rarity in 19th-century America. Social reformer Jacob Riis brought his camera to Minetta Street in the 1890s. He described the slums as "vile rookeries." Journalist Stephen Crane described Minetta Lane and Minetta Street as "two of the most enthusiastically murderous thoroughfares in the city."

The Italian village

Minetta Lane remained the heart of New York's Little Africa into the first decade of the 20th century. By then, many of the neighborhood's African American churches had relocated uptown to Harlem. In the place of black migrants, Italian immigrants streamed in. Developer Vincent Pepe found the tangled streets of Greenwich Village charming and sought to beautify the slum. He bought the tenements and razed them in 1924. In their place stood his artist-friendly development, **the Minettas**. On both sides of the street, Pepe designed townhouses with a common backyard used as a garden.

"The artist, the writer, the creator of beauty in any medium—these are the men for whom the Minettas should be preserved," Pepe wrote in a promotional brochure. A 1923 article in the *New York Times* described the development "as free from noise and as peaceful as though miles away." The picturesque quality of Minetta Street attracted artists, and Greenwich Village quickly became the bohemia of New York—the local version of the Left Bank in Paris.

A block to the east of the former stream, **Minetta Tavern** opened in doors in 1937. Among its early regulars were Ernest Hemingway, Ezra Pound, Eugene O'Neill, E. E. Cummings, and Dylan Thomas. A museum of neighborhood history as much as a restaurant, the interior walls are painted with scenes from the Greenwich Village of the 1920s.

A more recent arts-related destination that carries the stream's name is **Minetta Lane Theater** on Minetta Lane. The 393-seat performance space opened in 1984, occupying a former printing company.

Sixth Avenue subway

The expansion of the subway system through Greenwich Village extended Sixth Avenue to the south, toward Tribeca. Along the way, numerous row houses were demolished—including a few of Pepe's Minetta Street buildings—and the neighborhood was forcibly incorporated into the traffic and transit patterns of Manhattan.

The disruption of the Greenwich Village grid resulted in small triangular parcels that were assigned to the Parks Department. With support from local civic groups, **Minetta Green**, **Minetta Park**, and **Minetta Triangle** provided a naturalistic element that buffered adjacent apartment buildings from the traffic of Sixth Avenue. Inside Minetta Triangle, bluestone paths feature images of trout—the fish that were once found in Minetta Brook.

Across Bleecker Street is another pocket green space, **Winston Churchill Square**, bound by Bleecker Street, Sixth Avenue, and Downing Street. The park's namesake was the wartime British prime minister, whose mother was a New Yorker. Originally known as Bleecker Street Playground, this park was renamed as a complement to the adjacent **Downing Street**—an address synonymous with the prime minister's office. Prior to the park's development, Minetta Brook flowed from this point in a nearly straight line southwest, toward the Hudson River. That path is marked today by Downing Street.

Rediscovery

For a stream that has not seen daylight since the 1820s, Minetta Brook is quite the local celebrity. Not a drop of its water can be found above the surface, but walking tours conducted by urban explorers and historians dutifully follow its former course.

The first instance of Minetta Brook's reappearance in the public imagination was in 1865, when civil engineer Egbert L. Viele drafted his *Sanitary & Topographical Map of the City and Island of New York*. A veritable reference for architects and engineers to this day, it depicts every known inland waterway that existed in Manhattan. Prior to publishing this map, Viele served as the surveyor of what became Central Park and Prospect Park. His fame followed him throughout his life. After publishing his map of Manhattan, the retired brigadier general went on to serve as the city's parks commissioner and as a congressman. He is entombed with his second wife in a pyramid-shaped monument at the West Point military academy.

In 1883, the *New York Times* published the first of many articles on the water flowing through basements of homes built above Minetta Brook's course. "The engineers of those days evidently believed that the leveling of the hills, down the sides of which coursed the rivulets . . . would exterminate the stream. But they were mistaken," the article stated.

Viele serves as a prominent source in this story, having reported back in 1859 on the connection between hastily buried streams and fever outbreaks that occurred in buildings constructed atop the fill. Viele quotes an unnamed local doctor, who said, "I have practiced medicine for 50 years in the vicinity of Minetta Water, and I can trace the course of the stream by my practice in intermittent fevers." With the doctor's testimony in mind, Viele's map serves as a warning to engineers—and to doctors—on the hazards posed by buried streams.

In 1892, the *New York Times* revisited the issue of the brook, when drygoods merchant Solomon Sayles was developing his department store at 126 Sixth Avenue, near West 10th Street, and found the cellar flooded. Viele, interviewed again for this story, concluded that "such springs are as natural as the island's rock formations and cannot be dammed."

Over the course of the next century, nearly every infrastructure project that crossed the stream's path found itself facing the torrent associated with Minetta Brook. Across the street from Washington Square's Roman-style triumphal arch is **Two Fifth Avenue**, a massive apartment building that, in its lobby, has a glass cylinder pipe sticking out of the floor. A plaque on the wall says that occasionally, silted water from Minetta Brook can be seen rising up inside the pipe.

The story of Minetta Brook resembles that of Collect Pond—going from supporting early housing settlements to fostering conditions for premature death. Both were prominent in the experiences of slaves in the city: Where Collect Pond served as the execution site for slaves suspected of rebellion, Minetta Brook was home to the city's first free black community. Following their burials, both former waterways became the sites of slum districts and breeding grounds for disease. Despite this, both are now celebrated by their neighborhoods for their roles in the city's early history.

PLACES TO SEE:

+ **Washington Square Park** Bound by Washington Square North (Waverly Place), Washington Square East (University Place), Washington Square South (West 4th Street), and Washington Square West (Macdougal Street)
+ **Minetta Tavern** 113 Macdougal Street + 212-475-3850 + www .minettatavernny.com
+ **Minetta Lane Theater** 18 Minetta Lane + 212-420-8214 + minettalanenyc.com
+ **Minetta Green** Minetta Lane and Sixth Avenue + www.nycgov parks.org/parks/minettagreen
+ **Minetta Triangle** Minetta Street and Sixth Avenue + www.nycgov parks.org/parks/minettatriangle
+ **Winston Churchill Square** West side of intersection of Downing Street, Carmine Street, and Sixth Avenue + www.nycgovparks.org/ parks/M027
+ **Jefferson Market Library** 425 Sixth Avenue + 212-243-4334 + www.nypl.org/locations/jefferson-market

LEARN MORE:

+ **Greenwich Village Historical Society** www.gvshp.org
+ **The Village Alliance** villagealliance.org

MANHATTAN

+ **Bus**: M8, M1, M2, M5 at Fifth Avenue and 8th Street, walk south to Washington Square Park; M5 uptown at Sixth Avenue and West 3rd Street, walk south to Minetta Street
+ **Subway**: A, C, E, B, D, F, M at West 4th Street, walk south to Minetta Street
+ **Bike**: There are bike lanes on Macdougal, Bleecker, and Hudson Streets

4. Broad Street (Heere Gracht)

Near the southern tip of Manhattan, **Broad Street** is situated atop a buried inlet of the East River. The inlet began at Exchange Place, half a mile inland. Broad Street's name is a reminder of the navigable canal at the inlet's median, which was covered in 1676.

The first Dutch settlers arrived in Lower Manhattan in 1625 and quickly set about building a colonial outpost reminiscent of their home country. The capital of the Netherlands had a network of canals in its commercial center, so New Amsterdam would as well. The inlet provided a natural path between **Shaape Waytie**, or "sheep pasture," and the East River. Along the way, a smaller tributary called Beaver Path linked with the inlet. In 1646, the colonial government transformed the inlet into the **Heere Gracht**, Beaver Path became **Begijn Gracht**,

Broad Street, New York City, 17th Century

and the inlet's northernmost block was called the **Prinzen Gracht**—all named after canals in Amsterdam.

The canals were accessible only to small watercraft and quickly took on a less romantic role as a dumping ground for refuse. In 1664, New Amsterdam was acquired by England and renamed New York. The new masters of the colony did not care for restoring the city's canals and had all of them buried in 1676.

On today's maps, the only physical reminder of the Heere Gracht is **Bridge Street**, a two-block road that intersects with Broad Street. Prior to 1676, the intersection was a bridge spanning Broad Street's canal.

PLACES TO SEE:
+ **Fraunces Tavern** 54 Pearl Street + 212-968-1776 + www.fraunces tavern.com

LEARN MORE:
+ **Downtown Alliance** www.downtownny.com

GETTING THERE:
+ **Bus**: M15 to Water Street and Broad Street
+ **Subway**: 1 at South Ferry; R at Whitehall Street; 4, 5 at Bowling Green; J, Z at Broad Street
+ **Ferry**: Staten Island Ferry to Whitehall
+ **Bike**: There are bike lanes on Water Street; the East River Bikeway is also in proximity to Broad Street

5. Maiden Lane (Maagde Paatje)

Less than a half mile to the north of Broad Street, a brook flowed into the East River, its path marked today by **Maiden Lane**. The stream had its origins at Nassau Street and its mouth at Pearl Street. In colonial times, it was known as **Maagde Paatje**, Dutch for "a footpath used by lovers along a rippling brook," according to *The WPA Guide to New York City*. Other historians have a less romantic theory for Maiden Lane's name: that the river that ran there was used for washing sheets.

As the city crept north, the stream was buried and covered with a paved road in 1698. At its former confluence with the East River, a **flea market** developed, offering produce, fish, and meat. The market's name had nothing to do with the microscopic insect. Like Maiden Lane's name, the market's origins were also Dutch—the word "vleigh" for a meadow was corrupted into "flea."

In 1823, it was relocated to a new intersection with the East River known as the **Fulton Street Market**. Specializing in fish, it remained in this location for 183 years before moving to its current home in the Bronx. A smaller outdoor market, called the **New Amsterdam Market**, opened on the original site in 2005, maintaining the historical continuity of its colonial forebear. The surrounding neighborhood developed over the centuries into the Financial District, anchored by the **New York Stock Exchange** at the corner of Broad and Wall Streets.

Along Maiden Lane are two noteworthy parks. A block east of Maagde Paatje's former source is **Louise Nevelson Plaza**, a triangular park bound by William Street, Maiden Lane, and Liberty Street. It is the city's first park to have been named after a living artist. Dedicated in 1978, it features public sculptures by Nevelson. At the wider end of this triangular park is the **Federal Reserve Bank of New York**, a neo-Renaissance fortress completed in 1935.

At the end of Maiden Lane lies the recently redesigned **East River Waterfront Esplanade**, which transformed a seawall shore once lined with tour-bus parking into a postmodern landscape, accommodating a bike path, on the East River's Manhattan waterfront.

PLACES TO SEE:
+ **Federal Reserve Bank of New York** 33 Liberty Street ✦ 718-543-3344 ✦ www.newyorkfed.org/aboutthefed/visiting.html
+ **Louise Nevelson Plaza** Bound by Maiden Lane, William Street, and Liberty Street ✦ www.downtownny.com/louisenevelson

GETTING THERE:
+ **Bus:** M15 at Water Street and John Street
+ **Subway:** A, C, J, Z, 2, 3, 4, 5 at Fulton Street
+ **Bike:** There are bike lanes on Water Street; the East River Bikeway is also in proximity to Maiden Lane

6. Murray Hill Reservoir

At the corner of West 42nd Street and Fifth Avenue is the **New York Public Library**, a Beaux-Arts landmark that stands atop the foundation

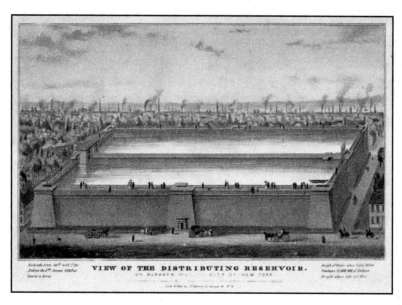

View of the Distributing Reservoir on Murray's Hill, 1842

of the decommissioned **Murray Hill Reservoir**. During its half century of service, the reservoir's four-acre pool was a popular attraction to residents and visitors alike. Behind the library, **Bryant Park** continues to serve as a pleasant oasis in the heart of Midtown Manhattan.

The land on which the reservoir sat was included in the 1686 Dongan Charter that allocated unclaimed and unused land in Manhattan to the government. The site's first use was in 1823 as a potter's field, after the older one in Washington Square reached capacity. This potter's field was decommissioned after less than two decades, in 1840, in preparation for the superblock's subsequent use as a reservoir.

From its earliest years, the city had difficulty maintaining a supply of freshwater for its growing population. With Collect Pond polluted, water companies stepped in, delivering barrels of drinking water to wealthier residents, as their poorer neighbors relied on wells and cisterns. The unclean quality of the groundwater resulted in routine outbreaks of cholera and yellow fever, droughts, and inability to combat fires. A bold solution was sought: to tap a clean source distant enough from the city to avoid being polluted and large enough to anticipate growth in population.

The 400-acre Croton Aqueduct tapped the Croton River in Westchester County, sending its water to the Murray Hill Reservoir in Midtown. Along the way, water dropped 13 inches every mile, using gravity to reach the city. On July 4, 1842, the city toasted to American independence with water from the Croton Fountain at City Hall Park. An ode to the $11.5 million aqueduct was sung, and prominent dignitaries in attendance included President John Tyler, former presidents John Quincy Adams and Martin Van Buren, and Governor William Seward. The aqueduct was considered the greatest civil engineering project in the United States since the Erie Canal. The aqueduct and the canal ensured New York's status as an economic power.

The reservoir in Midtown was designed by James Renwick Jr., whose career would include such Manhattan landmarks as Grace Church and Saint Patrick's Cathedral. Recognizing the scenic aspects of the hilltop site, he designed the reservoir walls in the Egyptian Revival style. Atop the walls, a promenade enabled visitors to admire the water and views of the city. The reservoir became a popular weekend destination for city residents.

The city's first world's fair

In bringing the nations of the world together, the Olympic Games promote unity through sports. Their cultural and industrial counterpart is a world's fair, which New York famously hosted in 1939 and 1964. Most New Yorkers are not aware that in the 19th century, an earlier world's fair, by a different name, took place at Bryant Park—or, as it was then called, Reservoir Square.

This fair operated between July 14, 1853, and November 14, 1854, as the **Exhibition of the Industry of All Nations**. It highlighted the advances of the Industrial Revolution in the United States. The central structure of the fair was the **New York Crystal Palace**, a copy of Joseph Paxton's Crystal Palace from the 1851 world's fair in London. On the north side of 42nd Street, the 300-foot-high **Latting Observatory** served as an observation deck for fairgoers.

Reservoir Square was renamed after parks advocate William Cullen Bryant in 1884.

Calls for demolition

With the northward expansion of the city, a second distributing reservoir was built in Central Park in 1877. In 1881, the state passed a bill authorizing the Murray Hill Reservoir's demolition, but periodic droughts necessitated its survival for another two decades. Reporting on the changing reputation of the reservoir, the *New York Times* described the former "crown of Murray Hill" in 1896 as a "colossal eyesore at what should be one of the most attractive spots in the city." The same year, the New York Public Library was proposed for the site—grander than the reservoir, and designed to rival the libraries of the great Old World cities.

By 1900, supporters of the library cheered the demolition of the obsolete reservoir. In 1911 the main branch building was completed, holding more than a million books on 75 miles of shelves. The Beaux Arts–style structure was designed by architects Carrère and Hastings, featuring architectural elements reminiscent of ancient Rome.

With the completion of the New York Public Library's main branch, the reservoir became a distant memory, overshadowed by the library and by the newer, much larger reservoirs uptown and upstate. At the time of its opening, the library was the largest marble building in the country.

The reservoir's foundation

Unknown to visitors, the foundation stones of the Murray Hill Reservoir serve as the underground platform on which the library stands. These ancient bricks became visible to the public in June 2002, when the South Court of the library was completed.

In 1999, library director Paul LeClerc and architect Lewis Davis of the firm Davis Brody Bond conceived of a postmodern-style facility inside the library's South Court that would provide space for research classes and orientations. The four-story steel-and-glass addition carefully avoids disturbing the main branch's marble walls, enabling visitors to admire these walls, and the foundation stones below, with natural light filtering in from above.

The exposed walls beneath the South Court are not the only recent reminder of the reservoir. In 2003, the **Croton Reservoir Tavern** opened at 108 West 40th Street, featuring an indoor mural of the reservoir and decorated with furniture evoking the 19th century. As the skyscrapers of Midtown grow taller, the tavern and the South Court offer a glimpse into a time when the area was on the city's outskirts.

PLACES TO SEE:

+ **New York Public Library—Stephen A. Schwarzman Building**
  Fifth Avenue at West 42nd Street + 917-275-6935 + www.nypl.org
+ **Bryant Park** Bound by Sixth Avenue, West 42nd Street, Fifth Avenue, and West 40th Street
+ **Croton Reservoir Tavern** 108 West 40th Street + 212-997-6835 + www.crotonnyc.com

GETTING THERE:

+ **Bus**: M42 at Fifth Avenue; downtown M1, M2, M3, M4, M5 at East 42nd Street; uptown M1, M2, M3 at 34th Street; uptown M5, M7 at West 42nd Street
+ **Subway**: B, D, F, M at 42nd Street–Bryant Park; 7 at Fifth Avenue
+ **Bike**: There is an eastbound bike lane on East 40th Street, a westbound bike lane on East 39th Street, and a northbound bike lane on Sixth Avenue

7. Sunfish Pond

On the East Side of Midtown, Park Avenue South runs between early-20th-century office buildings, with the Lexington Avenue subway line roaring beneath the pavement a block away—the city's first subway line, opening to the public on October 27, 1904. In today's overdeveloped landscape, it can be difficult to imagine that the corner of Park Avenue South and East 31st Street was, a century earlier, the center of **Sunfish Pond**.

The pond's source was a stream that originated at West 44th Street and Broadway in present-day **Times Square**. Its Dutch name was **t'Oude Wrack**, or "old wreck," named after a ship that was wrecked in the East River near the creek's mouth. This stream paralleled Broadway running toward **Herald Square**, then turned to the east, where it emptied into Sunfish Pond. The stream then continued toward **Kips Bay**, where it emptied into the East River. The bay's namesake was Dutch settler Jacobus Hendrickson Kip, whose 1655 farmhouse at Second Avenue and East 35th Street survived until 1851.

The site of Sunfish Pond is in an inland neighborhood known since colonial times as Murray Hill, named after shipping merchant Robert Murray, who built his **Inclenberg** farm on a nearby hilltop in 1762. To the east of the pond, Eastern Post Road meandered its way north along Manhattan's East Side, roughly along the route of today's Third Avenue. Sunfish Pond served as a rest stop for travelers on this road.

During the American Revolution, Robert Murray's Patriot wife, Mary Lindley Murray, is credited with saving the lives of Generals George Washington and Israel Putnam. Local lore suggests that as Washington was retreating uptown following his defeat at Brooklyn Heights, the

British attempted to cut him off by landing at Kips Bay. But Mrs. Murray invited General William Howe and Governor William Tryon to the mansion for tea, entertaining them long enough to enable the patriots to escape. "It has since become almost a common saying among our officers, that Mrs. Murray saved this part of the American army," wrote local doctor James Thatcher in his journal.

A plaque installed by Daughters of the American Revolution at **130 East 37th Street** marks the site of Inclenberg and commemorates Mrs. Murray. The mansion burned down in 1834, and a decade later the Murray family sold their land to developers. A restrictive covenant on the former farm listed clauses banning the use of the properties for slaughterhouses, glue factories, or circuses.

But outside of the Murray farm's borders, industry was creeping in. In 1821, Peter Cooper bought a glue factory near Sunfish Pond, just a few blocks south of the Murray farm, taking advantage of its proximity to **Bull's Head Market**, which had relocated from Collect Pond to the area in 1813. The market supplied Cooper's factory with cows' and calves' feet, which were used to produce glue, gelatin, and household cement.

As pollution and development increased, the pond was no longer a reliable supplier of water for the area. In 1838, the **New York House of Refuge**—the nation's first home for wayward youth, located near Sunfish Pond at present-day Madison Square Park—caught fire. People attempted to use water from Sunfish Pond to douse the flames, but after a few gallons, the pond was effectively drained; the water turned to mud. Cooper's glue factory's success had resulted in the pollution of the once-pristine skating pond, and in 1839 it was filled.

Sunfish Pond reemerged in the headlines in 1907, when the Pennsylvania Railroad was constructing the East River tubes connecting Long Island with Penn Station. Leaking walls forced workers to reinforce the tunnel beneath Park Avenue.

No park or pavement marker commemorates Sunfish Pond. When one stands at the corner of Park Avenue South and East 31st Street, fishing and ice-skating could not be further from one's mind.

PLACES TO SEE:

✦ **Inclenberg plaque** 130 East 37th Street
✦ **Kips Bay Library** 446 Third Avenue at East 31st Street ✦ 212-683-2520 ✦ www.nypl.org/locations/kips-bay

GETTING THERE:
+ **Bus**: M34 at Park Avenue; downtown M101, M102, M103 at East 34th Street; uptown M1, M2, M3 at 35th Street
+ **Subway**: 6 at 33rd Street
+ **Bike**: There is an eastbound bike lane on East 30th Street and a westbound bike lane on East 29th Street

8. Central Park Pond

In the center of Manhattan Island is Central Park, an 843-acre green space where natural bodies of water are replicated—though not exactly restored—in seven ponds. Some of these ponds were created atop existing streams, with the marshes drained and refilled with pristine-looking water from the city's aqueduct. In other locations, new ponds were created, serving as reflecting pools, boating venues, and ice-skating surfaces. A third category of water flowing in Central Park includes the reservoirs that were part of the city's aqueduct. All of the park's waterways are meticulously maintained to prevent silting, algae blooms, and erosion. Without human intervention, nature would turn these waterways back into the marshland that was there before Central Park was developed.

The Pond is the southernmost of Central Park's bodies of water, located within view of the **Plaza Hotel** and Manhattan's **Grand Army Plaza**, which are situated at the most heavily used entrance into the park.

The Pond was formed in a valley where **De Voor's Mill Stream** once flowed. This stream originated at the present-day corner of Columbus Avenue and West 69th Street and flowed in a southeast direction toward **Turtle Bay**, emptying into the East River. With the development of Central Park, starting in 1858, this stream was completely buried—with the exception of a 3.8-acre pond at the park's southeast corner. Dips in the landscape where the stream flowed can be seen at **Dalehead Arch** and **Driprock Arch**, two nearby bridges that carry the park's internal roadways above pedestrian paths.

De Voor's Mill Stream occasionally manifested itself in the basements of buildings along its former route. In 1963, employees of the **Delmonico Hotel**, at 59th Street and Park Avenue, claimed to have caught a sunfish in a cemented channel of the old stream. A pump system in the hotel's basement prevents the stream from overflowing beyond its tube.

Postcard, The Lake and Terrace, Central Park

Within Central Park, the Pond appears on maps as a backward L, topped at its northern end by the Wollman Rink and nestled in its interior elbow by the Hallett Nature Sanctuary. Near its northern tip, Gapstow Bridge forms a 44-foot span above the water. At the time of its completion in 1858, the Pond was much larger at its northern end and served as a popular destination for ice-skating. In the first half century of Central Park's existence, it received more visitors in winter than in summer, and trolleys heading in the direction of the park had signs indicating whether the water was frozen enough for ice-skating.

Wollman Skating Rink

The transformation of the Pond's northern bay into the **Wollman Rink**, replacing the natural skating surface, began in the Great Depression under Parks Commissioner Robert Moses, who believed that Central Park needed more active recreational facilities to attract the middle and working classes. By that time, winters in New York were much warmer, and the pond was no longer safe to skate on for a full winter season.

The namesake philanthropist responsible for the rink was Kate Wollman, a wealthy stockbroker's daughter. The facility made the record books when it opened in December 1950. At 28,000 square feet and a cost of $750,000—$600,000 of which was footed by Wollman—it was the world's largest and most expensive skating rink. The cost included landscaping improvements around the Pond and a new playground adjoining the rink.

Heavy usage by New Yorkers and deferred maintenance by the finan-

A gondola ride on Central Park Lake

cially troubled city forced the rink's closure in 1980. Drainage problems and rock formations beneath the original rink made the cost of fixing it balloon to $12 million. Two blocks to the south of the park, real estate developer Donald J. Trump looked at the site from his eponymous tower in disgust. In June 1986, he promised to fund the renovation and complete it in record time. "I have total confidence that we will be able to do it," Trump said at the time. "I am going on record as saying that I will not be embarrassed." Under Trump's guidance, the rink was reopened on October 31 of that year, two months ahead of schedule and $750,000 under budget. Since then, the Wollman Rink has demonstrated the effectiveness of a privately operated public facility, even as some detractors have expressed fears of encroaching privatization in the city's most famous green space.

Gapstow Bridge

Central Park is an urban explorer's dream, with nearly 40 bridges and arches that each feature unique architectural elements. The southernmost is **Gapstow Bridge**, which traverses the Pond's northern bay. It is one of the most recognizable crossings in Central Park because of its proximity to Midtown and the views it offers of skyscrapers above the treetops. In the summer, vines grow on the bridge, blending it with the surrounding landscape.

Hallett Nature Sanctuary

Inside Central Park are two nature preserves that occupy heavily forested hills. In the park's center, the Ramble enables visitors to enter a forest that obscures the skyscrapers and insulates one from the noise of the city. At the Pond, on the other hand, the 3.5-acre **Hallett Nature Sanctuary** is fenced off from human intruders, reserved solely for birds and other wildlife.

The preserve was designated as a bird sanctuary by Robert Moses in 1934 and renamed after George H. Hallett Jr. by Parks Commissioner Henry J. Stern in 1986. A leader of the civic watchdog group Citizens Union, Hallett was also an avid birdwatcher and naturalist. He died in 1985 at age 90.

Although Central Park does not have any natural corridors to connect with other parks, wild beasts from beyond the city have somehow detected the greensward in the heart of Manhattan. In 1999, a coyote wandered into the Hallett sanctuary. Stern dubbed him Lucky Pierre after the Pierre, a nearby luxury hotel that overlooks the park. Seven years later, another coyote wandered south into the park and was also discovered in the sanctuary. Named Hal as an abbreviation of Hallett, he eluded police for nearly a week before capture.

The sanctuary is open to tours on a limited basis.

PLACES TO SEE:

+ **Grand Army Plaza** Bound by Fifth Avenue, 60th Street, Grand Army Plaza, and 58th Street
+ **Central Park Zoo** 64th Street and Fifth Avenue + www.central parkzoo.com + 212-439-6500
+ **Wollman Skating Rink** www.wollmanskatingrink.com + 917-492-3856
+ **Hallett Nature Sanctuary** Entrance near the north shore of the Pond; tour information is available by calling 212-794-4064 or e-mailing tours@centralparknyc.org
+ **Gapstow Bridge** Northeast corner of the Pond

LEARN MORE:

+ **Central Park Conservancy** www.centralparknyc.org

GETTING THERE:

+ **Bus**: M1, M2, M3, M4 downtown at 59th Street; M1, M2, M3, M4 uptown at 58th Street and Madison Avenue, walk one block west and one block north toward Central Park
+ **Subway**: N, Q, R at Fifth Avenue–59th Street
+ **Bike**: There are bike lanes on East Drive inside Central Park

9. Central Park Lake (Saw Kill)

This 20-acre lake is the largest of Central Park's naturalistic water bodies, roughly located in the section of the park between 72nd and 78th Streets. Its zigzagging form occupies a valley through which the **Saw Kill** stream flowed. Popular in its early years as an outdoor ice-skating venue, it is the only inland pond in Manhattan accessible to the public by rental rowboats.

Saw Kill stream

Saw Kill is a Dutch name inspired by the abundance of timber along the stream. In the early years of New Amsterdam, slaves worked in the woods around this stream, supplying materials for homes and ships. Their presence is noted on the Manatus map of 1639, the first European map of Manhattan. Logs were floated down the creek to the East River and then transported downtown by boat.

The stream flows from two forks on the Upper West Side. The south fork originated on West 85th Street near Central Park West, while the north fork originated three blocks to the north. The forks merged on present-day East 75th Street to the west of Park Avenue.

Two blocks east and two blocks north of the confluence, Eastern Post Road crossed the Saw Kill in a picturesque location known to early residents as the **Kissing Bridge**. There were once several bridges on Eastern Post Road with this romantic name, but with the disappearance of Old Wreck Brook, Sunfish Pond, and De Voor's Mill Stream, one by one the "kissing bridges" over them also disappeared. The bridge crossing the Saw Kill was the last to carry the name. By the time Central Park was created, it too was gone, as Third Avenue had taken over as the straight, grid-compliant version of Eastern Post Road.

When Central Park was being constructed, the sources of the Saw Kill were buried beneath **Manhattan Square**, the future site of the **American Museum of Natural History**. Likewise, the outflow was dammed where the **Loeb Boathouse** in Central Park stands today. The remaining portion of the stream was drained, connected to the Croton Aqueduct, and refilled. This new body of water became **the Lake**, which opened to the public in December 1858. On its opening day, nearly 300 skaters filled the ice-covered pond.

Ladies' Pond

An ideal walk along the former Saw Kill would begin at **Explorers' Gate**, the park entrance at West 77th Street and Central Park West. Walking into the park, the street takes **Eaglevale Arch**, a bridge made of local gneiss that once crossed above **Ladies' Pond**. Today a small meadow stretching between 76th and 78th Streets, this used to be an inlet of the Lake where women could skate in privacy as an alternative to the more crowded and mixed social scene on the Lake.

The former Ladies' Pond was buried in 1936 and is now occupied by Naturalists' Walk, a series of rustic-themed trails. Another arch relating to this buried pond is **Balcony Bridge**, which carries West Drive above the inlet that connected Ladies' Pond and the Lake. On this bridge are two protruding niches with benches that provide picturesque views of the Lake and the Upper West Side skyline.

Bank Rock Bay

The northern tip of the Lake is called Bank Rock Bay, a marshy inlet crossed by **Oak Bridge**. Originally designed by Calvert Vaux in 1860, the bridge was made of wood and cast iron. In the 1970s, vandals made the bridge unusable, and the cash-strapped Central Park Conservancy replaced it with a utilitarian Bank Rock Bridge in 1982. By 2009, the park's caretakers were in more robust financial shape, and they rebuilt Oak Bridge according to its original design, using historical photographs for reference.

The Ramble

The northern shore of the Lake is lined by a wooded 38-acre expanse called **the Ramble**. In contrast to the Hallett Nature Sanctuary, the public is welcome to explore this preserve's hilly terrain, where they may stumble upon a whimsical 5-foot-wide arch, an artificial brook, and numerous flora and fauna. Off-limits to the public, however, is **Indian Cave**, a natural formation discovered during the park's construction. In the first half century of the park's existence, boaters were able to row into the cave's mouth and disembark on its flat surface. Over the decades, however, suicides, assaults, and hoboes turned the cave into a nuisance. It was sealed up in 1934.

Continuing farther along the Lake's shore, the trail goes over **Gill Bridge**, a rare wooden crossing in the park that has gone through several cycles of vandalism and repair. This bridge spans **the Gill**, an artificial tributary of the Lake. The Gill's source appears to emerge out of a rock reminiscent of a natural spring. In reality, this "spring" is a tap that can be turned off at any time. The Gill flows into Azalea Pond, a popular bird-watching location where the Central Park Conservancy takes care to remove invasive plant species and keep the pond clear of algae and silting.

Bow Bridge

At the southeastern corner of the Ramble is Central Park's longest crossing, **Bow Bridge**, a 60-foot wrought-iron span designed by Vaux and Jacob Wrey Mould. The form of the bridge resembles an archer's bow, rising slightly at the center. Appearing prominently in film, literature, and countless wedding photographs, this bridge competes with Gapstow Bridge for the title of the most-visited crossing in Central Park. The bridge connects the Ramble with **Cherry Hill** on the lake's southern side. Along its railings are sculptural elements that incorporate Gothic, Renaissance, and neoclassical designs.

Loeb Boathouse

Since March 1954, the **Loeb Boathouse** has stood at the eastern end of the Lake, built atop a dam that blocks the Saw Kill from continuing its eastward flow. A restaurant and a boat rental facility are inside the structure. The building's namesake, a philanthropist and investment banker named Carl M. Loeb, provided $305,000 for the construction of the neoclassical structure. It replaced an older wooden Gothic boathouse dating back to the early years of Central Park.

Bethesda Fountain

On the lake's southern side is a plaza paved with red bricks that forms the northern terminus of **the Mall**, a pedestrian promenade lined with statues that points toward the far-off Belvedere Castle, though it ends at the Lake. At the center of this plaza is **Bethesda Fountain**, which celebrates the city's clean water supply with Emma Stebbins's *Angel of the Waters* statue. The fountain's name references the Gospel of John, which speaks of an angel who purified the water of the biblical Bethesda Fountain—just as the Croton Aqueduct made the city's water supply much safer to consume, reducing instances of malaria and yellow fever. Stebbins is the only female sculptor to have a work of art on permanent display in Central Park. The model for the statue is believed to have been actress Charlotte Saunders Cushman, a lesbian who lived with Stebbins at the time of the statue's dedication in 1873.

A prominent location for film shoots, the fountain is the symbolic heart of Central Park—located midway between its east and west sides, at the end of a pedestrian boulevard, with a view of the Ramble's dense forest on the opposite shore of the Lake.

Historical conditions

The Lake was one of the first sections of Central Park that was completed and open to the public. The instant popularity of ice-skating on the lake in the winter, boating on it in the summer, and hiking through the adjacent Ramble demonstrated that the public craved a naturalistic experience in close proximity to home.

The natural conditions of the Saw Kill would not have allowed the Lake to remain as it is—sediment washing in from the surrounding landscape would have turned it back into a marsh. The early 20s subjected the Lake's shoreline to a series of unnatural "improvements," such as concrete shorelines to prevent erosion. In recent decades, the city has replaced the concrete with boulders and plants, enabling turtles to secure ledges along the shore. The bird sanctuary isle was restored, the water was aerated, and the Lake presently appears as timeless as the day when the first park visitors skated across its surface.

PLACES TO SEE:

+ **Naturalists' Walk** Terrace Drive just east of Central Park West, below Eaglevale Arch
+ **Eaglevale Arch** Terrace Drive just east of Central Park West
+ **Balcony Arch** West Drive above the Lake
+ **Oak Bridge** Trail at northeast corner of the Lake, above Bank Rock Bay
+ **Ladies Pavilion** Hernshead promontory on western side of the Lake
+ **The Ramble** Wooded area on northern side of the Lake, south of 79th Street Transverse
+ **Gill Bridge** Trail on northern side of the Lake, where the Gill empties into the Lake
+ **Bow Bridge** Trail across the middle of the Lake, connecting the Ramble to Cherry Hill
+ **Bethesda Fountain** South side of the Lake at the intersection of the Mall and Terrace Drive

✦ **Loeb Boathouse** East side of the Lake at East Drive ✦ 212-517-2233 ✦ www.thecentralparkboathouse.com

LEARN MORE:
✦ **Central Park Conservancy** www.centralparknyc.org

GETTING THERE:
✦ **Bus**: M1, M2, M3, M4 downtown at 72nd Street; M1, M2, M3, M4 uptown at 72nd Street and Madison Avenue, walk one block west toward Central Park, enter park at 72nd Street and continue toward Bethesda Fountain; M10, M72 at 72nd Street and Central Park West, enter park at 72nd Street and continue toward Bethesda Fountain
✦ **Subway**: B, C at 72nd Street
✦ **Bike**: There are bike lanes on West Drive and Terrace Drive inside the park
✦ **Boat**: Boat rentals and gondola rides are available at the Loeb Boathouse from April through November

10. Conservatory Water

To the east of the Loeb Boathouse, across East Drive, there is an oval reflecting pool with its own boathouse. The boats here are powered by the wind or by remote control—the **Conservatory Water** serves as Central Park's model boating pond. It is located on the path of the Saw Kill and is fed by water from the Lake.

Initially, this pool was intended to be filled with lilies as part of a conservatory garden planned for this section of Central Park. The pond was the only part of this garden that was realized, featuring a rocky shoreline and lilies floating on the surface. The Conservatory Garden was eventually completed in 1934 at a location farther uptown, at Fifth Avenue and East 105th Street. Around that time, the Conservatory Water was redesigned with a granite shoreline loosely based on the reflecting pool of Jardin du Luxembourg in Paris. In 1954, the **Kerbs Boathouse** was built on the pool's east side.

What the Conservatory Water lacks in size, it makes up with its social scene, composed largely of model-boating enthusiasts. Every Saturday at ten in the morning, races are held under the banner of the Central Park

Model sailboats on the Conservatory Water

Model Yacht Club. In contrast to most of the city's parks, Central Park has numerous regulations designed to ensure quiet and cleanliness. In this model boating pond, motorized boats are prohibited for their noise and disruption to wildlife.

For children, Conservatory Water is best known for appearing in the novel and film *Stuart Little*. The child-friendly setting of this pond extends to its western side, which has two popular sculptures: the 1959 work *Alice in Wonderland* by José de Creeft, and the 1956 sculpture of a seated **Hans Christian Andersen** by Georg John Lober.

PLACES TO SEE:

✦ *Alice in Wonderland* **sculpture** North side of the Conservatory Water
✦ **Hans Christian Andersen sculpture** West side of the Conservatory Water
✦ **Kerbs Boathouse** East side of the Conservatory Water

LEARN MORE:

✦ **Sail the Park** Model boat rentals ✦ 917-522-0054 ✦ www.sailthe park.com
✦ **Central Park Model Yacht Club** www.cpmyc.org

GETTING THERE:

+ **Bus**: M1, M2, M3, M4 downtown at 75th Street; M1, M2, M3, M4 uptown at 75th Street and Madison Avenue, walk one block west toward the 76th Street entrance to Central Park
+ **Subway**: 6 at 77th Street, walk west on 77th Street toward Fifth Avenue, walk south on Fifth Avenue toward 76th Street, then enter Central Park
+ **Bike**: There are bike lanes on East Drive inside Central Park

11. Turtle Pond

Located at a dramatic change in landscape in the heart of Central Park, **Turtle Pond** is a remnant of the receiving reservoir completed in 1842 for the Croton Aqueduct. Similar in design to the distributing reservoir in Bryant Park, the 35-acre **receiving reservoir** served the city until 1930. Seven years after the reservoir was demolished, the Great Lawn was laid across the site. Turtle Pond is all that is left of the water that was once here, and its purpose now is aesthetic: to reflect Vista Rock and Belvedere Castle, which both rise on its southern side.

York Hill and Seneca Village

Prior to the construction of the reservoir, this site was known as **York Hill**, home to a small African American community that was pushed out in 1838 to make way for the reservoir. Most of the residents relocated a block west to an existing community known as **Seneca Village**.

Seneca Village was located between Seventh and Eighth Avenues, stretching from 83rd to 86th Streets. Like Greenwich Village, it was a rare community where blacks owned property, voted, and worshipped in the same church as their white neighbors, mostly Irish and German immigrants. When the receiving reservoir was built on the village's eastern border, local residents worked on its construction; Seneca Village soon had its sunrises obstructed by the retaining wall of the rectangular double pool.

The demise of Seneca Village began in 1853, when state lawmakers authorized the creation of Central Park. The press regarded Seneca Village as a shantytown, but property owners held off condemnation in a protracted two-year court battle. In 1856, the nearly 300 residents were sent eviction notices. The *New York Times* did not hide the motives behind the inclusion of Seneca Village's land within Central Park: "The sole object of the authorities in making the Park is to procure their expulsion from the homes which they occupy."

Within a year, Seneca Village was cleared, and the land west of the receiving reservoir was redeveloped as a series of hilltops and valleys. Traces of Seneca Village were rediscovered in 2011 by professors and students from the City College of New York and Columbia University.

Frederick Law Olmsted, who designed Central Park along with his partner Calvert Vaux, regarded the reservoir as a "blank, uninteresting object that can in no way be made particularly attractive." He ordered trees planted along its perimeter and designed paths to lead away from it. The only spot where the public was able to view the reservoir was from Belvedere Castle at the pool's southwestern corner.

Following the construction of a larger reservoir to its north, the receiving reservoir became known as the Lower Reservoir.

Belvedere Castle

At the southwestern corner of the receiving reservoir was **Vista Rock**, an outcropping rising to 130 feet above sea level. Prior to the creation of Central Park, this hill was topped by a fire observation tower. During the reservoir's construction, the hill was left untouched, intruding slightly into the otherwise perfect rectangle of the reservoir.

In 1867, Vaux designed **Belvedere Castle**, a hybrid Gothic–Moorish castle, as an architectural folly, set atop Vista Rock. Serving as a visual landmark, it was topped with a flag and lined up with the Mall farther south in the park, designed to draw the park's visitors toward its center.

The elevated setting of Belvedere Castle also gave it purpose as a weather station. It fell into disrepair, plagued by graffiti and pierced by weeds, after the station was decommissioned in 1967.

Every landmark in Central Park has its literary defender. Just as E. B. White wielded his pen to preserve the Ramble, author Anna Quindlen wrote a July 17, 1980, op-ed in the *New York Times* to defend Belvedere Castle from further decay. "It looms above the landscape like the cover drawing on a gothic novel, a true castle in the air." The castle reopened to the public on May 1, 1983, as the **Henry Luce Nature Observatory**, teaching visitors about the plants and animals that live in Central Park.

Draining the reservoir

At the turn of the 20th century, the prevailing attitude in City Hall toward Central Park began to shift, with the appointment of social reformer Charles B. Stover as the Manhattan parks commissioner in 1910. Looking at the park, Stover proposed playgrounds, tennis courts, and concert stages to make the park more accessible to the middle and working classes. At the time of his appointment to the position, the Lower Reservoir was already regarded as obsolete, and the 20-year debate over its future was just starting.

Stover's proposal recognized that with two world-class museums on either side of the reservoir, a processional boulevard should link them, with a formal garden at the midpoint. "If that is done, New York can have the grandest setting for its museums of any city in the world," declared Stover. However, with his resignation in 1913, the proposal failed to gather momentum.

In 1917, the city was celebrating the completion of the Catskill Aqueduct, which augmented the existing Croton Aqueduct that provided water to the city. Looking toward the Lower Reservoir, architect Thomas Hastings proposed a sunken garden surrounding a lagoon as a monument to the new aqueduct. The design of this pool was inspired by the 1893 World's Columbian Exposition in Chicago, where buildings were arranged around a central lagoon. However, Hastings' proposal was denounced by preservationists and recreation advocates for intruding on the park's sacred landscape and failing to provide playgrounds.

Immigrant leaders had their own proposals that demanded more recreational space. Patrick J. Conway, president of the Irish-American Athletic Club, slammed the "high muckety-mucks wanting to build a flower garden in Central Park." His alternative sought to retain the reservoir as a swimming pool.

Following the First World War, Hastings modified his proposal as a war memorial, but it too was rejected. After all, if every war merited a monument in Central Park, its image as a naturalistic landscape would be compromised. "It is so hopeless to ever accomplish anything in the city of New York in the way of an improvement," lamented Hastings. "So much contention and disagreement upon things, that it is really disheartening."

In 1919, a new populist newspaper was founded, the *New York Daily News*. In the following decade, the newspaper continuously pushed for the Lower Reservoir to be redeveloped for recreational use, through articles, informal polls, editorials, and publicity stunts such as having actors canoeing on the reservoir and a diver exploring its 45-foot depths.

The final design, which eventually became reality, was submitted by the American Society of Landscape Architects, covering most of Lower Reservoir's footprint with the oval-shaped Great Lawn.

Depression shantytown

The decommissioning of the Lower Reservoir occurred during the country's greatest financial meltdown, when nearly a quarter of the population became unemployed. In 1930, a homeless encampment was set up on the dusty remnants of the reservoir. Although the police cleared up this settlement attempt, the shanties were quickly rebuilt. The builders were then taken to court in July 1931, but a sympathetic judge suspended the sentences of 22 unemployed men ticketed for sleeping in Central Park, and gave each man $2 out of his own pocket. In December of that year, seven more men arrested with the same charge were again dismissed in court.

The settlement received the public's admiration for resourcefulness alongside derision for its apparent disregard of the law. By April 1933, work on the reservoir's demolition resumed, and the park's most famous homeless encampment was cleared.

Belvedere Lake to Turtle Pond

Between 1930 and 1934, Central Park experienced the greatest alteration to its landscape since its creation—the Lower Reservoir was drained and replaced with the **Great Lawn**. The draining was conducted from the northern to the southern end, and the small portion that remained was named Belvedere Lake.

Unlike the Sheep Meadow and the North Meadow, the Great Lawn would not remain a grassy oval. The installation of six baseball diamonds in the 1950s, followed by three decades of public concerts, resulted in pollution of the small lake—dust settled on its bottom, and algae bloomed on its surface. The lake appeared as an oversized puddle, unable to reflect the crumbling castle looming above it.

Following the 1983 restoration and reopening of Belvedere Castle, turtles were introduced to the lake, and marshes were planted along its northern side to shield the water from the dust of the Great Lawn. In 1987, the lake took its present shape and was renamed Turtle Pond.

The discovery that dragonflies preferred mating on the pond's northern side enhanced the pond's role as a nature preserve within the park. A letter received by the *New York Times* in 1990 praised the dragonflies not only for their physical beauty but also for their use in curbing the mosquito population in the park. "A visit to Central Park gains from time spent observing these magnificent creatures," wrote Irene Hardwicke.

This remnant of the receiving reservoir once again welcomes visitors and wildlife to its shores.

PLACES TO SEE:

+ **Belvedere Castle and Vista Rock** South side of Turtle Pond at 79th Street
+ **Delacorte Theater** East side of Turtle Pond ✦ 212-539-8500 ✦ www.shakespeareinthepark.org
+ **Great Lawn** North side of Turtle Pond

GETTING THERE:

+ **Bus:** M1, M2, M3, M4 downtown at 78th Street, enter Central Park at 79th Street; M1, M2, M3, M4 uptown at 79th Street and Madison Avenue, walk one block west toward Central Park and continue toward the Great Lawn; M10, M79 at 81st Street and Central Park West, enter park at 81st Street and continue toward the Great Lawn
+ **Subway:** 6 at 77th Street, walk west on 77th Street toward Fifth Avenue, enter Central Park at 79th Street and continue westward toward the Great Lawn
+ **Bike:** There are bike lanes on East Drive and West Drive inside Central Park

12. Jacqueline Kennedy Onassis Reservoir

The largest body of water within the island of Manhattan holds more than a billion gallons of water. Completed in 1862, this 106-acre **reservoir** served the city until 1993. It has since been preserved as a reflecting pool ringed by a 1.58-mile jogging path atop its retaining wall.

Prior to the reservoir's construction, the site was a freshwater wetland drained by the northern branch of the Saw Kill. At the time that Central

Park was designated, this marshland was mapped as an upper reservoir, anticipating growth in the city's water consumption. It was at the urging of Egbert Viele that this new reservoir was laid out in a curvilinear shape that complemented the park's winding roads and paths.

As the city grew, new reservoirs were built farther uptown and upstate to collect, hold, and distribute the city's water supply. As early as 1926, the Central Park Association, a precursor to the Central Park Conservancy, called for this reservoir to be decommissioned and replaced with parkland.

The city's Department of Water Supply was not ready to give up the reservoir and instead beefed up patrols around it to prevent trespassing. An employee in a rowboat made his rounds, picking up objects such as dead birds, bottles, and a set of *Encyclopedia Britannica*. As the reservoir continued to serve the city's water needs, its scenic perimeter became a popular jogging track.

In 1993, the reservoir was finally decommissioned, following concerns from the federal government about pollution in addition to its no longer being considered essential due to the completion of Water Tunnel No. 3. In contrast to the Lower Reservoir, which became the Great Lawn, the fate of the Upper Reservoir was quickly decided in favor of the status quo following an outpouring of letters to city officials and the Central Park Conservancy. Although there were whimsical proposals that involved using the lake for boating and swimming or replacing it with land, none were part of the official conversation. More than a half century after the first calls to cover the pond failed, the public had become used to the reservoir's cooling and calming effect.

Jacqueline Kennedy Onassis, an outspoken historical preservationist widely credited with saving Grand Central Terminal, lived nearby on Fifth Avenue and frequently jogged around the reservoir. At the suggestion of her children, John F. Kennedy Jr. and Caroline Kennedy, the reservoir was renamed the Jacqueline Kennedy Onassis Reservoir in 1994, following her death.

Considering its size, perhaps in the future new proposals will arise to make the reservoir more accessible as a lake, swimming site, or field. To date, only one couple has received the city's permission to swim and scuba dive in the reservoir: Upper East Side residents George and Catherine Parry, who first dived in the water in 1996, collecting decades' worth of discarded objects on their cleanup mission.

Another aspect of the reservoir's unique appearance is the 60-foot-high fountain near its southern side. Constructed in 1917 in celebration of the completion of the upstate Ashokan Reservoir, it was switched off a year later following complaints from parkgoers who were hit by the spray. It is turned on only on special occasions, such as the park's 150th anniversary, which occurred in 2003, and the centennial of the Catskill reservoirs in 2007.

PLACES TO SEE:

✦ **John Purroy Mitchel memorial** 90th Street and East Drive

GETTING THERE:

✦ **Bus**: M1, M2, M3, M4 downtown at 90th Street; M1, M2, M3, M4 uptown at 89th Street and Madison Avenue, walk one block west toward the 90th Street entrance of Central Park
✦ **Subway**: 4, 5, 6 at 86th Street, walk west on 86th Street toward Fifth Avenue, then enter Central Park at 90th Street
✦ **Bike**: There are bike lanes on East Drive and West Drive inside Central Park

13. Montayne's Rivulet (the Loch)

In the northernmost section of Central Park is a ravine that once carried a natural stream. **Montayne's Rivulet** originated on West 101st Street, between Columbus and Amsterdam Avenues. It entered Central Park at West 101st Street and cascaded rapidly through a ravine known as **McGowan's Pass**. The stream merged with Harlem Creek at the northeast corner of the park, widening into a marshland as it approached the East River at East 106th Street. This extra-wide street lies atop landfill that has covered Harlem Creek.

The stream's namesake is Dr. Jean de la Montagne, a French Protestant who settled in New Amsterdam in 1637. De la Montagne quickly assumed prominence in New Amsterdam as the colony's sole physician, known to the Dutch-speaking colonists as Johannes de la Montagne. Over the decades, the doctor's name was corrupted into Montayne and applied to the creek that flowed through his farm.

Montayne's Rivulet had an additional source within Central Park: a natural spring bursting out of a rock, which provided drinking water to passersby into the mid-19th century. Known as Montayne's Fonteyn, the spring had an iron ladle chained to the rock from which the public could collect the water.

The Loch

Olmsted and Vaux recreated a waterway on the dried-up course of Montayne's Rivulet, fed by the city's aqueduct. This stream originated at **the Pool**, a deep pond near Central Park West and 101st Street. It continued through a ravine as **the Loch**—bestowed its name by the park's planners who, upon observing the hilly terrain around Montayne's Rivulet, were reminded of Scotland—and descended through a series of waterfalls on its way to **Harlem Meer**, an L-shaped lake at the park's northeast corner.

Upon leaving the Pool, the rivulet pours over **Glen Span Cascade**, a 14-foot artificial waterfall. The waterfall was painstakingly constructed by Vaux and Olmsted, and its original form was preserved in early photographs of the park. In a 1992 restoration of Glen Span Cascade and the nearby **Glen Span Arch**, these photos provided guidance for the designers. The arch carries West Drive over the Loch and marks the stream's entrance into Central Park's **North Woods**. In addition to Glen Span Cascade, the Loch descends through two additional waterfalls before leaving the forest through the **Huddlestone Arch**. Completed in 1866, this Vaux product is composed entirely of boulders piled atop each other, without any mortar. It carries East Drive above the stream.

Following this arch, the Loch disappears below the surface, traveling in a culvert beneath **Lasker Rink and Pool** toward Harlem Meer.

PLACES TO SEE:

+ **The Loch** Begins near 102nd Street and Central Park West
+ **Glen Span Cascade** Near West Drive crossing the Loch
+ **North Woods** Above the Loch between West Drive and East Drive
+ **Huddlestone Arch** East Drive crossing above the Loch

GETTING THERE:

+ **Bus:** M10 at Central Park West and 102nd Street
+ **Subway:** B, C at 103rd Street
+ **Bike:** There are bike lanes on East Drive and West Drive inside Central Park

14. Harlem Meer

The northernmost of Central Park's lakes occupies the point where Montayne's Rivulet merged with **Harlem Creek**. Together, the freshwater creeks widened into a brackish estuary that followed present-day East 106th Street, heading toward the East River. In the initial allocation of land for Central Park, the site of **Harlem Meer** would have been excluded from the park, and the confluence of the two creeks would likely have been buried beneath urban development. But in 1863, the park was expanded north to 110th Street, encompassing the North Woods, a set of abandoned fortifications from the War of 1812, and the marsh where the creeks met. With the construction of the park, Montayne's Rivulet and Harlem Creek were severed from their sources and mouths.

The marshland was carved into a lake, named Harlem Meer after the Dutch word for "lake." The neighborhood to the north of Central Park, Harlem, has Dutch origins; it was named in 1658 after a city of the same name in the old country. During the handover of political power to the British in 1664, New Amsterdam became New York and Fort Orange became Albany, but Harlem's name remained unchanged.

Today, the section of the park around the lake is known for its steep terrain, historical structures, and recreational venues.

McGowan's Pass

The southern side of Harlem Meer is a series of coves punctuated by rocky outcroppings. Between the hilltops crowned by Nutter's Battery and Fort Clinton is **McGowan's Pass**. Prior to the development of Central Park, this was a heavily trafficked colonial route through the hills on Eastern Post Road. It lives on today as a park trail.

Its namesake is Daniel McGown, who purchased land around the pass in 1756. The pass played a major role in the American Revolution as a passage for General George Washington's army for their retreat north in September 1776. Washington triumphantly returned to New York through McGowan's Pass in November 1783 following the conclusion of the Revolutionary War.

Fearing a repeat of the British invasion of 1776, nearly every cape, island, and peninsula around the city was fortified, along with smaller blockhouses on strategic hilltops. McGowan's Pass received three garrisons linked by four-foot-high earthwork walls: **Fort Clinton**, **Fort Fish**,

Charles A. Dana Discovery Center, Harlem Meer, Central Park

and **Nutter's Battery** flanked the pass, staffed by troops who had a commanding view of the Harlem Plain and Hell Gate.

To the west of the pass, another hilltop had **Blockhouse No. 1** built on it as an additional defense. It was completed on December 22, 1814, two days before the Treaty of Ghent was signed, ending the War of 1812. Ironically, this minor fortification is the only remaining structure in Central Park from this war, preserved by Olmsted and Vaux as a romantic ruin.

Charles A. Dana Discovery Center

On the north side of Harlem Meer, where Harlem Lane and Eastern Post Road once merged, is the **Charles A. Dana Discovery Center**, a nature education facility. Despite its historic appearance, it was completed in 1993 as a replacement for an earlier boathouse.

Lasker Rink and Pool

In December 1962, the city approved a combined ice-skating and swimming facility where the Loch enters Harlem Meer. It was named the **Lasker Rink and Pool** after Loula D. Lasker, whose estate funded $600,000 of the project's cost. In the summer of 1964, Harlem Meer was drained temporarily as the rink was being built, and two years later, the rink and pool opened.

The structure contains the only swimming pool in Central Park, located close to the low-income Harlem tenements and public housing projects whose residents it was intended to serve. The construction of the Lasker Rink and Pool shrunk the size of Harlem Meer from 14 acres to 11—an example of postwar construction projects in the park that preserved open space on land at the expense of the waterways.

Restoration

In the first century of Central Park's history, efforts to "improve" the waterways often ended up causing damage to the ecosystem, as fish, waterfowl, and amphibians found the altered lakes and ponds unlivable. For Harlem Meer, the construction of a concrete bottom and shore gave the lake an unnatural appearance. In 1990, Harlem Meer was dredged, redesigned, and restored with a soft shoreline of rocks, plantings, and a small beach. Since then, it has regained its image as a naturalistic lake that recalls Harlem's rural past.

PLACES TO SEE:

+ **Lasker Rink and Pool** East Drive near the Loch ✦ 917-492-3856 ✦ www.laskerrink.com
+ **Charles A. Dana Discovery Center** North side of Harlem Meer ✦ 212-860-1370
+ **Fort Clinton** Hilltop near the southwest corner of Harlem Meer
+ **Nutter's Battery** Hilltop near the southern side of Harlem Meer, between Lasker Rink and Fort Clinton
+ **McGowan's Pass** East Drive between Fort Fish and Fort Clinton

GETTING THERE:

+ **Bus**: M2, M3, M4 at Central Park North and Malcolm X Boulevard; M1 downtown at 5th Avenue and 112th Street; M1 uptown at Madison Avenue and East 111th Street, walk one block west toward Central Park
+ **Subway**: 2, 3 at Central Park North–110th Street
+ **Bike**: There are bike lanes on East Drive and West Drive inside Central Park

15. Morningside Pond

To the north of Central Park, a ridge separating the Harlem Plain from the heights to its west proved insurmountable for the street grid, and in 1867, city planner Andrew Haswell Green mapped out Morningside Park as a 13-block green ribbon that hugged the cliff separating Morningside Heights from Harlem. The design process of this park closely resembles that of Central Park, with the same cast of characters: Frederick Law Olmsted, Calvert Vaux, and Jacob Wrey Mould. In contrast to Central Park, their plan for Morningside did not envision waterways.

Morningside Pond within the park appears natural but in reality is a construction pit for a gymnasium that was never completed. Proposed by Columbia University in 1960, the 2.2-acre structure would have straddled the cliff. Columbia students would enter on Morningside Drive, and Harlem residents would enter at Morningside Avenue, nearly five stories below.

Eight years after the gym was proposed, the civil rights period cast the facility in a different light. People's discomfort with a wealthy university with a mostly white faculty and student body overlooking a low-income black neighborhood below was reflected in their perception of the gymnasium. In addition, while the university would own and operate the proposed gym on public parkland, it would only be open to Harlem residents during specified times. Very quickly, protest signs emerged, referring to the proposed building as "Gym Crow."

When construction began in February 1968, demonstrators rushed in to stop the project. Columbia University was forced to retreat and instead built a gym within its campus.

For the next two decades, the foundation pit was an eyesore in the park. In 1988, construction resumed on the pit, and it was transformed into a two-acre pond. This too was controversial, as Harlem residents feared the gentrification of the park, not wanting passive recreational spaces to replace basketball courts and baseball diamonds.

Designed by landscape architecture firms Quennell Rothschild and Bond, Ryder & Associates, the pond included a bird sanctuary isle and a 50-foot waterfall cascading down the Manhattan schist cliffs. Two baseball diamonds south of the pond were refurbished as part of the project. New residents of Harlem might reasonably presume that the pond was part of the original design for the park, unaware that its existence hides a divisive moment in the city's history.

PLACES TO SEE:

✦ **Morningside Pond** Inside Morningside Park, between West 113th and West 114th Streets

LEARN MORE:
+ **Friends of Morningside Park** www.morningsidepark.org

GETTING THERE:
+ **Bus**: M3, M7, M116 at Manhattan Avenue and West 114th Street
+ **Subway**: B, C at Cathedral Parkway–110th Street or 116th Street, walk west to Morningside Park
+ **Bike**: There is a bike lane on Frederick Douglass Boulevard (Eighth Avenue) one block to the east of Morningside Pond

16. Highbridge Reservoir

Situated on a bluff overlooking the Harlem River is a swimming pool that functioned as the **Highbridge Reservoir** between 1863 and 1917. The reservoir was named after **High Bridge**, the multi-arched pedestrian crossing that carried the Croton Aqueduct over the Harlem River. Completed in 1848, its design paid homage to Roman aqueducts in its appearance and function. It is the oldest standing bridge in the city.

In 1863, the state authorized the creation of High Bridge Reservoir and a pumping station that diverted some of the water from the aqueduct to serve upper Manhattan. In total, the 324-square-foot pool held 10 million gallons of water.

On the reservoir's eastern side, the **High Bridge Water Tower** rose to 125 feet, with pipes inside running toward a tank at the top of the tower. The structure was built in 1872 to provide water pressure to high-elevation locations in upper Manhattan. The water tank was hidden inside the tower's roof and functioned until 1949. Since then, a bell has been installed inside the tower. The tower is open periodically for guided tours.

In 1934, the obsolete High Bridge Reservoir was transferred to the Parks Department along with the Williamsbridge Reservoir in the Bronx. Using funds and labor provided by the Works Progress Administration, **Highbridge Pool and Recreation Center** was completed within two years on the site of the reservoir. The pool has the capacity to fit over 4,000 people, ideal for a hot summer's day.

After it ceased functioning as the city's water conduit, High Bridge continued to serve the public as a pedestrian bridge with panoramic views of the city's skyline.

PLACES TO SEE:

✦ **Highbridge Park** Bound by Amsterdam Avenue, Edgecombe Avenue, West 155th Street, and Dyckman Street ✦ www.nycgovparks.org/parks/highbridgepark

✦ **Highbridge Pool and Recreation Center** Inside Highbridge Park, on Amsterdam Avenue at West 173rd Street

✦ **High Bridge Water Tower** At the northeast corner of Highbridge Pool and Recreation Center

✦ **High Bridge** East side of Highbridge Pool

GETTING THERE:

✦ **Bus**: M101 at Amsterdam Avenue and West 173rd Street

✦ **Subway**: A, C, 1 at 168th Street and Broadway, walk east on 168th Street to Amsterdam Avenue, turn left and walk toward West 173rd Street

✦ **Bike**: There is a bike path inside Highbridge Park on the east side of Highbridge Pool

17. Sherman Creek

Although earthquakes are a rarity in New York, there are fault lines in upper Manhattan that run between the ridges facing the Hudson River. The **125th Street fault** runs through the Manhattanville valley in a northwestern direction that skews off the street grid. To the north, the **Dyckman Street fault** runs beneath Dyckman Street in a valley that separates Washington Heights from Inwood. To the east of Broadway, a brook widened into a salt marsh as it emptied into Harlem River. It was known to the Dutch as Half Kill and to early English colonists as Round Meadow Creek before taking the name **Sherman Creek**.

Battle of Fort Washington

Sherman Creek had its origins in a spring near West 184th Street and Broadway, flowing north in a valley that separated Fort Washington Ridge from Fort George Hill. During the American Revolution, blockhouses designed to block the northward British advance topped these highlands. To the west of Sherman Creek, the present-day site of **the Cloisters** museum was once **Fort Washington**. Farther west across the Hudson River, **Fort Lee** stood atop the Palisades cliff as a twin to

Fort Washington, aiming to fire at any British warship daring to sail north into the Hudson Valley. Additional batteries were placed on Cox's Hill in present-day **Inwood Hill Park** and at **Jeffrey's Hook**, a spit of land beneath the present-day George Washington Bridge.

Following up on their successful expulsion of the patriots from Brooklyn and Lower Manhattan in September 1776, British General Sir William Howe directed his army toward the redoubts of upper Manhattan. The Battle of Fort Washington on November 16, 1776, resulted in a victory for the combined British and Hessian forces. Fort Washington was renamed after Sir William Tryon, New York's last British governor.

Sherman Creek Power Plant advertisement

Sherman Creek's role in the battle was its topography as an ideal landing site for the Redcoats, who stormed Fort George and continued toward Fort Washington, conquering upper Manhattan in a day.

Long after the blood of the fighters had dissipated into Sherman Creek, local residents were digging up buttons from their uniforms along the stream. Another reminder of the battle can be found in the backyard of the **Dyckman Farmhouse Museum**, located at 4881 Broadway, at West 204th Street. Surrounded on all sides by apartment buildings, this museum is the last farmhouse in Manhattan. During the battle, Hessian troops destroyed the original Dyckman home and built an encampment on the property. A reconstructed Hessian hut with a historical marker reminds visitors of the seven-year military occupation that followed the battle.

The Dyckman family returned in 1784 and rebuilt their farmhouse in the Dutch colonial style. It became a museum in 1916.

Dyckman Oval

At the intersection of Sherman Avenue and Broadway, Sherman Creek turned northeast and then east at Dyckman Street as it gradually widened. In the late 19th century, Inwood was the last frontier of Manhattan, retaining a rural appearance long after most of the island was cut up by the street grid.

Change arrived in 1906, when the Seventh Avenue subway was extended north of 145th Street. At the **Dyckman Street station**, the subway emerges from the ground and runs as an elevated line toward its terminus at Van Cortlandt Park. The Dyckman Street station is note-worthy for its Beaux-Arts headhouse and tunnel portal and its public art. With the arrival of the subway, the streambed of Sherman Creek west of Nagle Avenue was filled in, and apartment buildings were developed on top.

To the east of Nagle Avenue, the marshland was partially filled by 1923, when the **Dyckman Oval** opened to the public. This early sports arena hosted boxing matches and was the home field for the New York Cubans, the local franchise of the Eastern Colored League. At the time, the major leagues were open only to white players, and people of Afri-can and Latin American descent played in the colored leagues. The oval closed in 1938, and the Dyckman Houses were completed on its site in 1951.

With the construction of the Dyckman Houses, Sherman Creek was reduced to an inlet of the Harlem River. Tenth Avenue was constructed atop the landfill, connecting Inwood with Harlem River Drive.

Sculler's Row
The present outline of the Sherman Creek inlet was carved in 1896 as part of a larger project that straightened and dredged the Harlem River into a navigable waterway. On Sherman Creek's northern shoreline, barges brought coal to a power plant that served the neighborhood. On the southern side, rowing clubs had their boathouses in a procession known as **Sculler's Row**. From the late 19th century through the 1950s, the section of the Harlem River between Sherman Creek and the 145th Street Bridge rivaled Philadelphia's Boathouse Row.

The presence of competitive boat racing brought thousands of spec-tators to the shores of the Harlem River, many of whom watched the processions from High Bridge Park and Fort George Hill. On May 11, 1902, a daylong rowing club procession included 150 boats powered by over 600 oarsmen representing 11 rowing and boat clubs.

Over the following decades, rowing declined on the Harlem River as pollution, highways, and parkland encroached on its once-tranquil shores. A *New York Times* article from 1941 listed only three rowing clubs remaining at the Sherman Creek inlet, all on land owned by the city's Department of Docks. The city sought to evict the boaters, looking to use this section of the shoreline as an ash dump. Ironically, Commissioner of Docks John McKenzie had himself been an avid rower in his youth, practicing the sport at Flushing Bay in Queens.

Along with boating and rowing clubs, local universities also had boathouses on the Harlem River. The last holdout was Fordham University, whose boathouse was destroyed by an arsonist in 1978.

Redevelopment

In the early years of electric power, generating plants were often built close to the shore in order to facilitate the delivery of coal from barges. By 1970, the turn-of-the-century **Sherman Creek Generating Station** was obsolete and ceased generating power. For the next three decades, it stood unused as a vacant Beaux-Arts structure. Its successor is the much smaller **Con Edison Academy Substation**, which opened in 2011. Seeking a design that blended into the neighborhood and acknowledged its history, the walls facing Sherman Creek feature sail-like sculptures, and above the main entrance is a rotunda resembling a lighthouse.

On Sherman Creek's southern shoreline, decades of neglect brought abandoned cars and boats to the inlet. Restoration efforts spearheaded by the New York Restoration Project began in 1996, seeking to clear the illegal dumping site and lay out a naturalistic landscape. Sandwiched between the Harlem River Drive and the shoreline, the five-acre **Swindler Cove** opened in 2003 and features a freshwater park, a cove, and a floating boathouse. The cove is a small indentation in the shoreline framed by a walkway bridge. Its namesake was garden advocate Billy Swindler, who introduced NYRP founder Bette Midler to the site. Swindler died of AIDS in 1997 at age 39.

Funding for this park came from the state, which contributed $10 million, and Midler, who raised another $2.3 million for the **Peter Jay Sharp Boathouse**. In recognition of the shoreline's history as Sculler's Row, the boathouse was designed in the late Victorian style by architect Armand LeGardeur, who looked to old photographs for inspiration. Its namesake was a New York hotel and real estate owner who was involved in a variety of civic causes.

"I saw pictures of the number of people engaged in sport on the Harlem River in its former incarnation," Midler said, "and then I saw the ghost town it had become. If it existed once, why not again?"

PLACES TO SEE:

✦ **Swindler Cove Park** Dyckman Street at Harlem River Drive ✦
www.nyrp.org/Parks_and_Gardens/parks/Swindler_Cove_Sherman
_Creek_Park/Park_Overview

LEARN MORE:

✦ **New York Restoration Project** www.nyrp.org

GETTING THERE:

✦ **Bus**: M100 at 10th Avenue and Harlem River Drive
✦ **Subway**: 1 at Dyckman Street, walk one block east on Dyckman
Street toward the Harlem River
✦ **Bike**: The Harlem River bike path follows the southern shoreline of
Sherman Creek inlet; there is a bike lane on Tenth Avenue on the
western side of the inlet

18. Spuyten Duyvil Creek

These days, circumnavigating Manhattan is as easy as taking a Circle
Line cruise. The tour boat rounds Manhattan in a counterclockwise
route that travels north on the Harlem River and turns west at Broadway
Bridge for the last three-quarters of a mile toward the entrance to the

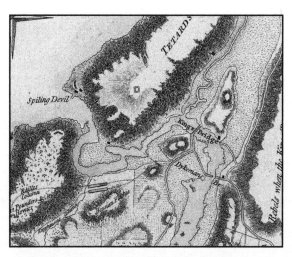

*Excerpt from the Battle of Fort Washington
Map showing original course of Spuyten Duyvil
Creek*

Hudson River. This stretch of the Harlem River flows between cliffs, with Marble Hill on the right and Inwood on the left. Beyond the Hudson River are the Palisades of New Jersey, rising to nearly 200 feet above the water.

Prior to 1895, this portion of the Harlem River was known as **Spuyten Duyvil Creek**, a twisting S-shaped route that was inaccessible to larger vessels. It was narrow enough to nearly connect Manhattan to the mainland and forced ships from upstate bound for Boston and Long Island to go around Manhattan's southern tip.

That year, the **Broadway Bridge** opened to traffic, replacing an ancient bridge and, later, carrying the Seventh Avenue Line across the new channel. The present Broadway Bridge is the third at the location, completed in 1962 as a lift span that rises from 24 feet to 136 feet above high tide.

Harlem River Ship Canal

With the completion of the Erie Canal in 1825, there was soon talk of shortening the route between the Hudson River and the Long Island Sound with a canal at Spuyten Duyvil. The work would straighten and widen the creek, in parts blasting through rock to make Manhattan a true island. Its shape was roughly that of a dollar sign—with the twist representing Spuyten Duyvil Creek and the straight line the **Harlem River Ship Canal**.

The Harlem River Ship Canal opened on June 17, 1895, to celebrations unmatched since the Erie Canal. The date chosen for the "wedding of the waters" was the anniversary of the Battle of Bunker Hill. The canal's opening included parades on land and water, fireworks, and musical compositions, such as "Prosperity to Our Canal."

As a result of the canal, the Manhattan neighborhood of **Marble Hill** was severed from the rest of the borough and transformed into an island, separated from the Bronx by a remnant of Spuyten Duyvil Creek. In 1913, the old creek was buried, and Marble Hill was fused to the continent. The hilly neighborhood has streets named after early Dutch settlers and was used as a fort during the Revolutionary War.

Buried with the creek was the original **King's Bridge**, namesake from which the adjacent Bronx neighborhood of Kingsbridge takes its name. The bridge was first constructed in 1693 as a toll crossing by settler Frederick Philipse and named as a token of loyalty to the king. The only reminder of this bridge is a plaque affixed to an exterior wall at Marble Hill Houses, a low-income development built atop the filled streambed of the creek that straddles the Bronx-Manhattan border.

Marble Hill's land border with the Bronx led to a campaign in 1939 by Bronx Borough President James Lyons to annex the 52-acre neighborhood. Local residents opposed the effort, describing it as an "anschluss," the term for Nazi Germany's heavy-handed takeover of neighboring Austria a year earlier. Although Marble Hill is still politically part of Manhattan, it shares the Bronx's 718 area code as well as its school board, community board, and police precinct.

Johnson Iron Works

Like many significant New York projects, the canal was unable to be realized as planned because of a recalcitrant property owner in the way. The canal's eastern half ran in a straight line, cutting off Marble Hill from Manhattan, but as it passed present-day Inwood Hill Park, the canal took a sharp southward jog around a peninsula, then twisted north around Inwood Hill before merging with the Hudson River. The 13.5-acre peninsula that the canal twisted to avoid was the site of the **Johnson Iron Works**, a smoke-belching foundry located at the midpoint of Spuyten Duyvil Creek.

Its story began in 1853, when industrialist Elias Johnson selected the site for his foundry. His son Isaac, fitting the pattern of a 19th-century industry captain, designed the neighborhood around his factory as a "company town," with employee housing, a school, a library, taverns, and a church. The Spanish-American War, the invention of automobiles, and the First World War continued to benefit the factory, whose workforce peaked at 1,600 in 1917.

But while the factory produced cannons, pistons, and auto parts, elected officials hadn't given up their goal of completely straightening Spuyten Duyvil Creek. In 1919, state lawmakers passed an act to straighten the canal. The factory waged a legal battle to keep its site, but it lost, despite all the jobs it created. A *New York Times* article from this period described the foundry as "a fair-sized industrial centre with a touch of the Pittsburgh atmosphere."

On June 9, 1923, the foundry produced its last order of steel, and its 1,200 workers were sent home. The straight canal route of today was opened to vessels in 1936 in a smaller celebration. The only remnant of the Johnson peninsula today is its southern tip, which is fused to Manhattan's Inwood Hill Park.

Letter C

Across from the former Johnson peninsula, there is a 100-foot cliff face that features the largest hand-painted letter on a natural surface. This **letter C** is a reminder of Columbia University's presence on the river. While the rowers of Fordham University had their boathouse near Sherman Creek, the city's oldest university has the **Baker Athletics Complex** on the southern side of Spuyten Duyvil Creek, facing the cliff.

Financier George Baker purchased the 26-acre complex for the university in 1921. Prior to his career with the New York Yankees, Lou Gehrig played at Baker Field as a Columbia engineering student. Besides rowing and baseball, the complex is used for football, lacrosse, and track events. Its largest facility, Wien Stadium, holds 17,100 spectators.

While Columbia has the distinction of occupying the northernmost tip of Manhattan Island, the opposite shore belongs to the Metro-North Railroad. Its predecessor company, New York Central, gave permission in 1952 to medical student and rowing team coxswain Robert Prendergast to paint the iconic 60-by-60-foot C in the school's trademark light blue color framed in a white border.

Inwood Hill Park

Taking up 196 acres on the southern side of Spuyten Duyvil Creek, **Inwood Hill Park** is one of the largest parks in Manhattan and contains numerous natural and historical features. Its natural forest, the last on the island, has rock shelters used centuries ago by the natives and more recently by homeless individuals. The park's location at the confluence of two streams made it an ideal fishing ground and trading post. In contrast to European settlement, which began at the southern tip of Manhattan, the native **Shorakapock** community was on the site of this park.

Within the park, the **Inwood Hill Nature Center** sits on the remnant of the peninsula between the ship canal and a cove that was part of Spuyten Duyvil Creek. The Depression-era structure was originally a boathouse.

The natural beauty of Inwood Hill Park is pierced by the noise of the **Henry Hudson Parkway**, which cuts through the park. The highway is a product of Robert Moses, the great city planner. He succeeded in completing the **Henry Hudson Bridge** over Spuyten Duyvil after three decades of opposition from local residents. The bridge was first proposed in 1904 ahead of the Hudson-Fulton Celebration of 1909 that would observe the tercentennial of Henry Hudson's discovery of the Hudson River and the centennial of Robert Fulton's steamship experiment on it.

Moses appropriated federal funding for "park access roads" by designing many of his highways to run through parks. His legacy is the city's parkway network, which is lined by green shoulders managed by the city's Parks Department. The Henry Hudson Bridge opened in 1936, an 840-foot steel arch crossing designed by David Steinman.

The third bridge over Spuyten Duyvil Creek is the Amtrak trestle that swings open for Circle Line boats. In its closed position, its average clearance is five feet, enough for a canoe to pass below. Completed in 1900, the single-track **Spuyten Duyvil Bridge** is used by the Empire Corridor service that runs between New York City and Buffalo. At the bridge's northern landing, the Amtrak line merges with the Metro-North.

The enlarging of Spuyten Duyvil Creek into the Harlem River Ship Channel sped up the urbanization of the surrounding landscape. At the same time, the preservation of Inwood Hill as a park and the exclave of Marble Hill provide plenty of natural and historical sites along the former creek.

PLACES TO SEE:

+ **Inwood Hill Park** Hudson River and Spuyten Duyvil Creek between Dyckman Street and Indian Road + www.nycgovparks .org/parks/inwood-hill-park
+ **Henry Hudson Bridge** Henry Hudson Parkway across Spuyten Duyvil Creek + web.mta.info/bandt/html/henry.html
+ **Baker Field** 533 West 218th Street + www.gocolumbialions.com
+ **Broadway Bridge** Broadway across Spuyten Duyvil Creek

LEARN MORE:

+ **Conservancy North** www.conservancynorth.org
+ **My Inwood blog** myinwood.net

GETTING THERE:

+ **Bus**: Bx7, Bx20, BxM1 at West 220th Street and Broadway; Bx7, Bx9, Bx20 at West 225th Street and Broadway
+ **Subway**: 1 at Marble Hill–225th Street
+ **Train**: Metro-North at Marble Hill or Spuyten Duyvil
+ **Bike**: There are bike routes within Inwood Hill Park and across the Henry Hudson Bridge; there is a bike lane on West 218th Street adjacent to Baker Field

19. Little Hell Gate

In the shadow of the Triborough Bridge and the Hell Gate Viaduct is a wide neck of land that connects Randalls and Wards Islands and the lesser-known Sunken Meadow Island. All three occupy a section of the East River known as Hell Gate. The main section of Hell Gate separates Wards Island from Queens, while **Little Hell Gate** once separated Wards Island from Randalls Island. Most of Little Hell Gate was filled, leaving only a small cove on the western shore of the combined Randalls and Wards Islands.

Little Hell Gate Bridge, 1996

The first proposal to fill the strait passed the state legislature in 1877 but was met with a swift letter of protest from the Society for the Reformation of Juvenile Delinquents, writing on behalf of the asylum on Wards Island. It argued that the use of trash for landfill would "probably bring disease and death among its inmates."

In 1916, the **Hell Gate Bridge** was constructed over the strait as part of the railroad's route to Penn Station. The section across Little Hell Gate was composed of four inverted bow-string arches, each spanning 300 feet. Today, it runs over reclaimed land.

The architect of this dramatic span, Gustav Lindenthal, had Othmar Ammann as his assistant. Ammann returned to Little Hell Gate in 1936 to celebrate the completion of his own creation, the **Triborough Bridge**, a series of three bridges that connect Randalls and Wards Islands with the Bronx, Manhattan, and Queens.

Between 1934 and 1970, Little Hell Gate was gradually filled in by the city, expanding parkland on both sides. In 1957 the city fused Sunken Meadow Island to Randalls Island at no cost by allowing contractors to dump construction debris in the section of Little Hell Gate between the islands. The filling of Little Hell Gate continued into the 1970s until only a small cove remained.

Hell Gate Bridge and the 4-span Little Hell Gate inverted bowstring arches in the foreground

With support from the Randalls Island Park Alliance, the private group that operates the city-owned island, a bike path was constructed along the cove, covering up a century's worth of landfill and hinting of a much larger strait that was there with a naturalistic shoreline.

PLACES TO SEE:

+ **Icahn Stadium** 20 Randalls Island ✦ www.icahnstadium.org
+ **Triborough (RFK) Bridge** Connecting to the Bronx, Queens, and Manhattan across the Bronx Kill, Harlem River, and East River ✦ www.nycroads.com/crossings/triborough

GETTING THERE:

+ **Bus**: M35 to Randalls and Wards Islands
+ **Subway**: 4, 5, 6 at 125th Street, transfer to M35
+ **Bike**: There are bike lanes on Randalls and Wards Islands that connect to Queens, the Bronx, and Manhattan via the Triborough (RFK) Bridge and the Wards Island Bridge

The Bronx

➤ **In the public imagination, crime films have secured** the Bronx's image as the most urban of the city's five boroughs, but it is also home to the world's most expensive baseball team, whose stadium stands atop a buried stream. Likewise, the Bronx cemetery, where numerous New York entertainers and society figures are interred, also has a hidden lake.

While Manhattan has Central Park, the otherwise-dense Bronx has the much larger trio of Van Cortlandt, Bronx, and Pelham Bay Parks, each with their own streams and stories. All streams in the Bronx run from north to south, reflecting grooves in the land left by the retreating glaciers of the last ice age. Individual ponds and lakes are the product of ice blocks that detached from the glaciers. In addition to natural watercourses, the Bronx has reservoirs that were part of the city's aqueduct.

The biggest waterway success story in the borough is the Bronx River: once a dumping ground for abandoned vehicles, now a showcase of postmodern landscape architecture. Near its mouth, a new trio of parks beckons visitors. With a renewed respect for nature, the developed landscape of the Bronx spans the spectrum—from forests with freshwater ponds to sandy beaches on the East River estuary.

* * *

20. Bronx River

The **Bronx River**, the longest freshwater stream in the Bronx, neatly bisects the borough in its run between the northern neighborhood of **Wakefield** and the south of the borough at **Hunts Point**. The river's downstream course offers a cross section of the borough—from its verdant north, into Bronx Park at the borough's center, emptying by the commercial and industrial warehouses of Hunts Point. In contrast to most of New York City's hidden streams, the Bronx River is more of a cause célèbre, largely thanks to the efforts of the Bronx River Alliance in promoting its restoration and developing new parks along its shores.

Known to the native Lenape as Aquehung, or "river of high bluffs," the Bronx River begins at **Kensico Reservoir** near Valhalla, which provides some of the drinking water for New York City. The excess water empties from the reservoir, flowing south in a nearly straight line toward the Bronx. Most of the stream's route is followed by the **Bronx River Parkway**, which was completed in 1925 as one of the nation's first limited-access highways, traveling through designated parkland along the stream.

The stream enters New York City at **Nereid Avenue**, which crosses the Bronx River with a dramatic set of concrete arches. Below the city line, the river continues through parkland, alongside a bike trail, toward Bronx Park. Known as **Muskrat Cove**, the section between the city line and Gun Hill Road is part of the Bronx River Greenway, a proposed 23-mile bike trail lining the Bronx River. The crossing over the river at Gun Hill Road was historically known as Williamsbridge, which has lent its name to the nearby Metro-North railroad station and neighborhood.

The 1.5-mile park strip north

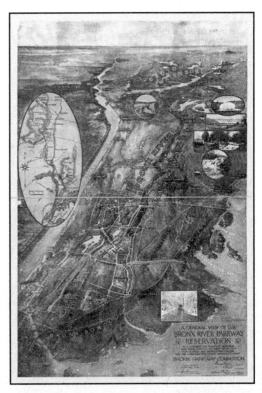

A general view of the Bronx River Parkway Reservation, 1915

THE BRONX

Bronx River Parkway at 174th Street, 1930

of Gun Hill Road is **Shoelace Park**, a portion of the stream straightened to make way for the Bronx River Parkway around 1918. Some of the sewers that had been flowing into the river were diverted when the stream was straightened, but at the same time, wetlands lining its shore were eliminated. Between 1950 and 1952, the Bronx River Parkway was extended below Burke Avenue toward Soundview. The original road on the stream's eastern bank is now a pedestrian and bike path.

Bronx Park begins below Kazimiroff Boulevard, planned as the borough's version of Central Park. Here, the river enters a two-mile stretch of thick forest in the borough's center. The park was acquired by the city around the same time as the parcels that later became the Van Cortlandt, Pelham Bay, Crotona, and Claremont Parks; the Mosholu, Crotona, and Pelham Parkways; and Grand Concourse. All were part of a "city beautiful" vision to provide green space for the Bronx. Bronx Park is home to the city's leading flora and fauna institutions: the **New York Botanical Garden** and the **Bronx Zoo**.

The 250-acre botanical garden is the largest in the city, containing a 40-acre natural forest, a waterfall, and a snuff mill built in 1840. The mill building and the surrounding park were once part of the estate of the Lorillard family, scions to a tobacco fortune. The family's tobacco firm is among the oldest in the world, dating to 1760. Today, the snuff mill is called the **Lillian and Amy Goldman Stone Mill**, after a generous family that funded its restoration. It is a popular wedding venue.

Within the botanical garden, a smaller body of water, **Twin Lakes**, feeds into the Bronx River.

Crossing Fordham Road, the stream enters the Bronx Zoo. At the zoo's northern edge, a bison range stands across from the **Mitsubishi Riverwalk**, where turtles can be spotted. A dam once used for a mill creates a pleasant waterfall here. This is one of two milldams within the zoo that resemble waterfalls; they slow the river, forcing waterborne travelers to portage around the cataracts. Behind the milldams, the impounded river is wide enough to have two named lakes: the six-acre **Lake Agassiz** and the 25-acre **Bronx Lake**. The former is named after Louis Agassiz, a noted Swiss-born geologist of the 19th century.

The stream is paralleled in the zoo by Boston Road, a colonial-period postal route that connected New York with Boston. Toward the southern edge of the zoo, the **Wild Asia Monorail** crosses the Bronx River. The river is then dammed at East 180th Street, its second cataract. At this location, a $12 million fish ladder was completed in March 2015, enabling the native alewife and blueback herring to swim farther upstream on the river. The fish ladder passes by the East 182nd Street dam, a barrier dating back to the 17th century.

Below this point, the water goes through **West Farms**, a heavily urbanized neighborhood with an ironically rural name dating to colonial times. The stream is narrow, with buildings and bridges keeping it in the shade for much of the day. The tight reach through West Farms includes River Park, a popular site for barbecues with the waterfall in the background.

Across East 180th Street is **River Garden**, a community garden with cornstalks lining the stream's eastern shore. On the western bank is **West Farms Rapids**, a narrow park trail hugging the shoreline. Elevated subway trains roar overhead, near the **East 180th Street station**, a former stop on the New York, Westchester, and Boston Railway that features a landmarked Spanish Mission–style station entrance and an abandoned platform formerly used by the railway. To the west of the station, the **Bronx Park South** neighborhood was once an example of urban devastation, famously documented by photographers Camilo José Vergara and Lisa Kahane, among others. Today, neo-urban townhouses share space with low-income projects and surviving prewar tenements.

Continuing downstream, the Bronx River dips beneath the Cross Bronx Expressway, reemerging in **Starlight Park**, a newly opened park that stands on the site of a former amusement park.

The new park is best reached by the **174th Street Bridge**, an arch bridge completed in 1928 which was designed to resemble an elevated subway trestle. The bridge spans the valley formed by the river and also crosses one of the city's shortest highways, Interstate 895 or the **Sheridan Expressway**, which is 1.2 miles long.

Continuing south, the next new park along the river is **Concrete Plant Park**, a narrow 1,900-foot length between Westchester Avenue and the Bruckner Expressway. Designed by landscape architect Jim Mituzas, the park features a trio of industrial relics as its centerpiece. Inside the park, austere white concrete deck chairs face the waterfront.

At the park's southern end, a single track branches off the Amtrak line, bound for Hunts Point. The drawbridge framing the park's edge carries the **Bruckner Expressway**. Its namesake is former Bronx borough president and congressman Henry Bruckner. South of the drawbridge, the eastern bank of the Bronx River was filled in with riprap and landfill between the 1920s and the 1960s, but today this largely undeveloped land makes up **Soundview Park**. It faces an industrial shoreline that continues to collect scrap metal and churn out concrete.

The neighborhood of Soundview takes its name from the Long Island Sound, which on older maps included the upper East River.

Traveling along Edgewater Road, the freight rail spur follows the street toward Hunts Point. At Lafayette Avenue is the second postmodern pocket park, **Hunts Point Riverside Park**, which transformed a dead end of Lafayette Avenue into a patch of green. The pocket park has a playground with a canoe theme, a pier, and a kayak launch.

At the mouth of the Bronx River is a 60-acre complex of warehouses that is the world's largest food distribution center, where trucks pick up meat, produce, and fish before dawn each day and distribute the food across the city's restaurants, supermarkets, and schools. Founded in 1967, the **Hunts Point Cooperative Market** is the successor to the older wholesale markets in Manhattan, but in spite of its location on the shore of the East River, the market does not utilize its waterfront. The main road ringing the complex is Food Center Drive—an excellent route for biking when the market is closed.

Recognizing belatedly that the shoreline by the market is inaccessible and unused, the city has begun reclaiming it for the public. A small example of this effort is **Hunts Point Landing**, a pocket park that opened in 2012, sandwiched between a former marine transfer station and the Fulton Fish Market, which relocated to Hunts Point from Lower Manhattan in 2006.

+ **Shoelace Park** Bronx Boulevard between East 233rd Street and Allerton Avenue
+ **New York Botanical Garden** 2900 Southern Boulevard ✦ 718-817-8700 ✦ www.nybg.org
+ **Bronx Zoo** 2300 Southern Boulevard ✦ 718-367-1010 ✦ www.bronxzoo.com
+ **Starlight Park** East 174th Street at Sheridan Expressway
+ **Concrete Plant Park** Bronx River between Westchester Avenue and Bruckner Boulevard
+ **Hunts Point Riverside Park** Lafayette Avenue at Edgewater Road
+ **Hunts Point Landing** Farragut Street at Food Center Drive

+ **Bronx River Alliance** One Bronx River Parkway ✦ 718-430-4665 ✦ www.bronxriver.org
+ **Bronx River Art Center** 2064 Boston Road ✦ 718-589-5819 ✦ www.bronxriverart.org
+ **Rocking the Boat** Every Saturday and Sunday from May through September, this group offers free rowing at Hunts Point Riverside Park ✦ 812 Edgewater Road ✦ 718-466-5799 ✦ www.rockingtheboat.org

+ **Bus**:
  ◇ Bx16, Bx31 at East 233rd Street
  ◇ Bx28, Bx30, Bx38, Bx41 at Gun Hill Road
  ◇ Bx26 at Kazimiroff Boulevard for New York Botanical Garden
  ◇ Bx12, Bx22 at Fordham Road for Bronx Zoo
  ◇ Bx9, Bx21, Bx36, Bx40, Bx42, Q44 at West Farms Square for Bronx Zoo
  ◇ Bx36 at East 174th Street and Bronx River Road for Starlight Park
  ◇ Bx4, Bx4a, Bx27 at Westchester Avenue for Concrete Plant Park
  ◇ Bx6 at Spofford Avenue and Halleck Street for Hunts Point Riverside Park and Hunts Point Landing
+ **Subway**: 2 at Wakefield–241st Street; 2, 5 at any of the stops between Nereid Avenue and West Farms Square–East Tremont Avenue; 6 at Whitlock Avenue

THE BRONX

+ **Train**: Metro-North at any of the stops between Wakefield and Botanical Garden
+ **Bike**: The Northern Bronx River Greenway extends south from Kensico Dam Plaza County Park in Valhalla toward the city line, and the bike trail continues south along the Bronx River toward Pelham Parkway; Concrete Plant Park also has a bike trail
+ **Boat**: The Bronx River is accessible by canoe along its entire length within the Bronx, with boat ramps at Shoelace Park, Fort Knox Park, Starlight Park, Concrete Plant Park, Hunts Point Riverside Park, and Hunts Point Landing; the clearance on the Bruckner Expressway drawbridge is 27 feet at mean high water

21. Tibbetts Brook

The valley that carries the Harlem River continues north of the river's bend at Inwood, with **Tibbetts Brook** taking up its floor. Originating in **Redmond Park** in Yonkers, this stream continues south into **Tibbetts Brook Park**, toward the city line, where it enters **Van Cortlandt Park**. The stream is named after colonial settler George Tippett. His descendants were loyalists and were expelled from New York following the American Revolution, but the misspelled name remained on the stream.

Within the park, the brook follows the **Old Putnam Trail**, an abandoned railway that operated between 1881 and 1980. The trail takes the route of the trains between Redmond Park and Van Cortlandt Park. Part of the trail uses a former trestle across **Van Cortlandt Lake**. Branching off from the trail is the **John Kieran Nature Trail**, which follows closer to the lake's shoreline. Continuing north, the Old Putnam Trail crosses the city line and becomes the **South County Trailway**. Vestiges of the railway include a rusty skeletal remnant of the Van Cortlandt Park train station and stone slabs intended for Grand Central Terminal that were placed in the park to determine whether they would survive against the elements.

Van Cortlandt Lake was formed in 1699 when Tibbetts Brook was dammed to power the Van Cortlandt family's gristmill. The mill ground its last wheat kernels in 1889, a year after the family estate and its mansion were purchased by the city for a public park. The **Van Cortlandt House** inside the park, today a museum, dates to 1748. During the Revolutionary War it hosted George Washington and his French allies, generals Rochambeau and Lafayette. A former grain plantation, it used slaves to cultivate the crops. The mansion includes an herb garden.

Flowing out of Van Cortlandt Lake, Tibbetts Brook continued south through the Kingsbridge neighborhood into **Spuyten Duyvil Creek**. Between 1891 and 1894, a sewer was built to channel the section of Tibbetts Brook south of Van Cortlandt Park beneath Tibbett Avenue.

If the stream were to be daylighted, it would probably run along a less developed eastern route following **Major Deegan Expressway** and the Putnam Line right-of-way. The creation of a park trail along a daylighted Tibbetts Brook would connect Van Cortlandt Park to the Harlem River, forming a green link to other parks along that waterway. Daylighting would also reduce the burden on the city's sewer system, into which the stream is presently channeled.

THE BRONX

PLACES TO SEE:
+ **Van Cortlandt House Museum** 718-543-3344 ✦ www.vchm.org
+ **Van Cortlandt Golf Course** 115 Van Cortlandt Park South ✦ 718-543-4595 ✦ www.golfnyc.com/vancortlandt_home/
+ **Basic Canoeing with the Urban Park Rangers** In the summer, the Parks Department offers basic canoeing courses in Van Cortlandt Lake; for more information, call 718-548-0912
+ **Kingsbridge Library** 291 West 231st Street ✦ 718-548-5656 ✦ www.nypl.org/locations/kingsbridge

LEARN MORE:
+ **Van Cortlandt Park Conservancy** www.vcpark.org
+ **Friends of Van Cortlandt Park** www.vancortlandt.org
+ **TrailLink Old Putnam Trail** www.traillink.com/trail/old-putnam -trail.aspx

GETTING THERE:
+ **Bus**: Bx9 and BxM3 to Broadway and West 242nd Street; Westchester Bee-Line buses 1, 2, 3 to Broadway and West 242nd Street
+ **Subway**: 1 at Van Cortlandt Park–242nd Street
+ **Bike**: There are bike lanes on Tibbett Avenue, within Van Cortlandt Park, and on the Putnam Line right-of-way

22. Westchester Creek

This stream's name recalls a time when the Bronx was part of Westchester County, before some of its towns gradually opted to join Greater New York. Adding to the geographic confusion, the colonial settlement of **Westchester**, located along today's Westchester Avenue in the Bronx, is

deep inside city limits, also orphaned from the county that shares its name. **Westchester Creek** originated near the intersection of Stillwell Avenue and Pelham Parkway, meandering south across land that later became the **Bronx Psychiatric Center** and the Lexington Avenue subway line's **Westchester Yard**.

The visible part of the creek emerges to the south of East Tremont Avenue, at **Herbert H. Lehman High School**, which was built in 1970 atop the stream. This 2.1-mile section of the stream still has an active role as a dock for small houseboats and oil barges. Near the former **Whitestone Cinemas** is the **Bruckner Interchange**, a twisting loop of ramps where five highways cross paths; and the historic **Saint Joseph's School for the Deaf**, part of a once-larger Catholic campus that was bisected by the **Whitestone Expressway** in 1936.

Westchester Creek, 1928

Farther down the shore is the one-block-wide **Ferry Point** enclave of homes and warehouses with unique street names such as Rohr, Senger, Wenner, and Yznaga Place. The 35-household neighborhood was once the estate of the Wenner family, subdivided in 1923. The legacy of the family remains in a street name.

Toward its end, the stream widens and is joined by **Pugsley Creek** just as it empties into the East River between Clason Point and Ferry Point.

Pugsley Creek originated near the Morrison Avenue–Sound View subway station on Westchester Avenue, meandering south on the sites of the present-day Monroe and Bronxdale housing developments. The stream emerges just south of Lacombe Avenue, within **Pugsley Creek Park**.

Continuing to Westchester Creek's southern tip, Brush Avenue enters **Ferry Point Park**, a 413-acre expanse of open space in the shadow of the Whitestone Bridge. As its name suggests, a ferry route plied the narrows in the East River between Ferry Point and Whitestone before the bridge opened in 1939. Turning eastward, the East River shoreline of the park forms a mile-long arc atop landfill that covered **Baxter Creek Inlet**, which once separated Ferry Point from Throggs Neck.

THE BRONX

PLACES TO SEE:

✦ **Herbert H. Lehman High School** 3000 East Tremont Avenue ✦ 718-904-4200 ✦ www.lehmanhs.com
✦ **Ferry Point Park** Entrance at Brush Avenue and Schley Avenue ✦ www.nycgovparks.org/parks/ferry-point-park

GETTING THERE:

✦ **Bus**: Bx5, Q44, or Q50 at the Bruckner Interchange
✦ **Subway**: 6 at Westchester Square–East Tremont Avenue, walk south on Commerce Avenue to reach the shore
✦ **Bike**: There are bike lanes on Brush Avenue and within Pugsley Creek Park and Ferry Point Park
✦ **Boat**: Westchester Creek is navigable by small watercraft; the clearance of the Bruckner Expressway drawbridge above the stream is 14 feet at mean high water

23. Rattlesnake Brook

Rattlesnake Brook's name takes the traveler back to a time when fearsome animals lived in the Bronx. The stream originated just north of Eastchester Road in the **Edenwald** neighborhood, flowing into a valley within the estate of the Seton family, relatives of Elizabeth Seton, the first American-born Catholic saint.

During the American Revolution, pitched battles raged across the eastern Bronx, with patriot raiding parties coming in from New England to attack loyalist positions.

A man-made waterfall was built to channel water from Rattlesnake Brook to the Setons' farm. The site of Seton Falls Park, where the waterfall still stands, was originally slated to become a hospital for contagious diseases, but community opposition scuttled the plan, and the land became a city park in 1930. The park is heavily wooded, with Edenwald public housing on its west and the suburban **Eastchester** neighborhood to the east.

South of the estate, Rattlesnake Brook crossed Boston Road, emptying into a 15-acre millpond where the Boston Secor housing development stands today. In the 19th century, **Holler's Pond** was a popular place for ice-skating and the manufacturing of ice blocks. The mill damming the brook was constructed in 1739 by Thomas Shute and Joseph Stanton. In 1790, Scottish settler John Reid purchased the mill, and it took on his name. This mill was destroyed in a storm in 1900.

Though the brook today goes back underground until its end at the Hutchinson River, the map reveals its history in street names, including **Reeds Mill Lane**, a one-block bend of old houses surrounded by modern high-rises.

Across the New England Thruway is a forested parcel that is surrounded by the high-rises of Co-op City. Comprising nearly 11 acres, **Givans Creek Woods** was saved from development by Friends of Givans Creek Woods, a group of local residents who wished to preserve a natural forest within walking distance of the massive apartments. It was designated as a park in 1995.

The preserve's namesake is Robert Givan, an immigrant from Scotland who settled in this area in 1795 and established a tidal mill near the forest. A mile to the south of the preserve, Givan Square, at the intersection of Eastchester Road and East Gun Hill Road, marks the location where the Givan family estate once stood. The creek runs beneath this forest and neighboring apartment buildings, emptying into the Hutchinson River.

PLACES TO SEE:

✦ **Seton Falls Park** Bound approximately by Baychester Avenue, East 233rd Street, Crawford Avenue, and Pratt Avenue ✦ www.nycgov parks.org/parks/seton-falls-park

GETTING THERE:

✦ **Bus**: Bx16 on East 233rd Street on the northern side of Seton Falls Park

+ **Subway**: 5 at Eastchester–Dyre Avenue, walk five blocks east on East 233rd Street toward Seton Falls Park
+ **Bike**: There are no bike lanes in or around Rattlesnake Brook

24. Hutchinson River

The second-longest freshwater stream in the Bronx originates in **Scarsdale**, flowing through three reservoirs before entering city limits. Known to natives as Aquacanounck, the **Hutchinson River** is the only stream in the country named after a woman: English settler **Anne Hutchinson**, a dissident Puritan who fled from Massachusetts. Her homestead was at Split Rock, on the site of Pelham Bay Park, where **Split Rock Golf Course** keeps the name of the natural landmark.

The widowed mother of 11 children was a casualty of the unpopular Kieft's War, where in 1643 governor Willem Kieft launched attacks against the Lenape natives. Among those killed in retaliation for the unprovoked attack were Hutchinson and 10 of her children. The lone survivor, Susanna Hutchinson, lived in captivity for a couple of years before the natives traded her back to the Dutch. Among her notable descendants is 2012 Republican presidential candidate Mitt Romney.

Speaking of Americana, the Hutchinson River once hosted a patriotic-themed amusement park on its western shore called **Freedomland**, which cost $65 million to build. The park operated for only four years, from 1960 to 1964— deep in debt and never a threat to Disney's amusement park empire. When it opened, it was the largest amusement park in the world, designed by a man who had been instrumental in creating Disneyland a few years before.

Hutchinson River, 1923

Following the closing of Freedomland, the marshland site was redeveloped into **Co-op City**, the largest housing development in the United

THE BRONX

States. Comprising 35 high-rise towers, seven townhouse clusters, and three shopping centers, Co-op City is an unusual blend of an urban appearance and a suburban lifestyle. The Cold War design exemplifies Le Corbusier's "towers in a park" concept, and more than two-thirds of the neighborhood is open space. In some ways, it is cut off from the rest of the Bronx: There is no subway access, and Co-op City is physically set apart by the New England Thruway.

In contrast to the Manhattan shoreline, which features park trails along nearly the entire length of the East and Hudson Rivers, the shoreline by Co-op City is virtually inaccessible to residents, covered by thick vegetation and construction equipment. Traveling by boat on the Hutchinson River, the view is a study in contrast, with towering apartments on one bank and the natural forest of **Pelham Bay Park** on the other. Farther upstream, a bus depot and car junkyards line the shore. Downstream, just before the Hutchinson River empties into Eastchester Bay is **Goose Island**, an uninhabited speck of land serving as a bird sanctuary. Its last permanent dweller, Abigail "Mammy Goose" Tice, vacated the island in 1884 at age 90. She died two years later on City Island.

Another island on the Hutchinson River, **Codling Island**, was located just south of Boston Road. By the mid-20th century, it was fused to the mainland.

GETTING THERE:

+ **Bus**: BxM7, Bx23, Bx28, Bx38, and Q50 on Co-op City Boulevard along the Hutchinson River
+ **Subway**: 5 at Gun Hill Road, transfer to Bx28 or Bx38
+ **Bike**: There are no bike lanes along the Hutchinson River
+ **Boat**: Hutchinson River is navigable for its entire length within the Bronx; the Pelham Parkway drawbridge has a clearance of 13 feet at mean high water; a bit upstream, the Amtrak railroad drawbridge has its closed-position clearance at 8 feet

25. Crotona Park (Indian Lake)

The 3.3-acre spring-fed **Indian Lake** is the centerpiece of **Crotona Park**, an expanse of forested hills in the midst of the South Bronx neighborhoods of Claremont and Tremont. Acquired by the city in 1888, its vicinity was known as Bathgate Woods, an outcropping that offered views of the Palisades cliffs and the distant towers of the Brooklyn Bridge, which was the city's tallest structure at the time.

As the Bronx developed, Crotona Park, with its boulders deposited during the last ice age, offered an escape for residents—woods in an area otherwise crowded with apartments. It features a Depression-period public swimming pool, tennis courts, and baseball fields.

The weed-choked lake had two major restorations: in 1984, when the Urban Park Rangers began offering tours of its natural elements, and in 2009, when a $200 million windfall of mitigation funds from the Croton Water Filtration Plant in Kingsbridge was used to improve parkland around the borough. Nearly $4.4 million was used to restore the lake and a tributary brook feeding into the lake. The concrete shoreline was replaced with plants gently sloping into the water, a boulder beach, and an underwater aeration system that restored its fish population.

The boathouse by the lake serves as a nature center, educating local students on the lake's ecology.

THE BRONX

PLACES TO SEE:

+ **Crotona Park** Bound by Crotona Park North, Crotona Park East, Crotona Park South, and Fulton Avenue + www.nycgovparks.org/parks/crotonapark

GETTING THERE:

+ **Bus**: Bx17, Bx11 at Crotona Avenue and Claremont Parkway inside Crotona Park; Bx15 at Third Avenue and 174th Street one block east of Crotona Park
+ **Subway**: 2, 5 at 174th Street one block east of the park
+ **Train**: Metro-North at Tremont
+ **Bike**: There are a bike lanes on Crotona Avenue, Prospect Avenue, and Park Avenue, and within Crotona Park

26. Jerome Park Reservoir

Located on a hilltop plateau, **Jerome Park Reservoir**'s eastern shore is the academic highland of the Bronx, with CUNY's **Lehman College**, the **Bronx High School of Science**, and **DeWitt Clinton High School** all occupying space there. The reservoir separates the neighborhoods of **Bedford Park** and **Kingsbridge Heights**.

Supreme Court ordered the sale of the Van Cortlandt Estate at the Jerome Park Reservoir in 1912

The strategic value of the reservoir's site was recognized in the American Revolution, with **Fort Four** on its south shore and **Fort Independence** on its north. The military use of the site ended in 1779 when the British occupiers, led by General Sir Henry Clinton, razed the forts. The land was the estate of the Bathgate family, which lent its name to a neighborhood and street in the borough.

The reservoir's next incarnation began on September 25, 1866, when Leonard Jerome's horse racing track opened to the public. Instead of the shape of a conventional track, the **Jerome Park Racetrack** had a "saddlebag" design, rounding a small hill, which Jerome preserved for scenery. For 30 years, the course was home to the American Jockey Club. The first Triple Crown races took place there, and in 1876, Jerome Park was also the site of the first outdoor polo race in America. On October 4, 1894, the racetrack closed in preparation for the land's next chapter as a body of water.

Like many of New York's great building projects, the reservoir was intended to be much larger than it ended up being. In its original plans, the reservoir had a circumference of three miles and a depth of 26 feet and was intended to hold two trillion gallons of water—enough to quench the thirst of Manhattan and the Bronx for ten days. During its construction, Division Engineer Daniel Ulrich compared his task to building the pyramids of Egypt.

But in its final state, the reservoir's circumference was two miles and its capacity only 773 million gallons; of the four proposed basins, only two were built. The site proposed for the unbuilt eastern basins later became Lehman College and the Concourse Train Yard.

The remainder of the eastern basin site remained empty until 1927, when Joseph V. McKee, president of the city's Board of Aldermen, proposed to use the land for civic projects including an uptown campus for Hunter College and a privately funded Museum of the Peaceful Arts. The former became reality, while the latter was never heard from again. The Bronx finally received its own museum of art in 2000.

Hunter was the women-only sister school to City College of New York, specializing in education. In a late hurrah for the collegiate Gothic style, the public works construction project proposed nine buildings for the campus, but by 1931 only four were completed. By that time, the Gothic architectural style had long been eclipsed by Art Nouveau, Art Deco, and other successor genres.

In 1951 the uptown Hunter College campus went coed and became a separate four-year liberal arts college. It received the name Lehman College in July 1968 and was subsequently expanded. The college was formally dedicated on March 28, 1969, the 91st anniversary of Governor Lehman's birth. The school's namesake was a four-term New York governor who later became a senator and was the first director-general of the United Nations Relief and Rehabilitation Administration. Lehman College is one of three CUNY colleges in the Bronx.

To the north of Lehman College is the Bronx High School of Science, which moved to its present campus in March 1959. It was one of the city's first specialized high schools, open to students citywide who pass an admission exam.

THE BRONX

PLACES TO SEE:

✦ **Lehman College—Arts at Lehman** 718-960-8000 ✦ www.lehman
.edu/arts/index.php

GETTING THERE:

✦ **Bus**: Bx1, Bx2, and Bx3 at Sedgwick Ave and Giles Pl; Bx22 and
Bx26 at Bedford Park Blvd and Goulden Ave
✦ **Subway**: 4 to Bedford Park Blvd—Lehman College
✦ **Bike**: There are currently no bike lanes on roads near the reservoir

27. Indian Pond

In the heart of the semiprivate **Fieldston** neighborhood, **Indian Pond** is tucked inside a privately owned park maintained by fees from local residents. The 140-acre neighborhood retains a bucolic character amid creeping urbanization in the rest of Greater Riverdale. Though a 2010 plan to build three new homes near the glacial pond set off protests among local residents, the pond is protected by the Fieldston Historic District, which is also a Special Natural Area District. It is located on Indian Road off Fieldston Road.

GETTING THERE:
+ **Bus**: Bx7, Bx10 at West 246th Street, walk east for three blocks on West 246th Street, turn left on Livingston Avenue, walk to a dead end to see the pond
+ **Subway**: 1 to 231st Street, transfer to Bx7 or Bx10
+ **Bike**: There are currently no bike lanes on roads near Indian Pond

28. Delafield Ponds

Located on either side of the private Delafield Way, **Delafield Ponds** are also on private property but are less accessible to the public. Between 1991 and 2004, they stood neglected in Delafield Estates, a partially completed residential development.

The kettle ponds' namesake is Major Joseph Delafield, a veteran of the War of 1812 who was a practicing attorney and president of the New York Lyceum of Natural History. The Delafields were a prominent New York family in the 19th century whose members contributed greatly toward the city's political, scientific, and social scenes. At the time that Delafield built his 257-acre estate at Fieldston, the area was part of Westchester County and resembled other Hudson Valley communities with its countryside mansions, river views, and sparse population.

Following the death of Delafield in 1875, his heirs subdivided portions of the estate. The community of Fieldston is one example of the grid-defying lanes lined with mansions amid thick foliage. In 1965, banker Edward Delafield donated what remained of the estate to Columbia University, and it was used by graduate students in the 1970s for a unique experiment where they raised a chimpanzee as a human.

Named Nim Chimpsky as a pun on linguist Noam Chomsky, he was trained to communicate with the students in American Sign Language.

Columbia sold the estate to a developer in 1984, who proposed building 33 smaller mansions in a circle around the Delafield mansion. Only nine were completed by 1991, when the main mansion burned to the ground, and the site was sold to builder Abraham Zion, who also struggled to complete the project. The estate was sold again in an auction in 2012.

The estates are located in a section of Riverdale designated for low-density houses to ensure the preservation of open space. At Delafield Estates, 70 percent of the property is undeveloped, including the ponds.

The ponds can be viewed by traveling on West 246th Street to the west of Independence Avenue. Here, the street curves and descends downhill toward the Hudson River. Delafield Way branches off to the left with the ponds located behind a guard booth at the entrance to the development. A few blocks to the east, Delafield Avenue also recalls the larger estate that presently totals just 10 acres.

THE BRONX

LEARN MORE:

✦ **Delafield Estates Homeowners Association** www.delafieldestates .org

GETTING THERE:

✦ **Bus**: Bx7 or Bx10 at West 246th Street, walk west for four blocks on West 246th Street and turn left on Delafield Way, and the pond is beyond the guard booth
✦ **Subway**: 1 to 231st Street, transfer to Bx7 or Bx10
✦ **Bike**: There are currently no bike lanes on roads near Delafield Ponds

29. Woodlawn Lake

Another glacial pond that is not on most maps is **Woodlawn Lake**, nestled near the northern edge of the historic **Woodlawn Cemetery**, the final resting place of numerous political, entertainment, social, and religious figures of New York. The cemetery was founded in 1863 as a nonsectarian burial ground and houses the remains of more than 300,000 people. Initially, the 400-acre cemetery had six lakes in it, with a brook draining from Woodlawn Lake into the **Bronx River**. The plan of the cemetery is akin to that of Central Park, containing wide, winding streets contrasting with the surrounding urban street grid. Woodlawn Lake is spanned by a stone bridge reminiscent of the Gapstow Bridge in Central Park.

The cemetery is a necropolis of the city's rich and famous, including business tycoons F. W. Woolworth, Isidor Straus, R. H. Macy, and Henry Lehman. It is the resting place of noted suffragette Elizabeth Cady Stanton, journalist Nellie Bly, and Uncle Sam illustrator James Montgomery Flagg. The main entrance to Woodlawn Cemetery is at Webster Avenue and East 233rd Street.

LEARN MORE:
+ **Woodlawn Cemetery** www.thewoodlawncemetery.org

GETTING THERE:
+ **Bus**: Bx16, Bx31 to East 233rd Street and Katonah Avenue; Bx34, BxM4 to East 233rd Street and Kepler Avenue
+ **Subway**: 4 to Woodlawn; 2, 5 to 233rd Street station, walk three blocks downhill on West 233rd Street, cross Webster Avenue, and the cemetery entrance is on the left
+ **Train**: Metro-North to Woodlawn, cross Webster Avenue, and the cemetery entrance is on the left

30. Williamsbridge Reservoir

Williamsbridge Oval is a park built atop the site of the oval-shaped Williamsbridge Reservoir, which once held up to 120 million gallons, serving the city between 1887 and 1934. The reservoir received its water from the **Kensico Reservoir**, located 15 miles upstream in Westchester County.

The reservoir was deemed obsolete by 1934 and was transferred to the Parks Department. The Williamsbridge Civic Association rejected a proposal to erect a stadium, as they believed that the arena would agitate local residents, and that "the gathering of large and noisy crowds in the stadium would seriously impair the efficiency and usefulness" of **Montefiore Hospital**, only a half mile away.

Williamsbridge Oval opened in September 1937. The former reservoir's name was inspired by the now-nonexistent **Williams's Bridge**—a bridge built by 18th-century settler John Williams across the Bronx

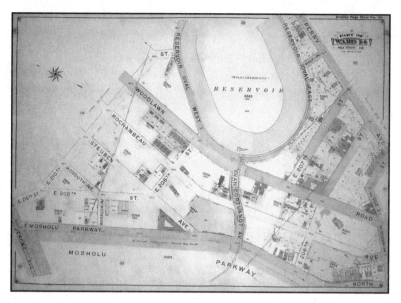

An atlas page showing the Williamsbridge Reservoir

River a quarter mile to the east (Williams's farm was on the east bank of the Bronx River in the vicinity of Gun Hill Road and White Plains Road). The bridge was rebuilt many times over the centuries, eventually losing its name while lending it to the surrounding community of **Williamsbridge**. The neighborhood of the oval is named Norwood, after an 1889 real estate development. On the map, two streets surrounding and leading to the park are Reservoir Oval and Reservoir Place, recalling the Oval's earlier use.

The park is home to the **Valentine-Varian House**, built in 1758 near Boston Road by Yonkers blacksmith Isaac Valentine. The house is made of native stone and provided its builder with a steady stream of customers on their way between New York and points north. Isaac Varian bought the house and its farm in 1792. Even after the reservoir became its neighbor, the farm continued to operate. By 1904, grandson Jesse Varian sold his lands to a developer. William F. Beller bought the house and the small parcel of land surrounding it in an auction in 1905. He maintained the house for nearly six decades. It was donated to the Bronx County Historical Society in 1965.

PLACES TO SEE:

✦ **Museum of Bronx History at the Valentine-Varian House** 3266 Bainbridge Avenue ✦ 718-881-8900 ✦ www.bronxhistoricalsociety .org/museumofbronxhistory

LEARN MORE:
+ **Bronx Historical Society** 3309 Bainbridge Avenue ✦ 718-881-8900 ✦ www.bronxhistoricalsociety.org

GETTING THERE:
+ **Bus**: Bx10, Bx16, Bx28, Bx30, Bx34, Bx38 at Bainbridge Avenue and Reservoir Oval East
+ **Subway**: D at Norwood–205th Street, walk two blocks north toward Reservoir Oval East
+ **Bike**: There is a bike lane on Mosholu Parkway, two blocks west of the park, and on the Bronx River Greenway, five blocks east of the park

31. Cromwell's Creek

The largest baseball stadium in the world stands atop the buried **Cromwell's Creek**, a stream known to natives as Mentipathe. The creek originated in **Morris Heights**, collecting runoff from nearby hills that lent their names to the neighborhoods of **Mount Eden** and **Mount Hope**. It then flowed south, following Jerome Avenue toward **Mullaly Park** and **Macombs Dam Park**, which were created in the late 19th century by filling in a saltwater marsh near the creek's confluence with the Harlem River. No trace of Cromwell's Creek remains today.

Its namesake is John Cromwell, nephew of England's Oliver Cromwell, who led a short-lived Puritan government that abolished the monarchy in Britain. John arrived from the Netherlands in 1685, settling in the future Bronx. Around 1770, his descendant James Cromwell built a mill on the creek, as well as the family homestead, which survived into the early 20th century.

Cromwell's Creek was gradually filled in the second half of the 19th century. By the time the first Yankee Stadium was completed in 1923, no trace remained of the stream. Its former path appeared on maps as a park occupying a valley between Jerome and River Avenues. In 2006, construction began on the new Yankee Stadium across the street from the old stadium, on 25 acres of parkland; and in 2010, the old Yankee Stadium was demolished and replaced with **Heritage Field**, a park containing three baseball diamonds. The park was designed to offset the loss of parkland on which the new stadium was built.

A few blocks to the north of Yankee Stadium, Cromwell Avenue preserves the name of the colonial family and the stream. Observing the local topography, Jerome Avenue runs along the floor of the valley where Cromwell's Creek flowed.

PLACES TO SEE:

✦ **Yankee Stadium** Tours available ✦ 1 East 161st Street ✦ 646-977-8687 ✦ newyork.yankees.mlb.com/nyy/ballpark/stadium_tours.jsp
✦ **Mullaly Park** Bound by Jerome Avenue, McClellan Street, River Avenue, and East 164th Street ✦ www.nycgovparks.org/parks/mullaly-park

GETTING THERE:

✦ **Bus**: Bx6 or Bx13 at East 161st Street and Gerard Avenue
✦ **Subway**: 4, B, D at 161st Street–Yankee Stadium
✦ **Train**: Metro-North at Yankees–East 153rd Street
✦ **Bike**: There are bike lanes on Edward L. Grant Highway, Grand Concourse, Gerard Avenue, and Walton Avenue

32. Mott Haven Canal

There is a Canal Street in the South Bronx, but you won't find Chinese food here. Prior to 1900, a canal though this neighborhood penetrated nearly a mile inland, lined with warehouses. Boats entered from the Harlem River, carrying coal from New England. Cranes picked up the freight and loaded the goods into warehouses. During the canal's heyday, **Mott Haven** was a burgeoning industrial neighborhood populated by Irish immigrants, with massive iron foundries and railyards along the shore and middle-class brownstones farther inland. Two bascule bridges spanned the narrow canal with lock-like tide gates underneath to keep out high tides. The neighborhood's namesake was Jordan L. Mott, whose **J. L. Mott Iron Works** arrived in the area in 1828, spurring the development of Mott Haven. Mott's firm produced many of the city's architectural forms, plumbing, and sculptures, including manhole covers. It relocated to New Jersey in 1902.

In contrast to the Gowanus Canal, which was originally a natural stream and has water steadily flowing from the East River, the Mott Haven Canal did not have a current, and its standing water quickly gained a reputation for its odor.

In 1896, the city's Board of Health declared the canal a public nuisance and urged the city to cover it. An objection was filed by the Bronx Electric Light Company—in which Tammany Hall chieftain Richard Croker had an interest—but the motion was denied, and Canal Place was paved over the buried waterway.

Only Canal Place and Canal Street remain as signs of this buried waterway.

PLACES TO SEE:

✦ **Mott Haven Library** 321 East 140th Street ✦ 718-665-4878 ✦ www.nypl.org/locations/mott-haven

GETTING THERE:

✦ **Bus**: Bx33 at East 138th Street and Canal Street; Bx1, Bx2, Bx21, Bx32 at 3rd Avenue and East 138th Street; Bx15 at East 138th Street and Lincoln Avenue
✦ **Subway**: 4, 5 at 138th Street–Grand Concourse, walk two blocks east on East 138th Street to Canal Place; 6 at 3rd Avenue–138th Street, walk three blocks west
✦ **Bike**: There is a bike lane on Third Avenue, two blocks east of Canal Place

33. Mill Brook

Known to the natives as Acrahung, **Mill Brook** originated just west of the present-day Fordham University campus, then followed the Metro-North Railroad's Harlem line south toward the village of Morrisania and continued along the eponymous **Brook Avenue** before finally emptying into the **Bronx Kill**. Toward the end of the 19th century, the stream was straightened and gradually covered as the Morrisania and Mott Haven neighborhoods developed. No trace of the streambed remains today.

At East 141st Street and Brook Avenue is **Brook Park**, acquired by the city in 1979. The park is maintained by the **Friends of Brook Park** as a community garden. The group also organizes canoe trips on the Harlem River and the Bronx Kill.

The group's blog features maps of the buried Mill Brook with a proposal to daylight a small section of the stream running below Brook Park, which would receive its water from rainwater collected on surrounding buildings. In partnership with the City Island–based **Gaia Institute**

of New York City, the group proposes to create a bioswale along the streambed in the one-block-wide park. The Gaia Institute has already developed a similar bioswale on Manhattan's Lower East Side, where the three-quarter-acre **Jardín del Paraíso** (Paradise Garden) features a pond with goldfish and turtles. Water for this pond comes from rainwater collection tanks and is piped in from a gutter of a nearby building.

Across the street from Brook Park is **Saw Mill Playground**, an uninspiring parcel of concrete that serves as the schoolyard for **Public School 179**. The playground opened to the public in 1968 and is used during the school year by students of the nearby Middle School 222 (formerly Public School 49).

PLACES TO SEE:

✦ **Brook Park** Brook Avenue at East 141st Street
✦ **Saw Mill Playground** East 140th Street between Willis Avenue and Brook Avenue ✦ www.nycgovparks.org/parks/sawmillplayground

LEARN MORE:

✦ **Friends of Brook Park** 646-648-4362 www.friendsofbrookpark.org

GETTING THERE:

✦ **Bus**: Uptown Bx15 at Willis Avenue and East 140th Street; Bx17 at Saint Ann's Avenue and East 140th Street; Bx33 at East 138th Street and Brook Avenue
✦ **Subway**: 6 at Brook Avenue, walk three blocks north to East 141st Street
✦ **Bike**: There are bike lanes on Saint Ann's Avenue, one block east of Brook Avenue; on Willis Avenue, one block to the west; and on 138th Street

34. Bronx Kill

Once a much wider tidal strait, the **Bronx Kill** inlet separates the Bronx from **Randalls Island**, which is politically part of Manhattan. The stream today is shallow enough to cross by foot at low tide and is used mainly by kayakers as a shortcut between the upper East River and the Harlem River. Prior to the early 1950s, when the inlet was wider, it was famed for its turbulent currents that had claimed the lives of a few individuals who ventured too far into its waters. The stream is crossed by the northern leg of the **Triborough Bridge** and by the Amtrak trestle that carries trains running between New York and Boston.

The same stream that swept away some wayward individuals also kept others from escaping. Between 1854 and 1935, Randalls Island hosted the state-funded **New York House of Refuge**, a juvenile detention facility. Its inmates often looked across the Bronx Kill to freedom, but only a few dared to challenge its currents.

Even as the stream was narrowed by land reclamation on both sides, it continued to pose a mortal threat to those who slipped on its rocks or tried to swim across. In contrast to the heavily developed South Bronx, Randalls Island is an expansive oasis of baseball diamonds—beckoning to youths who live north of the Bronx Kill, but nearly inaccessible from the Bronx other than by a sidewalk on the Triborough Bridge, which requires a steep and lengthy ascent.

The need for a more accessible pedestrian crossing between the Bronx and Randalls Island has been recognized since 1947, when the Parks Department filled in nearly 29 acres of water in the Bronx Kill, closing

the stream to navigation. In this project, they included a proposal for a bridge over the stream and over the rail yard on its northern shore. The pedestrian crossing, named Randalls Island Connector, opened in 2015.

To its north was the **Mott Haven Rail Yard**, which was built in 1866, when the Harlem River and Port Chester Railroad opened a train terminal in Mott Haven where commuters could connect to the Third Avenue El to continue farther downtown; following the completion of the Hell Gate Bridge, they could take the train all the way to Midtown Man-

Bronx Kill

hattan. The opening of the Lexington Avenue subway and other transit lines made the terminal obsolete, and it closed for passenger service in 1937.

PLACES TO SEE:

✦ **Randalls Island Park** www.nycgovparks.org/parks/randalls-island/highlights/6515

GETTING THERE:

✦ **Bus**: M35 to Randalls Island Park
✦ **Subway**: 4, 5, 6 to 125th Street, transfer to M35
✦ **Bike**: There are bike lanes on Randalls Island and on the Triborough Bridge
✦ **Boat**: The stream is accessible by kayak at high tide

THE BRONX

Queens

⟶ **The largest in size among New York City's five bor-**
oughs, Queens contains nearly 30 percent of the city's shoreline, whose
varied appearance includes the sandy beaches on the Rockaway Peninsula and the salt marshes of Jamaica Bay in the south. The more developed northern shore lines the East River, with numerous indentations
that lead to small streams. Glacial deposits left behind these inlets and
peninsulas, which date back to the last ice age. On the western shore,
facing Manhattan, the Dutch Kills and Anable Basin hearken to the
borough's industrial past.

Deeper within the borough are numerous kettle-shaped ponds that
were formed when chunks of ice broke off the glacier and melted. The
most prominent stream in Queens is Flushing Creek, which neatly divides
the borough into an eastern and western half and flows through Flushing Meadows–Corona Park, a 1,255-acre parcel that contains some of
the city's leading sports and cultural attractions.

The borough can also be divided into northern and southern halves
through the Ronkonkoma Moraine, a ridge that follows the southernmost extent of the Wisconsin glacier between Staten Island and the
South Fork of Long Island. Until 12,000 years ago, everything north of
Hillside Avenue was covered in ice, and to the south, a gradually sloping plain carried meltwater streams to the ocean. The moraine acts as a
watershed divide between streams flowing northward to the East River
and those flowing south into Jamaica Bay.

From the colonial period to the mid-19th century, streams in south-

ern Queens were dammed in order to power gristmills and later to provide drinking water for Brooklyn, which was an independent city before
1898. The construction of JFK International Airport filled in many of
these streams. Their only traces are streets bearing their names and
ponds within parks through which these streams once flowed.

35. Dutch Kills

Between Hunters Point to the south and Ravenswood to its north, the
section of Long Island City around Queens Plaza is gradually being
rebranded as **Dutch Kills**, reviving the name of a partially buried stream.
Across the United States, small streams are often named based on local
dialects. In the Deep South, a creek is a *bayou*, and in the eastern South,
a small stream is called a *run*. Throughout the former New Netherland,
kill was the commonly used term for creek and remains on the maps long
after Dutch authorities departed. The most prominent examples in New
York City are Arthur Kill and Kill Van Kull, two tidal channels separating Staten Island from New Jersey.

The Dutch Kills is presently an inlet of Newtown Creek that begins at
47th Avenue and 29th Street, a block to the south of **LaGuardia Community College**. The stream is lined by warehouses and parking lots and
crossed by three roadways and two train trestles. Prior to colonization,
local natives referred to this stream as Canapaukah, translated as "bears'
watering hole."

Below the surface

Originally, this stream had its headwaters at a point just north of present-
day Northern Boulevard and 33rd Street. Nor far from this corner are
the northernmost places in the neighborhood with monikers inspired by
the stream: the **Dutch Kills Playground** and **Dutch Kills School**. They
are located on Crescent Street between 36th and 37th Avenues. The playground features a design hearkening to the area's Dutch roots.

From there, the creek flowed south, past colonial farmhouses where
some of Long Island City's first European settlers lived. None of these
structures remain; all were razed by 1910 to make way for Sunnyside Yard,
the massive complex used by Amtrak, New Jersey Transit, and the Long
Island Railroad.

The only remaining trace of colonial farming along the Dutch Kills
is in the recently designed **Dutch Kills Green**, a traffic triangle near

Queens Plaza that holds two millstones that were once used to grind grain for local residents. Built sometime between 1643 and 1657, Jorrisen's Mill was the first gristmill in Queens; it used slave labor during the colonial period. Water from the Dutch Kills was diverted through a sluice to move the mill's stone wheels. In 1861, the mill was demolished to make way for the Long Island Railroad, and its owners, the Payntar family, had the stones moved west by 300 feet to avoid destruction. In 1913, the family's farmhouse was demolished during the construction of Queens Plaza, and the stones were embedded in a concrete traffic triangle for nearly a century. The traffic triangle would later become Dutch Kills Green.

Dutch Kills Green's design is a postmodern landscape of sculptured concrete benches and native wetland grass species that grew along the Dutch Kills before it was buried. The millstones, recently released from concrete, rest among shrubs in the park.

Crossing Northern Boulevard, the former streambed meandered through **Sunnyside Yard**, a 192-acre rail yard separating the neighborhoods of Long Island City and Sunnyside. Along its northern edges, massive industrial buildings with abandoned freight sidings have since been subdivided for office space and light industry.

Above the surface

A block to the south of LaGuardia Community College, the stream emerges from the ground alongside a concrete yard. But a hint of ecological restoration can be found across the street from the present headwaters. Since 2004, **Long Island City Roots Community Garden** has operated on a narrow sliver of land on 47th Avenue and 29th Street. The garden sits atop a former siding of the Degnon Terminal freight tracks that used to crisscross the blocks around the remaining portion of the stream. The garden serves as a memorial to local firefighter Michael E. Brennan, who was killed on September 11, 2001.

Continuing downstream, the **Hunters Point Avenue Bridge** carries 49th Avenue above the Dutch Kills. Part of this road is called Hunters Point Avenue, and it predates the street grid. When street numbers were assigned, the portion west of the Dutch Kills was numbered, but the subway and railroad station on it are still called Hunterspoint Avenue. The drawbridge is a bascule with a concrete bunker control tower.

The south side of this bridge offers excellent views of the Queens–Midtown Tunnel approach of the **Long Island Expressway**, where the highway emerges out of the tunnel onto a rapidly rising mile-long viaduct above the stream before descending back to the ground. The 106-foot-high clearance is a result of federal regulations requiring tall ships to pass beneath, though it is difficult to imagine how such a ship could navigate the Dutch Kills, considering the creek is only about as wide as the highway above it.

South of the Long Island Expressway is a rare engineering specimen: the **Borden Avenue Bridge**, one of only two bridges in New York City that moves on rails for boats to pass through. Across the United States, only four retractile bridges (including New York's two) remain. Prior to the construction of the Long Island Expressway, this bridge was the main east–west crossing connecting Hunters Point with Blissville and points east. The present bridge opened in 1908. Heading westward, Borden Avenue seems to point right toward the Empire State Building.

Farther downstream, the Dutch Kills passes beneath a couple of railroad trestles before emptying into Newtown Creek. Presently, most of the properties along the Dutch Kills are zoned for manufacturing use. The stream appears on the nameplate of a local watering hole: **Dutch Kills** bar at 27-24 Jackson Avenue. The bar, which opened in 2009, proudly connects itself to the stream's storied past.

Dutch Kills, 1940

Depending on the cleanliness of the water, perhaps in the future the community garden up at the head of the stream could become a launching site for canoes plying a restored Dutch Kills. A rezoning of properties along its shore could usher in residential development, with green spaces along the water's edge.

+ **Dutch Kills Green** Queens Plaza North at 41st Avenue
+ **LaGuardia Community College** 31-10 Thomson Avenue + 718-482-7200 + www.lagcc.cuny.edu
+ **Long Island City Roots Community Garden** 29-08 47th Avenue + www.grownyc.org/osg-rwh-licroots
+ **Dutch Kills Bar** 27-24 Jackson Avenue + 718-383-2724 + www.dutchkillsbar.com

GETTING THERE:
+ **Bus**: Q67 at 27th Street and Borden Avenue for the Borden Avenue Bridge; Q39 at Thomson Avenue and Skillman Avenue
+ **Subway**: 7 at Hunters Point Avenue station, walk on 49th Avenue toward the Hunters Point Avenue Bridge
+ **Train**: Long Island Railroad at Hunterspoint Avenue
+ **Bike**: There are currently no bike paths near the exposed section of the Dutch Kills
+ **Boat**: The stream is accessible by small watercraft; the clearance of the Borden Avenue Bridge is 3.94 feet above mean high water

QUEENS

36. Anable Basin

For much of the late 19th and early 20th centuries, the shoreline of the East River was lined with a series of piers and short inlets that served as docks for factories and railyards. In Long Island City, **Anable Basin** punctures the shore for nearly one city block, a reminder of a time before condo towers began to redefine the neighborhood. When the inlet was constructed in 1868, Long Island City was home to numerous oil refineries and factories that relied on the East River for deliveries. When the basin was dug out, a mastodon bone was found at the site. The basin's namesake is Henry Sheldon Anable, a prominent figure in local business and politics.

For much of the 20th century, the largest facility on the basin was the Pepsi-Cola bottling plant at the confluence of Anable Basin and the East River. In 1936, the Artkraft Strauss Sign Corporation installed the cursive ruby-colored neon-on-metal **Pepsi-Cola sign** atop the bottling plant, and it became an instant navigational landmark. The bottling plant closed in 1999, and in 2009 the iconic 120-foot-long sign was dismantled and reassembled within **Gantry Plaza State Park**, which lines the shore of the East River between Anable Basin and Hunter's Point.

The landscaping of Gantry Plaza preserves the industrial past of the site, most notably with a pair of gantry cranes that lifted railroad cars off barges and onto tracks. The decline of the waterfront rail yard began in 1910, when the **East River Tunnels** enabled passenger trains to take commuters directly into Midtown Manhattan. Freight operations persisted for another half century before trucking and cargo planes spelled the demise of boxcars and barges in Queens.

Anable Basin's next moment in artistic representation arrived in October 2007 with Chico MacMurtrie's temporary sculpture *A Tree for Anable Basin*. The 24-foot-high aluminum tree stood on a floating island verdant with local grass species. MacMurtrie is the founder of the Brooklyn-based arts and engineering collective, Amorphic Robot Works.

Anable Basin gained notoriety for sustainable agriculture in August 2012, when Cooper Union architecture student Karim Ahmed designed a hydroponic garden on a 20-square-foot raft. *Waterpod*, as the project was called, grew sunflowers, kale, corn, and a baby nectarine tree. The chinampa floating farms used in Aztec society inspired the project. Ahmed's raft was tethered where **Anable Basin Sailing Bar and Grill** is located, at the northwest corner of the basin. The eatery offers mooring for vessels, picnic tables by the waterfront, and a mixture of American and ethnic dishes.

As Long Island City's skyline grows, Anable Basin is also on the rise from its former status as an industrial backwater. Properties along the basin are capitalizing on views of Manhattan and cleaner water to attract customers.

QUEENS

PLACES TO SEE:
- **Anable Basin Sailing Bar and Grill** 4-40 44th Drive ✦ 646-207-1333 ✦ www.anablebasin.com
- **Gantry Plaza State Park** 4-09 47th Road ✦ 718-786-6385 ✦ nysparks.com/parks/149/

LEARN MORE:
- **Long Island City Community Boathouse** www.licboathouse.org

GETTING THERE:
- **Bus:** Q103 to 46th Avenue, walk one block west to Fifth Street, turn right, walk one block north to Anable Basin

+ **Subway**: 7 at Vernon Boulevard–Jackson Avenue, transfer to Q103
+ **Bike**: There are bike lanes on Vernon Boulevard, one block east of Anable Basin
+ **Boat**: The stream is accessible by small watercraft

37. Luyster Creek

On the northwestern corner of Queens is an inlet surrounded almost entirely by a power plant complex and within view of the nation's most famous piano manufacturer. The only point along the stream's shore that is accessible to the public is a dead end on 19th Avenue one block west of 37th Street, where the avenue hits the stream.

Prior to colonization, **Luyster Creek** was a tidal creek that flowed along present-day 19th Avenue, separating a small island on the north side of the avenue from mainland Queens. The stream's eastern mouth was near the present-day **Rikers Island Bridge**, where it emptied into Bowery Bay.

The first European settler here was Hendrick Harmensen in 1638, who established a farm by the shore. The old Dutch term for farm is *bouwerij*, which was anglicized to Bowery, the namesake of both Bowery Bay in Queens and the Bowery area in Lower Manhattan. Harmensen was killed by local natives in 1643. His widow remarried, and the island on the property was briefly called **Houwclicken** (Dowry Island).

The deacons of the Dutch Reformed Church bought the farm before 1654, to provide food for their poor; hence it was called Armen Bouwerie or "Poor Bowery." About 1688, the church sold its farm to Pieter Corne-lissen Luyster, who lent his name to Dowry Island and the nearby creek.

At Luyster Creek's western mouth was Berrien's Island. The Berriens were French Huguenots who settled in the Netherlands and later relo-cated to New York. Settler Corneulius Berrien purchased the island in 1727 and was buried on the island four decades later. The family ceme-tery has long since disappeared, and the island is fused to the mainland as part of the **Astoria Generating Station**.

Luyster's Island ceased to exist by the early 20th century, and most of it is now occupied by the **Bowery Bay Wastewater Treatment Plant**, which began operating in 1939. With its rounded windows and stream-lined corners, the facility is an example of the Art Deco style that was popular in prewar New York.

Overlooking Luyster Creek is an Italianate style mansion built in

1858 for downtown Manhattan optician Benjamin Pike Jr. He died in his home in 1864, leaving behind a collection of globes, telescopes, and other visual devices.

The development of Luyster Creek took off after 1870, when William Steinway relocated his **Steinway & Sons** piano manufacturing firm to the creek's shore, establishing a company town around the factory. Pike's home was renamed after Steinway, and his family resided there through 1926. Steinway's village housed nearly 400 workers in Victorian-style townhouses along Steinway Street. The village had a free kindergarten, a public library, and the **Steinway Reformed Church** at 41st Street and Ditmars Boulevard. Steinway also funded a trolley line linking the village to Astoria and to the ferry to Manhattan. To the east of the village, Steinway funded the **Gala Amusement Park**, which later became the site of **LaGuardia Airport**. The piano factory offers tours by reservation.

As the neighborhood became more industrial, land around the 27-room **Steinway Mansion** shrunk. By 1926, it was down to an acre when Jack Halberian bought it for $45,000. The building is a city landmark, but it continues to gradually deteriorate. As a landmark, the structure cannot be altered without the city's approval; however, much of the property was developed into warehouses in 2015, greatly reducing the mansion's once-sizable yard.

In 2012, the nonprofit organizations Green Shores NYC and the Trust for Public Land proposed a boat launch for Luyster Creek at the dead end of 19th Avenue. Other than colorful renderings of the proposed dock, there has not been any momentum to push the project forward.

PLACES TO SEE:

✦ **Steinway & Sons Factory** 18-1 Steinway Place ✦ 718-721-2600 ✦ www.steinway.com
✦ **Steinway Library** 21-45 31st Street ✦ 718-728-1965 ✦ www.queenslibrary.org/Steinway
✦ **Steinway Mansion (privately owned)** 18-33 41st Street

LEARN MORE:

✦ **Greater Astoria Historical Society** 35-20 Broadway ✦ 718-278-0700 ✦ astorialic.org

GETTING THERE:

✦ **Bus:** Q101 to Steinway Street and 20th Avenue; Q100 to 20th Avenue and 31st Street

✦ **Subway**: M, R at Steinway Street, transfer to Q100
✦ **Bike**: There are bike lanes on 35th and 36th Streets northbound and southbound, respectively, and on 20th Avenue
✦ **Boat**: The stream is navigable, but its proximity to a power plant could pose security restrictions

38. Sunswick Creek

In contrast to Brooklyn, which was an independent city prior to its 1898 merger into New York City, Queens was a county of towns and villages. The most developed municipality and only city in pre-1898 Queens was Long Island City; it encompassed Astoria, Ravenswood, Dutch Kills, Hunters Point, Steinway, and Sunnyside. Flowing through this city were numerous streams that powered gristmills supplying grain to colonial settlers. As the area became more developed, **Sunswick Creek** was gradually diverted into underground channels until it became completely hidden from view.

Sunswick is an English corruption of a native name denoting a powerful woman. No further information is known about the namesake. The stream originated just north of present-day Queens Plaza, meandering along 21st Street toward Broadway, where it turned west and emptied into Hallets Cove.

For much of the 19th century, Ravenswood's shore along the East River was dotted with mansions. During his stay in the neighborhood, James Fenimore Cooper authored *The Water-Witch*. Ravenswood's name can be traced to local clergyman Rev. Francis L. Hawks, who sought to honor his North Carolina colleague Rev. John S. Ravenscroft. With industrialization, the mansions gave way to brick factories and power plants. The local skyline is dominated by the **Ravenswood Generating Station**, known locally as Big Allis.

Near Sunswick Creek's source, the **Queens Library at Long Island City** offers plenty of literature on local history. The postmodern-style building opened in 2007 and features low-relief sculpture and art around its main entrance. Down the block from the library is **Sixteen Oaks Grove**, a triangular park on a very busy 21st Street. The park was acquired in 1939 and originally named after Anthony Leo Placella, a local resident who served in the First World War and died a few days short of the November 11, 1918, armistice.

Continuing north, the stream's path passes through the Queenswood

Co-op, as well as the **Ravenswood Houses**, a public housing campus of 31 buildings encompassing 2,167 households. The projects opened in 1951.

At Broadway, the buried stream enters a brick sewer tunnel dating to 1893. Large enough for a walk, its exploration by Steven Duncan was chronicled in *National Geographic*'s online series Change the Course, which addresses bodies of water around the world that have been affected by overdevelopment.

Long Island City High School takes up most of the superblock to the west of 21st Street. Built in 1995, it is an early example of the architectural transition in public school design toward postmodernism.

Near the former mouth of the stream at Vernon Boulevard and Broadway, a gristmill once stood. In 1957, workers uncovered two millstones and Spanish "pieces of eight" currency dating to 1797. Unlike the Dutch Kills millstones, which sit prominently in the Dutch Kills Green at Queens Plaza, there are no accounts on the fate of the Sunswick millstones. The first mill at Sunswick Creek was built in 1679.

At the creek's mouth is **Socrates Sculpture Park**, an artistic destination sitting atop a landfill. The park is the creation of local sculptors Mark di Suvero and Isamu Noguchi, who cleared the trash-strewn lot in 1986 and encouraged artists to decorate the site. The park offers spectacular views of the lighthouse at the northern tip of Roosevelt Island. Further in the background is Gracie Mansion, the official mayoral residence at the northern end of Manhattan's Upper East Side.

Crossing Vernon Boulevard back to the inland side, one can find the **Noguchi Museum**, which is home to sculptures, models, and photographs of Isamu Noguchi's work. The prolific sculptor's career spanned nearly six decades, and his works can be found around the globe. Places as distant as Jerusalem, Hiroshima, Munich, and Honolulu, among others, all have public art by Noguchi in their memorials, museums, and parks.

As neighborhoods around Sunswick Creek experience real estate resurgence, old names that had vanished from the map, such as Dutch Kills and Hunters Point, now prominently appear in advertising. At the corner of 35th Street and 35th Avenue is **Sunswick 35/35**, a tavern that opened in 2005 catering to the growing population of young professionals in Astoria.

In the form of sculpture, Sunswick Creek briefly reappeared on the landscape in Mary Miss's 2012 work *Sunswick Creek: Reflecting Forward*, commissioned by Socrates Sculpture Park and the Noguchi Museum.

With informative signposts and reflective mirrors along the creek's former path, Miss sought to connect pedestrians to the rich natural and human history buried beneath the concrete.

As western Queens continues to boom, perhaps Sunswick's name will appear on more attractions along its former path.

PLACES TO SEE:

+ **Queens Library at Long Island City** 37-44 21st Street + 718-752-3700 + www.queenslibrary.org/long-island-city
+ **Sunswick 35/35 bar** 35-02 35th Street + 718-752-0620 + www.sunswick3535bar.com
+ **Noguchi Museum** 9-01 33rd Road + 718-204-7088 + www.noguchi.org
+ **Socrates Sculpture Park** 36-01 Vernon Boulevard + 718-956-1819 + www.socratessculpturepark.org

GETTING THERE:

+ **Bus:** Q103, Q104 to Broadway and Vernon Boulevard for Noguchi Museum and Socrates Sculpture Park
+ **Subway:** N, Q at Broadway, transfer to Q104
+ **Bike:** There are bike lanes on Vernon Boulevard and 34th Avenue

39. Flushing Creek

Flushing Creek, also known as Flushing River, appears in a variety of forms, including freshwater marshes, man-made lakes, and an underground channel, before emptying into Flushing Bay, an arm of the East River. Prior to colonial settlement, the stream meandered through a wide freshwater marsh that mirrored the borders of Flushing Meadows–Corona Park. Its major confluences were Horse Brook, Kissena Creek, and Mill Creek.

Flushing Creek's human history includes a stint as an ash dump followed by the site of two World's Fairs. The stream flows past the home of the New York Mets baseball team and the US Open tennis championship site, and it is the location of the Hong Kong Dragon Boat Festival.

Prior to its use as a fairground, most of present-day Flushing Meadows–Corona Park was a salt marsh used as dumping ground by the Brooklyn Ash Removal Company. Its executive, John A. "Fishhooks" McCarthy, was an operative of the Tammany Hall political machine and benefited

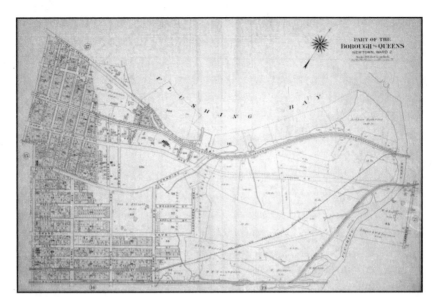

An atlas page from 1909 showing Flushing Creek

generously from various political deals. Eager to profit in every way from the dump, he charged scavengers a fee to pick through the trash. In 1929, the company proposed redeveloping the site into four 18-hole golf courses, but the plan failed to gain support.

The city purchased the ash dump in 1934 and leveled "Mount Corona" by distributing the ash across surrounding wetlands and Rikers Island, expanding the acreage of developable land. As for Brooklyn Ash Removal, the city found it more cost-effective to collect the refuse on its own rather than through the carting company. With the landfill operator condemned and compensated, the city then went after 150 smaller property owners at Flushing Meadows, such as a tavern owner on the park side of 111th Street, a gas station on Roosevelt Avenue, and a monument manufacturer near Mount Hebron Cemetery.

After the last 20 holdouts were evicted in August 1936, construction workers invaded the 897-acre site, flattening its ashen hills and constructing unique Art Deco–style exhibition structures for the 1939 World's Fair. New York was selected as the host of the fair on the occasion of the 150th anniversary of George Washington's inauguration as president, which took place in New York.

After the World's Fair closed on October 31, 1940, most of its buildings were razed, and the site was gradually developed into a park. From 1946 to 1951, the former fairground was briefly the world's convention center, as the United Nations used the New York City Building (later the **Queens Museum**) as its temporary headquarters. While there was an alternative plan to make Flushing Meadows the world's capital, at a much lower cost than Turtle Bay, the diplomats went ahead with the Manhattan location. Had the UN remained in Queens, one could easily imagine the working-class Corona and Flushing neighborhoods hosting consulates and diplomatic residences. At the same time, it would also mean that the park would be off-limits to the public and fenced off under tight security.

Willow Lake

Flushing Creek once emerged at a point just to the east of the **Kew Gardens Interchange**, a massive tangle of highway ramps where Union Turnpike, Van Wyck Expressway, Grand Central Parkway, and Jackie Robinson Parkways cross paths. This site was known in colonial times as the Head of the Vleigh (an old Dutch term for "meadow"). From here, **Vleigh Place** begins its route north along the drainage divide separating the Flushing Meadows watershed on its west from the swamp to the east where Kissena Creek originated. The road continues to cut through the street grid, but most of its traffic was taken by Main Street in the 1930s, which runs parallel to Vleigh Place, connecting Flushing with Jamaica.

Prior to development, this section of Queens was called Queens Valley, a landscape of farmland and golf courses that was redeveloped into the Kew Gardens Hills neighborhood. Traveling on the Grand Central Parkway just north of the interchange, the roadway beneath the subway trestle leading into **Jamaica Yard** is often flooded after heavy rain. The yard serves the Queens Boulevard subway line.

The construction of the yard buried some of the headwaters of the stream and a sizable portion of the wetlands, but it could have turned out much worse. In 1972, architect Charles Brickbauer was commissioned by developer Samuel LeFrak to design Willow Lake Village, a $250-million high-rise development above the yard. The towers would have cast shadows over Willow Lake, compromising the wildlife sanctuary. With only two roads leading into the proposed complex, local streets would have been overwhelmed, and the plan was shelved.

To the right of the roadway in the marshes is the present source of Flushing Creek. The marshlands open up into **Willow Lake**, a reservoir carved out for the 1939 World's Fair. Initially, the lake was ringed with trails and baseball fields that constantly flooded. In 1976, the city fenced off 106 acres around the lake as a nature preserve, open to the public only as part of guided tours. Insulated by highways and a train depot, the 47-acre lake is virtually undisturbed and is a magnet for a variety of bird species flying through the area.

The lake can be accessed through the **Willow Lake Trail**, which has entrances at 72nd Road and Grand Central Parkway in Forest Hills and 73rd Terrace and Park Drive East in Kew Gardens Hills.

Meadow Lake

Willow Lake empties into a narrow creek that runs beneath the interchange of Jewel Avenue and the **Van Wyck Expressway**, then flows into **Meadow Lake**. In the first World's Fair, Meadow Lake was known as Fountain Lake and had its own United States Army Field Band composition, *Fountain Lake Fanfare* by Robert Russell Bennett. It was carved out of the salt marshes along the creek as part of the master plan by architects Gilmore Clarke and Michael Rapuano.

With the start of the Second World War, maps of the fair subsequently labeled the reservoir as Liberty Lake. Fearing that the fair would not make a profit, its planners zoned the eastern shore of the lake as the amusement zone. Its highlights included the 250-foot **Parachute Jump**, a tower festooned with the logo of Life Savers candy. Chairs with parachutes tethered to cables rose to the top and then gently descended with their passengers. Following the fair's close, the tower was dismantled and reassembled at Coney Island, where it operated until 1964. It is today an official city landmark with a fresh coat of paint and nighttime illumination, but alas, no functioning parachutes.

In a time when nearly every country promoted its own brand of nationalism, many of the homegrown exhibits at the World's Fair also featured a patriotic flavor steeped in history. Washington Hall celebrated the 150th anniversary of George Washington's inauguration with a lakeside replica of his Mount Vernon home. Adjacent to it, the Cuban Village promoted tourism to the island nation with exotic dancers and musicians.

To the east of Meadow Lake is **Mount Hebron Cemetery**, formerly the Spring Hill estate of the Colden family, who arrived from Ireland and built a mansion here in 1763. The family's contribution to New York history includes colonial governor Cadwallader Colden and his grandson, Cadwallader David Colden, 54th mayor of New York City. Following the American Revolution, the loyalist Coldens gave up their manor, and the farm passed through several hands before becoming a cemetery in 1893.

The **boathouse** on Meadow Lake dates to the 1939 World's Fair and is one of only three buildings in the park remaining from that event. The boathouse reopened to the public in November 2011 after more than two decades in decay.

To its west is a grassy plaza with a circular pier marking the site of the **Aquacade**, a 9,000-seat stadium used for swimming and stage performances in both of the World's Fairs. Between and after the fairs, it served as a public swimming pool. The pool closed in 1977, a victim of deferred maintenance and a tight budget. Destroying the venue was cheaper than restoring it.

In the 1939 World's Fair, Broadway impresario Billy Rose hosted some of the best-known athletes of the time including Tarzan actor Johnny Weissmuller and Gertrude Ederle, Queens resident and the first woman to swim the English Channel. In its last years, the stadium was formally known as the **Gertrude Ederle Amphitheater**. In both World's Fairs, the Aquacade was the centerpiece of an amusement district that supplemented the national and corporate exhibits that dominated the venue.

For the 1964 World's Fair, Meadow Lake served as an afterthought. A much smaller amusement area was located on the north end of the lake, with most of its shoreline ringed by parking lots, a symbol of growing automobile usage and suburban migration. While the first World's Fair had railroads as its largest exhibit, car manufacturers dominated the second fair. Two decades after the fair, the lake nearly took on an automotive theme all over again when a grand prix racetrack was slated to surround its shoreline. Opposition from local residents and investigations by journalists hinting of a sweetheart deal between the racetrack promoters and politicians killed the project.

Between the boathouse and the Aquacade site, Meadow Lake empties into Flushing Creek in the form of a narrow channel flowing beneath the Van Wyck Expressway, its greenish water discouraging fishing, boating, or any other human activity. Twists of highway ramps above connect the Van Wyck and Long Island Expressways. The first road crossing at this location was **Strong's Causeway**, built in the 1850s. Laid out across the tidal marshland, it connected Flushing to Corona and was used by a trolley line whose route is marked today by the Q58 bus.

A Flushing judge in the mid-19th century, Benjamin Woodhull Strong lived for a time at Spring Hill, the former Colden estate. Strong's Puritan ancestors arrived in Massachusetts in 1630. In line with their faith's respect for the Old Testament, some of his ancestors had rare biblically inspired names such as Jedediah, Ebenezer, Selah, Zerubbabel, Asahel, and Benaiah. Judge Strong was an outspoken proponent of road improvements and railroad expansion in Queens, and it was fitting to name the causeway after him, as it passed by his home.

In 1928, the route that crossed Strong Causeway, Nassau Boulevard, was extended to eastern Queens. It was soon renamed for Horace Harding, the railroad executive who promoted the project. By 1954, the former causeway was renamed for the final time as the Long Island Expressway, a 71-mile route that runs for nearly the entire length of Long Island, from Midtown Manhattan to Riverhead. Like many of New York City's major infrastructure projects, this highway was never completed to its full extent. It is an interstate in name only; its extensions across the Long Island Sound into Connecticut and across Manhattan into New Jersey were never completed. As a result of its unrealized leg in Manhattan, the highway's first exit is number 13, at Borden Avenue in Long Island City.

The fairgrounds

Leaving the highway interchange, the stream goes underground, unceremoniously buried for the 1964 World's Fair and never uncovered. From this point, the creek runs through two pipes toward the pool known as Fountain of the Planets. Any attempt at daylighting would mean displacing two heavily used soccer fields.

In contrast, when the earlier 1939 World's Fair took place, Flushing Creek acted as a centerpiece in the Court of States, with unique pavilions representing various states. Among the highlights was Pennsylvania, with a scale replica of Independence Hall. The pavilion for New Jersey was a replica of George Washington's Trenton headquarters, while Texas was a copy of the Alamo. A bit downstream from the states, the creek expanded into the oval-shaped Lagoon of Nations, ringed by structures representing various countries. In the center of the lagoon, fountains illuminated by lights provided entertainment every night during the World's Fair.

Between the fairs, this segment of Flushing Creek flowed freely through the park, a natural touch on a radial axis of paths originating at the **Trylon and Perisphere**, a globe and obelisk that defined the first World's Fair. Demolished after the fair, the site is presently occupied by the **Unisphere**, a giant steel globe that was an emblem of the second World's Fair. Preserved after the fair, it serves as the unofficial symbol of Queens.

For the 1964 World's Fair, Flushing Creek was reduced to an afterthought, hidden behind the exhibits, and partially buried beneath the park's central section, with the oval-shaped Lagoon of Nations transformed into the circular **Fountain of the Planets**. This reflecting pool sits at the eastern end of a row of fountains connecting to the Unisphere. As in the previous fair, every evening jets of water spouted from the fountain, illuminated by lights with music synchronized to the display. However, after the 1964 fair ended, the pool was neglected. Today it collects trash, and the former fountain control structure in the center of the pool resembles an abandoned bunker.

On the pool's western side stand two extraordinarily tall flagpoles topped by metallic eagles. Their sleek shape and size and the roundels beneath the eagles led to rumors that the flagpoles were part of a never-built exhibit for Nazi Germany. A guidebook from the fair, however, attributes the eagles to sculptor Robert Foster. Mayor Fiorello LaGuardia used every opportunity to attack the Nazis in public, arguing that a "museum of horrors" was a more fitting location for Adolf Hitler.

Another legend explaining the flagpoles was the presence of other dictatorships, which sought to demonstrate their power through monumental architecture, such as axis pact members Japan and Italy. In particular, the Soviet pavilion featured a 188-foot pedestal with a 75-foot statue on top. That made it the third-tallest structure after the Parachute Jump and the Trylon. The apparent embarrassment to the United States may have resulted in the oversized flagpoles for Old Glory.

In the summer of 2012, the Fountain of the Planets reappeared in the news with a proposal by Major League Soccer to cover the circular pond with a $300 million, 25,000-seat stadium. Concerns about replacing the parkland that would be lost to the stadium and increased traffic to the games kept the project on hold. Within a year, the proposal quietly died after a spirited public battle, with the New York Yankees offering land in the Bronx for the soccer stadium.

From the circular pond, Flushing Creek dives back underground beneath a soccer field, reemerging in the **Flushing Meadows Golf Center**. At this point, the freshwater part of Flushing Creek is dammed by **Tide Gate Bridge**, also called Porpoise Bridge. The structure was built ahead of the 1939 World's Fair to keep incoming tides from reaching further upstream into the park.

The Long Island Railroad's **Port Washington Branch** also dams the stream, with only a small opening allowing East River tides to flow in. In preparation for the 1939 World's Fair, the railroad drawbridge was replaced with a trestle, and today trains speed through the storied landscape of Flushing Meadows.

Willets Point: the Iron Triangle

From the Long Island Railroad crossing to its mouth, Flushing Creek is a tidal inlet, barely navigable beneath the Van Wyck Expressway, which was extended north in 1963 as a concrete viaduct between the Kew Gardens Interchange and the Whitestone Expressway at Northern Boulevard. The highway descends beneath the Roosevelt Avenue drawbridge and then rises again above Northern Boulevard before merging with the Whitestone Expressway at the last bridge above Flushing Creek.

The **Roosevelt Avenue Bridge** rises above Flushing Creek and the Van Wyck Expressway. When it was completed in 1927, the double-decker bascule bridge was designed to accommodate large vessels in case Flushing Creek were upgraded to a canal or seaport. Penetrating nearly five miles into Queens, Flushing Creek was proposed as a cross-island canal, connecting the East River with an international seaport in Jamaica Bay. Part of the canal's path would have used the path of the future Van Wyck Expressway through southern Queens. The proposed canal ran into opposition from property owners in Richmond Hill who feared pollution. Further south, the plan to transform Jamaica Bay was also shelved in favor of Newark Bay, which continues to serve as the largest freight seaport on the East Coast.

A similar bridge designed for a never-built ambitious project is the **Marine Parkway Bridge**, which takes Flatbush Avenue over Rockaway Inlet. Completed in 1937, the lift bridge has a 55-foot clearance above high tide and 150 feet in its raised position, anticipating tankers and battleships that would never arrive.

Flushing Creek passes by a neighborhood in transition on its western bank. **Willets Point**, also known as the Iron Triangle, is an industrial district populated largely by automobile repair shops. The area has no sewers because, since the time of the first World's Fair, its property owners have successfully resisted efforts by the city to develop the area. Under Mayor Michael Bloomberg, efforts to revamp Willets Point picked up, as part of a vision to bring hotels, offices, and a convention center to Queens.

The leading proponent of redevelopment in Willets Point is the New York Mets, the National League baseball franchise that arrived in the neighborhood in 1964. Designed in time for the 1964 World's Fair, **Shea Stadium** was a modernist arena, fitted with retractable seats to accommodate the Jets football team and concerts. The arena ended up as a modest version of a much larger project; the plan had envisioned a round,

QUEENS

domed arena, similar to its contemporaries the Astrodome in Houston and the Kingdome in Seattle. The crescent-shaped outdoor stadium hosted its last game on September 28, 2008. Within two weeks, demolition commenced.

By February of the following year, the last chunks of rubble were gone, and all that remains of the stadium are engraved plates marking its field on the parking lot of its successor, **Citi Field**. The new stadium is a throwback to the history and heritage of the National League in New York. The exterior arches resemble Ebbets Field, and the green seats hearken to the Polo Grounds—where the Dodgers and Giants played, respectively, before both teams moved to California.

Willets Point received its name from Willets Point Boulevard, a route designed to run in a northeast direction from Roosevelt Avenue to **Fort Totten**, where the actual Willets Point is located—at the confluence of the East River, Little Neck Bay, and the Long Island Sound. The boulevard was never completed, and today it runs in two segments: a pockmarked five-block stretch through the Willets Point neighborhood and a longer segment that picks up in northern Flushing and terminates just short of Fort Totten.

The shore along the Willets Point neighborhood is polluted from runoff but is also inaccessible, with marshes growing on the water. Across from Willets Point is an iconic clock tower, familiar to airplane pilots landing at LaGuardia Airport and generations of Mets baseball fans. A former furniture and zipper factory, it is presently a U-Haul truck depot, with cement factories as its neighbors. Prior to the 1960s, College Point Boulevard was Lawrence Street, named after a colonial settler family whose estate stood on the shore of the stream until the early 20th century. Their estate entertained high-profile figures including the future King William IV and President George Washington—at separate events, of course.

The **Northern Boulevard Bridge** crossing Flushing Creek is an uninspiring highway overpass completed in 1980. There is only one sidewalk, on the northern shoulder. The bridge's predecessors were drawbridges, with the earliest dating to 1800. In 1880, it was upgraded to a swing bridge with one trolley track. This structure was replaced with a Beaux-Arts design in 1906, featuring round turret towers. The 1939 replacement was a concrete tower overlooking a bascule lift. The present design makes no pretensions about Flushing Creek, recognizing it as an inlet with little service as a shipping route.

QUEENS

The last bridge to cross Flushing Creek is the **Whitestone Bridge**, a four-lane drawbridge proposed for Willets Point Boulevard but almost immediately absorbed into the Whitestone Parkway, which connected Grand Central Parkway with the Whitestone Bridge. Completed in 1939, it enabled motorists from upstate and New England to access the first World's Fair in Flushing Meadows. In the postwar years, car ownership across the country increased, and an upgrade was necessary to transform Whitestone Parkway into an expressway. In 2008, it was replaced with a fixed span.

From this point, the river turns sharply to the west and empties into **Flushing Bay**, an arm of the East River. At its mouth, a city-owned concrete plant hugs the shore. From this point, the southern shore of Flushing Bay offers views of LaGuardia Airport from the promenade and the **World's Fair Marina**. The eastern shore has no parks; it is covered with commercial and industrial development.

Potential for revival

Between the two World's Fairs, this stream flowed through Flushing Meadows in its natural state. The major barriers preventing a boat trip from its source to its mouth were the Tide Gate Bridge and Long Island Railroad trestle. Since the 1964 World's Fair, the extension of the Van Wyck Expressway atop the stream has reduced the navigable portion to its two lakes and the reach north of Roosevelt Avenue. The burial of the creek through its fairgrounds section has rendered it invisible in the most prominent section of the park.

In November 2008, the Parks Department released the ambitious Flushing Meadows Corona Park Strategic Framework Plan, which included the daylighting of Flushing Creek's buried sections. The plan proposed covering the Fountain of the Planets under a lawn with the restored stream flowing around it.

A daylighted Flushing Creek could serve as a unifying element for the disparate sections of Flushing Meadows–Corona Park, from its source at Willow Lake to its mouth at the Flushing Bay promenade. It would reconnect park goers to the natural history of Flushing Meadows and provide better drainage of the park's two lakes, reducing algae and improving oxygen levels for its wildlife. At the same time, a daylighting project would displace two heavily used soccer fields and a portion of the park's golf course, and it would cost a lot. For now, the buried section of the stream will remain as is.

QUEENS

QUEENS

✦ **Flushing Meadows–Corona Park**
  ✧ Willow Lake preserve
  ✧ Meadow Lake boathouse
  ✧ Ederle Terrace (Aquacade site)
  ✧ Unisphere (site of the Trylon and Perisphere)
  ✧ Queens Museum (New York City Building) ✦ 718-592-9700 ✦ www.queensmuseum.org
  ✧ Tide Gate Bridge
  ✧ Flushing Meadows Golf Center and mini-golf
  ✧ Citi Field (site of Shea Stadium) ✦ 123-01 Roosevelt Avenue ✦ 718-507-6387 ✦ www.mets.com
  ✧ Billie Jean King National Tennis Center ✦ 718-760-6200 ✦ www.usta.com
  ✧ New York Hall of Science ✦ 47-01 111th Street ✦ 718-699-0005 ✦ www.nysci.org
  ✧ Queens Zoo ✦ 53-51 111th Street ✦ 718-271-1500 ✦ www.queenszoo.com
✦ **Willets Point** Willets Point Boulevard between Roosevelt Avenue and Northern Boulevard
✦ **Roosevelt Avenue Bridge** Roosevelt Avenue over Flushing Creek
✦ **Flushing Bay Promenade** Runs along Grand Central Parkway and Northern Boulevard
✦ **Mount Hebron Cemetery** 130-04 Horace Harding Expressway ✦ 718-939-9405 ✦ www.mounthebroncemetery.com

✦ **Bus**: Q48 at Roosevelt Avenue and College Point Boulevard; Q58 at College Point Boulevard and 57th Road; Q88 at Horace Harding Expressway and College Point Boulevard
✦ **Subway**: 7 at Mets–Willets Point
✦ **Bike**: There are bike lanes within Flushing Meadows–Corona Park
✦ **Boat**: The creek is navigable up to Roosevelt Avenue; Meadow Lake is accessible to canoeing and has a boathouse with rentals

40. Kissena Creek

Kissena Creek is an eastern tributary of Flushing Creek, also referred to on some maps as Ireland Mill Creek. It is buried for almost its entire path, with the exception of a small segment within Kissena Park. Nearly half of its path lies beneath parkland and could be daylighted without encroaching on private property. The stream had its headwaters in a swamp in Kew Gardens Hills. From there, the stream flowed across Fresh Meadows in a northeast direction before circling around Kissena Park and turning west toward Flushing Meadows, where it emptied into Flushing Creek.

Kew Gardens Hills

At Kissena Creek's start, the swamp was a sizable tract bound by Vleigh Place on the north and west, and Parsons Boulevard on the east. It served as a source for peat in the late 19th century, a fossil fuel related to coal that forms from decayed plant matter. As the neighborhood developed, the swamp shrank in size. The last remnant of the swamp was a 23-acre parcel where the **Opal Luxury Apartments** and **Lander College for Men** now stand, completed in 2004 and 2000, respectively. Across an open field, the 14-story Opal apartments promise opulence to those who can afford it and even to a few who wouldn't otherwise have been able to—six units are reserved for lower-income applicants as part of a tax abatement agreement between the building's developer and the city.

A couple of blocks to the northwest of the Opal is Aguilar Avenue, a crescent-shaped two-block road that carried the ancient Jamaica Road across the creek. This colonial-period path connected the settlements of Flushing and Jamaica and made a curve around the swamp. By the early 1950s, the route running past the former swamp was straightened and renamed Kissena Boulevard. The old curve remained under the name Aguilar Avenue.

Fresh Meadows

Crossing Parsons Boulevard, the stream meandered eastward across **Fresh Meadows**, a largely suburban-style neighborhood that derives its name from freshwater springs that dotted the landscape and contributed to Kissena Creek. At Utopia Parkway, the stream was joined by a tributary flowing north from the present-day site of **Utopia Playground**, which had a kettle pond. The pond was located at the junction of Utopia

QUEENS

Parkway and 73rd Avenue, which was known as Black Stump Road. The ancient name is a reminder of a time when local property owners marked their boundaries with burned-out remains of tree stumps.

On the shore of the pond were the Black Stump School and the volunteer Black Stump fire company. The pond was filled in 1941 in favor of the three-acre **Utopia Playground**. In the postwar period, Fresh Meadows rapidly developed, and there was a need for a new school for the neighborhood. In 1947, the city's Board of Estimate proposed one on the site of the playground. However, citing cost and the buried pond, Parks Commissioner Robert Moses opposed the idea, and the playground was saved. **Public School 173** was built a couple of blocks to the north, with **Fresh Meadows Playground** as its schoolyard.

Utopia Parkway's name hearkens to the Utopia Land Company, which purchased a 50-acre tract in Fresh Meadows in 1905 with the goal of building a cooperatively run Jewish community. A street grid was laid out with street names from the Lower East Side, such as Orchard, Houston, and Hester. The project failed to raise enough funds to get past the planning stage, and the land remained undeveloped for another three decades. The only street that retained its original name was **Utopia Parkway**, which runs parallel to and then merges with the colonial-period **Fresh Meadow Lane**.

Continuing downstream, Kissena Creek's path crosses the Long Island Expressway and enters the grounds of **Francis Lewis High School**, a modernist campus that takes up four blocks and includes an athletic field behind its building. The school opened in 1960 and is named after a Welsh-born American revolutionary who lived in Whitestone. His name appears on the Declaration of Independence on behalf of New York. In Queens, his name can also be found on **Francis Lewis Boulevard**, the longest north–south route in the borough; and **Francis Lewis Park**, a small waterfront oasis at the foot of the Whitestone Bridge.

Kissena Park

In places where topography is challenging, parks and cemeteries usually occupy the summits. To the west of the high school are **Mount Saint Mary's Cemetery** and the **Kissena Park Golf Course**. Separating the two hilltop sites is **Booth Memorial Avenue**, an ancient road once known as North Hempstead Turnpike. Following the completion of the Long Island Expressway in 1954, Booth Memorial Avenue became less trafficked; in the section running past the golf course it resembles a countryside road. Its namesake is Salvation Army founder William

Booth, an English Methodist pastor who founded the charitable organization in 1878.

Booth's ties to Queens go back to 1957, when the Salvation Army opened Booth Memorial Hospital at the corner of Main Street and the avenue now bearing his name. The facility offered services to unmarried mothers at a time when out-of-wedlock births were a rarity. In 1992, the Salvation Army divested itself of the hospital, and it is today called **New York-Presbyterian/Queens**.

As golf courses are concerned, **Kissena Park Golf Course** is a relative newcomer to a borough that once had nearly a dozen private clubs. One by one, they closed and moved east as development crept up around them. This golf course was commissioned by Robert Moses in 1935 as a public works project. It was designed by prolific golf course architect John Van Kleek. Prior to the Great Depression, Van Kleek operated in partnership with Wayne Stiles, creating more than 140 courses between Maine and New Mexico. More than 70 remain in use today. Van Kleek's imprint at public courses across the city also includes Silver Lake in Staten Island, Split Rock in the Bronx, and Dyker Beach in Brooklyn, among others.

Kissena Creek flows beneath Fresh Meadow Lane on the golf course's eastern border, making a left turn westward at its northeastern corner.

Beyond the northeast corner of the golf course is a large depression used by the city's Department of Transportation as a storage facility. Older aerial photographs and maps show the site as a reservoir and pumping station that supplied the town of Flushing with its drinking water. A bike trail follows the streambed between Fresh Meadow Lane and 164th Street along the northern edge of the golf course. Here, the stream reappears after heavy rains in the form of vernal pools. These temporary ponds provide a habitat for young amphibian creatures before they mature into frogs and salamanders.

The bikeway is part of the larger Brooklyn-Queens Greenway, a 40-mile bike path running from Coney Island to Fort Totten. Within Queens, a sizable portion of the trail runs through a 4.5-mile green linear park known as **Kissena Corridor Park**. This park connects Flushing Meadows with the **Queens Botanical Garden**, Kissena Park, and **Cunningham Park**.

A linear park was first proposed for Queens by urban planner Louis Risse in 1900. The park can be considered an early example of a rail trail, incorporating the right-of-way of the short-lived Central Railroad of Long Island, better known as the Stewart Line. Founded by department store magnate Alexander T. Stewart, it operated between Flushing and Bethpage between 1871 and 1876. Most of the Queens portion of this line was abandoned in 1879, with other portions incorporated into the Long Island Railroad. Acquisition of the railroad's right-of-way through the park began in 1938 and was completed within a decade.

From Cunningham Park, the bikeway continues eastward along the Vanderbilt Motor Parkway, an early highway abandoned in 1938 and repurposed as a park trail, to **Alley Pond Park**. From there, **Joe Michaels Mile**, a waterfront path along **Little Neck Bay**, takes the bike path to its conclusion at **Fort Totten**, at the northeastern tip of Queens.

Along this stretch of Kissena Creek, the northern border of Kissena Corridor Park is marked by Underhill Avenue, named after a prominent local family that provided intelligence for the patriots during the American Revolution. The streambed crosses 164th Street, entering the 235-acre Kissena Park, where it reappears above the surface as a lake.

For much of its preconsolidation history, Flushing had a reputation as a planting center. **Kissena Lake** was given the name by horticulturist Samuel Bowne Parsons based on a Chippewa word for "it is cold." Parsons operated a plant nursery within the future park from the early 1870s until his death in 1906. A 14-acre remnant of the nursery near Parsons Boulevard and Rose Avenue is known as the **Historic Grove**.

The earliest nursery opened in 1735, growing plants from exotic destinations. Operated by William Prince, it was named **Linnaean Gardens** after famed Swedish botanist Carl Linnaeus, who designed a classification order for all living things. The family business continued only into the 1870s, but on the map today, there is still a Prince Street in Flushing and an alley off it called Linnaeus Place. At its height, during the Civil War, the Prince family's nursery totaled 113 acres. Other plant-related sights on the map are the street names in Flushing, in alphabetical order with names such as Ash, Beech, and Cherry, ending with Rose.

Within the park, there are some 100 tree species from places as far as Japan and Iran, all a testament to Parsons's nursery. Many of the older trees growing in Central and Prospect Parks originated in this nursery.

The family is the namesake for Parsons Boulevard, a series of road segments running from Malba to downtown Jamaica. On the Queens street grid, boulevards are major roads running either askew to the grid or across long distances. Parsons Boulevard appears unfinished, with the largest gap being Kissena Park.

Located at the northwestern corner of the park, Kissena Lake was once fed by the creek and a smaller stream from the north that has since been buried with a playground built on top. Within the lake is a bird sanctuary isle, constructed following the lake's most recent restoration in 2003. The lake was used as an ice-skating and ice-harvesting site for much of the 19th century. Its use as a recreational site led the city to purchase land around it for a park in 1906.

In 1942, the Works Progress Administration drained the lake, cutting it off from natural sources, and redesigned it as a "bathtub lake," with a concrete shoreline and water piped in from the city's aqueduct. Lacking natural aeration and warmed by its shallower depth and concrete shoreline, the lake suffered a buildup of algae and had to be drained again in 1983 to clear away the invasive growth. In 2002, a $1.8 million restoration drained the lake in stages, resulting in its current appearance. At certain locations, a naturalistic shoreline was built. The isle in the middle was added, and wells and pipes were placed to provide new sources of water.

Prior to 1942, the lake drained into Kissena Creek beneath a stone bridge reminiscent of Gapstow Bridge in Central Park. Since then, it has drained into a short pipe that empties into a freshwater wetland. To the north of the wetland is the Parsons tree grove, and on the south is a vast meadow. Inside the grassland, the 400-meter **Kissena Velodrome** beckons professional bicyclists with an acrylic-covered track that hosted the 1964 Olympic Trials. The track is named after Flushing businessman and bicycle enthusiast Siegfried Stern. Velodromes were popular around the country at the end of the 19th century, but with the rise of automobiles, they gradually fell in number. Presently, there are only 26 such tracks in the United States, with the Kissena Velodrome as the lone holdout within New York City.

The wetland is separated from the meadow by the former Stewart Line embankment, which has a trail running above it. Amid the shrubs, the stream hits this concrete embankment and disappears through a metal grate, beneath the ground, and runs in the dark toward its confluence with Flushing Creek.

Kissena Corridor Park (west)

The streambed's next road crossing is the ancient Kissena Boulevard, where Kissena Park ends and the **western park corridor** takes over. Within the park corridor are three blocks of tract housing surrounded by parkland on three sides. These blocks are a holdover from the park's past, when it was a patchwork of privately owned parcels. The city gradually acquired each plot, but one apparently was developed before the city could attain it.

On the north side of the enclave is the Stewart Line right-of-way. The only hint of the rail line is an entrance to the park at Rose Avenue and Kissena Boulevard with a railroad-themed sculpture and paving elements. On the south side is a small wetland, atop the former streambed, and **Captain Mario Fajardo Playground**. A native of Ecuador, Fajardo resided in Flushing. On February 26, 1991, shortly before the Persian Gulf War ended, Fajardo and six of his comrades were killed during an operation to clear American land mines. Booth Memorial Playground was renamed after Fajardo the following year.

The land covering most of the western Kissena Corridor Park is landfill created in 1954 from excavations for the nearby Long Island Expressway. Prior to the filling work, the stream was still visible in this area and occasionally caused flooding in surrounding homes in the Queensboro Hill neighborhood. A trail covered in mulch offers a relaxing walk through forest and meadow sections of the corridor. On Colden Street between Geranium and Juniper Avenues, the environmental naming theme appears on **Rachel Carson Playground**, a tribute to the author of the 1962 book *Silent Spring*, which gave momentum to the environmentalist movement. Next to the playground is a community garden operated by local senior residents.

Queens Botanical Garden

The buried streambed continues beneath Main Street, entering the **Queens Botanical Garden**. With the exception of Manhattan, each of the city's boroughs has its own botanical garden, all containing streams and ponds as part of their layouts. For most of its history, the Queens Botanical Garden did not appear to acknowledge the stream that used to run through its property. The only bodies of water on display were small wetland gardens.

A sign of the garden's reconnection with Kissena Creek appears in its 2001 Master Plan, which proposes a self-sustaining ecosystem within the 39-acre garden. A stream would form from rainwater collected atop the roof of its administration building, flowing through pools toward a wetland at the garden's western edge. Runoff collected in the garden's parking lot and other locations would also contribute to the stream. Although this stream would not be connected with Kissena Creek, which runs in a sewer beneath the garden, its course mirrors the former streambed. The first phase of the plan, an environmentally friendly **Visitor & Administration Center**, was completed in 2007.

Flushing Meadows–Corona Park

Exiting Queens Botanical Garden, the phantom streambed enters the eastern panhandle of **Flushing Meadows–Corona Park**, located between College Point Boulevard and Van Wyck Expressway. A former wetland, this section was filled ahead of the 1939 World's Fair using soil dredged from Meadow and Willow Lakes. During the fair, this was the **Court of Peace**, a rectangular lawn flanked by buildings representing countries. At the head of this layout was the massive U.S. Pavilion with 13 columns at its entrance that symbolized the original states of the union. In the 1964 World's Fair, this space was a parking field, separated from the fairgrounds by the expressway.

At this point, the sewer carrying Kissena Creek enters a massive underground water treatment plant before emptying into Flushing Creek. Constructed at a cost of $291 million, the **Flushing Bay Combined Sewer Outfall Retention Facility** began operating in May 2007. It was designed to hold 43.4 million gallons of sewage from a 7,400-acre drainage basin that includes the Kissena Creek watershed.

Atop the seven-acre facility are a soccer field and the **Al Oerter Recreation Center**. This $50 million public gym opened in March 2009 and was named after the Astoria-born discus throw champion. In his athletic career, Oerter won gold medals at four consecutive Olympic Games between 1956 and 1968. With an annual membership fee of $50, the center has nearly 50,000 members using its two fitness rooms, indoor running track, racquetball and basketball courts, computer center, and classes teaching karate, gymnastics, and aerobic dancing.

PLACES TO SEE:

+ **Utopia Playground** Utopia Parkway at 73rd Avenue
+ **Kissena Park Golf Course** 164-15 Booth Memorial Avenue ✦ 718-939-4594 ✦ www.nycgovparks.org/parks/kissenapark/facilities/golf
+ **Kissena Park** Bound by Rose Avenue, Kissena Boulevard, 164th Street, and Booth Memorial Avenue ✦ 718-359-1297 ✦ www.nycgovparks.org/parks/kissenapark
  ◇ **Historic Grove** www.nycgovparks.org/parks/kissenapark/highlights/12242
  ◇ **Velodrome** www.nycgovparks.org/facility/cycling-tracks/kissena-velodrome

✦ **Queens Botanical Garden** 43-50 Main Street ✦ 718-886-3800 ✦ www.queensbotanical.org
✦ **Al Oerter Recreation Center** 131-40 Fowler Avenue ✦ 718-353-7853 ✦ www.nycgovparks.org/facilities/recreationcenters/Q099-NMD01

GETTING THERE:

✦ **Bus**: Q20A, Q20B, Q44 at Main Street and Elder Avenue for Queens Botanical Garden; Q65 at Oak Avenue and 164th Street for Kissena Lake; Q17, Q25, Q34 at Kissena Boulevard and Rose Avenue for Historic Grove
✦ **Subway**: 7 at Flushing–Main Street, transfer to Q20A, Q20B, Q44, Q65, Q17, Q25, or Q34
✦ **Bike**: There are bike lanes on Underhill Avenue and within Kissena Park as part of the Brooklyn-Queens Greenway, and on 164th Street

41. Mill Creek

The northern tributary to Flushing Creek empties into its source just a few feet shy of the point where Flushing River becomes Flushing Bay. It is one of many creeks in New York City that carries the name **Mill Creek**, a reminder of the many gristmills that dotted the colonial landscape of the future city.

The Mill Creek of Queens played a major role in the isolation of College Point from the rest of Queens due to a vast flooded meadow along the creek.

The northern source

The stream had two branches: one originating in the north, at the present-day **George U. Harvey Playground**, located where 20th Avenue intersects with the Whitestone Expressway. The nine-acre green space features a roller-skating rink, two baseball diamonds, and a basketball court. Its namesake served as Queens borough president from 1925 to 1941.

The playground sits on land acquired by the village of Whitestone in 1892 for its water supply system. The Parks Department took possession of the site in 1936 as part of its project in laying out the Whitestone Parkway, which was later upgraded to an expressway.

Leaving Harvey Playground, the phantom stream crosses the Whitestone Expressway, entering a massive triangular expanse that contains **College Point Corporate Park** and the abandoned **Flushing Airport**. The northern border of the former airport is marked by 20th Avenue, built on fill across a former wetland.

The southern source

The southern branch of Mill Creek originated near the intersection of Northern Boulevard and Main Street, flowing past the present-day **Leavitts Park**. The park is named after Flushing millionaire G. Howland Leavitt, who in 1912 took a $3,000-a-year job as the superintendent of Queens highways. Borough President Maurice Connolly presumed that Leavitt, with his wealth, would not be susceptible to corruption. Leavitt also sat on the board that approved the design of the Queens borough flag, which was unfurled in 1913. The flag features a tulip and rose as symbols of Dutch and English colonial rule.

Inside the park is a charming Victorian-period structure, the **Lewis H. Latimer House Museum**. A son of fugitive slaves, Latimer worked with his generation's most brilliant inventors, including Alexander Graham Bell and Thomas Edison. Although Edison is credited with inventing the light bulb, the filament was designed by Latimer. Constructed between 1887 and 1889, the home originally stood on Holly Avenue, a mile to the south. Threatened with demolition, it was relocated to Leavitt Park in 1988.

Running north, the stream flowed through another superblock where the **Mitchell Gardens apartments** are today. The middle-class 1,400-unit co-op complex is named after the Mitchell family, who once owned this land. Their old home, **Innerwyck**, was a farmhouse built in 1670 at the corner of Bayside Avenue and Union Street. The Mitchell family resided there between 1804 and 1921. The historic home was demolished in 1959. It was the second-oldest structure in Queens after the Bowne House.

Mill Creek's southern branch merged with its northern branch near the present-day corner of Linden Place and 28th Avenue and continued across the marshland toward Flushing Creek.

College Point

For the first two centuries after the arrival of white settlers, the **College Point** peninsula was known as Lawrence's Neck, after its most prominent colonial family. Its present namesake was the short-lived **Saint Paul's College** seminary, a creation of Episcopal pastor Rev. William

QUEENS

Augustus Muhlenberg. Ground was broken on the site in 1836, but a financial panic in the following year reduced donations for the school. The would-be college closed in 1850.

College Point's development rapidly increased following the arrival of rubber manufacturer Conrad Poppenhusen in 1854. Poppenhusen turned College Point into a company town, funding a steamboat line, a library, and the nation's first kindergarten. The latter two were located within the **Poppenhusen Institute**. A city-designated landmark, the facility was completed in 1868; it also housed the justice of the peace, the first College Point Savings Bank, German singing societies, a courtroom, a sheriff's office with two jail cells, and a grand ballroom.

In regard to Mill Creek, Poppenhusen reduced College Point's isolation by constructing a railroad and causeway across the wetlands, providing a southern connection to the mainland and a more direct route to Flushing.

What is today College Point Boulevard was a series of four connected roads renamed in 1969; previously they were 122nd Street, College Point Causeway, Lawrence Street, and Rodman Street. The last two were names of families that owned significant properties around colonial Flushing. The causeway portion of the boulevard is visible as a straight and flat portion between 27th Avenue and the Whitestone Expressway.

A forgotten railway

Between 1869 and 1932, the **Whitestone Branch** of the Long Island Railroad traversed the wetlands. The rail line terminated at Whitestone Landing, and each station featured charming Victorian architecture. In its early years, College Point was a summer destination valued for its beer gardens and waterfront resorts. With Prohibition, these economic mainstays shuttered, and ridership declined as well.

In comparison to other LIRR branches, Whitestone was an appendage —an unprofitable one-track spur that stretched four miles with numerous grade crossings that were costly to eliminate. In 1915, the LIRR proposed leasing the Whitestone Branch to the city for use as a subway line. Failing to gain City Hall's attention, the LIRR reduced the offer to $1 per year in 1926. Instead of following the examples of the Culver, Brighton, and West End lines in Brooklyn—rail lines that were absorbed into the subway system—the city rejected the offer, and the LIRR began proceedings to abandon the branch.

For the next four years, a civic group called the United Transit Committee, which represented local commuters, unsuccessfully sued the railroad and lobbied the city to connect the one-track line with the subway system. On January 4, 1932, the Supreme Court ruled in favor of the LIRR.

On February 16, 1932, the last train rolled across Mill Creek. In April, the right-of-way was purchased by a contractor, and the drawbridge over Flushing Creek was demolished, severing the right-of-way from the rest of the Long Island Railroad system.

Flushing Airport

While the railroad was in decline, runways were constructed atop the wetland for **Flushing Airport**. Mill Creek was reduced to a ditch that ran along the eastern runway. In the early years of aviation, nearly a dozen privately run airfields across the city competed for customers. Two of the airports were expanded and became the present-day **LaGuardia Airport** and **JFK International Airport**. An additional one, **Floyd Bennett Field** in southern Brooklyn, held on as a naval air station until 1971.

In contrast, Flushing Airport received no historical recognition, lacking the record-setting early flights and celebrity pilots. Since its closing in 1984, its edges were developed, while nature has reclaimed the hangars and runways.

The airport opened in 1927 as Speed's Airport, named after its founder, Anthony "Speed" Hanzlik. His company, Speed's Flying Service, operated on the city-owned site from 1937 until its closing. The airport's proximity to LaGuardia, neighborhood opposition, numerous accidents, and flooding on the runways plagued the airport throughout its existence. Its main clientele were private airplanes and blimps.

Mill Creek's meddling with the airport is exemplified in a 1960 comment by Charles Leedham, commissioner of the city's Department of Marine and Aviation, who described Flushing Airport as the "miasmal swamp of the Western Hemisphere." At the time, Leedham proposed a $6 million upgrade for the field, "so you won't need a seaplane license to land there."

The construction of an electric plant near the airport's northeast corner in the 1970s forced the closure of runway 4-22, leaving only one landing strip. When gusts exceeded 35 miles per hour, Hanzlik would close the airport. The airport also never operated at night, lacking the necessary lighting systems.

Benjamin Rosenthal, who represented Flushing in Congress between 1962 and 1983, heard numerous constituent complaints about the airport and was among the leading voices calling for its closure. "It's a built-in hazard," he told the *New York Times* in a 1970 interview. Hanzlik and his wife, Wilhelmina, stubbornly held on to the airport, running it as a mom-and-pop operation more fitting for a small town.

Between a blackout, a wave of arson in the Bronx, and ongoing financial troubles, 1977 was a watershed year for New York City. For Flushing Airport, this was its third year without Hanzlik, who had died three years earlier. He was succeeded by Clifford Rice. With each accident, the airport's reputation worsened. In January, a Piper Twin Comanche plane crashed into a warehouse north of the airport. In May, a light plane crashed into a nearby home, killing a teenage passenger. The city ordered the airport closed on August 19.

In defiance of the city's order, Rice reopened the airport on August 26 and welcomed a Piper Aztec piloted by supporter Fred Graff. However, an hour later, police arrived and threatened to arrest Rice. Rather than risk imprisonment, Rice declared the airport permanently closed, and a wooden cross was laid out on the runway. In January 1984, the airport closed permanently, in part because of accidents and flooding. For the next few years, ambitious plans for a heliport and airship terminal were debated among city officials as nature reclaimed the site. In October 1993, the city backed away from the heliport proposal, ending the last serious attempt to restore the site to aviation-related usage. From that point, the debate turned toward commercial use of the site. A 2004 proposal by the city to build a Korean-run wholesale distribution center to house 180 businesses was met with protests.

For now, the western edge has the **College Point Fields** sports park while the eastern side is home to the *New York Times* **printing plant**. This 515,000-square-foot industrial facility opened in 1997 at a cost of $280 million. Designed by James Stewart Polshek & Partners, it is covered with a corrugated-steel facade and large glass windows offering a peek at its automated press.

Linden Place used to run through the airport site but has been closed since the early 1990s as a result of flooding from Mill Creek. Crossing the remains of Linden Place at 28th Avenue, Mill Creek enters the 35-acre campus of the **New York Police Academy**. The massive $656 million facility includes a glass-enclosed bridge running above Mill Creek. The school brings various aspects of police training to a single location. At the time of its 2009 groundbreaking, the NYPD had its main academy near Gramercy Park, its shooting range at Rodman's Neck in the Bronx, and its driving course at Floyd Bennett Field in Brooklyn. Prior to construction, the site was a police tow pound that held nearly 3,000 vehicles.

Mill Creek runs through a straight culvert across the campus, making an L-shaped turn toward the south. The channel was constructed by the city in the early 1980s. Mill Creek disappears belowground at 31st Avenue, running through 72-inch pipes toward Flushing Creek.

College Point Corporate Park

A 300-acre expanse of superblocks to the southwest of the former airport was first proposed as a site for light industry in 1960 by James Felt, chairman of the City Planning Commission. The goal was to reduce the flight of manufacturers from the city and generate tax income from the undeveloped land. At the time, the marshland had "paper streets" on it—roads that were on the official map but never built. In the 1980s, **College Point Corporate Park** assumed most of its current buildings, following a $4 million drainage project by the Economic Development Corporation. Above the buried stream, **Crystal Window & Door Systems** has its factory and office. The company was founded in 1990 by Taiwanese immigrant Thomas Chen; its 165,000-square-foot facility includes a Chinese art gallery.

College Point Corporate Park was intended for industrial use, but today only three tenants have manufacturing facilities at the site: the *New York Times*, Crystal Window, and St. Lawrence Cement. Other tenants include building materials retailer Home Depot, a self-storage warehouse, a multiplex cinema, and a bus depot.

Mill Creek returns to the surface at College Point Boulevard, where it empties into Flushing Creek.

PLACES TO SEE:

+ **George U. Harvey Playground** 20th Avenue at the Whitestone Expressway + www.nycgovparks.org/parks/harvey-park
+ **Leavitts Park** Bound by Leavitt Street, 32nd Avenue, and 137th Street
+ **Lewis H. Latimer House Museum** 34-41 137th Street + 718-961-8585 + www.historichousetrust.org/house/lewis-h-latimer-house-museum
+ **Poppenhusen Institute** 114-4 14th Road + 718-358-0067 + poppenhuseninstitute.org
+ **Flushing Airport site** Bound by the Whitestone Expressway, Linden Place, 130th Street, and 20th Avenue
+ **College Point Fields** Bound by Ulmer Street, 130th Street, 23rd Avenue, and Linden Place

QUEENS

+ **New York Police Academy** 130-30 28th Avenue + 718-670-9100+
www.nyc.gov/html/nypd/html/police_academy/police_academy
.shtml
+ **Crystal Window & Door Systems** 31-10 Whitestone Expressway +
718-961-7300 + www.crystalwindows.com

GETTING THERE:
+ **Bus**: Q25, QM2, QM20, Q50 at Linden Place and Whitestone
Expressway; Q65 at College Point Boulevard and Whitestone
Expressway
+ **Subway**: 7 at Flushing–Main Street, transfer to Q25, Q50, or Q65
+ **Bike**: There are currently no bike lanes on roads near the path of
Mill Creek

42. Horse Brook

The western tributary to Flushing Creek flowed on land that is presently occupied by a number of superblock developments, including the **Queens Center** mall and **LeFrak City**. **Horse Brook** originated in Elmhurst, near the present-day corner of Kneeland Avenue and Codwise Place, flowing along the paths of Justice Avenue and the Long Island Expressway toward Flushing Meadows.

Similar to Sunswick Creek, this stream is remembered only on signs placed by individuals appreciative of its history. Otherwise, the only other traces of this stream are the large superblocks that defy the street grid. These blocks avoided development until technology enabled construction atop the high water table marking the former streambed.

In Elmhurst

The English settlement of Newtown was founded in 1652 as a replacement for an earlier failed attempt at Maspeth, where local natives chased out the European settlers in 1643. The settlement's official Dutch name was Middleburgh. The first mention of Horse Brook in local official documents was at an annual town meeting in 1662, where it was voted that "whosoever has cats or dogs or hogs lying dead in any place to offend their neighbors they must either bury them or throw them into the creek." From that point, the condition of the stream would progressively deteriorate from human activities.

When the colony switched to English rule in 1664, Hastings became the new official name, but the more popular moniker Newtown stuck around and remained in usage for two more centuries. The heart of this settlement was the block of Broadway between Justice Avenue and Queens Boulevard, pierced in the middle by Horse Brook. The town lent its name to the Newtown Pippin, a type of apple, and to **Newtown Creek**, the stream separating western Queens from Brooklyn.

From 1683 to 1898, the County of Queens was comprised of seven towns: Long Island City, Newtown, Flushing, Jamaica, Hempstead, North Hempstead, and Oyster Bay. The first four towns agreed in 1898 to be consolidated within New York City, while the remaining three seceded to form the suburban Nassau County. In turn, the Rockaway Peninsula seceded from Hempstead to join New York City.

The town of Newtown encompassed the land between Flushing Meadows and Sunnyside that includes present-day neighborhoods such as Forest Hills, Ridgewood, Corona, and Woodside, among others. In 1897, the town was renamed Elmhurst to disassociate itself from the foul-smelling reputation of Newtown Creek. The town's old name can still be found on **Newtown High School** and the Grand Avenue–Newtown subway station.

The former town seat was a courthouse at the corner of Justice Avenue and Broadway. After 1898, it became a police station; it was demolished unceremoniously in 1966. A street triangle on the site of the building bears the name **Libra Triangle**. Named by Parks Commissioner Henry Stern, it has a historical marker recalling the former stream.

Along the southern shore of the stream, **North Hempstead Plank Road** connected Maspeth with Flushing Meadows along present-day 57th Avenue, Hoffman Drive, 63rd Avenue, Apex Place, and Colonial Avenue.

At 55th Avenue, the former streambed is covered by the **Georgia Diner** parking lot. The popular diner opened in 1978 and has seen the neighborhood transform into a dense residential district at the turn of the 21st century. It is only a matter of time before the parking lot is developed.

Across this road, the coliseum-shaped **Queens Place** shopping center takes up nearly an entire block, featuring two spiral ramps leading to its rooftop parking lot. Around its white concrete facade, four levels of slot windows conceal another wall. Typical of postwar shopping mall design, there are no real windows.

Looking closer at the building, its southeastern edge contains a five-foot notch pierced by an HSBC bank branch. As a result, the 426-foot-diameter structure is not a perfect circle. This notch is the product of stubborn homeowner Mary Sendek, who lived on the corner of 56th Avenue and Queens Boulevard from 1922 until her death in 1980. When Mary and Joseph Sendek moved into the house, Queens Boulevard was still a two-lane road. A cemetery and church were their western neighbors, and Horse Brook rushed behind the backyard. Muskrat and an occasional fox could still be found along the creek's banks.

Urbanization and expansion of Queens Boulevard followed the arrival of the subway in 1933. By 1963, Sendek was a widow living with her dog, and Macy's had purchased all the other properties on her block for the mall. In her battle to stay, Sendek rejected exorbitant offers for her property, holding on to every inch, including the five-foot notch where her backyard would cut into the coliseum. Sendek reportedly turned down a $200,000 offer for a home that had cost her husband only $4,000 to purchase.

Architectural firm Skidmore, Owings & Merrill adapted to the situation, cutting an edge into the building. In 1980, Sendek's heirs sold her house to a developer. The replacement for Sendek's house greatly ruins the view of Queens Place for eastbound travelers on Queens Boulevard. Macy's left the building in 1996, moving to the nearby Queens Center Mall. The largest tenant at this time is Target.

Behind Queens Place is a small traffic triangle formed by 56th Avenue (formerly Horse Brook Road), Justice Avenue, and 90th Street. Dubbed **Horsebrook Island**, it keeps the stream on the map. On the other side of the triangle is the **Newtown High School athletic field**, an undeveloped block that features tennis courts, handball, soccer, and a running track. The sports field stands in contrast to the massive **Queens Center Mall** on the other side of 57th Avenue.

Located at the junction of two major boulevards, the Long Island Expressway, numerous bus lines, and a subway station, the mall's commercial success is entirely based on its central location. The mall contains nearly a million square feet of retail space, with Macy's and JCPenney anchoring the 175 businesses inside the structure. The mall's exterior features the names of neighborhoods in Queens, and in the basement, the World's Fare food court also gives a nod to the borough's history and diverse population.

Past what is now the Queens Center Mall, the stream expanded into a wide wetland as it turned east, running along the path of the Long Island Expressway toward Flushing Meadows. The massive roadway separates Elmhurst and Corona from Rego Park and Forest Hills.

In Rego Park

Across the highway, a pumping station on the corner of 62nd Avenue and Queens Boulevard once collected water from Horse Brook. Today, it is hidden beneath **Lost Battalion Hall**, a public recreation center built in 1939. The facility is named after a battalion of 301 American soldiers who were isolated from the rest of their unit during the Battle of the Argonne in the First World War. After five days, they successfully repelled a German offensive but lost one-third of their men. Alongside its recreational use, the building also houses the local chapter of Veterans of Foreign Wars.

In 1972, the city's Board of Estimate passed a resolution allowing American Telephone and Telegraph (AT&T) to place a telephone equipment center on land adjacent to Lost Battalion Hall, and in exchange, the communications company paid for the demolition of the sanitation garage behind the hall.

The AT&T facility stands on a raised embankment that makes it appear like an island rising above the traffic of Queens Boulevard. Its elevation and lack of windows were designed with security in mind, protection against human and natural threats.

Behind this facility is the third major shopping center built atop the buried stream. With its signature red color, **Rego Park Center** on Junction Boulevard is easily remembered by motorists on the Long Island Expressway, its current form a welcome change from what it looked like in the 1990s, when the mall was vacant following the bankruptcy of the Alexander's department store on an adjacent block.

In 2009, the 600,000-square-foot expansion of the former Alexander's transformed the undeveloped parking lot atop the streambed into a popular shopping destination that includes Century 21, Costco, and Kohl's. The expansion building is divided into two halves, one for parking topped by a residential tower and another for retail. Between them, a canopy-covered pedestrian corridor bisects the superblock.

In LeFrak City

Much of the clientele for Rego Park Center comes from **LeFrak City**, a massive housing development located across the Long Island Expressway. Built on 40 acres of land, the complex houses over 14,000 residents within 20 identical towers that are each 16 stories. A self-contained city built between 1960 and 1969, LeFrak City features its own office buildings, swimming pool, synagogue, mosque, church, and library.

The land on which LeFrak City sits was once a sprawling wetland where a stream from the north, originating at Alstyne Street and 98th Street, merged with Horse Brook. When developer Samuel J. LeFrak acquired the wetland in 1955, it was an undeveloped dumping ground temporarily lined with Quonset huts built for returning World War II veterans. Because of its soil conditions, land along the stream between 99th Street and Colonial Avenue had evaded development until this point. By then, much of the surrounding area was already laid out in a grid and covered by apartment buildings.

Construction on LeFrak City began in 1960, celebrated at the time as the largest privately financed apartment complex in the world, costing LeFrak $150 million. The ambitious development's plans included a shopping center, office tower, helipad, ten swimming pools, tennis courts, two theaters, numerous underground parking garages, a post office, fountains, and gardens. Concierges in top hats welcomed residents into buildings named after global destinations, such as Ceylon, Melbourne, London, and Mexico. The **LeFrak City Library**, located on 57th Avenue and 98th Street, offers newspaper clippings and books on the history of LeFrak City.

Park City Estates

Where a pedestrian bridge carries 99th Street between LeFrak City and Rego Park, one could imagine a winding stream instead of highway traffic. The section of Rego Park along the highway is defined by the Rego Park Center and a series of high-rise developments that appear to mirror LeFrak City. Among them are two schools with accompanying playgrounds.

Before 1923 this section of Rego Park was called Annadale Park. It was used by farmers from Chinatown who grew produce for grocery stores in their neighborhood. That year, the 27-acre Thomson farm at Queens Boulevard and 63rd Avenue was sold to the Rego Construction Company, headed by Henry Ludwig Schloh. Rego was short for "real good."

Between Queens Boulevard and the city line, the service road that follows the Long Island Expressway carries the name **Horace Harding Expressway**. Its namesake was a business executive credited with promoting the concept of a highway that stretched the length of Long Island. Harding began his career in finance in 1883 at age 20, and by the time of his death on January 4, 1929, he commanded leadership of a

QUEENS

multitude of companies, including American Express; American Metal Company; Ann Arbor Railroad; New York, New Haven, and Hartford Railroad; and New York, Ontario, and Western Railroad.

In 1923, Harding approached borough officials with his highway proposal and was turned down because the city lacked the budget to build the road. Undeterred, he reached out to fellow business leaders and commissioned a land survey for the road. In May 1929, the city renamed Nassau Boulevard after Harding.

The **Horace Harding Playground** and **PS 206 Horace Harding School**, located on 98th Street and 62nd Drive, also memorialize the highway promoter. Built in 1954, the school is an example of the modernist style promoted by Michael Radoslovich, who served as the in-house architect for the Board of Education between 1952 and 1969. In contrast to prewar U-shaped schools, Radoslovich advocated H-shaped buildings, where the space between the wings could be filled in as the buildings expanded.

Across the street from the school is **Park City Estates**, a development of five identical 16-floor towers built around a private traffic circle. Designed by Philip Birnbaum, the towers feature outdoor balconies that connect apartments, as well as underground garages beneath its private driveway and park.

At 108th Street, a second elementary school along Horse Brook's path is **PS 220 Edward Mandel School**. Its namesake was a school reformer in the early 20th century who coordinated the expansion of the city's public schools across the five boroughs. Mandel was a resident of Forest Hills and is buried at Maple Grove Cemetery.

Corona Park

Across the highway is a section of the Corona neighborhood where streets deviate from the grid and carry names instead of numbers. When the enclave of **Corona Park** was built in 1854, it comprised an eight-block grid designed around Broad Street (present-day Saultell Avenue). The settlement was located at the junction of Colonial Avenue and Corona Avenue, two ancient roads that merged to form Strong's Causeway. The western boundary of the village is still marked on the map today as Westside Avenue, a one-lane path that predates other local streets. Horse Brook marked the southern edge of the village, where a milldam interrupted the flow of the stream.

QUEENS

Forest Hills Houses

Across 108th Street from PS 220 is an 8.46-acre superblock that hosts the **Forest Hills Cooperative Houses** and **Queens Community House**. For a decade, the construction of this housing project exemplified the growing rift between black and Jewish communities in the city during the late 1960s.

At the start of the decade, this undeveloped block was used as a golf driving range. But in 1966, the mayor announced plans to turn the land into scattered-site housing—a public housing project in this middle-class neighborhood. Seeing the pattern of crime and white flight that accompanied the projects built in neighborhoods such as Brownsville and East New York, the predominantly Jewish community in Forest Hills rallied against the project. The revised plan turned the rentals into a co-op, but where the "owners" were selected by the Housing Authority, and when they moved out, they could only sell their units back to the agency. The completed towers were 12 stories, half the height originally proposed, with 40 percent of the units reserved for the elderly. Part of the compromise also included the creation of **Queens Community House** on the campus of the housing development. Working on a model of a settlement house, the facility offers a variety of social services and programs for local residents of all ages.

In the spring of 1975, the apartments and the community house opened to the public.

Colonial Avenue and Coe's Mill

Behind Forest Hills Cooperative Houses, the one-block **Colonial Avenue** skews off the grid; it was once part of the ancient North Hempstead Plank Road. For nearly three centuries, the road traversed a small island in the middle of Horse Brook. On the island were **Coe's Mill** and a hotel. In 1930, the Long Island Expressway obliterated all traces of the gristmill and its island. Colonial Avenue was cut into two segments by the highway. The northern three blocks were incorporated into the service road, and the southern segment continues to carry the name.

The story begins in 1652 when English settler Captain John Coe established a gristmill on the island to serve the residents of Newtown. His father, Robert Coe, had arrived in America with his three sons in 1634, settling in the Puritan colony of Massachusetts. A year later, the family relocated to Connecticut. The family migrated to Long Island in 1644 following a dispute within their church. Together with the Reverend Richard Denton, they founded the town of Hempstead. Coe was also among the founders of Newtown and Jamaica.

The border between the Dutch and English colonies was a blurry one, and the influx of dissident Puritans and Quakers to Long Island caused friction with the Dutch administration. Skirmishes occurred on the border, and following the native raid that destroyed Maspeth in 1643, English settlers accused New Amsterdam of not doing enough to protect them against native attacks.

In 1662, John Coe and his sons authored a letter on behalf of English settlers on Long Island requesting that their towns be annexed to the Connecticut colony. At the same time, the Newtown settlers elected delegates to meet Governor Stuyvesant to defuse tensions. The colonists swore loyalty to the Dutch, who in return approved of democratic elections within the settlements of Hempstead, Flushing, Newtown, and Jamaica. Nevertheless, mistrust and accusations of dual loyalty persisted as the number of English settlers on Long Island rapidly outgrew the Dutch.

In August 1664, four English frigates commanded by Captain Thomas Nicolls sailed into the harbor of New Amsterdam, and the colony peacefully surrendered to the English.

In his 1892 book *The Skillmans of New York*, author Francis Skillman visits the crumbling mill and imagines its past:

> *The Coe house is an historic house, and the Coes were of the stuff that make their mark by changing a dynasty; their particular job in this respect having been the ousting of the Dutch and the introduction of the English; the stifling of old Stuyvesant and, the advent of Governor Nicolls—all of which was accomplished "by those hearty men in twelve years—from 1652 to 1664."*

Skillman also noted that Coe's Mill was the site of the first recorded criminal sentence in colonial Newtown:

> *Captain Coe and his mill have left behind them a precedent in criminal jurisprudence as carried out in 1660, when a thief detected stealing corn from the mill was condemned to walk a certain distance, with two rods under each arm, to the sound of the official drum beaten before him.*

The mill operated until 1875, and for its last remaining decades it served as a hotel. Following the construction of the Long Island Express-

QUEENS

way, two gas stations were built on either side of the highway and are still there today.

Fairview apartments

The last street block atop Horse Brook's streambed is the Fairview block, which has the **Fairview Swim Club** and the 14-story cooperative **Fairview Apartments**. Both were completed in 1965, named after the World's Fair that was taking place in nearby Flushing Meadows. The apartment towers have a sizable underground garage covered by parklike grounds.

The last crossing above the former stream is a footbridge connecting the Grand Central Parkway service road with Colonial Avenue. From the bridge, looking west toward LeFrak City, one is standing above a highway, with Manhattan visible in the background. But to visualize this scene before 1930, imagine an island with a mill and the water of Horse Brook rushing past it. And looking east toward Flushing Meadows, imagine an expansive marsh where Horse Brook merged with Flushing Creek.

PLACES TO SEE:

+ **Queens Library at Elmhurst** 85-08 51st Avenue + 718-271-1020 +
  www.queenslibrary.org/elmhurst
+ **Queens Place Mall** 88-01 Queens Boulevard + 718-393-9400
+ **Queens Center Mall** 90-15 Queens Boulevard + 718-592-3900 +
  www.shopqueenscenter.com
+ **Lost Battalion Hall Recreation Center** 93-29 Queens Boulevard +
  718-263-1163 + www.nycgovparks.org/facilities/recreationcenters/
  Q401
+ **Rego Park Center** 61-35 Junction Boulevard + 718-275-2696 +
  www.regocenter.com
+ **Queens Library at LeFrak City** 98-30 57th Avenue + 718-592-
  7677 + www.queenslibrary.org/lefrak-city
+ **Horace Harding Playground** 62nd Drive at 98th Street + www
  .nycgovparks.org/parks/horace-harding-playground/
+ **Barrier Playground** 102nd Street at Horace Harding Expressway +
  www.nycgovparks.org/parks/barrierplayground/
+ **Queens Community House** 108-25 62nd Drive + 718-592-5757 +
  www.queenscommunityhouse.org
+ **Fairview Swim Club** 61-20 Grand Central Parkway +
  718-592-0263

+ **Bus**: Q11, Q21, Q29, Q38, Q52, Q53, Q59, Q60 at Hoffman Drive and Woodhaven Boulevard for Queens Center mall; Q72, Q88, at Junction Boulevard and Horace Harding Expressway for Rego Park Center or LeFrak City; Q23, Q58, Q88 at 108th Street and Horace Harding Expressway for Forest Hills Houses
+ **Subway**: M, R at Grand Avenue–Newtown for Queens Place mall; M, R at Woodhaven Boulevard for Queens Center mall; M, R at 63rd Drive–Rego Park for Rego Park Center
+ **Bike**: There are currently no bike lanes near the former Horse Brook streambed

43. Strack Pond

Strack Pond, a kettle pond located inside **Forest Park**, was buried in 1966 and restored four decades later—a rare example of a restored body of water in New York City. Traffic from Woodhaven Boulevard can be heard by the pond but not seen, as a ridge separates the bowl-shaped natural depression from the busy roadway.

The pond's namesake was a Woodhaven resident killed in the Vietnam War. It is located at a point to the west of Woodhaven Boulevard and south of Forest Park Drive in a natural depression.

Forest Park was acquired by the city of Brooklyn in 1895. Its main thoroughfare, **Forest Park Drive**, was designed by landscape architect Frederick Law Olmsted and features a design similar to Central Park and Prospect Park. The third-largest park in Queens, it includes a historic carousel, a greenhouse, a band shell, a golf course, sports fields, and monuments. In its early years, the park contained five ponds, three of them within the golf course.

Strack Pond was given its name in February 1969 in honor of Private First Class Lawrence George E. Strack, the first Woodhaven resident to die in the Vietnam War. Strack spent his summers playing for the Rich-Haven Little League and in the winter, ice-skated on what was then an unnamed pond. He volunteered to serve as a paratrooper in 1966. Strack was killed in a firefight on March 3, 1967, during a combat parachute jump in Vietnam.

In 1966, the lake was converted to a field; after Strack's death a year later, this field was named for him. For many years, the Rich-Haven Little League played there. However, the field often flooded after heavy rains, making it frequently unusable. In May 2004, the restored pond was opened to the public as a three-acre nature preserve with a trail descending to the pond.

Within the western part of Forest Park, visitors to Strack Pond can ride on the historic **Forest Park Carousel**, carved in 1903 by Daniel Muller. The ride was designated as a city landmark in 2013. Nearby, the **George Seuffert Bandshell** hosts the Queens Symphony Orchestra in the summer season. The seating area accommodates 3,500 spectators.

Most of western Forest Park is occupied by the park's 110-acre **golf course**, which contains three ponds on its grounds. The course was designed in 1896 by Tom Bendelow. The Scottish-born designer favored a "naturalistic" approach that embraced the contours of the terrain, a style that complemented Olmsted's vision for Forest Park. Bendelow's work in popularizing the sport and designing courses across the country earned him the nickname "The Johnny Appleseed of American Golf."

The course opened in 1901 as the 9-hole Forest Park Links. It expanded to 18 holes in 1905. In its early days, many of the numbered holes had nicknames, such as "Camelback," "Cabbage Patch," "Bunker Hill," "Lover's Lane," "Old Glory," and "San Juan Hill" (the latter named after a battle in the recently fought Spanish-American War).

To the south of the golf course is **Oak Ridge**, a Dutch Colonial–style building completed in 1905. Formerly the clubhouse for the golf course, it contains the park's administrative offices and offers space for community events.

PLACES TO SEE:

+ **Forest Park Carousel** Woodhaven Boulevard at Forest Park Drive + 718-788-2676 + www.forestparkcarousel.com
+ **George Seuffert Bandshell** Forest Park Drive west of Woodhaven Boulevard + www.nycgovparks.org/parks/forest-park/highlights/12782
+ **Forest Park Golf Course** 101 Forest Park Drive + 718-296-0999 + www.golfnyc.com/forestpark_home/
+ **Oak Ridge** 1 Forest Park Drive + 718-235-4100 + www.nycgov parks.org/parks/forestpark/highlights/12555

GETTING THERE:
+ **Bus**: Q11, Q21 at Forest Park Drive
+ **Subway**: J, Z at Woodhaven Boulevard, transfer to Q11 or Q21
+ **Bike**: Forest Park Drive

44. Jackson Pond

The eastern half of Forest Park comprises mostly natural forest covering a postglacial knob and kettle terrain. In this section of the park, Forest Park Drive is closed to vehicles and allows pedestrians and bicyclists to travel through the woods on a wide roadway. At the intersection of Myrtle Avenue, Memorial Drive, and Park Lane South, a large plaza was laid out, accompanied by two playgrounds, a First World War monument, and a pine grove behind the plaza.

Occupying a depression on the north side of Myrtle Avenue, **Jackson Pond Playground** sits atop the buried **Jackson Pond**, which was once a popular site for ice-skating and model boating. To the south of the pond is Richmond Hill, a neighborhood developed in 1869 by developer Albon Platt Man and landscape architect Edward Richmond. The latter was the suburb's likely namesake, with a possible inspiration from Richmond upon Thames, an upscale suburb of London.

At the time, the Forest Park Lodge stood on the pond's shore. Once a summer home of former congressman and then mayor Abram S. Hewitt, it later became the office of the park's first superintendent, Jarvis Jackson, the namesake of the pond. The mansion was demolished in 1941.

In 1922, the Parks Department proposal to fill in Jackson Pond received an impassioned letter of protest from Wallace Fox, a young local resident. The letter appeared in the *Richmond Hill Record*, the neighborhood newspaper that operated from 1903 to 1948.

> *From my point of view the pond is the most attractive spot in Forest Park. Jackson's Pond is the only pond in Richmond Hill where we boys and girls, and very often grown-ups, too, can go skating in the winter. . . . Why not leave it as it is?*

As the population of Richmond Hill grew, the city "improved" the pond in 1931 by covering the muddy bottom with brownstone pebble

QUEENS

gravel. In 1941, a concrete shoreline was installed in a design similar to Kissena Lake and Bowne Pond.

In 1966, the lake was dried and covered with concrete after the city determined it to be an unsafe ice-skating site. Basketball courts were installed on the oval-shaped outline of the lake. The playground was renovated in 2001 with two small fountains to commemorate the pond that was once there.

In the center of the plaza intersection, a bronze statue of a soldier looks to the south. Designed by Joseph Pollia, this First World War memorial was dedicated in 1925. Known as *My Buddy*, it depicts a serviceman pausing to look down at the grave of a fallen comrade. The statue stands on a pedestal designed by William Van Alen, the architect of the Chrysler Building. On the pedestal, a plaque lists the names of the 71 Richmond Hill residents killed in the war.

Stretching between downtown Brooklyn and Richmond Hill, **Myrtle Avenue** is among the longest and oldest streets in Queens. It opened in 1854 as Jamaica Plank Road. "Plank" refers to tollbooth gates where travelers paid a toll for using the road. Myrtle Avenue became free of charge toward the last decade of the 19th century.

PLACES TO SEE:

✦ **Jackson Pond Playground** Myrtle Avenue at Memorial Drive and Park Lane South
✦ *My Buddy* **monument** Myrtle Avenue at Memorial Drive and Park Lane South

GETTING THERE:

✦ **Bus**: Q11, Q54 at Park Lane South and Myrtle Avenue
✦ **Subway**: J, Z at 111th Street, transfer to Q11
✦ **Bike**: There are bike lanes on Forest Park Drive

45. Bowne Pond

In the northern section of Flushing, the street grid gently rolls across a landscape of tall trees and early-20th-century mansions. In the center of this quiet neighborhood is Bowne Park, an 11.8-acre green space that was a private estate until 1925. It belonged to the Bowne family, which has roots in Flushing going back to John Bowne, who arrived in 1631. The Bownes were Quakers, an England-based Christian sect. In 1657, the Quaker residents of Flushing wrote the Flushing Remonstrance, a document that demanded religious tolerance from the government. Although Bowne's name does not appear among the signatories, his home was used for prayer gatherings in defiance of Dutch authorities. The **Bowne House** was inhabited by his descendants until 1945. **Bowne Pond** is located a mile to the north of the house.

Bowne's descendants owned substantial land around Flushing. Among them was Walter Bowne, who served as the mayor of New York from 1829 to 1833. He kept a summer residence near the southern shore of the pond. By 1925, Bowne Park was a holdout as the surrounding area was mapped for development. The vacant mansion burned down in March of that year. Three months later, the city acquired the land for a park.

In a pattern similar to Kissena Lake and Jackson Pond, the shoreline was lined with concrete, and two fountains were installed at the center of the pond. Instead of a natural spring, an aqueduct now provides the pond's water supply. Without the fountains, water in the pond becomes warm and stagnant, resulting in algae growth. Alongside water quality, pollution and poaching have also affected wildlife in the pond.

PLACES TO SEE:
+ **Bowne Park** Bound by 29th Avenue, 159th Street, 32nd Avenue, and 155th Street + www.nycgovparks.org/parks/bowne-park

GETTING THERE:
+ **Bus**: Q16 at 29th Avenue and 157th Street
+ **Subway**: 7 at Flushing–Main Street, transfer to Q16
+ **Bike**: There are currently no bike lanes around Bowne Pond

46. Goose Pond

To the west of affluent Jamaica Estates is the slightly more affordable neighborhood of Jamaica Hills, which also sits atop the terminal moraine of the last glacier. The southern limit of the moraine is marked by Hillside Avenue. On the north side of this road is a knob-and-kettle terrain, while the southern side has a landscape that gently slopes down toward the ocean.

The only remaining kettle pond in Jamaica Hills, **Goose Pond**, is located inside **Captain Tilly Park**, a nine-acre site perched on a slope beneath Jamaica High School. In the center of Goose Pond is a bird sanctuary isle that is the smallest island within the smallest natural body of water in the city.

The land around the park belonged to its namesake family in the 19th century and later to the Highland Park Society, an organization of local landowners that maintained the park. Captain George H. Tilly served in the Army Signal Group during the Spanish-American War of 1898. The war was a resounding victory for the United States, which gained the Spanish colonies of Puerto Rico, Cuba, Guam and the Philippines.

The Cubans were promised independence, and native Filipino forces expected the same from their American ally. Instead, they found one colonizer replacing another and launched an insurgency. On May 27, 1899, Tilly and a small unit landed in the town of Escalante on Negros Island to repair a damaged telegraph cable. They were told that the residents were supportive of the United States, and initially the residents welcomed Tilly's party. But upon entering the cable building, Tilly's men were fired upon from all sides; they retreated back to the beach and swam toward their boat as rebels chased after them in their canoes. All but Tilly escaped alive. His mutilated body was buried near the village.

Back at home, the pond was transferred as a park to New York City in 1908 as Highland Park. To avoid confusion with another Highland Park on the Brooklyn-Queens border, it was renamed Upland Park in 1912. The park was renamed after Tilly in 1935, at the same time that the pond was renovated with a concrete shoreline. In 1941, a monument in memory of the Spanish-American War was unveiled in the park, and it became the site of a ceremony each Memorial Day.

Over the decades, Goose Pond lost its natural source of water, and algae bloomed in it. Much of the surrounding park had also fallen into disrepair. In 1996, the Jamaica Hill Community Association and Councilman Morton Povman allocated funding for the park. The restoration included draining and deepening the pond and installing a new clay liner and filtration system. Carp and bluegill sunfish were reintroduced to the pond, among other native wildlife. A new well provided water for the pond, and an island in its center served as a wildlife sanctuary. Each fall, the park hosts Jamaica Family Day, a fair for local residents.

On the northern side of Goose Pond, the **Jamaica High School** campus occupies the former Clark estate on a hilltop location overlooking much of southern Queens. The Georgian Revival structure was completed in 1927 and accommodates more than 4,000 students. An official city landmark, it was designed by William H. Gompert. Inside, there are murals painted in 1930 by Suzanne Muller, showing the history of

Long Island. The beaver is the school's mascot, in honor of the native name for the neighborhood: Jameco, which translates to "beaver."

The curvy road separating Jamaica High School from Captain Tilly Park is **Chapin Parkway,** named after local pastor Dr. Edwin Chapin. In 1869, his widow established the **Chapin Home for the Aging** in Manhattan. It relocated to Jamaica in 1912, at a site two blocks from the park.

Once a largely Jewish neighborhood, Jamaica Hills is presently home to a sizable Bangladeshi Muslim community, with mosques dotting the residential section and numerous ethnic clothing shops along Hillside Avenue. To the west of Goose Pond are a number of light blue colored homes and storefronts, indicating the presence of Sri Chinmoy's followers. The Bengali meditation master established his **Sri Chinmoy Centre** in Jamaica Hills in 1968, and it continues to attract visitors interested in Chinmoy's music, art, and teachings.

Although the pond is very shallow and surrounded by development, it offers a hint at the landscape that covered Jamaica Hills for nearly 10,000 years.

QUEENS

PLACES TO SEE:
+ **Captain Tilly Park** Highland Avenue at 165th Street; Chapin Parkway at 85th Avenue.
+ **Hillside Arts and Letters Academy (former Jamaica High School)** 167-01 Gothic Drive + 718-658-1249

GETTING THERE:
+ **Bus**: Q65 at 164th Street and Highland Avenue, walk one block east on Highland Avenue to 165th Street; Q1, Q2, Q3, Q36, Q43, Q76, Q77 at Hillside Avenue and 165th Street, walk one block north on 165th Street to Highland Avenue
+ **Subway**: F at 169th Street, walk one block north on 169th Street, turn left and walk five blocks east to 165th Street
+ **Train**: Long Island Railroad at Jamaica, transfer to Q43 or Q65
+ **Bike**: There are currently no bike lanes near Goose Pond

47. Crystal Lake

To the north of Richmond Hill is Kew Gardens, a neighborhood founded by Albon P. Man's sons Alrick and Albon Jr. in 1868. The historic commercial center of this village-style neighborhood is the Lefferts Boulevard overpass above the Kew Gardens railroad station. Inspired by the Ponte Vecchio in Florence, Italy, the bridge is lined by shops as it crosses the main line of the Long Island Railroad.

Prior to 1909, the site of Kew Gardens station was **Crystal Lake**, a kettle pond formed after the last ice age. It was buried in favor of a track-straightening project for the railroad that included a new station the following year.

When Man developed Richmond Hill, land around Crystal Lake was not yet ready for development, regarded as too hilly and used as a golf course by the **Richmond Hill Golf Club**. The railway initially avoided the pond, running to its north.

The same year that the Kew Gardens station opened, the Long Island Railroad was extended to Penn Station, resulting in a speedy half-hour commute to Midtown Manhattan. On the southern side of the station, the **Homestead Hotel** was built atop the former pond in 1921. At the time, railroads were the leading form of transportation between cities, and many local stations had hotels built next to them. Designed in a neo-Georgian style in the appearance of a manor, the hotel gave a historic appearance to a new neighborhood. The building is presently a residence for seniors.

While the tracks running through Kew Gardens are nearly straight, streets to their south are crooked, designed to follow the contours of the landscape. In this knob-and-kettle terrain, it is possible that other ponds existed prior to development.

With one of the nation's busiest commuter railways running above its site, it would be impossible to restore Crystal Lake in its original state. One possibility for a revival could come in the form of a fountain on the site of the station's parking lot. However, with few parking spots available in the surrounding neighborhood, even this idea would likely be considered impossible.

PLACES TO SEE:
+ **Kew Gardens station** Austin Street at Mowbray Drive
+ **Maple Grove Cemetery** 127-15 Kew Gardens Road (entrance at Kew Gardens Road and Lefferts Boulevard) + 718-285-6107 + www.local-cemetery.com

GETTING THERE:
+ **Bus**: Q10 at Austin Street and Lefferts Boulevard

- **Subway**: E, F at Union Turnpike–Kew Gardens, transfer to Q10
- **Train**: Long Island Railroad at Kew Gardens
- **Bike**: There are currently no bike lanes around the site of Crystal Lake

48. Jackson's Mill Pond

Throughout Long Island, large grassy meadows stood out in contrast to the mostly forested environment of the larger region. The largest of all was the **Hempstead Plains**, a natural prairie stretching across central Nassau County. Within Queens, such open spaces included **Fresh Meadows** and a now-forgotten area called **Trains Meadow**, which occupied a section of East Elmhurst between Northern Boulevard and Astoria Boulevard. The origin of this name is unclear, but it could be a corruption of Drains Meadow, after a stream flowing through it.

The first European settler in Trains Meadow was Rev. William Leverich, who arrived in 1662 to serve as pastor of the First Presbyterian Church of Newtown. Typical of English settlers in New Netherland, Leverich was a "nonconforming" Christian who initially immigrated to New England.

The first road across the plain was laid out in 1672 and remained in use into the 1930s, when the numbered grid erased most of **Trains Meadow Road**. Other homes along this path included that of the Barclay family, who later built horse-racing tracks in the area, and that of Welsh-born settler John Hazard, who served as a local judge.

The construction of Junction Boulevard and 94th Street made Trains Meadow Road obsolete. Two short segments of the old road remain in East Elmhurst, cutting through the grid as Jackson Mill Road. These segments survived because of their past use as a trolley right-of-way.

Jackson's Mill

The stream that drained Trains Meadow originated near the present-day intersection of Broadway and 58th Street in Woodside. It flowed in a northeastern direction toward Flushing Bay. Its native name was Sackhickniyeh.

Near its mouth at Flushing Bay, Dutch settler Warner Wessels constructed a dam in 1655, with an undershot wheel providing power to grind wheat and corn for local residents. The site of the reservoir behind

QUEENS

the mill, **Jackson's Mill Pond,** is on the northeastern side of the inter-section of Ditmars Boulevard and 94th Street.

The mill had three names during its existence: Kip's Mill, Fish's Mill, and Jackson's Mill. The latter was in memory of its last owner, Samuel Jackson. The mill operated until 1870. The road atop the milldam con-nected Trains Meadow with Sanford Point, a tip facing the East River that separated Flushing Bay from Bowery Bay. This road is today called 94th Street and continues south for nearly four miles as Junction Boule-vard. To locals, the land around Jackson's Mill Pond was affectionately dubbed "Frog Town" to describe the noisy wildlife that prevented people from sleeping.

North Beach amusement district

A few years after the mill's closing, Frog Town entered its second phase in 1886 as **North Beach.** A northern rival to Brooklyn's Coney Island, North Beach featured numerous beer halls, hotels, amusement rides, and the first Ferris wheel on the East Coast. At the tip of Sanford Point, a ferry pier brought in travelers from East Harlem, the Bronx, and Lower Manhattan.

The amusement district's decline can be attributed to pollution and the prohibition on alcohol in the 1920s. In contrast to Coney Island, where ocean tides keep the beach relatively clean, on the East River, sew-age takes much longer to dissolve. Coney Island had an advantage over North Beach, which could only offer bathhouses and swimming pools as alternatives to the dirty East River. The 1920 enactment of Prohibition forced the closure of all taverns and beer gardens on North Beach as the drinking public moved to underground venues for the next decade.

Glenn Curtiss Airport

With the closing of the Gala Amusement Park, a new tenant arrived in 1929: aviation pioneer Glenn Curtiss. The early rival to Orville and Wilbur Wright, Curtiss was a bicycle and motorcycle inventor before going airborne.

The 105-acre airfield was named the **Glenn Curtiss Airport,** and the city contributed to its expansion by adding landfill. For the local ecology, the airport was a disaster. In September 1929, nearly 6,000 abandoned cars from across Queens were dumped in Bowery Bay to form a bulk-head. The airport served as a base for airborne police operations and a year after its opening was the scene of the first manhunt by air.

The airport featured passenger flights to Floyd Bennett Field, Newark, Atlantic City, and Philadelphia. The service was unprofitable, but the city saw potential in Glenn Curtiss Airport because of its proximity to Manhattan and bought the site in 1935, changing its name to North Beach Airport. It was eventually expanded and reopened as LaGuardia Airport in 1939.

Holmes Airport

Just as North Beach Airport grew to the north of Jackson's Mill Pond, another airfield competed to the west of the pond. Founded in 1929, just a few months before Glenn Curtiss Airport, the **Holmes Airport** of Jackson Heights doggedly fought to survive. Failing at commercial flights, Holmes was used for sightseeing, flying schools, and as a blimp hangar. Ambitious in advertising, the airport dubbed itself Grand Central Air Terminal, in homage to the busy railway terminal in Midtown Manhattan.

Like many early airports, Holmes had its own contribution to precedent-setting flights: In 1936 the first aerial traffic reports were provided by a blimp based at Holmes. But as the example of Flushing Airport demonstrated, two airports cannot operate safely in proximity to each other. The city saw the potential to expand Glenn Curtiss Airport through landfill; Holmes airport, by contrast, was hemmed in by advancing residential development.

What remained of Jackson's Mill Pond was drained on the west side of 94th Street and expanded on the eastern side into an inlet of Flushing Bay under the name **Jackson Creek Basin**. This inlet was filled by 1964, replaced with parking lots and an expanded central terminal for LaGuardia Airport. Although LaGuardia is considered small in comparison to the two other Port Authority–operated airports in the metropolitan region, it remains a vital hub for domestic and Canada-bound flights.

With airport structures and highway lanes covering up the path of Jackson's Mill Pond, it is impossible to restore the pond at its former location.

GETTING THERE:

+ **Bus**: Q33, Q72 at 94th Street and Ditmars Boulevard; M60 at 94th Street and 23rd Avenue
+ **Subway**: 7 at Junction Boulevard, transfer to Q72

QUEENS

✦ **Bike:** There are currently no bike lanes near the historic path of Jackson's Mill Creek

49. Linden Pond

A block to the south of the **103rd Street–Corona Plaza subway station** is a park that predates Manhattan's Central Park by five years, built around a kettle pond.

Linden Park marks the historic center of Corona, a village founded as West Flushing in 1853 and renamed in 1868 for its hilltop location as a symbolic "crown" on the landscape. In its early years, the village's main attraction was the **National Race Course**, a horse-racing park that lent its name to National Street, which runs to the west of Linden Park.

With a depth of only two feet in most places, **Linden Pond** was a safe place for ice-skating at the turn of the 20th century. The pond was drained in 1947 as part of an improvement project that brought new playground structures and a baseball field. At the turn of the 21st century, Linden Park was renamed **Park of the Americas**, an unimaginative name that erases the pond from public memory.

PLACES TO SEE:

✦ **Park of the Americas (Linden Park)** Bound by 103rd Street, 41st Avenue, 104th Street, and 42nd Avenue ✦ www.nycgovparks.org/parks/park-of-the-americas/map

GETTING THERE:

✦ **Bus:** Q23 at Roosevelt Avenue, walk three blocks south to 42nd Avenue
✦ **Subway:** 7 at 103rd Street–Corona Plaza, walk three blocks south to 42nd Avenue
✦ **Bike:** There are currently no bike lanes around the site of Linden Pond

50. Shady Lake

Shady Lake kettle pond is mentioned in Francis Skillman's book *The Skillmans of New York* as a point where Corona Avenue begins its descent toward Flushing Meadows. It was located near the present-day intersection of Corona Avenue and 108th Street. Unlike Linden Pond, Shady Lake was on privately owned land. It was drained in the early 20th century. In its day, it was used for ice harvesting; ironically, the corner of Corona Avenue and 108th Street is the location of the **Lemon Ice King of Corona**, a popular purveyor of Italian ices founded in 1944.

Although the site of the lake is covered by development, on the north side of the intersection is **William F. Moore Park**, a well-kept space with a bocce court used by the neighborhood's older Italian residents. Their strong connection to this space has earned it the nickname "Spaghetti Park."

The park's namesake was reportedly the first Corona resident killed in World War I, during the Battle of Belleau Wood. A plaque underneath the park's flagpole commemorates 49 local residents killed in the war. The plaque was paid for by the Corona Heights Civic Association, which represented businesses and residents around the site of the former Shady Lake.

PLACES TO SEE:
+ **Lemon Ice King of Corona** 52-02 108th Street ✦ 718-699-5133 ✦ www.thelemonicekingofcorona.com
+ **William F. Moore Park** Corona Avenue at 108th Street ✦ www .nycgovparks.org/parks/william-f-moore-park

GETTING THERE:
+ **Bus**: Q23 at Corona Avenue and 108th Street; Q58 at Corona Avenue and 51st Street
+ **Subway**: 7 at 103rd Street–Corona Plaza, and transfer to Q23
+ **Bike**: There are currently no bike lanes around the site of Shady Lake

51. Alley Pond Park

Along the northern shore of Long Island, there are several fjord-like inlets carved during the last ice age and filled with silt deposits. Examples of such inlets and valleys in Nassau County are Cold Spring Harbor, Hempstead Harbor, and Manhasset Bay.

In Queens, Little Neck Bay was formed in the same fashion, with its headwaters located in the valley separating Bayside from Douglaston. During the colonial period, this valley was known to European settlers as "the

Alley Pond, 1927

Alley." Today, it is located entirely within **Alley Pond Park**, which extends south to Union Turnpike. Within the 635-acre park, there are seven additional ponds in addition to Alley Creek, which flows through the bottom of the valley. The valley is lined by the largest virgin forest in Queens, with trees dating to the colonial period.

The names reflect local flora and fauna: Turtle Pond, Muskrat Pond, Lily Pad Pond, Cattail Pond, Windmill Pond, Little Alley Pond, and Alley Pond. Most of these were formed as kettle ponds after the last ice age. To explore all the ponds and distinctive natural features of Alley Pond Park in one day, it is ideal to begin the hike at Springfield Boulevard and Kingsbury Avenue and work your way north.

The bridge crossing the boulevard is the **Vanderbilt Motor Parkway**, a linear park that covers the route of the country's oldest limited-access highway. Built in 1908 as a two-lane route, the privately operated 45-mile toll road ran between Fresh Meadows and Lake Ronkonkoma. At the time, most of eastern Queens was farmland, and the parkway offered wealthy car owners a quick route to points east. In the parkway's early years, the Vanderbilts hosted grand prix races on the highway, making it one of the first racetracks in the Americas. The highway was abandoned in 1930 after the city built the toll-free Grand Central Parkway as a parallel alternative. Today the parkway serves as a link connecting Cunningham Park and Alley Pond Park.

At the point where the Vanderbilt Motor Parkway turns south, there is a staircase descending into Alley Pond Park. Coming into view is

Little Alley Pond, a lily-covered kettle pond that abuts Grand Central Parkway. The pond is surrounded by thick vegetation and appears untouched by the city.

Turning north, there are signs pointing to the **Alley Pond Park Adventure Course**, a set of ropes, climbing walls, and a zip line designed to promote exercise and teamwork skills. The course is the only one of its kind in New York City; it opened in 2007. Its highest ropes carry users 45 feet above the ground.

"First came skate parks, then surfing, then hiking and camping, then mountain biking. Now you can zip through the treetops and balance among the branches . . . all without leaving New York City," Parks Commissioner Adrian Benepe said at the opening of the facility. At the time, the Parks Department was promoting alternative sports alongside traditional offerings such as basketball and softball.

Farther north inside the thickly forested park are **Turtle Pond** and **Cattail Pond**. Their appearance and condition resemble that of Little Alley Pond—preserved in their natural state with little interference. The first road you will pass that traverses the Alley is West Alley Road, which slopes down into the valley, running past Alley Pond. Prior to the Long Island Expressway, West Alley Road was one of only two routes crossing the Alley. In the woods to the north of the Long Island Expressway is the tallest and oldest known tree in New York City, a tulip poplar (*Liriodendron tulipifera*) known as the **Queens Giant**. In contrast to the now-dead weeping beech in downtown Flushing and the Camperdown elm of Prospect Park, the Queens Giant is hidden from public exposure for its own protection.

In 2002, forest ecologist Bruce Kershner estimated the circumference of the tree to be 19 feet; using a laser to measure the height, he recorded it at 134 feet and still growing. The age of the tree is more than 430 years, predating European settlers by nearly a century.

Crossing back to the southern side of the Long Island Expressway, travelers can descend into the valley on West Alley Road. At the southwestern corner of the interchange of the Cross Island Parkway and the Long Island Expressway is **Alley Pond**. In the colonial period, the pond was a scenic stop on West Alley Road and an important commercial location. Gristmills were built along the creek, harnessing the flow to grind wheat. The last of the mills was built by James Hedges in the 1760s, damming the creek to form Alley Pond. The structure burned down in 1926. Next to the mill, the Buhrman general store operated from 1828 to 1929. At the time of its opening, it was the only store in the area. It was demolished after the Alley was acquired by the Parks Department in 1929.

With a number of silent screen stars living in nearby Bayside, the pond was an ideal location to film. In 1923, resident Gloria Swanson starred in *ZaZa*, with a French village set constructed around the pond.

Four years later the city's Board of Estimate authorized the purchase of Alley Pond Park in a package that also included Crooke's Point and Wolfe's Pond on Staten Island. The park opened to the public in 1935.

Within two years, Alley Pond was reduced in size as the Cross Island Parkway was constructed along its eastern shore. The historic pond was completely buried in 1954, when the Long Island Expressway crossed the valley. Maps produced after 1954 showed Alley Pond on the northern side of the Long Island Expressway—a replacement pond that was never completed. The interchange atop the former pond was an inconvenient one, featuring three cloverleaf ramps tightly spiraling upward from the valley floor. A marshy patch of vegetation marked the site of Alley Pond.

The tight traffic conditions and poor drainage were addressed by the state in 2000, when it began a $165 million reconstruction of the interchange. The five-year effort returned 12 acres to the park. The restored pond absorbs runoff from the surrounding landscape and channels it into Alley Creek.

On the northern side of the expressway, the creek flows through a wide freshwater marsh that forms the largest section of the park. Although a part of the park since 1929, it was never developed and regarded as an eyesore in its early years. Change happened in 1972, when Douglaston couple Joan and Hy Rosner began leading tours through the swamp. Alongside other local supporters, the Rosners founded the **Alley Pond Environmental Center** to promote conservation of the wetland.

On the grounds of the nature center is a 40-foot windmill that was built in 2005 as a replacement for an older windmill dating to the 1870s. The original structure was built on the Douglaston peninsula to pump water to local farms using wind power. As farmland was transformed to suburban housing in the early 20th century, the former mill became a residential dwelling. In 1986, the mill was spared demolition after an outcry from local residents. Relocated to Alley Pond Environmental Center, it provided water for **Windmill Pond**. Two years later, an arsonist destroyed the historic structure. Undeterred, members of Committee to Save the Windmill raised funds to build a replica.

Across the backyard of the nature center is a concrete pipe that carries outflow from Oakland Lake into Alley Creek. Once an exposed tributary, it was buried following the construction of the Cross Island Parkway. A boardwalk runs atop the covered stream, ending with a pier that juts into Alley Creek. Looking down, one can see water from the tributary entering the creek.

The creek leaves Alley Pond Park at **Little Neck Bridge**, a masonry-and-metal structure that carries Northern Boulevard across the creek. The first version of this bridge was constructed in 1826 by local landowner Wynant Van Zandt. About 1,000 feet farther downstream, the Port Washington Branch of the Long Island Railroad crosses the stream at nearly the same clearance as Little Neck Bridge.

To the east of Little Neck Bridge is the **Alley Pond Golf Center**, a driving range built on the site of a former dump. The golf center has operated at this site since the early 1950s. It is one of the busiest driving ranges in the city, with 70 stalls.

The last crossing over Alley Creek is the Long Island Railroad trestle carrying the Port Washington Branch. The only branch in the system that does not run through Jamaica, this line was constructed in 1854, terminating in Flushing. The line was extended to its terminus at Port Washington in 1898. Beyond the railroad trestle, the creek widens into Little Neck Bay.

QUEENS

PLACES TO SEE:

✦ **Little Alley Pond** Kingsbury Avenue at Grand Central Parkway
✦ **Alley Pond Park Adventure Course** 718-217-4685 ✦ www.nycgov parks.org/programs/rangers/adventure-course
✦ **Queens Giant** East Hampton Boulevard at Horace Harding Expressway (north side)
✦ **Alley Pond** West Alley Road at Douglaston Parkway
✦ **Alley Pond Environmental Center** 228-06 Northern Boulevard ✦ 718-229-4000 ✦ www.alleypond.com
✦ **Alley Pond Golf Center** 232-01 Northern Boulevard ✦ 718-225-9187 ✦ www.alleypondgolf.com

LEARN MORE:

✦ **Alley Pond Environmental Center** 228-06 Northern Boulevard ✦ 718-229-4000 ✦ www.alleypond.com

GETTING THERE:

✦ **Bus:** Q12 at Northern Boulevard and 227th Street for Alley Pond Environmental Center; Q27, Q88 at Springfield Boulevard and

Kingsbury Avenue, walk east on Vanderbilt Motor Parkway to reach the park; Q30, QM5 at Douglaston Parkway and 65th Avenue
+ **Subway**: 7 at Flushing–Main Street, transfer to Q27 or Q12; F at 169th Street, transfer to Q30; E, F at Kew Gardens–Union Turnpike, transfer to Q46
+ **Train**: Long Island Railroad at Flushing–Main Street, transfer to Q27 or Q12
+ **Bike**: Cloverdale Boulevard, East Hampton Boulevard, Joe Michaels Mile, and Vanderbilt Motor Parkway are part of the Brooklyn-Queens Greenway

52. Oakland Lake

Among the five community colleges within the City University of New York, the most spacious campus is that of **Queensborough Community College**, which occupies a former golf course overlooking **Oakland Lake**. Since the college's arrival to Bayside in 1964, it has played a vital role in the preservation and restoration of this glacial kettle lake.

The lake received its water from a natural spring and a feeder stream that originated at 223rd Place and the Horace Harding Expressway, flowing into a ravine that widened into the lake. An outflow stream took excess water from the lake east toward Alley Creek, which emptied into Little Neck Bay.

The first European settler near the lake was Englishman John Hicks, who received a patent from Dutch authorities to claim the lake in 1645. In 1827, William Douglas purchased land around the pond and the lake became known as Douglas Pond. His last name can be found today on the map in Douglaston, an upscale neighborhood located a mile to the east of the lake.

The lake's current name comes from **the Oaks**, an estate owned by Frederick Newbold Lawrence on the lake's southern shore. A veteran of the Civil War and briefly a president of the New York Stock Exchange, he descended from a prominent colonial family whose cemetery is located a mile to the north at 216th Street and 42nd Avenue.

In 1896, the 180-acre Lawrence property was transformed into the **Oakland Golf Club**, which hosted its first game on April 10, 1897. From its early years, the club welcomed women as members and staff. At the time, women's suffrage was a hotly debated topic around the country, and as late as 1922, a local school principal protested the hiring of young

QUEENS

women as caddies. "If they were young it interfered with their school work," wrote Principal Jennie Potter, "and if they were beyond the school age, it interfered with their domestic work." But at local civic meetings, the female caddies were defended by their mothers. "They have been found to be more attentive to their duties than boys and they give better service," one mother argued.

The caddies were paid "liberally" by the club, whose membership included powerbrokers Bernard Baruch, Robert Wagner Sr., and highway promoter Horace Harding. The expressway bearing Harding's name runs a few blocks to the south of the club, and historians speculate that perhaps Harding wanted the expressway built to facilitate access from the city to this golf course.

Below the golf course, Oakland Lake supplied drinking water for the town of Flushing, with a pumping station built at its mouth. The lake was transferred to the Parks Department in 1934, which then citified the lake in a design resembling Bowne Pond and Kissena Lake—the shoreline was lined with concrete, and the lake was cut off from its natural sources. Encroaching development around the lake contributed further to its deterioration.

In 1952, the Oakland Golf Club disbanded, and the course survived as a city-run public course for only another nine years. Most of the course was then developed into 600 units of tract housing, with 14 acres slated for **Benjamin N. Cardozo High School** and 35 acres for a college campus. The stream that fed into Oakland Lake was buried beneath the school's running track. An additional school, **Public School 203**, was also built atop the ravine, with a small playground adjoining it. On the campus of Queensborough Community College, the old golf clubhouse serves as the art gallery, situated at the highest point on campus.

In its first decade, the college made history for having the youngest president in the City University system, when 31-year-old Dr. Kurt R. Schmeller was appointed in 1968. Schmeller remained president of the college until 1999, earning distinction as the longest-tenured president of a public college in the country. The college library carries his name.

The most recent addition to the campus is the **Kupferberg Holocaust Resource Center**, a postmodern structure completed in 2011. Clad in Jerusalem stone and irregularly shaped panes of glass, the design commemorates Kristallnacht, the 1938 pogrom in Nazi Germany known as the Night of the Broken Glass. The research center provides exhibits, speakers, and literature on the holocaust.

In 1969, the Alley Restoration Committee was formed, providing tours around Oakland Lake and Alley Pond Park. Its founding chairman was Queensborough Community College Dean John O. Riedl, who organized the tours. The first Walk in the Alley, conducted in 1969, attracted 2,000 supporters. Recognizing the outpouring of support, the Parks Department stabilized the slopes around Oakland Lake to prevent further erosion.

In the half century since Oakland Lake's acquisition by the Parks Department, its most outspoken champion was Bayside resident Gertrude Waldeyer, an educator and environmentalist who mapped out the buried wetlands surrounding the lake in hope of their eventual restoration. Through the effort of Waldeyer's group, the Oakland Lake and Ravine Conservation Committee, $1 million was raised to restore the lake to its natural state, which replaced the concrete shore with natural materials, and to reintroduce catfish, carp, perch, bass, and sunfish. The nature trail around the shore was renamed after Waldeyer following her death in 1987.

The restoration of Oakland Lake was more than a cosmetic effort; the lake is a vital component of the storm drainage infrastructure in eastern Queens. In May 2011, the city's Department of Environmental Protection announced the opening of the first Bluebelt system in Queens, where excess storm damage is channeled through landscaped corridors resembling natural streams, ponds, and wetlands to Oakland Lake, and from there to Alley Creek. The city's first Bluebelt opened in 1997 on Staten Island.

With Oakland Lake's deep ravine location, homes surrounding the lake are hidden from view, creating an illusion of being outside the city. The lake is an example of a successful stream restoration project that was made possible as a result of common goals between restoring the lake to its natural appearance and using it as a storm drainage outlet.

PLACES TO SEE:

✦ **Oakland Lake** Parkland bound by Cloverdale Boulevard, 46th Avenue, Springfield Boulevard, and Queensborough Community College

✦ **Queensborough Community College Art Gallery** 222-05 56th Avenue (Oakland Building) ✦ 718-631-6396 ✦ www.qcc.cuny.edu/artgallery

✦ **Queensborough Performing Arts Center** 222-05 56th Avenue (Humanities Building) ✦ 718-631-6311 ✦ www.qcc.cuny.edu/QPAC

LEARN MORE:

✦ **Friends of Oakland Lake and Ravine** friendsofoaklandlake@gmail
   .com
✦ **Bayside Hills Civic Association** www.baysidehills.info
✦ **Bayside Historical Society** www.baysidehistorical.org
✦ **Alley Pond Environmental Center** www.alleypond.com

GETTING THERE:

✦ **Bus**: Q27 at Queensborough Community College; Q12 at Northern
   Boulevard and Springfield Boulevard, walk south on Springfield
   Boulevard to Oakland Lake
✦ **Subway**: 7 at Flushing–Main Street, transfer to Q27 or Q12
✦ **Train**: Long Island Railroad at Flushing–Main Street, transfer to
   Q27 or Q12
✦ **Bike**: Cloverdale Boulevard has bike lanes as part of the Brooklyn-
   Queens Greenway

53. Golden Pond

Prior to 1954, land around **Golden Pond** was a private estate, one of
many along the northern shore of Queens that were part of Long Island's
"Gold Coast." The pond is located in **Crocheron Park**, a sizable green
space on the eastern edge of Bayside that overlooks Little Neck Bay. On
the northern shore of the pond, 35th Avenue extends into the park as a
winding "lover's lane."

Between 1695 and 1899, land around the pond belonged to descendants of colonial settler John Crocheron. The family has roots in France,
where their Huguenot sect was persecuted at the time.

In the 19th century, two of his descendants served in elected office.
Henry Crocheron served in Congress for one term in 1815, and Nicholas
Crocheron was elected to the State Assembly forty years later. Another
family member, Joseph Crocheron, owned racing horses and attracted
a clientele of political leaders to his **Crocheron House Hotel** on the
Crocheron estate.

Among the patrons at the Crocheron House clambakes was Tammany Hall boss William M. Tweed, who hid in the hotel after escaping
prison in 1875. From Bayside, Tweed made his way to Spain as a sea-

man. The hotel was sold in 1899 to William M. Thomas, also a racehorse owner. In 1907, the hotel burned down, and the property sat unused until the city purchased it in 1924 for a park.

Within the scenic park is a tree planted on Memorial Day in 1933 in honor of James Corbett, a heavyweight boxer and local resident who died in February of that year. "Gentleman Jim" is known to historians as the father of modern boxing for pioneering many of the moves that are common to the sport. Corbett and his wife, Vera, resided a block to the south of the pond on a road that now bears his last name. In front of **221-04 Corbett Road** is a boulder with a plaque installed in 1971 to denote its celebrity occupant.

To the north of the pond is **John Golden Park**, also named after a local celebrity, who wrote scores for Broadway shows. With a career that spanned nearly 40 years, Golden produced over 150 musicals and shows, starting with *Turn to the Right* in 1916. Golden died on June 17, 1955, bequeathing his 17-acre estate to the city as a park. John Golden Park is adjacent to Crocheron Park, creating a single green plot with tennis courts, seven baseball diamonds, and a playground.

Both parks lie along **Joe Michaels Mile**, a waterfront promenade that connects the parks with **Little Bay Park** to the north and **Alley Pond Park** to the south. The promenade offers views of Little Neck Bay facing the upscale communities of Little Neck and Great Neck on the opposite shore. The namesake of the promenade was a local doo-wop singer and marathon runner who survived seven heart attacks before succumbing to one at the age of 45. Michaels often trained on the shore of Little Neck Bay and on the Vanderbilt Motor Parkway. Teaming up with other local runners, Michaels was among the founders of the Alley Pond Striders, a running group based out of the park, and the Cardiac Runners, an organization to help others "run away from heart disease." Michaels died in 1987, and the promenade was renamed after him a year later. With so much nature around it, the landscape around John Golden Pond does not seem like New York City at all.

PLACES TO SEE:

✦ **John Golden Park** 33rd Road at 215th Place ✦ 212-639-9675 ✦ www.nycgovparks.org/parks/john-golden-park
✦ **Crocheron Park** 35th Avenue at Corbett Road ✦ www.nycgovparks .org/parks/crocheron-park
✦ **Joe Michaels Mile** Enter at 35th Avenue at the Cross Island Park-

way ✦ www.nycgovparks.org/parks/crocheron-park/highlights/
12644

✦ **James Corbett House (privately owned)** 221-04 Corbett Place

GETTING THERE:
✦ **Bus**: Q13, Q31 at 35th Avenue, walk east on 35th Avenue to a
  dead end
✦ **Subway**: 7 at Flushing–Main Street, transfer to Q13
✦ **Train**: Long Island Railroad at Bayside, transfer to Q13
✦ **Bike**: There are bike lanes on Joe Michaels Mile along Little Neck
  Bay as part of the Brooklyn-Queens Greenway

54. Gabler's Creek and Aurora Pond

In the hilly terrain separating the Douglaston and Little Neck neighborhoods, **Gabler's Creek** runs through a ravine on its way to Little Neck
Bay at Udalls Cove. The marsh at the stream's mouth straddles the city
line. Thanks to determined local residents, the stream runs undisturbed
within the **Udalls Cove Park Preserve**.

In a depression tucked between Sandhill Road and the Long Island
Railroad's Port Washington Branch is **Aurora Pond**. The pond's namesake is local resident Aurora Gareiss, who fought to save the ravine
around Udalls Cove from development. The artificial pond was formed
when Sandhill Road was paved through the ravine, damming Gabler's
Creek. Excess water from the pond flows north through the creek toward
Udalls Cove.

Prior to development in the area, Gabler's Creek originated near the
intersection of Thornhill Avenue and Overbrook Street. The latter road
was constructed around 1930, taking its name from the creek buried
below it. Land around Gabler's Creek was inhabited by the Matinecocks, an indigenous tribe whose lands stretched along the northern
shore of Long Island to the east of Flushing. In the cemetery of the Zion
Episcopal Church is a monument with the inscription, "Here lie the last
of the Matinecock."

But the inscription is false. The presence of Native Americans in Little Neck persisted much longer than in the rest of what became Queens.
In 1656, the last flicker of native resistance in Queens was extinguished
at the Battle of Madnan's Neck, near the corner of Northern Boule-

QUEENS

vard and Marathon Parkway. The commander of the English settlers was Thomas Hicks, whose descendants settled across Queens and Long Island, including the future settlement of Hicksville. But the Matinecocks did not disappear completely, retaining a small cemetery at Northern Boulevard and Jesse Court, an alley near Browvale Lane. Its last caretaker was James Waters, who also went by the name Chief Wild Pigeon. When Northern Boulevard was widened in 1930, the native graves were relocated to the Zion Episcopal Church's cemetery.

At Alameda Avenue, the buried stream runs below the property of **Saint Anastasia Roman Catholic Church**, a parish founded in 1915. The church used to own land across Northern Boulevard as well, seeking to build a high school on the site. Instead, the city condemned the land in 1983 for a wildlife preserve. The church was awarded $1,375,000 in compensation for the land by an appellate court.

A second church with a strong geographical connection to Gabler's Creek is **Zion Episcopal Church**, located a block to the west of Saint Anastasia on the north side of Northern Boulevard. The countryside-style church sits on land donated by landowner Wynant Van Zandt in 1829. Behind is a cemetery that includes early African American residents, Civil War veterans, and the relocated Matinecock graves. The present church structure dates to 1925, designed in the New England style.

Returning to Saint Anastasia Church, the site of its never-built high school is part of the 17-acre Udalls Cove Ravine, a tight space hemmed in by tract houses, which was saved through gradual acquisition by the city between 1978 and 1990. The stream emerges from the ground, passing underneath the railroad, and spills into the picturesque **Aurora Pond**.

Aurora Gareiss, the pond's namesake, was the cofounder of the Udalls Cove Preservation Committee, which she formed with her neighbor Virginia Dent in 1969 to protest further encroachment on the ravine.

At the time, the Queens portion of the marsh was threatened by illegal dumping and development. Across the city line, a proposed golf course would have covered the marsh with landfill. The committee purchased 1,200 copies of *Audubon Magazine*, which had a cover story about the value of salt marshes, and distributed them to village residents in an effort to convince them that marshland was worth preserving.

Traversing the park is Sandhill Road, a one-lane winding road listed on older maps as the more ambitious-sounding Bayshore Boulevard. On the eastern side of the marsh, Little Neck Parkway extends four blocks north of the railroad toward **Virginia Point**, named after Dent. Weathered pilings in Udalls Cove stand as remnants of a past when the shore was dotted with fishing piers, and littleneck clams were harvested by local businesses. By 1893, the local clam industry was forced to close as a result of pollution. Nevertheless, the term "littleneck" is still used as a size category for clams, regardless of geographic origin.

To the east of Virginia Point, a smaller stream originating in the University Gardens section of Great Neck flows underneath parking lots and behind backyards on its way to Udalls Cove. This unnamed creek passes by a water pumping station near the site of Bloodgood Haviland Cutter's gristmill. A lifelong resident of Great Neck and Plandome, he was a prolific poet and friend of Mark Twain. The "Poet Lariat" character in Twain's *Innocents Abroad* is said to be based on Cutter. Cutter died in 1906 at age 89 and is buried in the Zion Episcopal Church cemetery. His mill is memorialized by Cutter Mill Road and **Cutter Mill Park** across the city line in Great Neck.

At Virginia Point, Gabler's Creek widens into Udalls Cove, an inlet that narrows into a creek during low tide. Its namesake is Richard Udall, a local landowner who purchased the **Saddle Rock Grist Mill** in 1833. The mill was owned by his descendants until 1950; today it operates as a museum. It is located a mile downstream from Udalls Cove in the village of Saddle Rock.

Although the history of Udalls Cove since 1969 appears to be a success story, it is not resolved. With 15 privately owned lots remaining within the ravine, development remains a threat to the cohesion of the preserve. Over the past half century, the city and state have acquired private parcels in a piecemeal manner. In order to ensure a unified master plan for Gabler's Creek and Aurora Pond, these remaining lots should be acquired in one shot.

QUEENS

PLACES TO SEE:

✦ **Udalls Cove Park Preserve**
  ◇ **Virginia Point** Northern tip of Little Neck Parkway
  ◇ **Aurora Pond** Sandhill Road, a block east of Little Neck Parkway
  ◇ **Udalls Cove Ravine** Northern Boulevard at 245th Street
✦ **Zion Episcopal Church and cemetery** 243-01 Northern Boulevard
  ✦ 718-225-0466 ✦ www.zionepiscopal.org
✦ **Saint Anastasia Roman Catholic Church** 45-14 245th Street ✦ 718-631-4454 ✦ www.stanastasia.info

LEARN MORE:
✦ **Udalls Cove Preservation Committee** www.littleneck.net/udalls cove

GETTING THERE:
✦ **Bus**: Q12 at Northern Boulevard and 245th Street
✦ **Subway**: 7 at Flushing–Main Street, transfer to Q12
✦ **Train**: Long Island Railroad at Little Neck
✦ **Bike**: There are currently no bike routes near Udalls Cove Park Preserve

55. Fort Totten Ponds

On the northeastern tip of Queens is an ear-shaped peninsula that served as a military base from 1859 to 1995, designed to protect Queens from a foreign naval invasion that never came. On the isthmus connecting **Fort Totten** to the mainland are two freshwater ponds that would be inundated with salt water from Little Neck Bay in the event of a storm surge. A smaller unnamed lake is covered with algae, while **Fort Totten Lake** is ringed by marshland that links it with the bay.

The best place to see the lakes within the fort is on Duane Road, which separates them. Outside the fort, the larger pond can be seen from **Joe Michaels Mile**, a path that runs along the western shore of Little Neck Bay.

The peninsula's first European owner was English settler William Thorne in 1640; his descendants lived on it until 1829, calling the peninsula Thorne's Neck. In 1829, Thorne's descendants sold the peninsula to Charles Willet, and the parcel was renamed Willets Point. In the 20th century, the name migrated five miles west to an industrial neighborhood as a result of Willets Point Boulevard, a discontinuous road that was meant to run between Fort Totten and the present-day "Willets Point." The original Willets Point became Fort Totten after an official renaming in 1898. The **Willets Farmhouse** still stands but is in dire need of renovation.

Following the British invasion of New York during the American Revolution, the federal government feared another invasion and planned a series of defenses at points of entry to the city. This fort on the site of

the Willets farm and Fort Schuyler on **Throggs Neck** were both constructed to protect against an approach from the East River.

The fort in Queens initially did not have a name; it was dubbed Camp
Morgan after Governor Edwin D. Morgan. As the Civil War raged
in the South, construction on the fort halted in 1864 as advancements
in masonry-penetrating ordnance made it obsolete. The fort served as
a staging area in transporting troops to the front lines and a testing
ground for defense weapons. In 1995, Congress voted to close the military base and transfer it to the city, which opened Fort Totten to the
public in 2001.

The peninsula is shared by the U.S. Army Reserve, the New York
City Fire Department, the Coast Guard, and the Parks Department.
Most of the residential dwellings were demolished by the city, leaving
standing only structures of historical and architectural value, clustered
around the smaller pond.

Among the structures is castle-like **Officers' Club**, which was completed in 1887. Its uses included an officers' mess hall, a clubhouse for the
U.S. Army Corps of Engineers, and a Job Corps center. Its design was a
tribute to the engineers, whose logo resembles the building. Its present
occupant is the Bayside Historical Society.

QUEENS

PLACES TO SEE:

✦ **Fort Totten Park** Totten Avenue at the Cross Island Parkway ✦
www.nycgovparks.org/parks/fort-totten-park
◇ **Bayside Historical Society** 208 Totten Avenue ✦ 718-352-1548
✦ www.baysidehistorical.org
◇ **Willets Farmhouse (closed at this time)**
◇ **Water Battery**
✦ **Little Bay Park** Cross Island Parkway between Utopia Parkway and
Totten Avenue ✦ www.nycgovparks.org/parks/little-bay-park

GETTING THERE:

✦ **Bus**: Q13, Q16 at Fort Totten
✦ **Subway**: 7 at Flushing–Main Street, transfer to Q13 or Q16
✦ **Bike**: There are bike lanes on Joe Michaels Mile along Little Neck
Bay as part of the Brooklyn-Queens Greenway

56. Potamogeton Pond

Also known as Pea Pond, the glacial kettle pond **Potamogeton Pond** is tucked into a narrow strip of parkland in Hollis Hills alongside Grand Central Parkway; it is named after an aquatic plant. It was once a stop on a bridle trail that connected Cunningham Park to Alley Pond Park, but when local stables closed, the trail was abandoned. Nearby Vanderbilt Parkway became the preferred corridor between these two major parks.

Completed in 1936, Grand Central Parkway runs along the top of the glacial ridge where the ice sheet terminated. Potamogeton Pond can be found at 86th Avenue and 217th Street. The completion of Grand Central Parkway reduced this once-popular ice-skating site to a bog. The roadway cut off some of the water that fed the pond, resulting in less water intake. The perch, carp, and catfish that lived in the pond died off in 1963 as the parkway was widened in conjunction with the World's Fair in Flushing Meadows, which would take place the following year. Silt covered up the pond, and plants grew atop its former surface.

Science teacher Thomas Schweitzer's Hollis Hills Civic Association teamed up with ecology professor Andrew Greller's Queens College Ecology Club to lobby the city, which by 1970 determined that "the area known as Pea Pond . . . no longer receives sufficient water to maintain a pond." Undeterred, advocates for the pond enlisted the support of the Boy Scouts, the Queens Village Centennial Association, and local high school nature clubs, succeeding in blocking the state and city's plans to cover the pond's site.

The pond is presently overgrown with phragmites and cattails. Entrances to the Potamogeton Pond Trail can be found on Grand Central Parkway at either 217th Street or 82nd Avenue. The lack of natural water sources for this pond indicates that in order to maintain its natural appearance it must be maintained constantly by the city in a manner similar to Kissena Lake and Bowne Pond.

LEARN MORE:
✦ **Hollis Hills Civic Association** www.hollishillscivic.com

GETTING THERE:
✦ **Bus**: Q27, Q88 at Springfield Boulevard and Grand Central Parkway north service road, walk west on Grand Central Parkway to 82nd Avenue; Q46 at Union Turnpike and Bell Boulevard, walk

south three blocks on Bell Boulevard to Grand Central Parkway, turn left and walk east to 217th Street

+ **Subway**: E, F at Kew Gardens–Union Turnpike, transfer to Q46
+ **Bike**: There are currently no bike routes around Potamogeton Pond

57. Old Mill Creek

Also known historically as the west branch of Hook Creek, Forest Stream and Simonson's Creek, **Old Mill Creek**'s most prominent appearance is within Brookville Park in Rosedale, where it widens into Conselyea's Pond.

Old Mill Creek originated near the **Belmont Park racetrack** in Elmont, less than a mile to the east of the city line. A water pumping station originally operated by the Jamaica Water Supply Company stands on Hempstead Turnpike near Plainfield Avenue, collecting groundwater that contributed to Old Mill Creek. The extra water emerges out of the ground two blocks to the south of the water tanks at Belpark Avenue near Joan Court, where it flows for nearly a mile though a concrete channel constructed in 1933.

Old Mill Creek goes underground at Linden Boulevard and meanders through the helix interchange of the **Cross Island Parkway** and **Southern State Parkway**. From this point, the stream flows entirely within Queens, running south parallel to Brookville Boulevard toward its end. Prior to the construction of Belt Parkway in 1934, the stream flowed through two reservoirs that connected to Brooklyn Water Works and served the community of Foster's Meadow. Since the highway was built, the stream resembles a ditch in the road's shadow.

The stream disappears in certain spots beneath the Belt Parkway until the highway's sharp turn westward, where it connects with Sunrise Highway. Together with Conduit Avenue, Sunrise Highway is part of State Route 27, a series of roads running between Gowanus in Brooklyn and Montauk Point at the easternmost tip of Long Island.

To the south of this bend in the highway, Old Mill Creek emerges in the naturalistic setting of **Brookville Park**. Prior to Rosedale's incorporation into New York City in 1898, the parkland belonged to Brooklyn Water Works. At the point where the creek widens into **Conselyea's Pond**, a pedestrian bridge crosses it. This bridge is a remnant of the **Cedarhurst Cutoff**, a spur of the Long Island Railroad that operated from 1872 to 1880 and again from 1928 to 1934.

At the park's southern end, Old Mill Creek passes beneath a narrow overpass carrying 147th Avenue and enters **Idlewild Park**, a wetland that covers 180 acres between Rosedale and JFK Airport. Inside this park, the creek meanders among the marshes, with tributaries feeding into it. The stream used to merge with Hook Creek before emptying in Head of Bay. But with the construction of Brookville Boulevard through the wetlands, Old Mill Creek was redirected south, emptying into **Thurston Basin**, an arm of **Jamaica Bay**.

PLACES TO SEE:

+ **Brookville Park** Brookville Boulevard between South Conduit Avenue and 147th Avenue + www.nycgovparks.org/parks/brook ville-park
+ **Idlewild Park** Brookville Boulevard between 147th Avenue and Rockaway Boulevard + www.nycgovparks.org/parks/idlewild-park

GETTING THERE:

+ **Bus**: Q85 at Brookville Boulevard and South Conduit Avenue; Q111, Q114 at 147th Avenue and 235th Street
+ **Subway**: E, J, Z at Sutphin Boulevard–Archer Avenue, transfer to Q85, Q111, or Q114
+ **Train**: Long Island Railroad at Rosedale, walk one block west on South Conduit Avenue to Brookville Boulevard
+ **Bike**: There is a bike trail within Brookville Park

58. Thurston Creek

Thurston Creek had its origin near Springfield Boulevard and 121st Avenue, across from **Montefiore Cemetery** in the Saint Albans neighborhood. It flowed south along Springfield Boulevard for nearly three miles, emptying into Jamaica Bay. Today, the only visible part of the creek can be found in **Springfield Park**, which contains Cornell's Pond. From the pond, the creek flows south through the grounds of JFK Airport, widening into Thurston Basin before emptying into Head of Bay.

The cemetery had its first Jewish internment in 1908. It envelops the much older **Old Springfield Cemetery**, a nonsectarian burial ground dating to 1761. Its first burial is 77-year-old Jean Cornell, marked by a brownstone monument. She was the wife of settler William Cornell, whose descendants include Cornell University founder Ezra Cornell and his son Alonzo, who briefly served as governor between 1880 and 1882.

The stream flowed past the hotels and farms of Springfield to empty into **Springfield Pond**, a body of water formed by a milldam in the mid-18th century. Development arrived in the isolated community following the completion of Penn Station in 1910, which enabled residents to reach Midtown Manhattan in a half hour. Springfield was renamed Springfield Gardens in 1927, billed as an attractive suburb served by two branches of the Long Island Railroad.

In the 1920s, the neighborhood's population rose dramatically from 3,046 to 13,089. Sections of Thurston Creek north of Springfield Pond were channeled into a sewer, and the pond was buried in the following decade. The pond's site remained undeveloped, and in 1959, the city acquired it for parkland. **Montbellier Park** is named after one of the leaders of the campaign for the park. Albert Montbellier was a civic activist and founder of the Springfield Gardens Taxpayers and Citizens Association. He died in 1963, and the park was named after him the following year.

To the south of Springfield Pond, a tributary stream fed into Thurston Creek. Originating near 131st Avenue and 224th Street, this unnamed stream fed into **Baylis' Pond**, a popular ice-skating spot at 219th Street and 141st Avenue that was formed by the dam of a gristmill operated by the Higbie family. The Baylis family also had property along the pond's shore. This stream and pond were filled in the 1920s. As with Springfield Pond, no trace of this smaller pond remains. Tract housing covers its location.

Continuing south along Springfield Boulevard, the next plot of open space along the former streambed is the **Springfield Gardens Educational Campus**, a modernist square-shaped structure dating to 1963. A block to the south of the school is the Belt Parkway, flanked on its shoulders by Conduit Avenue. The avenue follows the path of the Brooklyn Water Works aqueduct that carried water from Massapequa to Brooklyn.

On the southern side of the Belt Parkway, **Collaborative Arts Middle School** also occupies the streambed, built a year before the high school. Thurston Creek emerges to the surface south of 145th Road, where it enters the 24-acre **Springfield Park**. The stream winds through the park in a brick channel, emptying into Cornell Pond. The park offers passive recreation and sports facilities for baseball, tennis, and basketball.

QUEENS

QUEENS

Across the Idlewild marshes

Leaving the park, Thurston Creek enters the **Idlewild marshes**, where it detours around airport freight warehouses that were built in the early 1970s. This section of the stream was recently redesigned to collect storm water from nearby streets as part of the Bluebelt plan managed by the city's Department of Environmental Protection. Springfield Boulevard shrinks into Springfield Lane, a colonial trail that disappears into the marshes. It used to connect with Rockaway Turnpike, linking eastern Queens with Far Rockaway. At 149th Avenue and 223rd Street is the **Idlewild Cricket Field**, a recent addition built in response to a growing Indo-Caribbean population in the area.

Prior to the construction of JFK Airport, Thurston Creek flowed south through the marshes toward Jamaica Bay. To the south of Rockaway Boulevard, the creek was lined in the first half of the 20th century by fishing shacks and bungalows in a development called **Springfield Dock**. No trace of this neighborhood remains. All of it is covered by JFK Airport's Cargo Area D.

With the airport covering most of the streambed below Rockaway Boulevard, daylighting in this section would be impossible. The section where it would be easiest to restore natural conditions is between Springfield Park and Rockaway Boulevard, presently a narrow channel bound by landfill.

PLACES TO SEE:

+ **Montbellier Park** Springfield Boulevard at 139th Avenue + www.nycgovparks.org/parks/montbellier-park
+ **Springfield Park** Springfield Boulevard between 145th Road and 147th Avenue + www.nycgovparks.org/parks/springfield-park
+ **Idlewild Park** Springfield Lane at 149th Avenue www.nycgovparks.org/parks/idlewild-park

GETTING THERE:

+ **Bus:** Q77, Q85 at Springfield Boulevard and 145th Road
+ **Subway:** F at 169th Street, transfer to Q77
+ **Bike:** There are currently no bike lanes along the path of Thurston Creek

59. Cornell Creek

Cornell Creek, also known historically as Jamaica Creek, had its origin near the commercial center of Jamaica at **Beaver Pond**, following Sutphin Boulevard south toward **Baisley Pond**, where additional tributaries flowed in from the east. From there, the stream continued south, emptying into Jamaica Bay. With the exception of Baisley Pond, the rest of the creek is entirely buried beneath local streets, homes, and JFK Airport.

Beaver Pond

The history of central Queens is closely tied to **Beaver Pond**, whose native name, Jameco—the Lenape word for beaver—was corrupted into Jamaica by English settlers. They arrived in the area in 1656 with permission from the New Netherland government to build a settlement, which the Dutch named "Rustdorp." Following the English takeover of the colony in 1664, the settlement's popular name, Jamaica, became official. The town became the seat of Queens County in 1683.

On the village's southern edge was Beaver Pond, a natural lake whose namesake was a vital component in the colonial economy. Beaver fur attracted Dutch colonists to the region; the animal even appears on the seal of New York City. In the 18th century, Beaver Pond was the site of horse races and public executions.

On the estern side of the pond was **Prospect Cemetery**, in operation since 1668. Its dead include American revolutionaries, Civil War veterans, and members of prominent local families such as Van Wyck, Sutphin, and Brinkerhoff. The last burial took place in 1988.

At the turn of the 20th cenutry, the pond was used as an ice-harvesting site. City authorities considered the industrial use of Beaver Pond a health hazard, as its outflow contributed to the Brooklyn Water Works. In April 1906, a grand jury recommended filling in this "menace to the health of the community."

Although Beaver Pond was filled, land atop the site remained undeveloped for another couple of decades. As with other filled-in lakes such as Collect Pond, the neighborhood atop the fill was largely industrial, covered with auto repair shops, slaughterhouses, and undeveloped lots used for storage. Beaver Road, which traces the former pond's northern shore, is the only physical reminder of the historic body of water.

QUEENS

Baisley Pond

From Beaver Pond, Cornell Creek flowed south for nearly two miles to **Baisley Pond**, centerpiece of a 109-acre park named after the pond. The pond was created in the 18th century to power local gristmills. The pond's namesake was local landowner David Baisley, who sold the pond to Brooklyn Water Works in 1852. A year later, as the pond was being engineered to contribute to Brooklyn's water supply, six molar teeth and small bone fragments attributable to mastodon were found in the pond. A paleontological study of the location determined that the extinct pachyderm died after the Pleistocene ice sheets receded, likely trapped in a bog.

Following Brooklyn's consolidation into Greater New York in 1898, the pond's use as a reservoir declined, and in 1914, the pond was transferred to the Parks Department. In June of that year, four young swimmers were arrested for bathing in the pond. One of the swimmers, May Gluck of Jamaica, told the officer, "The water was cool and it looked so good that we just took a plunge. We wore very proper bathing suits, too." The magistrate dismissed trespassing charges, reminding the officer that the pond was no longer a reservoir and that the water supply of Brooklyn was not in danger. Patrolman Albert Gauss then attempted to charge the swimmers with disorderly conduct. The magistrate dismissed all charges.

During the Great Depression, Parks Commissioner Robert Moses redesigned the park with a concrete shoreline around the pond, playgrounds, and baseball diamonds.

In the postwar years, the streets around Baisley Pond filled up with housing ranging from single-family tract homes to the **Baisley Park Houses**, a low-income development situated atop the streambed that fed into the pond. The housing development consists of five towers on a superblock, in a design nearly identical to most NYCHA projects around the city.

Baisley Pond Park offers a variety of recreational options that include basketball, handball, tennis, a running track, four playgrounds, and cricket fields. A sculpture of a mastodon in one of the playgrounds serves as a teaching tool on the park's history. In a design inspired by the Mall in Central Park, there is a tree-lined walkway leading to a First World War memorial that was unveiled in 1921.

The portion of the park south of Rockaway Boulevard was acquired by the Parks Department in the 1960s. Around that time, the stream was buried in this section and covered with fill on which park goers run and play baseball and football.

Across the Idlewild marshes

Below Conduit Avenue, the buried stream passes beneath JFK Airport. Prior to the airport's opening in 1948, 150th Street followed Cornell Creek along its eastern bank from Rockaway Boulevard to the creek's mouth at Jamaica Bay. The old name for this street was Three Mile Mill Road. Similar to the Meadowmere enclave at the mouth of Thurston Basin and the long-gone Springfield Dock, a small fishing community existed at the mouth of the stream prior to the construction of JFK Airport. Where the streambed ran to the bay is now the 2.5-mile-long **JFK Expressway,** one of the city's shortest highways, connecting the Belt Parkway with the airport.

PLACES TO SEE:
✦ **Baisley Pond Park** North Conduit Avenue and 116th Avenue between Sutphin Boulevard and Baisley Boulevard ✦ www.nycgov parks.org/parks/baisley-pond-park

GETTING THERE:
✦ **Bus**: Q6, Q7 eastbound at Rockaway Boulevard and 150th Street; Q6 westbound at Rockaway Boulevard and Baisley Boulevard; Q7 westbound at Rockaway Boulevard and Sutphin Boulevard
✦ **Subway**: E, J, Z at Sutphin Boulevard–Archer Avenue, transfer to Q6; A to Rockaway Boulevard, transfer to Q7
✦ **Train**: Long Island Railroad at Jamaica, transfer to Q6
✦ **Bike**: There are bike lanes within Baisley Pond Park

60. Hawtree Creek

Across the train tracks, **West Hamilton Beach** clings to the eastern bank of Hawtree Basin, an inlet lined with small boats and crossed by the arc-shaped **Hawtree Basin Bridge**, which connects the small neighborhood with Old Howard Beach; and by 102nd Street, which connects it to the Ramblersville section of Howard Beach. **Hawtree Creek**'s name is an Old English word synonymous with hawthorn, a tree common in this region.

A pedestrian walkway spanning the stream along the Rockaway Line provides a scenic shortcut between the Howard Beach station and West Hamilton Beach. Prior to 1955, the Long Island Railroad had a station at Hamilton Beach, marked by a wooden shed on the platform. Its proximity to Howard Beach and lack of usage resulted in its closing.

The neighborhood has its own volunteer fire department and ambulance corps, a source of pride to local residents since 1928. The main road in West Hamilton Beach is 104th Street, which has ten dead-end streets

branching from it. Some were assigned numbers, while others kept their names. At the southern end of 104th Street, a loop enables Q11 buses to turn around on their return to the mainland. **Hamilton Beach Park** provides a scenic overlook at the confluence of Hawtree Creek and Jamaica Bay. The park is a unit of **Gateway National Recreation Area**, a national park comprising islands in Jamaica Bay and parks around its shore.

The bridge to Hamilton Beach

On the northern side of the footbridge, Hawtree Basin splits into three branches, the longest originating near the train tracks. The only road linking West Hamilton Beach to mainland Queens is 102nd Street, which crosses the northernmost branch of the inlet using a short and narrow bridge. It is likely the shortest automobile-accessible crossing in the city with an official name. For much of the 20th century, it was known as **Lenihan Bridge**, named after local Alderman

Hawtree Creek, 1940

John Lenihan, who served from 1924 to 1935. The narrow bridge and its neighboring dead-end roads often appeared in newspaper accounts as a traffic hazard.

Prior to 1995, West Hamilton Beach was one of a handful of neighborhoods in the city that was not connected to its sewer system. The much-anticipated installation of sewers required a controversial replacement for Lenihan Bridge in order to accommodate trucks carrying construction materials. Augustine Barry, a homeowner whose property abutted the bridge, opposed the project because a temporary bridge would be placed within four feet of his home. For Mr. Barry, the project smacked of injustice, as he had moved to West Hamilton Beach 40 years earlier after his prior home was demolished to make way for the Long Island Expressway in Elmhurst.

The construction of the temporary bridge resulted in cracks on the foundations of Barry's home. Diesel exhaust from passing buses added to his aggravation. In June 2006, the city's Department of Buildings declared the home unsafe, ordering Mr. Barry and his wife, Ann, to vacate. The city's chief engineer, Robert J. Ronayne, offered his Brooklyn apartment to Barry, but it was turned down. Barry chose to sleep in his car instead, in order to guard his home and his chickens from potential vandalism.

The story had a happy ending a year later. "All's well that ends well," said the city's transportation commissioner, Christopher R. Lynn. The city repaired the home to the tune of $455,000. Estimating the cost of the house at $150,000, Mr. Barry was pleased to move in but felt sorry for the taxpayers who had footed the bill. As his brother Eugene summed it up, "All's well that ends well, sure. But this all could have been avoided."

A final chapter in this bridge's saga is its name change in 2001. By then, John Lenihan was long forgotten, and the crossing was renamed the **Ramblersville-Hawtree Memorial Bridge** to honor seven soldiers from the neighborhood who were killed in the Second World War.

Hawtree Creek Bridge

Prior to 1963, West Hamilton Beach had a second automobile connection with Howard Beach at 165th Avenue, also known as Lockwood Court. The **Hawtree Creek Bridge** was a notorious traffic hazard, resulting in the death of a local motorist in 1956. A year later, the city banned buses and trucks from using this bridge, described in news reports as "decrepit." It was replaced in 1963 with the present **Hawtree Basin Bridge**, a pedestrian crossing in the form of a bright blue arc across the channel at Rau Court.

In October 2012, Superstorm Sandy caused extensive damage in the neighborhood, resulting in the loss of all but one of the vehicles belonging to the West Hamilton Beach Volunteer Fire Department. The department raised funds and received donated vehicles, and a year later, its fleet was up to nine—five ambulances and four fire trucks.

As global weather patterns suggest an increase in large storms, envi-

QUEENS

ronmental and urban planning groups have proposed a combination of man-made and natural barriers to mitigate storm surge damage. The natural element involves introducing reefs and marshes to serve as sponges in absorbing massive waves. The man-made element is inspired by existing examples in the Netherlands, where movable barriers are located at the mouths of streams. In this case, barriers installed at the mouths of inlets along Jamaica Bay would keep storm surges away from homes along the shore of Hawtree Creek and Shellbank Basin.

PLACES TO SEE:

+ **Hawtree Basin Bridge** Hawtree Creek between Davenport Court and Rau Court
+ **Hamilton Beach Park** 165th Avenue at 104th Street
+ **Ramblersville-Hawtree Memorial Bridge** 102nd Street between Broadway and Russell Street
+ **West Hamilton Beach Volunteer Fire Department** 102-33 Davenport Court + 718-843-9863 + www.whbvfd.org

GETTING THERE:

+ **Bus**: Q11 to 104th Street and 165th Avenue in West Hamilton Beach or 99th Street and 163rd Avenue in Old Howard Beach
+ **Subway**: A at Howard Beach, walk south along walkway to West Hamilton Beach or transfer to Q11
+ **Bike**: There are currently no bike lanes in West Hamilton Beach; the nearest is on 102nd Street and 159th Avenue, which connects to other bike routes

61. Shellbank Basin

The inlet of **Shellbank Basin** penetrates nearly a mile inland into the neighborhood of Howard Beach. The inlet's east bank is lined with mansions, while the western side has commercial properties sandwiched between the stream and Cross Bay Boulevard. The basin was carved out in the 1890s by glove manufacturer William J. Howard, who transformed parts of his 150-acre goat farm into a resort community.

Prior to Howard's arrival, the marshland landscape had pockets of housing in Ramblersville, Remsen's Landing, and Hamilton Beach— neighborhoods that have been absorbed into present-day Howard Beach.

The growth of early Howard Beach is tied closely to its namesake, who opened the **Hotel Howard** in 1899 at the present-day site of Frank M. Charles Park. The hotel stood on a narrow spit of land on Jamaica Bay between Shellbank Basin and Hawtree Creek. The hotel was accessible by railroad and ferry, offering what were then innovative amenities such as electric lights. The hotel burned down in October 1907, and in its place the residential community of Howard Beach Estates was mapped out.

While the eastern bank of Shellbank Basin features homes from the prewar period, the western bank was developed largely in the 1950s, when marshlands between the basin and the Brooklyn–Queens border were drained and mapped.

Cross Bay Boulevard serves as the commercial spine of Howard Beach—a six-lane highway that runs for 11 miles, from Elmhurst to Rockaway Beach. Prior to 1924, the Rockaway peninsula was connected to mainland Queens only by the railway, with vehicles having no option other than a circuitous early route around Jamaica Bay. Recognizing the need for a road across Jamaica Bay, the city's Board of Estimate approved the project in June 1918.

Although local residents strongly supported its construction, the presence of oyster beds along the road's path resulted in delays. Owned by the state, the oyster beds were assigned long-term leases to fishermen. The city had no authority to remove the beds and could only attempt to move the beds in a way that would not disturb the creatures. The completion of the **Cross Bay Bridge** in June 1939 greatly increased the number of summer visitors to the Rockaways, benefiting communities along the route, including Howard Beach, where the road follows the western shore of Shellbank Basin.

At Cross Bay Boulevard and 158th Avenue is an air compressor installed in 2012 to aerate the water of Shellbank Basin. Before the pump was constructed, stagnant water resulted in massive fish deaths, leaving hundreds of dead fish floating on the surface and producing a smell that offended shoreline property owners. The odors occur when a sudden drop in temperature raises the basin's colder water to the surface. The $3.5 million structure pumps air bubbles into Shellbank Basin, mixing the cooler water of its bottom with warmer surface water.

Adjacent to the boxy structure is a unique **Starbucks** coffee franchise, located at 157-41 Cross Bay Boulevard. Instead of a typical brick box, this Starbucks is located inside a facility resembling a beach shack that includes a waterfront promenade and rooftop balconies. The structure was completed in 1995, designed by Maspeth-based architect Thomas F. Cusanelli for developer Vincent Luccisano. The amount of open space

QUEENS

and public access to the shoreline is the result of waterfront zoning legislation passed by the city council in 1993. Under this law, properties along waterfronts were required to provide a certain percentage of open space accessible or visible to the public.

A former archery range, the Luccisano property featured volleyball courts following the completion of the restaurant facility. When the restaurant became a Starbucks, parking spaces were paved atop the volleyball courts. Nevertheless, the property includes publicly accessible waterfront space as a result of legislation could offer a hint to the future of the city's shorelines, where privately owned lots on the water's edge are accessible to the public.

Along the narrow strip between Cross Bay Boulevard and Shellbank Basin are a series of restaurants with waterfront views. Most have an Italian menu that reflects the historic demographics of Howard Beach. Examples include **Roma View Catering, Cross Bay Diner**, and **Lenny's Clam Bar**. The biggest of them all is **Russo's on the Bay**, a palatial catering hall occupying nearly an entire block between 162nd and 163rd Avenues. The facility opened in 1987 and has expanded and undergone renovations since then, each time growing in size and opulence.

Prior to his arrest and sentencing in 1992, organized crime leader John Gotti resided in Howard Beach. Although the connection between the mob and Russo's catering hall was well known among residents, many civic groups held their dinners at Russo's, including elected officials who pleaded ignorance when asked about this by the press. At the 2004 trial of Gambino crime family scion Peter Gotti, informant Michael "Mikey Scars" DiLeonardo testified that the Gambino family received $1 for every person who showed up at Russo's.

At 162nd Avenue, the **Old Mill Yacht Club** is housed in a modest brick facility. Behind it, a row of small boats is its fleet. The club was founded in 1894 and merged in 1910 with the Pleasant Point Marine Club, adopting the formal name Old Mill Yacht Club of Pleasant Point. The club is used for a variety of community events throughout the year.

Two blocks farther downstream, the **Surfside Motel** offers rooms with views of Shellbank Basin. Its neighbor is **Vetro Restaurant & Lounge**, located near the basin's mouth at Jamaica Bay. A smaller but equally opulent spinoff of Russo's, this catering hall offers waterfront and rooftop dining options.

Across Shellbank Basin, the isthmus known as Old Howard Beach ends at **Frank M. Charles Park**, which is surrounded by water on three sides. Originally a city-owned park, it was named after the first Howard

Beach resident to be killed in combat during the First World War. In the early decades of the 20th century, the Charles family owned bungalows in the neighborhood and rented them out to summer tenants. The tip of the isthmus was the site of William Howard's Casino building, a beachside recreation center with showers, refreshments, and space for functions. The park was acquired by the National Park Service in 1972 as part of **Gateway National Recreation Area**, a set of parks ringing Jamaica Bay and Lower New York Bay. At the time, the city was nearly bankrupt, and local residents hoped that with federal ownership, the park would receive proper maintenance.

With legislation requiring open space along waterfronts and the architectural examples of Russo's and Vetro, it is likely that Shellbank Basin has a solid future as a destination for dining and social events. Perhaps it is fitting that Howard Beach, with its historical Italian identity, has its canal inspired by Venice, where the waterways are lined with palaces.

PLACES TO SEE:
+ **Frank M. Charles Park** 165th Avenue between 95th Street and 99th Street in Old Howard Beach

GETTING THERE:
+ **Bus**: Q52, Q53 on Cross Bay Boulevard, anywhere between 157th Avenue and 163rd Avenue; Q21, Q41 at Cross Bay Boulevard and 159th Avenue; Q11 at Frank M. Charles Park
+ **Subway**: A at Howard Beach, transfer to Q11, Q52, or Q53
+ **Bike**: There are bike lanes on 91st and 92nd Streets, one and two blocks to the west of Cross Bay Boulevard

62. East and West Ponds

Between Howard Beach and the Rockaway Peninsula is the only inhabited island in Jamaica Bay—1,200 acres divided between the Jamaica Bay Wildlife Refuge and the neighborhood of Broad Channel. Within the refuge are two ponds carved out of the marshy landscape, serving as a habitat for fish and migrating birds.

The ponds were formed after New York City Transit took over the Rockaway Branch from the Long Island Railroad in 1955, following a trestle fire in May 1950, and converted it for subway use. During the reconstruction of the rail line, the island took its present shape. Channels separating three islands—Ruler's Bar Hassock, The Raunt, and Broad Channel—were filled in, and the remaining parts of these channels became ponds. The 45-acre **West Pond** is better known to visitors because of its proximity to the refuge's visitor center and parking lot. The pond is ringed by a trail offering views of Manhattan in the distance.

East Pond is the larger twin, at 117 acres. Separated from West Pond by the busy Cross Bay Boulevard, it receives fewer visitors. Along the eastern shore of this pond, the Rockaway Line passes through the longest stretch of track between stations, at 3.5 miles, between Howard Beach and Broad Channel.

Prior to May 1950, the marshes around East Pond were dotted with fishing shacks set up by squatters in an unofficial community known as **The Raunt**. The Long Island Railroad did not mind the presence of shacks along its trestle and even set up stations to accommodate (and gather revenue from) these residents. The Raunt's name is likely a Scandinavian product, from the Danish word *rogen*—pronounced "raun"—which translates to roe; this area was a spawning ground for fish.

This settlement lost most of its structures in a 1931 fire. By 1938, the census recorded only 100 remaining residents. When the city condemned The Raunt in 1950, there were 15 structures left. An embankment was constructed for the railway, creating a single island out of Ruler's Bar Hassock, Goose Creek Island, Big Egg Marsh, and The Raunt. This newly formed landmass was given the name **Broad Channel** after the neighborhood at its southern tip. What remained of the channels separating these former islands was transformed into landlocked ponds.

The Raunt was condemned in 1950 after being rezoned as a bird sanctuary. Its last holdout, Agnes Rafferty, rowed away for the final time in October 1954. Most of her former neighbors resettled nearby in Howard Beach and Broad Channel. Over the decades, the spit of land on which The Raunt was located has eroded into Jamaica Bay, leaving no trace of the former neighborhood.

The first subway trains on the refurbished Rockaway Line rolled into Broad Channel on June 28, 1956. The trains bypass the wildlife refuge billed as a "man-made Galapagos." In 1972, Congress designated Broad Channel as part of the 27,000-acre **Gateway National Recreation Area**.

Broad Channel's ponds are carefully managed by custodians who maintain their levels and keep out encroaching saltwater from Jamaica Bay, but accidents still happen. In early 2010, pipes connecting the ponds with Jamaica Bay burst, resulting in saltwater pouring into the ponds. And in October 2012, the ponds took another hit when the storm surge from Hurricane Sandy destroyed the subway embankment and breached into the ponds. Since the storm, the breach in East Pond has been repaired as a result of the subway trestle reconstruction. West Pond, however, remains breached and flooded with saltwater. At this time, the National Park Service is evaluating options for the pond—between keeping it salty or restoring its water to brackish or fresh.

The history and nature of both ponds is depicted at the **Visitor Contact Station**, an environmentally friendly structure completed in 2007.

PLACES TO SEE:

✦ **Jamaica Bay Wildlife Refuge Visitor Contact Center** 718-318-4340 ✦ www.nyharborparks.org/visit/jaba.html

GETTING THERE:

✦ **Bus:** Q52, Q53 to the Visitor Contact Center at Jamaica Bay Wildlife Refuge
✦ **Subway:** A at Broad Channel, walk along Noel Road to Cross Bay Boulevard, turn right and walk about three-quarters of a mile to the Visitor Contact Center; A at Rockaway Boulevard and transfer to the Q52 or Q53
✦ **Bike:** There is a bike route along Cross Bay Boulevard into Broad Channel

QUEENS

Brooklyn

➤ **The northwestern corner of Brooklyn has been shaped** as much by the natural forces of the past ice age as by a century's worth of industrialization, which transformed salt marshes along the East River into canals that brought barges and oil tankers to Brooklyn. Although the neighborhoods along the shores of these waterways have largely shed their industrial character, the high cost of restoring these streams to their natural condition has kept them isolated and unusable to most local residents. However, with federal funding and gentrification of coastline neighborhoods, these streams are slowly returning to the public consciousness in a positive light.

The geological landscape of southern Brooklyn resembled that of southern Queens, with streams flowing south into Jamaica Bay across a gently sloping plain. As the streams approached the bay, they became inlets, separating the mainland from sandbars formed by ocean currents. As urbanization encroached, all of these creeks were severed from their natural sources and reduced solely to their inlets connecting to Jamaica Bay. Many of these inlets today are lined with either nature preserves or boating facilities that enable the public to interact with restored landscapes and waterways.

The terminal moraine that marks the southernmost extent of the Pleistocene ice sheet runs across Brooklyn in a northeast–southwest direction that separates the gently sloping coastal plains to the south from rolling hills and valleys to its north. Along this ridge are large cemeteries and parks that take advantage of the scenery. When the city of Brooklyn needed places to store its water supply, reservoirs were constructed atop this ridge to enable the water to flow into low-rise homes below using gravity. Along the length of the Harbor Hill Moraine, loose chunks of the retreating ice sheet melted to form kettle ponds.

In Brooklyn, most of the terminal moraine has been covered with dense residential development that appears on the map as Cypress Hills, Crown Heights, Prospect Heights, and Bay Ridge. The major exceptions are the cemetery belt on the Queens border that includes Highland Park and, toward the center of Brooklyn, Prospect Park, Green-Wood Cemetery, and Sunset Park. As neighborhoods developed, kettle ponds were filled, leaving Brooklyn's only remaining examples within Green-Wood Cemetery.

While urbanization encroached, a sizable parcel between Crown Heights and Park Slope was preserved as Prospect Park. Inside the park is an artificial stream that flows through the hilly terrain, carrying three names before emptying into a 40-acre lake. The stream is reminiscent of Central Park's streams except that it has no natural history prior to the park's creation.

63. Newtown Creek

Although Brooklyn and Queens share a common land border that straddles the middle of numerous streets and cemeteries, the westernmost 3.5 miles of this border is marked by **Newtown Creek**, a tributary of the East River that once had its own network of feeder streams such as English Kills, East Branch, Maspeth Creek, Whale Creek, and Dutch Kills. The creek and its tributaries today are entirely lined with concrete bulkheads, and the former system of streams is presently an estuary of the East River. Because there is no inflow, the only movement of water in Newtown Creek is the result of tidal action. Otherwise, the water is essentially "dead," with debris and pollution collecting in the waterway and having no opportunity to flow out or dissolve.

English Kills
The farthest inland reach of Newtown Creek is **English Kills**, an inlet that presently originates out of a storm drain behind 465 Johnson Avenue in East Williamsburg. The storm drain is known in official terms as a combined sewer overflow or CSO—used to discharge raw sewage from homes, streets, and businesses in the event of excessive rainfall. This par-

BROOKLYN

ticular CSO site is among the city's busiest, discharging 344.4 million gallons of sewage into the stream.

The present path of the English Kills inlet was proposed in the 1860s and carved out in 1890 as an improvement project that straightened its shoreline and kept the width of English Kills to 100 feet.

A few feet farther downstream is the **Montrose Avenue Rail Bridge**, a low-clearance trestle that carries the **Bushwick Branch** of the Long Island Railroad across English Kills. The rail line has a long history of serving northern Brooklyn, but since 1924 it has been reduced to a single-track freight spur whose main client is Waste Management, a carting firm that transports the city's commercial trash.

At Ten Eyck Street, the stream turns 90 degrees to the right and then to the left as it approaches the **Metropolitan Avenue Bridge**. While English Kills was named after the area's early English settlers, many local streets and neighborhoods carry names dating back to the Dutch rule of the region. Examples include: Bushwick, which is a corruption of the 17th-century Dutch name Boswijck, meaning "little town in the woods"; Ten Eyck, a prominent landowning family whose name in Dutch means "at the oak"; and, near the bridge, Vandervoort and Varick Avenues contribute additional Dutch names to the local landscape.

Originally known as the **Williamsburgh and Jamaica Turnpike**, Metropolitan Avenue was laid out in 1814 as an eight-mile toll road connecting these two early settlements. The present bascule drawbridge was completed in 1933. On both sides of the bridge, Grand Street merges with Metropolitan Avenue, and traffic from both roads uses this bridge.

East Branch

The **East Branch** of Newtown Creek presently originates beneath the intersection of Metropolitan Avenue and Onderdonk Avenue, four blocks to the east of English Kills. In times of excessive rainfall, a CSO drain beneath this intersection dumps 586 million gallons of sewage annually into the stream.

On its eastern bank is the Consolidated Revenue Facility of the Metropolitan Transportation Authority, the public transit agency of the metropolitan region. Constructed in 2002, this fortresslike structure is ringed by a parking lot and has no relation to Newtown Creek. Considering the polluted state of the water, the architects had no ambition to install walkways along the shore, and the building apparently turns its back to it. The revenue facility abuts a concrete manufacturing plant and school bus parking lots.

Less than 1,000 feet to the north of Metropolitan Avenue, the East Branch flows beneath the **Grand Street Bridge**, an antiquated 1903 swing bridge that has only one vehicular lane in each direction. The width of the bridge is less than half of Grand Street's width on either shore, forcing traffic to slow down as vehicles cross the span.

The first version of this bridge opened in 1875 and quickly became dilapidated from lack of maintenance. Fifteen years later, a replacement was completed in its place, but it was regarded by the War Department as an "an obstruction to navigation." As a swing bridge, the span sits atop an artificial island in its center and swings sideways to allow tall ships to pass through.

The current bridge is likely to be replaced in the near future. A fixed span will likely be built, lacking the industrial charm and metal grating surface of the 1903 bridge.

Maspeth Plank Road

Less than 100 feet from the confluence of the East Branch and English Kills, Newtown Creek proper passes by ruins of a wooden pier and abutments on either bank where **Plank Road** once crossed. On the western bank is a massive superblock that was once the site of the Maspeth Holders gas tanks, and on the eastern side is the former **Furman's Island**. Prior to 1875, Maspeth Plank Road was one of the busier crossings on Newtown Creek, surrounded by glue and fertilizer factories that carelessly polluted the stream. Among them was Peter Cooper's glue factory, which produced early versions of edible gelatin. Having caused the demise of Sunfish Pond in Manhattan, the same factory brought pollution to Newtown Creek toward the end of the 19th century.

A likely hazard to navigation, Maspeth Plank Road's bridge was cleared, and a dock used for transporting animal carcasses was temporarily installed in its place. Today, on both sides of the creek where the road used to be, Maspeth Avenue simply dead-ends by the water. In recent years, the city has transformed waterfront dead-end streets into pocket parks. In neighborhoods where much of the waterfront is off-limits to the public, these parks provide recreational space and a location where boats can launch into the water.

In April 2015, the North Brooklyn Boat Club and the Newtown Creek Alliance jointly transformed the dead ends of Maspeth Avenue into a park that would provide a "soft edge" on the otherwise bulkhead shoreline.

BROOKLYN

Maspeth Holders

Following the departure of the glue factory, the land on the west bank of Newtown Creek was acquired by the Brooklyn Union Gas Company, which built the twin **Maspeth Holders gas tanks** on the property. Completed in 1927 and 1948, they towered at nearly 400 feet as the world's largest gas tanks; they were an easy point of reference for traffic reporters. Together, the tanks held 32 million cubic feet, enough to supply up to 160,000 homes for a month with a constant pressure that kept pilot lights from going out. With advances in technology, similar tanks around the city were decommissioned and demolished. The Maspeth Holders were taken down in a controlled implosion on the morning of July 15, 2001, forever altering the local skyline. In their place, smaller gas storage tanks were built, but most of the site, presently owned by the successor utility company National Grid, remains underdeveloped, held as a reserve for possible future utility use in a city where there is little land left for such development.

Furman's Island

On the eastern bank of the former Plank Road crossing is a sanitation garage and FedEx Ground distribution facility. As late as the 1930s, these parcels of land were known as **Furman's Island**, a marshy expanse ringed by Newtown Creek, Maspeth Creek, and **Shanty Creek**.

In 1638, it was one of the first English-speaking settlements within New Netherland. Officially called Arnhem after a city in the Netherlands, it was known to natives and settlers as Maspeth, from the Munsee term *mespaetches*, or "bad water place." In 1643, the Maspeth natives massacred the settlers, and the community was abandoned.

This native victory was temporary, as the Englishmen returned a decade after the massacre, in 1652, to build the nearby community of Middleburgh, known informally as Newtown. As the town grew, the creek that led travelers to it became known as Newtown Creek.

Furman's Island was the subject of dispute between the towns of Bushwick and Newtown, mirroring the larger conflicts taking place between the Dutch and English colonies. On January 7, 1769, the colonial legislature delineated the border, placing the island in Newtown, Queens. A physical reminder of this decision is **Arbitration Rock**, a glacial boulder that marked the future Brooklyn-Queens border and can be found today in the yard of the **Vander Ende-Onderdonk House**, a colonial farmhouse located at 18-20 Flushing Avenue in Ridgewood.

In its early years, the island also carried the names Smith and Mott, after its early landowners. Its final name was adopted in 1815, when Judge Garrit Furman purchased the 57-acre island. Furman also took credit for reviving the name Maspeth on local maps nearly two centuries after the last local natives were expelled. Furman built a mansion overlooking Newtown Creek and entertained local leaders with excerpts from *The Maspeth Poems*, which he composed. One such poem predicted the environmental decay to come, titled "Petition of the Shell-Fish, on Maspeth Island, for Protection Against the Turnpike-Makers, That Are Working the Williamsburgh Turnpike." The poem was in jest, as Furman was a partner in the construction of the turnpike that became Maspeth Avenue.

In 1855, the first bone-processing plant arrived on the island, producing ink, soap, glue, and gelatin for the public. The Furman estate gradually shrunk until the last parcel was sold in 1899. The arrival of oil refineries, tanneries, and acid manufacturers further degraded an island once known as a countryside retreat. With industrial development, Newtown Creek took on a negative reputation, and nearby Newtown was renamed Elmhurst in 1897. By the 1930s, Shanty Creek was completely filled in. Its former streambed would have approximately followed the route of 49th Place between Maspeth and Grand Avenues.

Mussel Island

At the confluence of Maspeth Creek and Newtown Creek was **Mussel Island**, an uninhabited patch of marshland that survived into the 1940s. As the shoreline of Newtown Creek industrialized the late 19th century, the island was regarded as a navigation hazard.

In 1919, a bill was introduced in Congress to dredge and widen Newtown Creek in order to improve navigation for larger vessels. The legislation passed in 1921. In the place of Mussel Island, a "turning basin" was carved out from the surrounding shoals. By the late 1930s, the project was completed.

Maspeth Creek

Maspeth Creek, a tributary of Newtown Creek originated in an elevated hilltop known as the **Ridgewood Plateau**, which marked the dividing point between the Newtown Creek and the Flushing Creek watersheds. Presently, only 1,000 feet of this stream remain on the surface, connected to Newtown Creek. Its only source of water is a CSO drain that spews out raw sewage during excessive rainfall.

The stream's history is closely intertwined with that of the native Lenape peoples who lived along its banks. Much of that history is tragic. Though the natives achieved an initial victory in Kieft's War in 1643—destroying the settlement at Newtown Creek—tribes throughout New Amsterdam and Long Island subsequently suffered heavy losses under the command of Governor Willem Kieft and English settler Captain John Underhill. By 1662, massacres and smallpox had eradicated the last native communities on western Long Island.

The creek reappeared in the public discussion in the mid-19th century, when local glue factory magnate Peter Cooper proposed a canal to link Maspeth Creek and Newtown Creek, bypassing the perilous reefs of Hell Gate. William H. Nichols, vice president of the Manufacturers' Association of Kings and Queens Counties, revived the plan in 1895. "People sneer at Newtown Creek, but they should not, for it is now one of the most important shipping centers in the country," said Nichols. The proposed canal sought to cleanse the stagnant water of Newtown Creek by providing flow from Flushing Creek, in addition to creating a transportation corridor for vessels through northwest Queens.

However, the proposal to dig a canal faced inland opposition, where property owners feared an encroachment of industry on the pastoral landscape. Maspeth Creek was truncated and partially covered with fill, reduced to an inlet of Newtown Creek.

Phelps Dodge Laurel Hill Works

The largest property on the north bank of Newtown Creek is a 37-acre former copper smelting plant that operated from 1871 to 1983. In the century that it operated by the creek, the factory complex soaked the ground with cadmium, chromium, copper, lead, mercury, petroleum hydrocarbons, and PCBs, among other contaminants. Like the gas tanks across the creek, the smokestack of the **Laurel Hill Works** also had a superlative record as the world's tallest when it was built in 1901.

Following nearly two decades of neglect, the property was declared a federal Superfund site in 2010, a first step toward cleaning up and developing the waterfront parcel.

Kosciuszko Bridge

The highest crossing over Newtown Creek is **Kosciuszko Bridge**, one of two bridges over the stream that carry the names of Polish patriots who fought in the American Revolution. This bridge opened to traffic as the Meeker Avenue Bridge on August 23, 1939, nine days shy of the German invasion of Poland, which triggered the Second World War. At the time, Greenpoint was already home to a burgeoning Polish immigrant population.

In July 1940, the city officially renamed the bridge after Tadeusz Kościuszko. The ceremony took place on September 23 of that year, with Polish parades on both side of the creek and a rousing speech by Mayor Fiorello La Guardia. "Insofar as the American people and the American government are concerned," said La Guardia, "the free government of Poland still lives and will continue to live."

The enormous 125-foot clearance of this bridge was a requirement set by the federal government. An extra-tall bridge enabled tall ships to pass underneath, providing materials to the theaters of war.

By the turn of the 21st century, the bridge was becoming obsolete and created a traffic bottleneck, carrying the Brooklyn-Queens Expressway near its junction with the Long Island Expressway. The state Department of Transportation engaged the public with four designs for a replacement bridge. All of the designs incorporated plenty of concrete; the one that was eventually accepted proposed a cable-stayed bridge that would become an instantly recognizable scenic landmark. A pedestrian lane on the southbound side of the bridge would provide panoramic views of Midtown Manhattan. The new Kosciuszko Bridge is expected to be completed by 2020.

Penny Bridge

One block to the west of the Kosciuszko Bridge, Meeker Avenue dead-ends on the shore of Newtown Creek, separated by the 200-foot-wide channel from Laurel Hill Boulevard on the Queens side of the stream. Prior to 1939, a crossing that carried numerous funerals connected these two roads. A predecessor to the Kosciuszko Bridge, the humble crossing was known as **Penny Bridge**, and it carried funeral processions from Brooklyn to Calvary Cemetery on the Queens side of Newtown Creek.

The site of Penny Bridge shares a common history with Furman's Island and the settlement of Newtown as a non-Dutch settlement in New Netherland. The oldest structure at this location was the **Duryea House**, a Dutch-style farmhouse built in 1681 by Huguenot couple Joost (George) Durie and his wife Magdalena Le Febre. A ferry had been operating at this location since 1670. The one-and-a-half-story structure had a lower floor made of stone and a wooden main floor. Located outside of a settlement, it served as an emergency stockade—protection against potentially hostile natives. Between the stones of the lower floors

BROOKLYN

were holes through which muskets could shoot at the attackers. Mr. Durie lived at this home until his death in 1727. This historic structure, the oldest along Newtown Creek, survived into the early 20th century.

In 1803, a toll bridge was constructed at the foot of Meeker Avenue, charging a penny toll. The wooden bridge was replaced with a steel-frame structure in 1894 that survived until the Kosciuszko Bridge replaced it in 1939. The name Penny Bridge survived on a nearby Long Island Railroad station until March 1998, when it closed because of light usage.

Calvary Cemetery

On the northern side of the former Penny Bridge is a hilltop historically known as **Laurel Hill**. From colonial times until 1845, it was the homestead of the Alsop family, who kept a small mansion on the summit. When the estate was sold to the **Calvary Cemetery**, the small **Alsop family plot** predating the Catholic graveyard was willed to its new owners, who continue to maintain it. The previous name of this hilltop survives in Laurel Hill Boulevard—a pre-grid roadway, hidden beneath the elevated Brooklyn-Queens Expressway, that connects Newtown Creek with the Woodside neighborhood.

The cemetery's first burial took place on July 31, 1848, and since then it has interred more than three million individuals. In the 19th century, local outbreaks of cholera, influenza, and tuberculosis resulted in mass burials. The Calvary Monument, a city-owned park tucked inside the cemetery, honors veterans of the Civil War. The tiny plot of land for the monument was purchased by the city in 1863 and reserved for Civil War veterans who died in city-run hospitals. Designed by Daniel Draddy, the 50-foot spire was dedicated in 1866, making it one of the city's earliest Civil War memorials.

Greenpoint Avenue Bridge

A half mile downstream from the site of Penny Bridge is the **Greenpoint Avenue Bridge**, known officially as the J. J. Byrne Memorial Bridge. This crossing connects Greenpoint with **Blissville**, a little-known Queens neighborhood sandwiched between Newtown Creek and the Long Island Expressway. The bascule-lift structure has a clearance of 26 feet above high tide and is a popular location for watching the Fourth of July fireworks.

The first bridge at this location was built in the 1850s by developer Neziah Bliss, whose name is preserved in the Blissville neighborhood. The current bridge was completed in 1987 and is the sixth structure to cross Newtown Creek at this location. The bridge's honorary namesake, James J. Byrne, was a lifelong civil servant whose positions included commissioner of public works and a term as the borough president of Brooklyn. He died an untimely death in 1930, and his name was assigned to the Greenpoint Avenue Bridge that same year.

Newtown Creek Wastewater Treatment Plant

The gas tanks on Newtown Creek were gone in 2001, but nine years later, eight 140-foot **digester eggs** were completed at the **Newtown Creek Wastewater Treatment Plant**, giving Greenpoint its latest recognizable industrial structure. These egg-shaped cones process the city's sludge, transforming it into useful fertilizer. At 54 acres, it is the largest of the city's 14 wastewater treatment plants. Following a renovation that employed world-class architects such as James Stewart Polshek and Vito Acconci, the facility has a visitor center and a quarter-mile **Newtown Creek Nature Walk** that features sculptures and signs detailing the natural history of Newtown Creek.

Within the campus of the plant is **Whale Creek**, an arm of Newtown Creek that once extended as far as Greenpoint Avenue and Humboldt Street. In August 1888, this inlet welcomed the Joggins raft, a massive, cigar-shaped bundle of logs transported by sea from Port Joggins, Nova Scotia, by contractor James D. Leary. The record-setting seagoing float attracted crowds throughout its 11-day voyage. It was 595 feet in length, with a girth of 150 feet and a depth of 38 feet. The great mass of logs was bound together by iron chains and steel wire.

Pulaski Bridge

The final bridge across Newtown Creek is the **Pulaski Bridge**, connecting Long Island City with Greenpoint. The bridge is the successor to the Vernon Avenue Bridge, which was located one block to its west and had a much lower clearance.

At the time of its construction, two competing bills in the City Council sparred over its name. Councilman Jeremiah T. Bloom proposed the functionalist Newtown Creek Bridge, in line with numerous other crossings around the city named after their locations and destinations. His colleague Joseph T. Sharkey proposed honoring Polish patriot Casimir Pulaski. The latter succeeded, and the bridge opened in September 1954. These days, the 2,726-foot crossing is best known as the approximate halfway point on the New York City Marathon.

At the southern approach to the former Vernon Avenue Bridge, Manhattan Avenue widens to a dead end at the shoreline. In 2009, this quiet dead end was transformed into a waterfront park that occupies the site of the long-gone bridge. In contrast to Pulaski, this green plot has a very geographic name: **Manhattan Avenue Street End Park**. Perhaps in the future it will find a more memorable namesake.

Beyond this park, Newtown Creek continues for another third of a mile before merging with the East River at Hunters Point.

PLACES TO SEE:

+ **Metropolitan Avenue Bridge** Metropolitan Avenue at Grand Street
+ **Grand Street Bridge** Grand Street crossing East Branch of Newtown Creek
+ **Kosciuszko Bridge** Brooklyn-Queens Expressway crossing Newtown Creek
+ **Site of Penny Bridge** Meeker Avenue at Newtown Creek (Brooklyn) or Review Avenue at Laurel Hill Boulevard (Queens)
+ **Calvary Cemetery** Main entrance is at Gale Avenue and Greenpoint Avenue
   ◇ **Calvary Monument** Inside Calvary Cemetery
+ **Greenpoint Avenue Bridge** Greenpoint Avenue crossing Newtown Creek
+ **Newtown Creek Wastewater Treatment Plant** 329 Greenpoint Avenue + 718-595-5140 + http://www.nyc.gov/html/dep/html/environmental_education/newtown_visitors_center.shtml
+ **Newtown Creek Nature Walk** Dead end of Paidge Avenue, near Provost Street + http://www.nyc.gov/html/dep/html/environmental_education/newtown.shtml
+ **Pulaski Bridge** Connects McGuinness Boulevard in Brooklyn with 11th Street in Queens
+ **Manhattan Avenue Street End Park** Northern dead end of Manhattan Avenue, near Ash Street

GETTING THERE:

+ **Bus**: B32, B62 for the Pulaski Bridge; B24 for the Greenpoint Avenue Bridge; Q54, Q59 for the Grand Street Bridge
+ **Subway**: G at Greenpoint Avenue, walk north on Manhattan Avenue toward Newtown Creek
+ **Bike**: There are bike lanes on Grand Street, Greenpoint Avenue, and the Pulaski Bridge

BROOKLYN

✦ **Boat**: The stream is navigable by small watercraft for nearly its entire length

64. Gowanus Canal

To the south of downtown Brooklyn, a 1.8-mile-long canal zigzags through the street grid, its seemingly lifeless water emitting a repulsive odor and a kaleidoscope of colors broken up by the slow-moving current. The **Gowanus Canal** represents the challenge of constructing an inland waterway that had no flow and is an example of early attempts to force the water to circulate in order to reduce pollution. The canal has inspired numerous books, songs, poems, and urban renewal attempts. In the 21st century, the stream is experiencing a revival as the surrounding neighborhoods are redeveloped for commercial and residential purposes and the federal government has committed funding toward cleaning up the stream.

The canal was originally a tidal inlet of Upper New York Bay, ringed by marshland that collected water from the highlands of Cobble Hill and Park Slope. Its namesake was Gouwane, a chief of the local Canarsee tribe, whose membership lived on lands between the East River and the Jamaica Bay neighborhood of Canarsie. In the 1860s, developer Edwin Litchfield straightened the creek into a canal. With its freshwater sources cut off and its route confined to the street grid, the water became less fluid, with less oxygen circulating. Runoff from oil and gas refineries killed off its marine wildlife, turning the Gowanus Canal into a toxic stew useful only to vessels docking on its shores.

The pumping station

The farthest inland point on the Gowanus Canal is the **pumping station** at 201 Butler Street. When this Beaux-Arts structure was completed on June 21, 1911, the neighborhoods of Gowanus and Cobble Hill celebrated its opening with parades and flags. Isolated from the tides of Upper New York Bay and lacking its own sources of inflow, the water of the Gowanus Canal was stagnant and had been collecting toxic matter for nearly half a century by that point.

Dubbed South Brooklyn Day, the festival included an automobile parade on land and a boat procession on the canal. It also featured Miss Gowanus—nine-year-old Jeanne T. Haviland, the daughter of the naval parade's commodore—who was chosen to drop lily petals on the water.

BROOKLYN

Brooklyn in 1766, including Gowanus Creek

Mayor William J. Gaynor greeted the girl, announcing that the "hitherto corrupt waters will now be as pure as that flower."

Beneath the pumping station is the eastern end of the **Gowanus Canal flushing tunnel,** a 12-foot-diameter conduit that runs under Degraw Street. Using an electric-powered turbine, water is pumped out of the Gowanus Canal and routed to **Buttermilk Channel**, an arm of the East River located 1.2 miles to the west. Completed three years before the Panama Canal, this tunnel was hailed as a local engineering marvel, designed to facilitate the flow of water in the Gowanus Canal. The pumping station worked until 1963, when the propeller broke down. From that point, industrial runoff and physical detritus turned the canal into a toxic stew, nicknamed "Lavender Lake" by locals. It took nearly four decades to restore it to service.

The pumping station and its tunnel were repaired in 1999, with the flow reversed—now water from Buttermilk Channel is directed into the Gowanus Canal. This change created a flowing current in the canal, but after decades of pollution, a layer of muck had settled on its bottom, continuing to deter a full revival of local marine wildlife.

Wildlife in the canal

Following the passage of the Clean Water Act in 1972 and the decline of industry along the city's shores, native marine plants and wildlife began to reappear in the water throughout New York City. But in the Gowanus Canal, the water can still be fatal.

The Gowanus Canal in 2014

In April 2003, a harp seal was swept into the canal and emerged on shore covered in blood, with lesions on its flipper. The seal was rescued by the Riverhead Foundation for Marine Research and released into the Long Island Sound. In April 2007, a 12-foot minke whale nicknamed Sludgie was separated from its mother in New York Harbor and ended up in the canal. It died after hitting submerged rocks. And in January 2013, a 7-foot dolphin attracted crowds of onlookers who prayed for its safety as it navigated the murky water in search of food. For eight hours, the struggling cetacean had the world's attention. Following its death, a necropsy found that the dolphin was at an advanced age with multiple illnesses before it ended up in Gowanus Canal.

In the early colonial period, the stream was known as Gowanus Creek and was valued by local settlers for its bivalve oysters. They were harvested in abundance and shipped to the markets in Manhattan for consumption. Along with oysters, other native wildlife that have returned to the canal include white perch, herring, striped bass, crabs, jellyfish, and anchovies. However, creatures living in the canal have a much lower life expectancy and greater difficulty finding food than those in the harbor.

Union Street Bridge

There are seven bridges spanning the stream, including a rare retractile bridge and the city's highest subway viaduct. From the canal's headwaters to its mouth, the bridges increase in length and traffic capacity.

The **Union Street Bridge** is a bascule lift completed in 1905. On its

BROOKLYN

eastern bank, 543 Union Street is a former packing box factory repurposed as an art exhibition space. On the western bank, a former automobile repair shop at 501 Union Street has been repurposed as a private event space called **501 Union**. At the corner with Bond Street, a former brass foundry has also been transformed into an event space. Between the two venues, **Showroom Gowanus** exhibits artworks in a similar industrial space that retains most of its original appearance.

Carroll Street Bridge

The oldest bridge crossing the Gowanus Canal, **Carroll Street Bridge**, is also the oldest of the four surviving retractile bridges in the United States. Such bridges have rails on the shore that move the bridge away from water to allow vessels to pass. In 1888, the wooden span at this location had become too dangerous for vehicles and was slated for replacement. George Ingram and Robert Van Buren, the chief engineer of the Brooklyn Department of City Works, designed the retractile crossing in its place. It functioned continuously until 1986 when maintenance issues forced the city to keep it in the open position. Prior to its closing, the bridge had a cameo appearance in the 1985 comedy film *Heaven Help Us*. In 1989, the bridge reopened in a restored appearance that includes Belgian block pavement on either side, an antique lamppost, and a regulation sign. It reads: "Any person driving over this bridge faster than a walk will be subject to a penalty of five dollars for each offence." When this rule was instituted, horse carriages traveled across the span. The penalty is not enforced but the sign remains as a nod to the bridge's history.

The bridge is an official city landmark, its preservation enshrined by city law. Among other superlatives that it enjoys is that it is the last bridge in the city that has a wooden deck on which automobiles travel. On the western side of the Carroll Street Bridge is Lavender Lake, a bar that takes the canal's pejorative name and revels in its neighborhood's industrial past.

The namesake of Carroll Street and the nearby Carroll Gardens neighborhood is Charles Carroll, a signer of the Declaration of Independence representing Maryland. Because his state's regiment played a key role in the Battle of Long Island, Carroll was put on the map of Brooklyn.

Fourth Street Basin

Gowanus Canal had a branch, the **First Street Basin**, that provided coal to a **Brooklyn Rapid Transit power station** on its western bank. The power station is currently awaiting renovation ahead of its new role as an art venue. Three blocks south, **Third Street Bridge** is identical to the Union Street Bridge in its design and age.

Another 200 feet to the south of this bridge, the Gowanus Canal splits in two, with the main branch continuing toward the harbor and the **Fourth Street Basin** branching off to the east. On the northern side of this basin is the **Third and 3rd Whole Foods**, the local branch of the upscale food retailer named for its location at the intersection of Third Street and Third Avenue. Located on a former brownfield site, it took many years of cleaning up and regulatory approval before the store opened its doors in December 2013. The first Whole Foods in Brooklyn, this location features several unique characteristics designed for local audiences: an enclosed rooftop greenhouse that grows the store's vegetables, a rooftop beer hall, an outdoor restaurant, and a walkway that overlooks the Fourth Street Basin.

Until the mid-20th century, this inlet extended toward Fourth Avenue on the edge of Park Slope. In colonial times, it was Denton's Mill Pond, which was fed by **Vechte's Brook**. Its namesake, the Vechte family, was a Dutch family who lived nearby; their house, today known as the Old Stone House, has a history rooted in the American Revolution.

Revolutionary battle site

The earliest colonists built farmhouses along the inlet's shore and harvested its oysters, sending the seafood to markets in Manhattan. One of these farmhouses is the Vechte-Cortelyou House, better known as the **Old Stone House**. The structure is a replica of a 1699 farmhouse that was demolished in 1897 and lovingly restored three decades later. It is the centerpiece of **Washington Park**, a playground that occupies a portion of the vast field on which the Battle of Long Island took place.

The house originally stood next to a tributary stream that was later named the Fourth Street Basin. At this location, a key confrontation in the Battle of Long Island took place. Splitting up his troops between the passes of Gowanus, Flatbush, Bedford, and Jamaica, British General William Howe ordered his top planner, General James Grant, to march toward the Old Stone House. Grant's force was met by the 1st Maryland Regiment, led by General William Alexander, a patriot who also went by his self-declared nobility title Lord Stirling.

With the British and Hessian forces outflanking the patriot line at Gowanus, George Washington ordered a retreat, with a rear guard of about 270 men remaining to stall the British advance. Outgunned and outnumbered, Lord Stirling was taken prisoner along with his troops. Those who tried to retreat found themselves bogged down in the marshes of Gowanus Creek, and they were either killed by musket fire or captured alive. Only a few dozen men succeeded in crossing the stream and reuniting with Washington's main force. In this bloodbath, 256 of the Maryland Regiment were killed and buried by local residents, who were drafted by the British for the task. Their precise burial site remains hidden; historians are determined to find the bones in the hope of designating the site as a memorial.

Stirling survived his captivity and was released in a prisoner exchange six months after the battle. He is remembered in **William Alexander Middle School 51**, which adjoins Washington Park.

The Old Stone House enjoyed a long postwar history linked with prominent Brooklyn individuals and institutions. Edwin Litchfield purchased it from the Cortelyou family in 1852 as a real estate investment. Litchfield's other prominent holding included the future Prospect Park. In 1883, the Brooklyn Dodgers baseball team established Washington Park on the property, with the historic structure serving as its clubhouse. The Dodgers departed for Ebbets Field in 1913, and the Washington Park stadium was demolished within two years. Its name was retained for the parkland surrounding the Old Stone House.

The industrial landscape

The transformation of Gowanus Creek into a canal began in 1847, when Major David B. Douglass proposed to straighten the creek and fill in the surrounding marshes. Part of Douglass's plan included tidal basins at the head of the canal to ensure a current. The basins were never built—an oversight that later resulted in the pollution of the canal.

Following the Civil War, the Gowanus Canal Improvement Commission carved a 6,000-foot channel from Douglass Street to Percival Street and constructed the first bridges across the stream. Litchfield led the Brooklyn Improvement Company, which carved out basins that branched off from the canal.

At Ninth Street, two bridges cross over the Gowanus Canal—one carrying Ninth Street and, above it, the other carrying the highest subway station in the city. The **Ninth Street Bridge** is a nondescript lift bridge that was completed in 1999 as a replacement for an older bascule drawbridge at the same location. It is overshadowed by the **Culver Viaduct**, a short section of the Culver subway line that rises out of the ground in Carroll Gardens, running over the Gowanus Canal before dipping beneath the surface in Park Slope.

At the viaduct's highest point is the **Smith–Ninth Streets station** on the F and G lines, the only station in the city that sits atop a waterway. At 87.5 feet above street level, it is the highest subway station in the world, providing excellent views of downtown Manhattan and the Statue of Liberty.

The station is a rarity among the IND or Independent City-Owned stations, which were built between 1925 and 1937, because it was built aboveground. The steep dip in topography between Cobble Hill and Park Slope made a tunnel impractical, and a viaduct had to be high enough to permit tall ships to pass underneath, in accordance with federal regulations. Unlike the city's older, privately built elevated stations, the Culver Viaduct is almost entirely clad in concrete, with little architectural embellishment.

Following a renovation of the viaduct in 2013, the Smith–Ninth Streets station was included in the MTA Art for Transit program where Red Hook–based artist Alyson Shotz installed etched-glass panels in the station's 26 windows that carry images of old nautical maps of New York Harbor. The collection is titled *Nautical Charts—Gowanus & Red Hook from 1733–1922.*

Paralleling the Culver Viaduct is the **Brooklyn-Queens Expressway**, a ribbon of concrete that runs through all five of the city's boroughs under the designation of Interstate 278. The road is part of an ambitious beltway design by urban planner Robert Moses that connects to the Belt Parkway and the Cross Island Parkway. At the Gowanus Canal, the expressway is at its widest point, absorbing the traffic of the Prospect Expressway, Brooklyn-Battery Tunnel, and Gowanus Expressway. The bridge rises steeply above the canal and, similar to the Culver Viaduct, it towers over a bascule twin drawbridge. The outermost of the crossings over the waterway, the **Hamilton Avenue Bridge** has its control tower between its twin roadways and neon-like lights on each side serving as beacons for boats.

Beyond the Hamilton Avenue Bridge, the Gowanus Canal widens into the Gowanus Bay, part of the larger Upper New York Bay, also known as the New York Harbor. On the western side of the bay is a massive abandoned structure towering over ball fields and vacant docks. Unused since 1965, the **New York State Barge Canal Grain Elevator** looms above the landscape with 54 concrete grain silos, each 90 feet tall;

BROOKLYN

the terminal stretches 430 feet long. The structure was the last in a series
of grain silos that brought grain by barge from Midwestern terminals.

At the time of its construction, the Erie Canal system was in decline
as railroads became the primary mode of transporting grain. Constructing a waterfront grain silo failed to reinvigorate the state-owned canal.
When the structure opened on September 1, 1922, Governor Nathan
Miller recognized that the building would not fulfill its purpose. "Even
if the barge canal were never used in normal times, it is a good thing to
have it in case of emergencies," he said.

The structure was bought by concrete executive John Quadrozzi Jr. in
1997 in a failed bid to turn the grain silo into a concrete plant. Over the
half century of its abandonment, the structure has been used as rooftop
sunning deck, graffiti wall, and concert venue, among other illicit uses.

PLACES TO SEE:
+ **Carroll Street Bridge** Carroll Street between Nevins Street and
  Bond Street
+ **Old Stone House** 336 Third Street ✦ 718-768-3195 ✦ www.theold
  stonehouse.org
+ **Third and 3rd Whole Foods** 214 Third Street ✦ 718-907-3622 ✦
  www.wholefoodsmarket.com/stores/brooklyn
+ **501 Union** 501 Union Street ✦ 347-529-6486 ✦ www.501union
  .com
+ **Smith–Ninth Streets station** Smith Street at Ninth Street
+ **Hamilton Avenue Bridge** Hamilton Avenue between Hamilton
  Place and Smith Street

GETTING THERE:
+ **Bus**: B37 on Third Avenue at either Third Street or Degraw Street,
  walk west toward the Gowanus Canal on either of these streets
+ **Subway**: 2, 3, 4, 5, B, D, N, Q, R at Atlantic Avenue–Barclays
  Center, transfer to B37; F, G at Smith–Ninth Streets, walk down-
  stairs to the stream
+ **Bike**: There are bike lanes on Smith Street, Third Avenue, Union
  Street, Third Street, and Ninth Street
+ **Boat**: The stream is navigable for small watercraft for nearly its
  entire length; Hamilton Avenue Bridge has a vertical clearance of
  19 feet above mean high water in its closed position

BROOKLYN

65. Bushwick Creek

Prior to development, the lands that became the neighborhoods of Williamsburg and Greenpoint were separated by **Bushwick Creek**, an inlet of the East River that is undergoing a partial restoration as its industrial shoreline is rezoned for parkland and high-density residential structures.

Since the late 19th century, the remaining portion of this stream has been known as Bushwick Inlet, an indentation of the East River that extends for nearly 1,000 feet inland between the neighborhoods of Williamsburg and Greenpoint. The present-day neighborhood of Bushwick is located more than a mile to the east of this inlet. In 1683, Bushwick was one of the six original townships that were designated within Kings County. The most populated of these, Breukelen, which was anglicized as Brooklyn, had annexed the other five towns by 1896. At that point in time, Brooklyn and Kings County became coterminous.

Colonial farms

The stream originated in two sources—one to the south of McCarren Park and another within the site of the park. The branches merged and widened into a salt marsh that flowed toward the East River. Settled during the Dutch rule of the region, Bushwick is the anglicized name of the Dutch name Boswijck, meaning "little town in the woods" or "heavy woods." Land for the town was acquired from the native Lenape residents in 1638, with Dirck Volkertsen de Noorman and his wife Christina Vigne setting up the first farm in 1645. The couple exemplified the diverse immigrant population of New Netherland, as the husband was Norwegian and his wife was Walloon. The stream that ran through the farm was informally known as Noorman's Kil in its early years. The original name can still be found on the map as **Noorman's Kil**, a historical-themed tavern located at 609 Grand Street. The farm is believed to have stood on the northern shore of Bushwick Creek, at the present-day corner of Franklin and Calyer Streets.

Industry along the stream

The East River shoreline of Greenpoint and Williamsburgh was known in colonial times as the Strand—an antiquated term for beach—where Brooklyn farmers transported their produce to the markets of Manhattan. Toward the middle of the 19th century, the inland sections of

Bushwick Creek

Bushwick Creek were filled, while industries were established along the area closer to the creek's mouth. The section near the East River served as a harbor for oil tankers docking at **Astral Oil Works**. Established by Charles Pratt in 1857, the docking site remained in use into the early 21st century, when it was rezoned for parkland. A prominent name on the Brooklyn landscape, the oil millionaire founded **Pratt Institute**, an art, architecture, and engineering college located in the Clinton Hill neighborhood. Closer to Bushwick Creek, Pratt financed the **Astral Apartments**, located at 184 Franklin Street, a historic residence built for his company's workers.

In Civil War history, Bushwick Creek was the launch site of the USS *Monitor*, the first ironclad warship in the United States, which was constructed in 101 days in 1862 at the **Continental Iron Works**. The construction of the vessel took place in the midst of an arms race against the Confederate Navy, which retrofitted the *Merrimack* into the ironclad *Virginia*, threatening the northern blockade effort. Shipbuilding at Bushwick Inlet ceased by 1889, but on the local landscape there are four reminders of the legendary vessel: Monitor Street in Greenpoint; a monument to the ship in McGolrick Park; a monument in Manhattan's Battery Park for the ship's inventor, John Ericsson; and the naming of John Ericsson Middle School 126 in Greenpoint.

In 1839, Kent Avenue was extended over the creek, and wetlands to the east of this bridge were filled in the following decades. Between 1903 and 1905, the city acquired 42 acres of marshland to the east of Kent Avenue for Greenpoint Park, which was renamed and developed as **McCarren Park** in 1909. Its namesake is Senator Patrick McCarren, who lived in Brooklyn and died in 1909.

Throughout its history, Bushwick Inlet has seen its share of sensational stories related to its use as a dock. On September 26, 1893, a herd of dehydrated Texas steer bound for a Williamsburg slaughterhouse spilled across the railing at Kent Avenue "into the ooze and mud of Bushwick Creek, where their frantic struggles only mired them the deeper." The timing was fortunate—the steer avoided drowning by the tide going out. The animals' handlers fed them fresh water in buckets and extricated them from the mud. In all likelihood, the steer probably ended up becoming someone's dinner. In more recent times, when livestock escape their date with the butcher, society tends to be more sympathetic by sending the lucky creatures to a farm or petting zoo.

During Prohibition, the coves and inlets of New York served the rumrunners who delivered their cargo under the cover of night to eager consumers. On August 16, 1924, the police impounded bootlegger tugboat *Lorraine Rita* at Bushwick Creek. The tug was described by authorities as "one of the most annoying rum runners entering the harbor." It carried a cargo of champagne, scotch, and rye whiskey estimated at $250,000. Previously known as the *Albatross*, the ship was destined for the scrapyard but somehow ended up in the hands of smugglers.

History highlighted

Toward the last decade of the 20th century, the once-booming waterfront of Brooklyn fell silent as seagoing vessels relocated to Port Newark and factories moved to other states and countries. While oil tanks remained active on the southern side of Bushwick Inlet, the rest of the shoreline was unused and awaiting ambitious proposals for reuse.

Seeking to reimagine the stream as a historical park honoring the USS *Monitor*, Greenpoint couple George J. Weinmann and Janice Lauletta-Weinmann spent nearly two decades gathering artifacts and documents for their dream, the **Greenpoint Monitor Museum**. The land on which the museum is proposed was the site of Continental Iron Works, last used as an oil storage facility. For Mr. Weinmann, the cause is very personal. His ancestor was an assistant surgeon aboard the ship and survived its sinking off Cape Hatteras. In 2003, the oil company Motiva Enterprises, a partnership of Shell Oil and Saudi Refining, offered an acre of its land between Bushwick Inlet and Quay Street for the museum.

The Weinmanns' dream lacked funding, in part due to a conflict with the city's Parks Department, which is acquiring waterfront parcels between Bushwick Creek and Newtown Creek for a 28-acre park. The museum is instead chartered by the state and operates as a traveling exhibit.

Although the city differs with the museum on where the facility will be located, it promises to incorporate the *Monitor* into the design of the park.

Future of the stream

The design of Bushwick Inlet Park promises a naturalistic appearance of the shoreline with wetlands, a beach, and riprap in the place of rotting piers and a crumbling bulkhead. As land values along the shore increase, the process of acquiring land will take longer than expected, and the final park may not be as ambitious as the one proposed on paper. Along with a soft shoreline, the placing of a kayak launch will ensure public access to a stream that for much of the past century has been guarded by fences and industry. To the south of Bushwick Inlet, the state is providing assistance in acquiring land along the waterfront with the seven-acre East River State Park abutting the unfinished Bushwick Inlet Park.

PLACES TO SEE:

+ **East River State Park** Kent Street and North Ninth Street + nys parks.com/parks/155/details.aspx
+ **McCarren Park** Bound by Nassau Avenue, North 12th Street, Bayard Street, Lorimer Street, and Manhattan Avenue + www.nyc govparks.org/parks/mccarren-park
+ **Noorman's Kil** 609 Grand Street + 347-384-2526 + www.noor manskil.com

GETTING THERE:

+ **Bus**: B32 at Franklin Street and Meserole Avenue
+ **Subway**: J, M, Z at Marcy Avenue, walk to Williamsburg Bridge Plaza for B32
+ **Bike**: There are bike lanes on Kent Avenue and Franklin Street
+ **Boat**: The inlet is navigable for small watercraft

BROOKLYN

66. Wallabout Creek

A half mile to the south of the Williamsburg Bridge, the East River makes a turn to the southwest with a wide cove at this knee-shaped bend. Known as **Wallabout Bay**, it was the site of a notorious floating prison during the Revolutionary War; the Brooklyn Navy Yard still stands there today. At the northwestern corner of this property, a deep channel cuts inland as the only remnant of **Wallabout Creek**. The stream's name is an English corruption of *Waal boght*, meaning "Walloon bay," after Walloon settlers who immigrated to New Netherland in the 1630s. This French-speaking Protestant community originated from Belgium, leaving their homeland in search of religious freedom. The first Walloon to settle near this stream was Joris Jansen de Rapalje in 1637. Spelling variations on his last name include Rapalle, Rapalye, and Rapelye.

Rapalje purchased a 335-acre tract called Rennegachonk from the local natives and established a farm on the site. This bay was soon renamed Wallabout Bay. Rapalje's descendants owned the land until 1781. The creek that ran across the farm originated nearly a mile inland, following a path that is the present-day Wallabout Street.

Wartime prison

When the United States declared independence in July 1776, New Yorkers supporting the revolution hastily set up fortifications on hilltops overlooking the harbor. In Brooklyn, a chain of defenses was set up between the headwaters of Gowanus Creek and Wallabout Bay that turned downtown Brooklyn and Brooklyn Heights into a redoubt. The only one of the four forts whose name is present on today's maps is **Fort Greene**, which lent its name to a neighborhood and a hilltop park overlooking the bay.

On August 22, 1776, British warships landed at Gravesend Bay, and the redcoats marched north toward Brooklyn. Splitting into three prongs, the imperial forces engaged the patriots on three approaches to the town: Gowanus Road, Flatbush Road, and Bedford Road, which respectively today are **Green-Wood Cemetery**, **Prospect Park**, and **Crown Heights**. The battle slowed the British advance enough to allow George Washington and 9,000 men to flee Brooklyn under the cover of a nightly fog on August 29.

For the remainder of the Revolutionary War, Brooklyn remained

BROOKLYN

firmly in British control. Wallabout Bay was transformed into a floating prison colony with at least 16 prison ships holding thousands of American prisoners. The most notorious of these ships was the HMS *Jersey*, a former warship that was officially a hospital ship but was known to its inmates as "Hell." Over the course of the war, more than 11,000 prisoners died aboard these ships—more than in all the battles combined. The dead were unceremoniously buried in shallow graves on the shoreline mudflats. Survivor Christopher Vail wrote that the death rate was eight people per day.

After the war, the ship was burned and sank to the bottom of the bay. It was rediscovered in October 1902 during construction on a new dock. The remains of the prisoners were exhumed in 1808 by Benjamin Romaine and the Tammany Society, a political club that later monopolized New York's leadership. A humble monument was built in nearby **Vinegar Hill** to hold the remains. A century later, they were again uncovered and transferred to the summit of Fort Greene Park, reburied beneath the **Prison Ship Martyrs' Monument**.

Designed by architect Stanford White, the 149-foot monument was the world's tallest Doric column at the time of its completion, topped with a 22.5-foot-tall funerary urn by sculptor Adolph Alexander Weinman. The urn is lit by an "eternal flame" that has been solar powered since 1997.

Brooklyn Navy Yard

After the Revolutionary War, Wallabout Bay remained an underused corner on the otherwise busy East River. Change arrived in 1801, when the federal government purchased land around the bay for the New York Naval Shipyard, better known as the **Brooklyn Navy Yard**. From 1806 until 1966, it designed some of the country's most famous warships. The Navy Yard reshaped the contour of Wallabout Bay, filling in the marshes around its shore and building dry docks for the construction of warships.

In the center of Wallabout Bay, ballast was deposited by merchant ships, forming two fan-shaped islands, **Cob Dock** and **Ordnance Dock**, which were later fused together. *Harper's New Monthly Magazine* in 1870 reported that the island was completed in 1866, at a cost of $1.9 million. Cob Dock was connected to the mainland by a ferry. By the mid-20th century, the growing size of the ships built in the dry docks required the partial dismantling of Cob Dock. Its northern third was fused to the mainland and reshaped into an elongated pier that separated Wallabout Bay from Wallabout Channel, a remnant of the creek.

Following the Second World War, the Brooklyn Navy Yard became obsolete, as Cold War–period battleships were too tall to pass beneath the Brooklyn Bridge. In 1966, the navy divested itself of the site, and it became an industrial park whose tenants included shipbuilders, construction companies, warehouses and, most recently, the **Steiner Studios**. Founded in 2004, it is the largest film studio in the United States outside of California. Since its opening, the studio complex has grown to occupy nearly 10 percent of the Navy Yard's territory. The studio is located near the southern side of Wallabout Channel with its parking lot situated atop the filled streambed.

Although most of the Brooklyn Navy Yard remains off-limits to the public, sections of it are opening up to those interested in learning about the film industry and the history of the site. Since 2011, Building 92 has been open to the public as the **Brooklyn Navy Yard Center**, where visitors can learn about Wallabout Bay's use as a Revolutionary War–era prison, a naval shipyard, and an industrial park.

At the mouth of Wallabout Channel, the condominium development **Schaefer Landing** includes a waterfront park and dock for the East River Ferry. The development is named after the beer brand that operated a brewery at this site from 1915 to 1976, the last of the pre-Prohibition breweries to operate in Brooklyn. Beer making in Brooklyn resumed in 1996, when Brooklyn Brewery opened its facility in northern Williamsburg to plenty of fanfare as a symbol of the borough's revival.

With small businesses booming in Williamsburg and the ever-rising popularity of neighborhood markets, another possible historical institution that could reappear on the map would be the Wallabout Market, a wholesale and retail hub that operated at the southeast corner of the Brooklyn Navy Yard from 1884 to 1941. It was located in a Dutch Revival structure designed by William Tubby that was demolished when the market closed.

As the Brooklyn Navy Yard gradually opens to the public and residential buildings are developed on its eastern periphery, it is likely that in the future, the Wallabout Channel could be redeveloped as a centerpiece of a new neighborhood with parkland along the shoreline. Boat landings and kayak launches could transform this navigable waterway for public use.

BROOKLYN

PLACES TO SEE:
+ **Steiner Studios** 15 Washington Avenue + 718-858-1600 + www
  .steinerstudios.com

+ **BLDG92 Brooklyn Navy Yard Center** ✦ 63 Flushing Avenue ✦ 718-907-5992 ✦ www.bldg92.org

+ **Bus**: B67 at Clymer Street and Kent Avenue; B62 at Wythe Avenue and Clymer Street
+ **Subway**: A, C, F at Jay Street–MetroTech, transfer to B67 or B62
+ **Bike**: There are bike lanes on Kent Avenue and Flushing Avenue
+ **Boat**: The stream is navigable by small watercraft for nearly its entire length

67. Coney Island Creek

The eastern seaboard of the United States has a relatively uniform appearance between Cape Cod and Key West: a coastal plain lined with barrier islands, shaped by waves and constantly shifting in dimension. Examples of these natural coastal barriers include Fire Island, Jones Beach, and the Rockaway Peninsula. At the southern tip of Brooklyn, Coney Island was originally an island, separated from the rest of Brooklyn by **Coney Island Creek**. As Coney Island developed into a waterfront summer resort followed by a year-round urban community, the inlet and its accompanying wetlands were gradually filled, and the island was fused to the mainland.

Only two portions of the tidal stream remain. On its eastern end, a mile-long inlet carries the name Sheepshead Bay. On the western side of Coney Island, a polluted stub of Coney Island Creek emerges beneath the intersection of Shore Parkway and Shell Road and takes a winding route toward Gravesend Bay. While the ocean-facing side of Coney Island is known worldwide for its amusement district, the stream that once separated the island from mainland Brooklyn is known only to a few urban explorers.

In 1937, the section of Coney Island Creek between Shell Road and Sheepshead Bay was filled, with the Belt Parkway running atop the former waterway. With just seven roads crossing the highway, the neighborhood of Brighton Beach seems as cut off from mainland Brooklyn by the Belt Parkway as it was when there was a stream on the road's path.

Prior to the 1840s, land around Coney Island Creek was devoid of settlement, as it was too distant from freshwater and subject to storm surge flooding. The native Canarsee tribe combed the beach for clams, whose meat they ate and whose shells they used as currency. Their name for Coney Island was Narrioch, "the place where there are no shadows," as sunlight always shone on the south-facing island. With its outlying location, it was the first place in New York City where European explorers dropped anchor.

In tracing the path of Coney Island Creek, an ideal starting point would be **Shell Road**, a thoroughfare built as a toll road in 1829 that was paved with discarded seashells in the 19th century and placed under the shadow of the elevated Culver Line in 1919. Prior to that, a surface railway ran on Shell Road between Green-Wood Cemetery and Coney Island. Both the railway and the subway line, presently used by the F train, connected downtown Brooklyn with the beach resorts of Sea Gate, Coney Island, Brighton Beach, and Manhattan Beach.

The subway station closest to this location is the **Neptune Avenue station**, known prior to 1995 as Neptune Avenue–Van Sicklen. The earlier name was derived from a family that owned land and a hotel near the station when it was built. Their name appears on the map in other parts of New York, as the family dates back to the New Netherland colony.

From this location, Coney Island Creek turns southwest, then northwest. Its southern bank is lined with parking facilities that turn their backs to the stream.

On the northern bank is a former landfill that is part of **Coney Island Yard**, the largest rail yard in the city's subway system. In contrast to most of the city's subway lines, which are named after the streets, lines terminating at Coney Island carry historical weight, with names of railroad developers and long-defunct hotels. The lines served by this yard are the West End, Sea Beach, Culver, and Brighton Lines.

By 1920, these four railway lines were incorporated into the subway system, all ending at the **Coney Island–Stillwell Avenue terminal**. The massive station underwent a reconstruction between 2001 and 2005 that resulted in a European-style makeover, featuring public artwork, a soaring arched ceiling covered with solar panels, and architecture that hints at the historical amusement parks of Coney Island. The terminal is located a quarter mile to the south of the **Stillwell Avenue Bridge**, which crosses the creek. A quarter mile to the west, the final bridge over Coney Island Creek carries Cropsey Avenue across a bascule lift structure that probably has not been opened in decades.

On the northern side of the creek beyond Cropsey Avenue, auto

BROOKLYN

repair shops stand side by side with remnants of **White Sands**, a bungalow colony dating to the late 1920s, on the land that is today sandwiched
between Coney Island Creek and the Belt Parkway. It was regarded as
one of the city's least-known neighborhoods. The construction of the
highway followed by a devastating hurricane in 1938 further reduced
the tiny enclave.

In 2000, 41 of the community's 68 homes were demolished to make
way for a 130,000-square-foot Home Depot megastore. The process of
acquiring 13.75 acres of the neighborhood took six years for the country's largest home improvement retailer. In exchange for securing the
approval of the City Council, Home Depot constructed a pedestrian
walkway along the shoreline of Coney Island Creek, providing public
access to the waterfront.

Home Depot's walkway passes by sunken hulls of small boats that
surround a metal conning tower from a **yellow submarine** constructed
by White Sands resident Jerry Bianco. In 1970, the 45-foot vessel was
launched with the mission of salvaging the sunken cruise ship *Andrea
Doria*. Lacking a substantial amount of ballast, the *Quester* I keeled to
the side and settled on the shallow bottom of the creek. Since then,
the yellow paint has peeled off, but it remains an unofficial landmark of
Coney Island Creek.

Beyond the submarine, Coney Island Creek widens into Gravesend
Bay. At the south side of the mouth of the creek is **Kaiser Park**. It was
named in memory of Leon S. Kaiser, a beloved principal at **Mark Twain
Junior High School**, who died in 1951. Across from Kaiser Park, on the
north side of the creek, is **Calvert Vaux Park**, named after the legendary
landscape architect who drowned at this location in 1895. The 85-acre
park is sited on reclaimed land constructed from soil excavated during
construction of the Verrazano-Narrows Bridge.

Following a devastating storm surge caused by Hurricane Sandy in
October 2012, the city published a resiliency plan for its shoreline communities. Among the proposals in the report is a tide gate for Coney
Island Creek, to be located between Kaiser and Calvert Vaux Parks.
Renderings of the structure show restored wetlands along the creek, with
additional pedestrian trails crossing a lush marshland. As it appears, the
plan would expand parkland, restore a natural habitat, and protect properties along a stream that has long been neglected, overshadowed in the
public consciousness by the ocean-facing side of Coney Island.

BROOKLYN

+ **Cropsey Avenue Bridge** Cropsey Avenue crossing Coney Island Creek
+ **Home Depot waterfront promenade** 2970 Cropsey Avenue
+ **Calvert Vaux Park** Shore Parkway between Bay 44th Street and Bay 49th Street
+ **Kaiser Park** Neptune Avenue and Bayview Avenue between West 23rd Street and West 32st Street
+ **Coney Island Creek Park** Bayview Avenue between Sea Gate Avenue and West 33rd Street

+ **Bus**: B82 at Cropsey Avenue and Hart Place
+ **Subway**: D, F, N, Q to Coney Island–Stillwell Avenue, walk north on Stillwell Avenue toward Coney Island Creek
+ **Bike**: There are bike lanes on Cropsey Avenue and Neptune Avenue
+ **Boat**: Coney Island Creek is navigable up to Cropsey Avenue Bridge

68. Sheepshead Bay

To many of the recent Russian residents of southern Brooklyn, **Sheepshead Bay** is known affectionately as "the canal," based on its firm bulkhead shoreline. This inlet separates the waterfront seafood restaurants of the Sheepshead Bay neighborhood to its north from the pricey neighborhood of Manhattan Beach to its south. Prior to the early 20th century, this bay was the eastern section of Coney Island Creek that separated Coney Island from the mainland of Brooklyn. In colonial times, the bay was known as "the Cove" and was fed by Squan, Hubbard, and Williams Creeks. All three of these tributaries have long been buried beneath the street grid. The last remaining one, Squan Creek, followed Sheepshead Bay Road until it was filled in the 1920s. Its name is derived from a species of fish that can be found along the Eastern Seaboard.

Head of the bay
At the head of Sheepshead Bay is **Holocaust Memorial Park**, a nod to the sizable Jewish community in Brooklyn. Inside the city's first public memorial to this genocide, a sculpture resembling a lighthouse eternally shines at the midpoint of the bay.

BROOKLYN

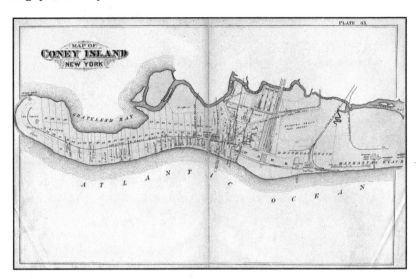

Sheepshead Bay

Proposed by the locally based Holocaust Memorial Committee, the memorial was designated in 1986 and dedicated on June 22, 1997, by Mayor Rudolph Giuliani. The date coincided with the 56th anniversary of the Nazi invasion of the Soviet Union; many of the attendees at the event were born in the Soviet Union.

Landscape architect George Vellonakis designed the memorial's central structure: a tower of granite, exposed steel, and bronze that appears as a lighthouse from a distance. A closer view reveals a steel frame with bricks on the bottom, reminiscent of a death camp smokestack. Surrounding this tower are memorial stones listing the camps, ghettoes, and massacre sites of the Holocaust.

The northern side of Sheepshead Bay is paralleled by Emmons Avenue, where seafood restaurants and fishing boats maintain the neighborhood's maritime identity. The best-known example of Sheepshead Bay's seafood culture is the **Lundy Brothers Restaurant** at 1901 Emmons Avenue. Completed in 1934, this official city landmark once seated over 2,400 patrons. The original restaurant closed after the death of founder Frederick William Irving Lundy in 1977. From that point, it fell into disrepair, though Brooklynites lamented losing this beloved institution. The Spanish Colonial Revival building was designated a city landmark in 1989 and now contains smaller restaurants, shops, and offices.

Ocean Avenue Footbridge

After the Wards Island Bridge in Manhattan, the second-longest pedestrian-only crossing in New York City is the **Ocean Avenue Footbridge**, which connects the Sheepshead Bay and Manhattan Beach neighborhoods. The first bridge on this site was built in 1880, when Long Island Railroad executive Austin Corbin wanted a footbridge to connect the mainland with his Manhattan Beach Hotel. At the time, Manhattan Beach was part of an island landmass that also included the present-day neighborhoods of Coney Island, Sea Gate, and Brighton Beach.

That same year, the Oriental Hotel was built on Manhattan Beach. By contrast, across the water on the mainland side, the construction of the Sheepshead Bay Racecourse brought gambling and lower-class hotels to the area. Seeking to preserve the elite atmosphere of Manhattan Beach, Corbin attempted to demolish the bridge in order to keep out Jews and other minorities. The town of Gravesend argued that the privately built bridge was a public highway. Corbin sent workers to demolish the bridge anyway, but Gravesend had it rebuilt. In 1881, New York's Commission of Highways ruled that the bridge was a public highway, and the Supreme Court issued an injunction against its demolition.

Since then, it has remained a charming and unchanged feature of Sheepshead Bay, even as the waterway was reduced to a bulkhead-lined inlet.

Sheepshead Bay Piers

Prior to 1934, **Emmons Avenue** had the appearance of a racing resort turned fishing village, with bait-and-tackle shops sharing the street with yacht clubs and seafood restaurants. Sheepshead Bay was by then only an inlet of the ocean; earlier plans for a Coney Island canal had been discontinued in the face of development, and instead the Belt Parkway was being constructed along the streambed.

In the following three years, the city reshaped the bay's shoreline by constructing a bulkhead on all of its shores, moving all structures along the Emmons Avenue waterfront to the west of East 27th Street, and constructing 10 piers on Emmons Avenue to serve fishing and excursion boats. The widening of Emmons Avenue resulted in a payout of $1,618,114 to the owners of 546 parcels along the avenue's path.

In 1990, the city installed art designed by artist Scott Burton on the piers. His project added weathervanes at the tip of each pier and medallions of local fish pressed into the sidewalk at the pier entrances.

BROOKLYN

For example, Pier 1 is marked with an image of a fluke, and Pier 10 is marked with a horseshoe crab.

Near Pier 1 is **Driscoll Tucker Place**, an extension of East 27th Street that was transformed into a minipark in 1953. This sitting area affords views of the bay at the point where the shoreline switches from piers to private properties. The park's namesake, Driscoll Tucker, was a local political and civic activist who died in 1945. In his time as a leader, he was known as the "Mayor of Sheepshead Bay."

Boat clubs and bungalows

Farther east on Emmons Avenue are the clubhouses of the bay's four remaining yacht clubs, each of which has a long history in Brooklyn.

Varuna Boat Club was originally located in Bay Ridge. It had its first regatta in 1875 and was incorporated in 1877. The house where it is presently headquartered is a remnant of a much larger community from the late 19th century known as Millionaire's Row, where wealthy businessmen established their summer homes along Emmons Avenue. The Varuna house is the former residence of the Froeb family, who made their money in liquors.

The nearby **Sheepshead Bay Yacht Club** has its headquarters at the former summer vacation home of Albert and Julius Liebmann of Rheingold Brewery. **Miramar Yacht Club** dates back to 1938 and had 93 members in 1998, according to its then commodore John Tesoriero. Finally, the **Baron DeKalb Knights of Columbus** chapter was founded in 1906, taking the name of a German-born French officer who supported the patriots in the American Revolution. DeKalb's name also appears on a prominent street in central Brooklyn.

Farther east on Emmons Avenue is **Webers Court**, a pedestrian lane sandwiched between bungalow residences on the water's edge. In the 1920s, the former racetrack resort community attracted middle-class vacationers as a result of improved subway and trolley connections.

At Ford Street is the newest chapter in Sheepshead Bay's history as a residential community. **The Breakers** is a condominium complex that opened in 2008—with a private waterfront promenade, much to the disappointment of other Sheepshead Bay residents who had hoped for public access to the shore.

At Brigham Street, the neighborhood comes to an end, and Emmons Avenue merges with the Belt Parkway. At this location, Sheepshead Bay widens into the Rockaway Inlet. Boaters familiar with the channel rec-

ognize not to steer too close to Plumb Beach, which has a shallow sand-
bar that extends for quite a distance from the shore.

Manhattan Beach

On the southern side of Sheepshead Bay, the **Manhattan Beach** peninsula extends for nearly a mile toward the Rockaway Inlet. The former site
of Austin Corbin's Manhattan Beach Hotel, its alphabetically sequenced
streets were given English names—such as Amherst, Beaumont, and
Norfolk—by Corbin, who wanted the neighborhood to have an upper-
class feel.

At the tip of Manhattan Beach, **Kingsborough Community College** occupies a 70-acre campus that includes the city's newest lighthouse, completed in 1990. The beacon is perched on a rounded, skeletal
tower atop the **Marine and Academic Center** rotunda. The light stands
at 114 feet above sea level and has a range of 11 miles. Along with the
beacon, the campus also has its own aquarium and a beach staffed by
student lifeguards. It is the only college campus in New York that has its
own beach, dock, and lighthouse.

Kingsborough is located at the eastern tip of the landmass once
known as Coney Island. While the former island's western tip in Sea
Gate was historically called Norton's Point, the eastern tip never had
a formal name. Until the 1940s, this tip was a sand spit that extended
farther east, but the ocean's currents altered it. These currents, which run
east to west, continue to move the barrier islands and peninsulas of Long
Island's South Shore, as seen in the gradual westward drift of Breezy
Point and Fire Island.

Although dense residential development is erasing elements of Sheepshead Bay's past as a vacation and fishing village, the piers and boat clubs
continue to connect the neighborhood to its namesake waterway.

BROOKLYN

PLACES TO SEE:
+ **Holocaust Memorial Park** Shore Boulevard and Emmons Avenue
+ **Lundy's Restaurant building** 1901 Emmons Avenue
+ **Ocean Avenue Footbridge** Crossing Sheepshead Bay between
  Emmons Avenue at East 19th Street and Shore Boulevard at Exeter
  Street
+ **Sheepshead Bay Piers** Emmons Avenue between Ocean Avenue
  and East 27th Street + www.nycgovparks.org/parks/sheepshead-bay
  -piers

+ **Driscoll Tucker Place** Emmons Avenue at East 27th Street
+ **Varuna Boat Club** 2806 Emmons Avenue
+ **Miramar Yacht Club** 3050 Emmons Avenue ✦ 718-769-3548 ✦ www.miramaryc.com
+ **Sheepshead Bay Yacht Club** 3076 Emmons Avenue ✦ 718-891-0991
+ **CUNY Kingsborough Community College** 2001 Oriental Boulevard ✦ 718-368-5000 ✦ www.kbcc.cuny.edu

LEARN MORE:

+ **Sheepshead Bay Library** 2636 East 14th Street ✦ 718-368-1815 ✦ www.bklynlibrary.org/locations/sheepshead-bay
+ **Sheepshead Bites** www.sheepsheadbites.com

GETTING THERE:

+ **Bus**: B4 at Emmons Avenue anywhere between Shore Parkway and Bragg Street; B44 at Emmons Avenue anywhere between Nostrand Avenue and Bragg Street; B49 at either Holocaust Memorial Park or Kingsborough Community College
+ **Subway**: B, Q to Sheepshead Bay, walk south on Sheepshead Bay Road
+ **Bike**: There are bike lanes on Emmons Avenue, Neptune Avenue, Bedford Avenue, and Oriental Boulevard
+ **Boat**: Sheepshead Bay is navigable for its entire length

69. Plumb Beach Channel

To the east of Knapp Street, the Belt Parkway leaves its tight urban right-of-way and begins its ribbon-shaped route around Jamaica Bay, traveling through the Jamaica Bay Wildlife Refuge. Within this preserve, the highway crosses over six inlets of Jamaica Bay that are remnants of streams that once drained into the bay. The westernmost of these inlets is **Gerritsen Inlet**, which includes **Plumb Beach Channel** as a tributary.

Gerritsen Beach

Plumb Beach Channel has its head at Allen Avenue and Knapp Street. This innermost reach of the channel is also known as Shell Bank Creek.

Its course was carved in 1923 as part of Realty Associates' development of **Gerritsen Beach**. Named after 17th-century Dutch settler Wolfert Gerritsen, this community is composed almost entirely of unattached single-family homes with docks, tightly clustered in a local grid of alphabetically named streets. Isolated from mainland Brooklyn by Shell Bank Creek, the neighborhood has the only volunteer fire department in Brooklyn.

At the center of the neighborhood, the **Gotham Avenue Canal** splits Gerritsen Beach into an older southern half and a newer half to the north. At the head of the canal, **Gerritsen Beach Library** serves as a community center. Completed in 1997, the $4.2 million facility marked the end of a 65-year effort to provide the local library branch with a permanent home as it moved from one storefront to another. The library features a neo-Romanesque main entrance, a clock tower, and community garden. Its architecture is reminiscent of a church.

Near the southern tip of Gerritsen Beach, the community has its own private beach at Post Court and Madoc Avenue. Known as **Kiddie Beach**, the park is maintained by the Gerritsen Beach Property Owners Association.

Plumb Beach

On the mainland Brooklyn side of Shell Bank Creek, a shoreline that would otherwise be developed for luxury residences is lined with a sanitation depot and water treatment plant.

At Harkness Avenue, the local TGI Friday's, a family-owned **Jordan's Lobster Dock**, and a Cold Stone Creamery all share space in a structure that has a decorative lighthouse behind it. The short dead-end street is named after Harry Harkness. An heir to his father's oil fortune, Harkness was a professional racecar driver and an amateur aviator. In 1915, he transformed the failing **Sheepshead Bay Race Track**, which was used for horse racing, into the **Sheepshead Bay Speedway,** an early racetrack for cars. Harkness died of influenza in January 1919, and the racetrack closed soon after. The memory of this racetrack lives on not only in Harkness Avenue's name but also in the Sheepshead Bay Stakes, an annual thoroughbred race held at Belmont Park that has its origins in Sheepshead Bay.

Shell Bank Creek passes the **Venice Marina**'s crowded dock, which holds dozens of small boats, and **Clemente's Maryland Crab House,** both of which are located on a dead end of Emmons Avenue that is separated from the rest of the strip by the Belt Parkway. Prior to 1937, **Hog Creek** ran across this site, a shallow channel that separated **Plumb Beach** from mainland Brooklyn. Depending on the mapmaker, bureaucrat, or property owner, the community was also sometimes spelled as Plum Beach.

In the early 1930s, the city attempted to fill in Hog Creek and transform Plumb Beach into a peninsula. On the morning of December 3, 1933, three buses carrying Gerritsen Beach residents pulled up to the location of Hog Creek and, in a coordinated effort, nearly 1,000 volunteers dug up the former streambed. A resident of Plumb Beach awoke to the sight of his home severed from the mainland. He telephoned local precinct commander Captain Edward Walsh, who sent officers to Plumb Beach. The Gerritsen Beach residents argued that a promised dredging of Shell Bank Creek had never occurred, and its stagnation was becoming a health hazard. The city's Dock Commissioner John MacKenzie agreed with the protesters and gave them permission to dig, provided that they built a footbridge for Plumb Island residents.

Owned by the federal government since the 1890s, Plumb Island was intended to become a fort but instead became a squatter colony accessible only by a five-cent ferry across the creek during high tide. A 1924 *New York Times* article on Plumb Island describes the rowboat operation as a "Toonerville Ferry"; it was the shortest ferry route in the city.

Having failed at building a fort on the island, the government leased the land in May 1907 to former judge Winfield S. Overton for five years. Overton charged the squatters rent and used the federal property to conduct activities that were illegal anywhere else in New York, such as gambling and boxing matches. To evict those not paying rent, Overton persuaded a company of soldiers from nearby Fort Hamilton to "invade" and expel the squatters.

The government broke its lease with Overton and appointed a new administrator for the island, Frank Dotzler. The 95 squatter families then were divided into Dotzlerite and Overtonian factions, paying rent to either man.

The colorful settlement did not survive long after that. Between hurricanes and Robert Moses' plans to build the Belt Parkway, Plumb Beach was doomed. The last squatters were evicted by 1940. In 1974, Plumb Beach was included within Gateway National Recreation Area. The beach now has no residents, though it is open during daytime hours as a popular swimming and windsurfing location.

To the north of Plumb Beach, Shell Bank Creek expands into Plumb Beach Channel. It merges with Gerritsen Inlet, passing underneath the Belt Parkway and emptying into the Rockaway Inlet at a location called Point Breeze.

PLACES TO SEE:
- **Jordan's Lobster Dock** 3165 Harkness Avenue ✦ 718-934-6300 ✦ www.jordanslobster.com
- **Venice Marina** 3939 Emmons Avenue ✦ 718-646-9283
- **Clemente's Maryland Crab House** 3939 Emmons Avenue ✦ 718-646-7373 ✦ www.clementescrabhouse.com
- **Plumb Beach Park** Belt Parkway eastbound between Emmons Avenue and Flatbush Avenue
- **Kiddie Beach (private)** Post Court at Madoc Avenue
- **Gerritsen Beach Library** 2808 Gerritsen Avenue ✦ 718-368-1435

GETTING THERE:
- **Bus**: B4 at Voorhies Avenue and Knapp Street; B31 at Gerritsen Avenue and Gerritsen Beach
- **Subway**: B, Q to Sheepshead Bay, transfer to Sheepshead Bay–bound B4; B, Q to Kings Highway, transfer to Gerritsen Beach–bound B31
- **Bike**: There are bike lanes on Gerritsen Avenue and the Jamaica Bay Greenway along the Belt Parkway
- **Boat**: Plumb Beach Channel is navigable for its entire length

70. Gerritsen Inlet

In contrast to Plumb Beach Channel, **Gerritsen Inlet** is entirely enveloped within Marine Park, with a bird sanctuary island located at its midpoint. Prior to development, this tributary of the Rockaway Inlet originated nearly a mile farther inland, in the present-day **Midwood** neighborhood, where the grid-defying Bay Avenue and Olean Street predate the neighborhood and follow the direction of the former creek. By the early 20th century, the stream appeared to emerge from the ground near the intersection of Kings Highway and Bedford Avenue, flowing in a southeast course. Crossing Nostrand Avenue, the stream widened as it flowed through the future Marine Park neighborhood,

BROOKLYN

which was developed in the late 1920s; its distance from the subway has allowed this neighborhood to retain a suburban appearance of detached single-family homes.

To the south of Fillmore Avenue, Gerritsen Creek crossed into a 150-acre parcel of green space that was purchased in 1917 by Frederick B. Pratt and Alfred T. White. The philanthropic duo bought the marshland as a gift to the city to preempt its development into a port. Its size and undisturbed landscape yielded promise that Marine Park could be the area's answer to Prospect Park.

In 1931, Mayor Jimmy Walker approved the selection of Charles Downing Lay as the park's architect. In his selection of Lay, the mayor rebuffed an effort by former State Senator Nathan Straus Jr. to conduct a nationwide architectural competition for the park. Seeing neighborhoods developing around the park's site, Walker sought an architect who would be able to complete the project in a speedy manner.

In the construction of Marine Park, Gerritsen Creek north of Avenue U was covered, and on top of the fill, an oval field ringed by a track now serves as a destination for local bikers and joggers. Around the periphery of this section, tennis courts, basketball courts, and softball fields appeal to sports enthusiasts. The extant section of the creek to the south of Avenue U is known today as Gerritsen Inlet or Marine Park Creek.

Across Avenue U, Lay proposed a T-shaped head to Gerritsen Creek, with boathouses and a marina. This proposal never went beyond planning stage, but it was impressive enough to be selected as the Silver Medal finalist in the art exhibition at the 1936 Summer Olympics in Berlin. Describing his project to the *New York Times*, Lay spoke about the balance between rustic and urban: "I am interested in everything about the city. I do not believe in the back-to-the-land movement carried to extremes. Far more practical is it to bring the country into the town."

The head of the truncated Gerritsen Creek has a naturalistic shoreline, with the **Salt Marsh Nature Center** near its tip. The $4 million educational facility opened in 2000, hosting classes on the natural history of Marine Park.

In the 17th century, the present-day head of Gerritsen Inlet was the site of a millpond dammed by **Gerritsen's Mill**. Built in the 1640s by Hugh Gerritsen, it is believed to have been the earliest tide-powered mill in America. At the time, the creek was known as Strome Kill, and its surroundings were being contested between Dutch farmers and the native Canarsee people. The last natives departed by the 1680s.

Gerritsen's Mill operated until around 1890, then passed into the ownership of William C. Whitney in 1899. Whitney used the land around the mill as a country home. In Gerritsen Beach, Whitney Avenue carries on the memory of this property owner. The mill stood until 1935, when vandals brought it down. Wooden pilings standing in a line across the channel mark the side of the milldam.

On the western side of Gerritsen Inlet, the parkland includes **Public School 277**, baseball fields, a playground, and a model airplane field operated by the **Radio Control Society of Marine Park**.

The eastern side of Gerritsen Inlet has a 210-acre golf course lying atop landfill that fused mainland Brooklyn with Barren Island. Prior to being filled, the Mill Creek and Deep Creek channels flowed here, connecting Gerritsen Inlet with Mill Basin. Between them, a vast salt marsh known as **Riches Meadows** formed its own island amid a maze of smaller landforms and inlets. The filling work began in 1917, as contractors extended **Flatbush Avenue** farther south toward Barren Island in anticipation of its crossing the Rockaway Inlet toward Fort Tilden. Originally a native trail, Flatbush Avenue begins at the foot of the Manhattan Bridge and ends by the shore of the Atlantic Ocean. Along with Kings Highway, Flatbush Avenue is as essential to Brooklyn's identity as Broadway is to Manhattan's.

The golf course opened in 1963 and includes a driving range. The original plans, however, were more ambitious—they proposed an additional nine-hole course on a manmade island in Gerritsen Inlet, which was known as **White Island** in honor of Alfred T. White. The island's golf course was never built, but a temporary bridge was constructed on its east side, whose pilings continue to impede boaters today. White Island had its origins in 1934, when the city was barred from dumping trash into the ocean and redirected the refuse into the marshes. White Island was formed from this landfill.

To the south of White Island, Gerritsen Inlet merges with Plumb Beach Channel, passing beneath the Belt Parkway overpass. The stream enters Rockaway Inlet at Point Breeze, a spit of sand that marks the tip of Plumb Beach. To the east of Point Breeze is **Dead Horse Bay**, a colorfully named cove that was formed out of refuse that included the city's dead horses. The Gateway Marina occupies this cove and is the largest in Brooklyn.

From its head at the Salt Marsh Nature Center to its mouth at Point Breeze, Gerritsen Inlet affords views of a restored natural landscape—one that resembles Brooklyn as it was for centuries, before it became a city.

BROOKLYN

+ **Salt Marsh Nature Center** 3301 Avenue U + 718-421-2021 +
www.nycgovparks.org/parks/marine-park/facilities/naturecenters
+ **Marine Park Golf Course** 2880 Flatbush Avenue + 718-252-4625
  + www.golfmarinepark.com
+ **Radio Control Society of Marine Park** Gerritsen Avenue between
Seba and Lois Avenues
+ **Plumb Beach Park** Eastbound Belt Parkway, east of exit 9
+ **Gerritsen Beach Library** 2808 Gerritsen Avenue + 718-368-1435
  + www.bklynpubliclibrary.org/locations/gerritsen-beach

+ **Bus**: B4 at Voorhies Avenue and Knapp Street; B31 Gerritsen Avenue and Gerritsen Beach
+ **Subway**: B, Q to Sheepshead Bay, transfer to Sheepshead Bay–bound B4; B, Q to Kings Highway, transfer to Gerritsen Beach–bound B31
+ **Bike**: There are bike lanes on Gerritsen Avenue and the Jamaica Bay Greenway along the Belt Parkway
+ **Boat**: Gerritsen Inlet is navigable for its entire length

71. Mill Basin

The only inlet of Jamaica Bay to have a drawbridge, **Mill Basin** originates from two branches, both lined with luxury housing, full of yachts plying the water in the neighborhood that shares the inlet's name. Prior to development, there was no Mill Basin—its location was a labyrinth of marshland islands and streams such as Mill Creek, Irish Creek, Dam Creek, Little Flat Creek, and Big Flat Creek. Amid these waterways was Mill Island, whose elevated topography kept it above the high tide.

Schenck House

The first permanent structure on Mill Island was the **Jan Martense Schenck House**, a Dutch colonial structure that accompanied a mill located at the head of Mill Creek. Completed in 1677, it was among the dozen farms that comprised Nieuw Amersfoort, a settlement that was later renamed Flatlands. Jan Martense Schenck was a scion of Dutch nobility and chose the location for its potential as a port. Further inland, farms grew grain that was processed at the tidal gristmill and dock near the Schenck House.

Because Flatlands had an economy dependent on agriculture and a small population, it relied heavily on slave labor. At slavery's height in 1790, nearly 30 percent of residents in Kings County were African American, the majority enslaved. Among the counties of New York, Kings County had the largest proportion of slaves to owners.

The Schenck family owned the house for three generations, finally selling it in 1784. Ownership of the home passed to the Martense family, followed by retired general Philip S. Crooke. In 1909, the Atlantic, Gulf, and Pacific Company acquired the house and surrounding land as it sought to transform the marshland into a thriving industrial seaport. The house fell into disrepair. In 1952, the **Brooklyn Museum** rescued the house—the borough's oldest structure—and reassembled it inside the museum. The site of the Schenck House is today **Public School 236**, located a block from the head of Mill Basin.

Along the shoreline

Along the northern side of Mill Basin, Avenue U frames the shoreline, which is fenced off from the sidewalk and overgrown with weeds. Closer to the Kings Plaza Mall, the Skyway Marina makes use of the waterway. On the shore, the retail properties face Avenue U, providing no access to the water, with the exception of Lowe's Home Improvement—it has a pedestrian walkway with benches on the shore.

At the corner of Avenue U and Flatbush Avenue, Mill Basin makes an elbow-shaped turn to the south. Since 1970, the massive **Kings Plaza** shopping center has occupied the corner. Standing out amid the unattached suburban-style homes, it faced opposition from local residents during its construction. When it opened on September 11, 1970, local residents blocked the surrounding streets, fearing that the mall would inundate their quiet neighborhood with traffic congestion.

On the opposite side of Mill Basin, the shore near Strickland Avenue is lined with commercial and parking facilities that contrast with the rest of Mill Basin. The most visited venue on this side of Mill Basin is **El Caribe Country Club Caterers**, a palace used for weddings that also has a pool overlooking the basin.

In the late 19th century, the Crooke family inherited the Schenck House through marriage. While Civil War veteran and Congressman Philip Schuyler Crooke lived in the home, his family member, Robert L. Crooke, operated a lead-smelting factory on Mill Basin.

BROOKLYN

The factory inspired other industries to set up shop along Mill Basin, including National Lead Company and the Gulf Refining Company. After the Atlantic, Gulf, and Pacific Company brought the land around the Schenck House in 1909, it filled in the surrounding marshland in anticipation of its transformation into an industrial seaport. The former marshland prepared for development, but the railroad connection never materialized, and only a few factories arrived in Mill Basin.

In the 1950s, Mill Basin was sold to residential developers. The former Mill Island, now a 300-acre peninsula, was covered with 1,500 homes built on two crescent-shaped grids. The larger grid to the north envelops **Lindower Park**, the community's public green space. The smaller grid to the south is tighter in formation and has waterfront homes with docks on its outermost streets. One of the streets, National Drive, is named after the long-gone National Lead Company. Quite the opposite of industry can be found on this road today—postwar suburban ranch homes have been replaced with upscale tract mansions. Among them is **2458 National Drive**, the most expensive unattached house in the city, which was listed for sale in 2013 at $30 million.

As the Mill Basin stream approaches the Belt Parkway, it widens and merges with East Mill Basin, a straightened waterway that separates the Mill Basin neighborhood from Bergen Beach. On the southeastern side of the merged basin is **Four Sparrow Marsh**, an undeveloped wetland that was acquired by the city's Parks Department in 2000. The 63-acre marsh was initially slated for development, but plans were changed as a result of opposition from local residents and environmental groups. The marsh is named in honor of the four native sparrow species found there: sharp-tailed, seaside, swamp, and song sparrow.

Mill Basin was the only inlet of Jamaica Bay that had a drawbridge at its outlet, enabling tall vessels to pass through. Completed in 1940, the **Mill Basin Drawbridge**, which carried the Belt Parkway between Barren Island and Bergen Beach, had a clearance above water at high tide of 35 feet (when it wasn't raised). The state is currently in the process of replacing this drawbridge with a fixed bridge, which will have a clearance of 60 feet. The replacement of the drawbridge is expected to alleviate traffic congestion on the Belt Parkway and create wider lanes for motorists and pedestrians.

On the Jamaica Bay side of the Belt Parkway, the National Park Service, as part of Gateway National Recreation Area, administers the parkland. The northern side of the basin's mouth at Jamaica Bay has the **Jamaica Bay Riding Academy**, where the public can take horseback rides on trails along the shoreline.

PLACES TO SEE:

+ **Kings Plaza Shopping Center** 5100 Kings Plaza + 718-253-6842
  + www.kingsplazaonline.com
+ **Lindower Park** Bound by Mill Avenue, East 60th Place, and Strickland Avenue + www.nycgovparks.org/parks/lindower-park
+ **Four Sparrow Marsh** Wildlife preserve bound by Flatbush Avenue, Mill Basin, and the Belt Parkway
+ **Mill Basin Bridge** Belt Parkway crossing Mill Basin
+ **Jamaica Bay Riding Academy** 7000 Shore Parkway, on eastbound Belt Parkway between Flatbush Avenue and Rockaway Parkway exits + 718-531-8949 + www.horsebackride.com

GETTING THERE:

+ **Bus**: B2, B3, B9, B41, B46, B47, Q35 at Kings Plaza; B100 at National Drive and Mill Avenue
+ **Subway**: B, Q to Kings Highway, transfer to B2 or B100
+ **Bike**: There are currently no bike lanes in the Mill Basin vicinity
+ **Boat**: Mill Basin is navigable for its entire length

72. Paerdegat Basin

BROOKLYN

The longest in length among Jamaica Bay's inlets, this straight waterway derives its name, **Paerdegat Basin**, from the Dutch for "horse's gate." Prior to the 1920s, the inlet was fed by a freshwater creek that originated even farther inland, near present-day **Paerdegat Park** and the **Flatbush Gardens** apartment development in East Flatbush.

This land was developed in 1940 by Fred C. Trump. Before he bought it, the parcel was known as **Paerdegat Woods** and alternately as **Vanderveer Estate**, named after a Dutch settler family that owned this land into the early 20th century. Their estate comprised dense woodland once used by the native Canarsee people for hunting bear and deer. Although the Dutch claimed the forest in 1624, the Canarsee continued to use it until 1670. That year, a localized conflict arose with the Rockaway natives, who nearly exterminated the Canarsee.

A century later the forest, then known as Flatbush Woods, was the scene of a pitched battle in August 1776 between 3,000 patriots and 17,000 British and Hessian troops.

Within the woods was **Paerdegat Pond**, a source of water for the town of Flatbush that was developed in 1881 as a pumping station by **Flatbush Water Works**. In contrast to the highly rated Croton water that was consumed by Manhattanites, Flatbush residents found their water to be salty, hard, corrosive, and having a high lime content. By 1913, the pumping station diluted its supply with Croton water to make it more palatable. The city could not shut down the pumping station, however, because Flatbush Water Works had a 99-year contract with the defunct town of Flatbush. In 1941, a lawsuit against the monopoly was filed. On June 27, 1947, the 350,000 residents of Flatbush were finally released from the contract. Three days later, Mayor William O'Dwyer and Brooklyn Borough President John Cashmore toasted the end of Flatbush Water Works at Brooklyn Borough Hall, raising glasses filled with "Ye Olde Flatbush Cocktail." Speaking to a *New York Times* reporter, one resident remarked, "Flatbush water is wonderful to drink, but it's kind of hard on the pipes."

In the 1940s, when Trump was looking to develop Paerdegat Woods, it was recognized as the last "old time" forest in Brooklyn. At the time, four local high schools were campaigning to have the site reserved for an athletic field. The developers won this battle and in 1949, the construction of 59 apartment buildings began at the 30-acre site. The only portion of the old forest that was reserved for parkland was a corner tract at Nostrand and Foster Avenues, which opened in 1953 as **Nostrand Playground**.

At the head of Paerdegat Basin, the city's Department of Environmental Protection maintains the **Paerdegat Basin Combined Sewer Overflow Facility** where excess sewage is stored in massive underground tanks and sifted through for floating rubbish like water bottles. Completed in May 2011, the $404 million facility stores 50 million gallons of storm water from surrounding sewers. The CSO facility is one of four in the city, built to reduce pollution in the city's waterways. The interior of the main building features tile patterns inspired by the Canarsee people, and the exterior includes a walkway along the shoreline.

The present form of Paerdegat Basin was carved out in the 1920s in preparation for its use as a seaport. Although the project for an international port at Jamaica Bay had the support of all local elected officials, on the federal level, Port Newark in New Jersey had a more convincing case. In the 1960s, the city sold off its parcels along the Canarsie shores to residential developers, who designed 15 one-block streets unimaginatively titled by numbers—Paerdegat 1st Street, Paerdegat 2nd Street, and so on.

On the western side of Paerdegat Basin, the residential neighborhood of **Bergen Beach** occupies the neck of land between Mill Basin East and Paerdegat Basin. Named after a colonial landowning family, the neighborhood is among the most isolated in Brooklyn. Prior to 1918, Bergen Beach was an island amid the marshland, with an amusement park built around the historic Bergen house. The sole physical connection to mainland Brooklyn was Island Avenue, later renamed Veterans Avenue. While numerous rails and roads served Coney Island, Bergen Beach had only a single trolley line on Island Avenue as its link. In 1951, the trolley was replaced with the B41 bus.

The isolation of Bergen Beach ensured that it would never compete with Coney Island. Between 1930 and 1939, the Bergen house and amusement park were razed to make way for the Belt Parkway, which bypasses the neighborhood. The approximate site of the amusement park is still used for recreation as the **Joseph T. McGuire Fields**, a public sports complex for soccer, baseball, hockey, and tennis.

On either side of Paerdegat Basin are boating clubs with marinas for small vessels. The **Hudson River Yacht Club** is on the Bergen Beach side, operated privately on city land. On the Canarsie side, the **Sebago Canoe Club** offers rentals for the public. Another public facility on the Canarsie side is **PacPlex**, the informal name of the Paerdegat Athletic Club. Inside this facility is Brooklyn's largest indoor swimming pool along with other recreational opportunities. To the immediate south of PacPlex is **Canarsie Park**, a green parcel that buffers the neighborhood of Canarsie from the Belt Parkway.

The Belt Parkway is the only road that crosses Paerdegat Basin, using a gracefully curving concrete bridge. The **Jamaica Bay Greenway** follows the Belt Parkway, running over Paerdegat Basin near its confluence with Jamaica Bay.

With the entire length of Paerdegat Basin owned by the city, its shoreline could be transformed into a linear park with different habitat zones designed to attract a diverse selection of wildlife. At the head of the basin, the CSO facility could be opened for public tours to educate visitors on the city's role in maintaining the ecosystem of this waterway.

BROOKLYN

+ **Paerdegat Park** Bound by Albany Avenue, East 40th Street, Farragut Road, and Foster Avenue + www.nycgovparks.org/parks/paerdegat-park
+ **Paerdegat Basin Combined Sewer Overflow (CSO) Facility** 1961 Bergen Avenue
+ **Joseph T. McGuire Fields** Bergen Avenue between Avenue V and Avenue X + www.nycgovparks.org/parks/joseph-t-mcguire-park
+ **Hudson River Yacht Club** 2101 Bergen Avenue + 718-251-9791
+ **Sebago Canoe Club** 1400 Paerdegat Avenue North + 718-241-3683 + www.sebagocanoeclub.org
+ **Canarsie Park** Seaview Ave between Paerdegat Basin and East 93rd Street + www.nycgovparks.org/parks/canarsie-park

+ **Bus**: B17, B103, BM2 at East 80th Street and Avenue M, walk one block south to Paerdegat Avenue North
+ **Subway**: 2, 5 to Flatbush Avenue–Brooklyn College, transfer to B103, BM2
+ **Bike**: There are currently no bike lanes in the vicinity of Paerdegat Basin
+ **Boat**: Paerdegat Basin is navigable for its entire length

BROOKLYN

73. Fresh Creek

Separating the neighborhoods of Canarsie and Spring Creek Towers, **Fresh Creek** gently winds its way through restored marshland. Along its western side is East 108th Street, the highest number on the east–west grid that begins in the Gravesend neighborhood six miles to the west.

On the eastern side is **Spring Creek Towers**, a 153-acre planned neighborhood of 46 high-rise apartments built along Pennsylvania Avenue. The community was known as Starrett City from its completion in 1974 until a change of ownership in 2002.

The neighborhood stands atop a former landfill and functions independently, with its own building address system, private patrol schools, and a shopping center. However, it does not have a subway connection to the city. It is a contemporary of other high-rise complexes on the city's periphery that are densely built but isolated from the subway, like Co-op City in the Bronx and North Shore Towers in Queens.

On the western side of Fresh Creek is a minigrid of streets whose names unimaginatively resemble those of the Paerdegat Basin grid, starting with Flatlands 1st Street and counting to Flatlands 10th Street.

Prior to development, Fresh Creek originated near the present-day intersection of East 105th Street and Avenue D. By 1950, the section of Fresh Creek to the north of Flatlands Avenue was filled with the **Breukelen Houses** development and the adjoining **Breukelen Ballfields** constructed atop the former streambed. Both take their name from the original Dutch name for Brooklyn.

In contrast to Mill and Paerdegat Basins, Fresh Creek's shoreline is not straight. It was designed with islands and peninsulas to attract birds to the 42-acre salt marsh that lines the shores of this stream.

Around the shores of Jamaica Bay, the marshland served as a dumping ground for victims of organized crime. On July 19, 1934, local fishermen uncovered the body of Willie Shapiro, 24, a Brownsville resident. Shapiro was found beaten to death, his head encased in a pillowcase and his body bound in a sitting position, likely to prevent an escape.

At the time, Brownsville was a hotbed of organized crime, best known for the hit squad Murder, Inc. In the Shapiro family, two older brothers, Meyer and Irving, were killed two years earlier. The brothers were recorded in news accounts as having "bullied shopkeepers." Fresh Creek appears calm these days, the longtime resting place for those who happened to be on the wrong side of the law.

PLACES TO SEE:

✦ **Fresh Creek Park** Louisiana Avenue between Twin Pines Drive and Seaview Avenue ✦ www.nycgovparks.org/parks/fresh-creek-park

74. Hendrix Creek

A narrow inlet not used by boats, **Hendrix Creek** separates Spring Creek Towers from Gateway Center, the most recent development near Jamaica Bay. The 7,000-foot-long channel is paralleled by Hendrix Street, which travels through the East New York neighborhood to the head of the inlet. Once fed by natural sources, the inlet now receives water from the **26th Ward Wastewater Treatment Plant** at its head. In 2014, a colony of oysters was introduced to the creek to act as a natural water filter. The plant's name hearkens back to the wards that comprised the city of Brooklyn prior to its consolidation into New York City in 1898.

The eastern side of Hendrix Creek is **Gateway Center**, a mixed-use development—mostly a shopping center—completed in 2002. Rainwater from its parking lot is collected into a 42-acre "rain garden" park around its periphery that filters out pollutants and then drains into Hendrix Creek. The edge of Gateway Center is part of **Spring Creek Park**, a ribbon of parkland along the Belt Parkway between Hendrix Creek and Spring Creek.

Originally a marshland, Hendrix Creek was gradually covered with sand beginning in the 1930s, receiving the informal name Vandalia Dunes, after nearby Vandalia Avenue. In 1967, the dunes were declared an urban renewal area and slated for development as a state psychiatric hospital. Instead, the site lay unused until the City Council approved **Gateway Estates** in 1996. The loss of habitat at Vandalia Dunes was swapped by the city for White Island in Marine Park, where trash was cleared and plants favorable to a bird sanctuary were introduced.

The neo-urban design of Gateway Estates and Gateway Center takes into account the presence of Hendrix Creek and follows a naturalistic drainage pattern of filtering rainwater from the community's streets into a wetland that flows into the stream.

PLACES TO SEE:
+ **26th Ward Wastewater Treatment Plant** 12266 Flatlands Avenue
+ **Spring Creek Park** Gateway Drive along Hendrix Creek
+ **Gateway Center** 409 Gateway Drive + 718-235-0467

GETTING THERE:
+ **Bus**: B13, B83, B84, Q8 to Gateway Center
+ **Subway**: A, C, J, Z, L to Broadway Junction or 3 to Pennsylvania Avenue, transfer to B83
+ **Bike**: There is a bike trail along Gateway Drive, connecting to the Jamaica Bay Greenway

BROOKLYN

75. Spring Creek (Old Mill Creek)

Two informational greeting signs on the Belt Parkway mark the overpass at **Spring Creek** as the border between Brooklyn and Queens.

Spring Creek

Westbound travelers see a "Welcome to Brooklyn" sign that carries the slogan "Home to Everyone from Everywhere!" Going in the opposite direction, a "Leaving Brooklyn" sign has "Fuhgeddaboudit" as the send-off. Both signs are the brainchild of former Brooklyn borough president Marty Markowitz, an outspoken booster for tourism in Brooklyn.

Spring Creek is the least developed of the inlets flowing into Jamaica Bay; its shoreline is crooked and lined with wild vegetation. The stream is a remnant of **Betts Creek** and **Ralph Creek**, which had their origins farther inland in City Line and Ozone Park.

Prior to development, Spring Creek emerged out of the gently sloping terrain to the south of the glacial terminal moraine at Jamaica Avenue. Its winding path fell roughly along today's Eldert Lane, the road that presently marks the border between Brooklyn and Queens.

A third tributary stream in the Spring Creek watershed was **Bull Creek**, which merged with Spring Creek near the present-day intersection of Cozine Avenue and Crescent Street. A short one-block alley running behind the homes on the southern side of Cozine Avenue is marked on the city's map as **Old Mill Road**, with three addresses registered on it. The long-gone namesake of this road was **Van Wicklen Mill**, a structure dating to at least 1770. The gristmill was powered by a tidal gate on the creek into the late 19th century.

Alongside the mill, the Van Wicklen family also owned a hotel, with both serving as centerpieces to a community of fishing shacks perched tightly along the creek. The location is listed in the 1865 J. H. Colton map as Van Wicklen Landing. In the early 20th century, it became

BROOKLYN

known simply as Old Mill. No trace of the mill remains other than Old Mill Road's intersection with Crescent Street, its approximate location.

In the place of a mill, there is now a different sort of water management facility at the head of Spring Creek. **Spring Creek Water Pollution Control Plant**, run by the city's Department of Environmental Protection, maintains a sizable pumping station that discharges treated water into the stream.

Nearly a mile to the northeast, a trio of Jewish cemeteries occupies the spot where Betts Creek emerged. Filled to capacity, the **Acacia**, **Bayside**, and **Mokom Sholom** cemeteries are not as well maintained as active cemeteries, and are frequent targets of vandals and subject to the ravages of nature. When the cemeteries accepted their first internment in 1865, the name Bayside was fitting, as the streams flowing into Jamaica Bay were in close proximity to the graves.

The western side of Spring Creek is followed by Fountain Avenue, a road that begins in Cypress Hills and descends toward the marshland around Spring Creek. To discourage illegal dumping, much of the shoreline along Fountain Avenue is fenced off by the Parks Department. Along this stretch of road is the **Brooklyn Developmental Center**, a mental health facility in a sprawling modernist campus run by the state. In 2014, the state announced that it would close the center.

The southern end of Fountain Avenue is a desolate stretch of tall grass and reeds that served as a dumping ground not only for trash but also for bodies—conveniently isolated, it was a good place for victims of kidnappings and organized crime to be unceremoniously deposited.

Through the 1970s, mobster Roy DeMeo disposed of his victims in the marshes along Fountain Avenue. DeMeo's income originated from loan sharking, car theft, and narcotics sales. His victims, believed to number around 200, included rivals, those who he thought disrespected him, and members of his crew suspected of cooperating with authorities.

DeMeo himself was killed in January 1983 at the order of archenemy Paul Castellano. The long roster of deaths DeMeo was responsible for inspired the 2006 film *Fountain Avenue* and a book by DeMeo's law-abiding son Albert, *For the Sins of My Father*.

Although mob activity declined in the years following DeMeo's murder, Fountain Avenue remained a dumping ground for murder victims. On February 26, 2006, an anonymous tip to the police alerted officers to the bound body of forensic psychology student Imette St. Guillen. Through DNA evidence, suspect Darryl Littlejohn was arrested for her murder. St. Guillen's murder inspired increased regulation and law enforcement in relation to the city's nightclubs and bouncers; despite Littlejohn's lengthy rap sheet, he had been working as a bouncer at the nightclub where St. Guillen was last seen in public.

On the southern side of the Belt Parkway, the grassland rises in a manmade landscape that covers up three decades of landfill operations. The Fountain Avenue Landfill operated between 1961 and 1985, in its final year collecting 40 percent of the city's refuse. At their highest point, the mounds rise to 130 feet above Jamaica Bay. In 1974, the city deeded the site to the federal Interior Department as part of Gateway National Recreation Area, which started the process of closing the landfill. This process was finally completed in 2004, when the city's Department of Environmental Protection covered the Fountain Avenue Landfill and the nearby Pennsylvania Avenue Landfill with a layer of plastic and soil. Atop the cover, 33,000 trees and shrubs were planted in the new 400-acre nature preserve. At a cost of $200 million, the project will incorporate the former dump into Gateway.

Considering the haunted history of Spring Creek in the 20th century, it is a welcome sight that the landscape is now being beautified as a park—perhaps a comforting notion to the relatives of those buried along the waterway.

PLACES TO SEE:
+ **Spring Creek Park (under construction)** Fountain Avenue at Seaview Avenue

GETTING THERE:
+ **Bus**: B13, B84, Q8 to Fountain Avenue and Brooklyn Development Center
+ **Subway**: A, C to Euclid Avenue, transfer to B13 and Q8
+ **Bike**: The Jamaica Bay Greenway is in proximity to Spring Creek

76. Prospect Park Waterways

While Central Park has numerous unconnected waterways that were adapted from natural streams on-site, Brooklyn's 585-acre **Prospect Park** has only one waterway, carved entirely from the terrain. Its water was originally sourced from a well; later it was hooked up to the city's water supply system. Its landscaping was inspired by the Adirondack wilderness, with a heavily forested rocky terrain that carries the stream

BROOKLYN

Prospect Park, 1872

through numerous waterfalls, rapids, and lakes.

Prior to development, the site of Prospect Park resembled the site of an undeveloped Central Park—goat farms, forests, swamps, and shanty residences. Construction began on July 1, 1866, with 1,800 men furiously reshaping the land. As the park was being built, clay pipes were installed beneath the future meadows, which channeled up to two inches of rain per hour into a drainage system feeding into the park's waterway.

Excavation of Prospect Park Lake began in 1867. A five-acre section of the lake opened in 1868, attracting 200 ice-skaters. By 1871, the lake was expanded to 30 acres. It was the largest construction project within the park. While its icy surface was a success in winter, in the hot summer the lake nearly evaporated. A clay layer mixed with silt was laid across the lake's bottom to retain the water.

The source of the stream

At the foot of Lookout Hill is a modest brick structure that was once accompanied by a 60-foot high smokestack and a 70-foot-deep well. The **Well and Boiler House** was completed in 1869 and contained the machinery that pumped 750,000 gallons of water into the park's waterways. In the 1930s, the city's aqueduct was connected to the park's water system, and the well was no longer needed. The building's underground reservoir and smokestack were torn down, while the building itself remained standing as a forgotten structure. In 2013, it was given a new use as an eco-friendly restroom that recycles human waste into fertilizer. The $1.8 million green latrine is expected to be completed by winter 2015.

The waterway emerges half a mile to the north in **Fallkill Falls**, a carefully constructed descent that plunges into **Fallkill Pool**. The name of the stream is inspired by New York's Dutch past, as many local streams use the toponym *kill* from the Dutch word for "creek." Within New York State, there is a natural Fall Kill in Poughkeepsie—a 38-mile stream that empties into the Hudson River. The Prospect Park waterfall descends from **Quaker Hill**, a forested terrain that contains a pocket cemetery that predates the park by nearly 20 years.

The stream flows out of Fallkill Pool beneath the wooden **Fallkill Bridge**, entering the larger **Upper Pool** and then a smaller **Lower Pool**, which are populated by a marsh and other water plants, where migratory birds rest. The Upper Pool features a small sandy area called the Dog Beach, where the public and pets can approach the water's edge. On the western side of the Lower Pool is a vast, rolling lawn called **Long Meadow**. This 90-acre feature of the park is the Brooklyn counterpart to Central Park's Sheep Meadow; it stretches for a mile from the park's northern end at **Grand Army Plaza** to its western end near **Bartel-Pritchard Square**. Once used for sheep grazing, lawn tennis, and croquet, the meadow's present-day activities include picnicking, sunbathing, barbecuing, and baseball.

Esdale Bridge marks the stream's exit from the Lower Pool and entry into the **Prospect Park Ravine**, a gorge that plunges the stream through the terminal moraine. Here, the stream takes on the name **Ambergill** and descends through **Ambergill Falls**. Olmsted personally chose the name. The Ravine is the section of Prospect Park that corresponds to the Ramble in Central Park, a seemingly wild terrain composed of rocks, forests, and streams. The landscape must be carefully managed; as erosion takes its natural course, sediment collects in the 100-foot-wide gorge, blocking the stream. Only through human intervention does the stream continue to flow uninterrupted through the Ravine.

Ambergill leaves the Ravine beneath **Nethermead Arch**, a bridge carrying Center Drive, which cuts through the park, across three arches— one for the stream, the second for the pedestrian path, and the third for the bridle trail. The Nethermead is the smaller meadow in Prospect Park, where Olmsted planted Osage orange trees as a defining feature. From this point, the stream is called **Binnen Water**, its name chosen by Olmsted from the Dutch for "within," indicating its location deep inside the park. The wood-framed **Music Grove Bridge** crosses Binnen Water in proximity to the **Music Pagoda**, an elongated octagonal structure built in the 1880s for concerts. At Binnen Bridge, pedestrians stand atop Binnen Falls, watching the stream descend to its final reach before it enters the Prospect Park Lake.

Prospect Park Boat House, 1910

This reach is the **Lullwater**, named for the calm pace of the water. At Lullwater is the **Boathouse**, a historic landmark completed in 1905. The architecture firm of Helme & Huberty designed the structure in the Beaux-Arts style, with the library of Saint Mark's Cathedral in Venice as the inspiration. In the years following the Second World War, public use of the boathouse declined sharply, and the building was slated for demolition in 1964. The demolition was approved by the City Planning Commission, the Board of Estimate, and the mayor, but opposition mobilized to save it.

Among those defending the structure were the Brooklyn borough president, the Municipal Art Society, the Brooklyn Bird Club, and numerous local civic organizations. Manhattan attorney Robert Makla defended the structure, describing Prospect Park as a work of art: "It's a creation just as a work of music or a theatrical piece." Makla's description of the park stands in stark contrast to an earlier description of the Boathouse in the *New York Times* as a "gaslight relic."

The building presently serves as an education center run by the Audubon Society, which reopened the boathouse on April 26, 2001—the shared birthday of both John James Audubon and Frederick Law Olmsted.

To the south of the Boathouse is **Lullwater Bridge**, the longest crossing in Prospect Park. The bridge, completed in 1906, is made of cast iron, reminiscent of Bow Bridge in Central Park. A larger cast-iron creation, **Terrace Bridge**, takes Wellhouse Drive over Lullwater. Beneath the bridge, a walkway lines the water's edge. As the water passes under the bridge, it widens into the 55-acre **Prospect Park Lake**, a sizable expanse of water in a borough that has fewer lakes than Manhattan (natural and manmade).

At the northeast corner of the lake is **Music Island**, an island that was conceived in the park's original design, then demolished, and only recently restored. Located inside a circular cove, it was meant to serve as a stage for musicians who rowed to the island with their instruments; spectators could watch their performances from a location on the shoreline called **Concert Grove**. As Olmsted envisioned it, park goers would pass by the music-playing island and imagine that the park had its own ambient soundtrack that complemented the landscape.

Poor acoustics drove the musicians to other locations in the park. Then, in 1960, ice-skating was no longer safe on the lake, and Parks Commissioner Robert Moses eliminated the half-acre island—and the east end of the lake—by constructing the Kate Wollman Rink on top of it. The Concert Grove paths that approached the lake's shore now faced a chain-link fence, as did the Abraham Lincoln statue that once faced the island. A 1967 guidebook to the park by its former curator described the state of Concert Grove as a "catastrophe," "wrecking," "desecration," and "obliterating."

In the first decade of the 21st century, the nonprofit Prospect Park Alliance proposed a $70 million project called **Lakeside**. The largest project in the park since the 19th century, Lakeside restored the filled-in portion of the lake, as well as Music Island, which is now a bird sanctuary; the ice-skating rink was moved to an underused parking lot nearby. Nearby **Teardrop Island** was also included in the shore restoration.

In a nod to philanthropy, the October 19, 2012, ribbon cutting for Lakeside added the following names to the park's map: Chaim Baier Music Island, Shelby White and Leon Levy Esplanade, and the Samuel J. and Ethel LeFrak Center at Lakeside. The facility's designers were the celebrated husband-and-wife team of Billie Tsien and Tod Williams along with landscape architect Christian Zimmerman.

Within the lake, other islands that serve as bird sanctuaries are Duck Island, Three Sisters Islands, and West Island. The shoreline of the lake has numerous coves and peninsulas, appearing as an inland sea.

PLACES TO SEE:
+ **Well House** 200 Wellhouse Drive, north side of Prospect Park Lake
+ **Fallkill Falls and Fallkill Pool** Between Quaker Hill and Long Meadow
+ **Upper and Lower Pools** Between Quaker Hill and Long Meadow

BROOKLYN

+ **Long Meadow** Western side of Prospect Park
+ **Esdale Bridge** Between the Ravine and Long Meadow
+ **Prospect Park Ravine** Between Long Meadow and the Nethermead
+ **Ambergill Falls** Inside the Ravine
+ **Nethermead Arch** Between the Ravine and the Nethermead
+ **Binnen Water** Between Nethermead Arch and Binnen Bridge
+ **Music Grove Bridge** Crossing Binnen Water
+ **Prospect Park Boathouse** 101 East Drive + www.prospectpark.org/ visit-the-park/party-venues/weddings-and-special-events/boathouse
+ **Lullwater Bridge** Crossing Lullwater
+ **Terrace Bridge** Wellhouse Drive crossing Lullwater
+ **Music Island** Facing Concert Grove by Prospect Park Lake
+ **Lakeside** 171 East Drive + 718-462-0010 + www.lakeside brooklyn.com

LEARN MORE:

+ **Prospect Park Alliance** www.prospectpark.org

GETTING THERE:

+ **Bus**: B41 at Empire Boulevard and Flatbush Avenue or B43, B48 at Empire Boulevard and Washington Avenue;
+ **Subway**: B, S, Q at Prospect Park
+ **Bike**: There are bike paths within Prospect Park

77. Green-Wood Cemetery

A short distance from Prospect Park is the 478-acre **Green-Wood Cemetery**, a parklike landscape of trimmed lawns, trees, and the tombs of New York's leading citizens. Designed by David Bates Douglass, the cemetery's paths follow the contours of the terminal moraine and preserve its kettle ponds as decorative features. In the initial decades following the cemetery's first interment in 1836, it was the secondmost visited destination in the United States after Niagara Falls.

Sixty years before its first burial, the hills of Green-Wood Cemetery were the scene of a bloodbath, as the patriots attempted to halt the British advance toward Brooklyn. Their efforts are commemorated with a monument at **Battle Hill**, the highest point in Brooklyn, located inside the cemetery.

The cemetery had its origins in the garden cemetery movement that

Sylvan Water, Green-Wood Cemetery, 1873

respected natural contours and scenery, creating a parklike environment for the dead at a time when cities did not have sizable public parks. In its first decade, hordes of picnickers took horse cabs and trolleys to reach Green-Wood Cemetery, creating momentum for the city to set aside Central and Prospect Parks.

Although initially proposed as Necropolis, it was named Green-Wood by its trustees; they felt that a single word, Greenwood, was unromantic and less impressive on the mind than its hyphenated version. Like in a city, every natural and constructed feature of the cemetery has a name. An 1868 article in the *New York Times* provides 52 names for the cemetery's "hills, ridges, dells and waters" that could be reached by 49 named avenues and 156 named paths.

At the time, the cemetery had seven named ponds: Alpine, Arbor, Crescent, Dale, Meadow, Sylvan, and Valley. Presently, only four remain: **Crescent Water** and **Dell Water** on its southern side, **Valley Water**, the largest of the pools, near its west, and **Sylvan Water** at the southeast. Dell Water was the most recent pond to have been filled in.

It has been more than a century since Green-Wood Cemetery was the city's most visited tourist destination, but for admirers of Gothic architecture, bird-watching, and celebrated public figures from the past, the country's second-oldest garden cemetery continues to welcome visitors with ample space for burials.

BROOKLYN

PLACES TO SEE:

✦ **Crescent Water** Bound by Crescent Avenue and Vale Avenue
✦ **Dell Water** Bound by Vale Avenue, Crescent Avenue, and Primrose Path

Lily pads on Green-Wood Cemetery Pond

+ **Valley Water** Bound by Lake Avenue, Landscape Avenue, Valley
  Avenue, and Walnut Avenue
+ **Sylvan Water** Located closest to Sylvan Avenue and Lake Avenue

LEARN MORE:
+ **Green-Wood Historic Fund** 500 25th Street + 718-210-3080 +
  www.green-wood.com

GETTING THERE:
*The entrance nearest to the four remaining ponds of Green-Wood Cemetery
is the main entrance at Fifth Avenue and 25th Street. The directions below
indicate the best way to reach this entrance.*
+ **Bus:** B63 at Fifth Avenue and 24th Street
+ **Subway:** R at 25th Street, walk one block east on 25th Street to the
  entrance
+ **Bike:** There are bike lanes on Fifth Avenue

78. Ridgewood Reservoir

Tucked amid dense foliage between Highland Park and the cemetery
belt of the Brooklyn-Queens border, **Ridgewood Reservoir** occupies
a hilltop location on the glacial terminal moraine. Between 1858 and
1898, this reservoir stored the water that flowed from collection res-

BROOKLYN

ervoirs on Long Island's South Shore. Following the consolidation of Brooklyn into New York City, the reservoir served as backup storage for the borough's water supply until its abandonment in 1990. In 2004, the Parks Department was assigned responsibility for the reservoir site.

Cemetery Belt

The terminal moraine where the reservoir lies stretches the length of Long Island and includes sizable green spaces within the city, such as Prospect Park, Forest Park, and Cunningham Park. On the Brooklyn-Queens border, the ridge appears as a cemetery belt that takes advantage of having property in two counties at once. The largest of these is the **Evergreens Cemetery**, a 225-acre burial park designed by noted 19th-century landscape architects Andrew Jackson Downing and Alexander Jackson Davis. Similar in design to Green-Wood and Woodlawn Cemeteries, it has roadways that follow the topography and allows plenty of space between graves. In contrast to its contemporaries, however, this cemetery does not have any bodies of water.

Another 225-acre cemetery along the county line is **Cypress Hills Cemetery**, which also opened in 1848. Cypress Hills had a pond in its northern section until the 1980s.

Another pond in the cemetery belt that no longer exists was **Banzer's Pond**, a partially manmade lake located on a tract that is presently within **Union Field Cemetery**. Prior to the construction of the Interborough Parkway, this pond was encircled by **Cypress Hills Park**, a privately owned picnic park located to the southeast of Cypress Avenue and Cypress Hills Street. The lake was used for boating in the summer and ice-skating in the winter. The pond was named after Charles Banzer, who operated a hotel by the pond in the late 19th century.

LAYING A WATERMAIN FROM RIDGEWOOD RESERVOIR.

Laying a watermain from Ridgewood Reservoir.

All cemeteries have their ghost stories. For Cypress Hills Cemetery, the spook could be Mary Wunder. On March 19, 1884, Wunder walked into Banzer's hotel asking for lodging, bleeding from a gunshot wound to the head. Wunder had become a widow nearly a year before the incident, and it was believed that she had attempted suicide at her husband's Cypress

Hills grave. No gun was found at the cemetery. Her two sons also were never seen in public after their father's death. In the year after the loss of her husband, Wunder wandered aimlessly around the country; a *New York Times* article following the incident said that she had "for some time been looked upon as insane."

The anti-German sentiment of the First World War and the enactment of Prohibition shortly thereafter greatly reduced the patronage at Cypress Hills Park, which was located in a largely German area of the city. The 13-acre park continued to operate as a picnic ground until around 1933, when the Interborough Parkway's right-of-way took over a portion of the park. The remainder was acquired by Congregation Emanu-El, a historic Manhattan synagogue, for one of its cemeteries, and the pond was drained.

The Interborough Parkway was renamed after Jackie Robinson in 1997, on the fiftieth anniversary of his entry into Major League Baseball. He is buried in Cypress Hills Cemetery, near the parkway's route.

Ridgewood Reservoir

Within the cemetery belt, Highland Park was acquired by the city of Brooklyn in 1856 as part of its Ridgewood Reservoir site. In 1905, the park was expanded as the city acquired the Schenck estate to its south. Within the park are monuments, picnic grounds, playgrounds, and softball fields that combine the naturalistic Olmsted layout with more recent needs for recreational uses.

On the northeastern side of the park is its most recent acquisition, the Ridgewood Reservoir site, which was annexed to the park in 2004. In its heyday, the reservoir was operated by Brooklyn Water Works, receiving up to 10 million gallons of water every day. The conduit originating in Nassau County terminated at Atlantic Avenue and Logan Street in East New York, where a steam-powered pumping station forced the water uphill through a "force tube" toward Ridgewood Reservoir. The pumping station was demolished in the 1960s, but the tunnels connecting it to the reservoir are remembered on the map as Force Tube Avenue.

In 1917 and again in 1936, tunnels were constructed to connect the reservoir with the city's Catskill-based aqueduct. The reservoir's function was reduced to backup storage, and two of its three basins were drained. Over the decades, as nature reclaimed the empty basins, the filled one has been used as an illegal swimming hole. This use resulted in the reservoir's repeated appearance in news reports covering drowning deaths in its water.

Left to its own devices, the stagnant pool of water turned into a wet-land; the National Audubon Society recorded that it was a habitat for 137 birds. Around its perimeter, invasive plant species colonized the site, hiding the brickwork beneath thick vegetation. In 1990, the city's Department of Environmental Protection decommissioned the reservoir.

In the 14 years between the reservoir's official closing and its revival as a park, it remained a place for illicit trysts, bird-watching, and home-less encampments. When in 2004 it was announced that Highland Park would annex the reservoir—adding 50 additional acres to the 140-acre park—the *New York Times* spoke with one squatter whom the city had asked to pull up stakes and move elsewhere. "It's totally different living here," 31-year-old Luis Rodriguez told the *Times*. "You're in the city, but you're far away from it." Further distancing himself from the city, Rodriguez nightly lowered himself down the reservoir's steep 40-foot walls into the heavily forested basin where he kept his tent.

The occasion for Rodriguez's interview was Highland Park's annex-ation of the reservoir on July 7, 2004, a handover that added 50 addi-tional acres to the 140-acre park.

In 2008, the Parks Department courted controversy when it proposed to turn the 31-acre third basin into a sports field as part of the city's effort to combat childhood obesity. The $50 million proposal meant cut-ting down nearly 500 trees. The other two basins would remain nature preserves ringed by trails. An outcry from environmental, preservation-ist, and community groups led to the plan's cancellation.

Since then, nature's reclaiming of the reservoir continues, while the city combats invasive plant species and preserves the historical aspects of the site.

BROOKLYN

PLACES TO SEE:

✦ **Highland Park** Bound by Jamaica Avenue, Jackie Robinson Park-way, National Cemetery, and Salem Fields Cemetery ✦ www.nyc govparks.org/parks/highland-park

GETTING THERE:

✦ **Bus**: Q56 at Jamaica Avenue and Highland Boulevard
✦ **Subway**: A, C, J, Z, L at Broadway Junction, transfer to Q56
✦ **Bike**: There are bike paths within Highland Park that are part of the Brooklyn-Queens Greenway

79. Dyker Beach Park

To the south of Bensonhurst, west of Bath Beach, and east of the Fort Hamilton army base is **Dyker Beach Golf Course**, one of Brooklyn's two oldest public golf courses (the other being Marine Park).

Prior to development, Dyker Beach was a salt marsh separating the terminal moraine of Bay Ridge and the coastal plain of Bath Beach. Its namesake is uncertain but believed to originate either from a Van Dyke family that settled in nearby New Utrecht or the dykes constructed by Dutch settlers to hold back tides. **Dyker Beach Park**, which is mostly taken up by the golf course, was acquired by the city of Brooklyn in 1895 and gradually expanded to its present size by 1934.

Initial plans for the park were drafted by the firm of Olmsted, Olmsted & Eliot, proposing a 50-acre lagoon from the salt marsh, along with playgrounds, bathhouses, lawns, and the golf course. As the park was reworked over the years, the lagoon was filled in 1918, leaving behind only one pond, in the golf course. Designed by golf course architect John Van Kleek, the links opened to the public in 1920.

The Norman French–style clubhouse, completed in 1934, is located on its own grid-defying road, De Russy Drive. The road, which cuts through a corner of Dyker Beach Park, was named by the Parks Department in 1997 in honor of General René De Russy, the military engineer who developed nearby Fort Hamilton in 1825 and owned land adjacent to the base. De Russy was born in 1789, the year that George Washington became president, and died in 1865, the year that the American Civil War concluded   a life that spanned some of the most critical moments in the early history of the United States.

In 1888, developer Frederick Henry Johnson purchased a section of the De Russy estate for a suburban development, Bensonhurst-by-the-Sea. When he died in 1893, his son Walter Loveridge Johnson continued developing the hilly terrain under the name **Dyker Heights**. Bound by Bay Ridge Avenue on the north and Fourteenth Avenue to the east, the neighborhood still retains its suburban appearance. It is best known for its extravagant Christmas decorations and the Italian American heritage of its community.

PLACES TO SEE:

✦ **Dyker Beach Golf Course** 86th Street and Seventh Avenue ✦ 718-836-9722 ✦ www.dykerbeachgc.com

GETTING THERE:

+ **Bus**: B4 or B6 at Bay Parkway and Stillwell Avenue; B82 at Kings Highway and West 12th Street; B1 at 86th Street and Eleventh Avenue
+ **Subway**: R at 86th Street, transfer to B1; D at 20th Avenue, transfer to B1
+ **Bike**: There are bike lanes on Seventh Avenue, Poly Place, and along the Belt Parkway

80. Japanese Hill-and-Pond Garden

Like the nearby Brooklyn Public Library, the **Brooklyn Botanic Garden** had a delayed opening at its present location. Its 39 acres were reserved by the state in 1897, but it didn't open to the public until 1911. Within the garden is a watercourse that echoes its larger counterpart in nearby Prospect Park. Alfred T. White, the philanthropist who also purchased land in southern Brooklyn and which became Marine Park, funded the pond's construction.

The most popular attraction within the Brooklyn Botanic Garden is the **Japanese Hill-and-Pond Garden**, designed by architect Takeo Shiota in 1915. A brook flows out of the pond, passing by the Bluebell Wood, the Rock Garden, the Plant Family Collection, and the South Garden. Fed by the city's aqueduct, Japanese Pond is enveloped in a miniature landscape that incorporates a variety of architectural and landscaping forms used in Japanese Gardens. A pavilion on the eastern side is based on the architecture of a teahouse. From its small windows, visitors see a tall wooden structure, the tori-mon, which indicates an approach to a Shinto temple. In the background are three constructed hills symbolizing heaven, earth, and humanity. Waterfalls add to the naturalistic scene.

Water flows out of the pond through a constructed ravine toward a lawn where two pipes, fed by rainwater, emerge to the surface between rocks. This was designed to resemble natural springs. The stream terminates at the Water Garden, first entering a forebay pond before pooling in the Water Garden pond. This new garden, designed by Michael Van Valkenburgh Associates, captures not only the stream's water but also runoff from throughout the garden, channeling some of it back to its source. Together with the Water Garden, Van Valkenburgh also designed an expanded Children's Garden and a redesigned Flatbush Avenue entrance.

PLACES TO SEE:

+ **Brooklyn Botanic Garden**: Entrances at 150 Eastern Parkway and 990 Washington Avenue + 718-623-7200 + www.bbg.org

GETTING THERE:

+ **Bus**: B41 at Flatbush Avenue and Grand Army Plaza
+ **Subway**: 2, 3 at Eastern Parkway–Brooklyn Museum
+ **Bike**: There are bike paths on Eastern Parkway

81. Mount Prospect Reservoir

Sandwiched between the Brooklyn Public Library and Brooklyn Botanic Garden is a steep hilltop park, **Mount Prospect Park**. Presently, it is regarded as a hidden park, its once-panoramic views blocked by the library, the **Brooklyn Museum**, and the apartments on Eastern Parkway. The hill is located inside a triangular superblock that was initially slated for inclusion in Prospect Park but became a reservation for the borough's leading cultural institutions.

Prior to development, the eight-acre site was known as the second-highest point in Brooklyn, at 200 feet. To its southeast, Flatbush Avenue passes through the heavily forested terminal moraine that is preserved within Prospect Park. During the American Revolution, Mount Prospect served as a lookout point for Washington's army as it stood above Flatbush Pass.

In 1856, the city of Brooklyn acquired the site for a reservoir, and within four years, the reservoir was made part of Prospect Park on the belief that the greensward would shield the drinking water from encroaching development. Water for the reservoir originated in the dammed streams of southern Nassau and Queens Counties, flowing through a conduit toward Ridgewood Reservoir and then through another conduit toward Mount Prospect.

The demand for water in the growing city led to calls for a water tower, which would boost property values and prevent fires. A Gothic-style tower made of pink granite was completed in 1892 by architects Henry W. Thayer and William J. Wallace. Another architectural curiosity built near the reservoir was its gatehouse, a classical structure that housed a water-testing laboratory.

Following Brooklyn's consolidation into New York City in 1898, Mount Prospect Reservoir became obsolete, and plans were made for its demolition. In 1930, the water tower was demolished to make way for the expansion of the Brooklyn Public Library's main branch. In 1940, the reservoir was transferred to the city and was quickly redeveloped into Mount Prospect Park.

From Grand Army Plaza, the view of Mount Prospect is concealed by the **Brooklyn Public Library**, which was the subject of modified plans and lengthy delays prior to its 1941 opening. Ground was broken for the facility in 1912, promising a Beaux-Arts design by Raymond F. Almirall. Unfortunately, from day one, budget cuts slowed the construction, and the Great Depression completely halted it. In 1935, the city hired Alfred Morton Githens and Francis Keally to simplify Almirall's design. The result was an Art Deco design with very little ornamentation, no dome, and only two of the three building wings that were present in the original triangular floor plan.

The isolation of Mount Prospect Park from Prospect Park by Flatbush Avenue could be resolved with a pedestrian bridge. The historic landscape of Prospect Park, however, is carefully guarded by the park's advocates and by the city as an official scenic landmark. For the foreseeable future, Mount Prospect Park will remain an afterthought tucked behind the borough's defining institutions, with no trace of the reservoir that occupied its summit.

BROOKLYN

PLACES TO SEE:
* **Mount Prospect Park** Eastern Parkway between the Brooklyn Public Library and Brooklyn Botanic Garden * www.nycgovparks.org/parks/mount-prospect-park
* **Brooklyn Museum** 200 Eastern Parkway * 718-638-5000 * www.brooklynmuseum.org
* **Brooklyn Public Library—Central Library** 15 Grand Army Plaza * 718-230-2100 * www.bklynlibrary.org/locations/central

GETTING THERE:
* **Bus**: B41 at Flatbush Avenue and Grand Army Plaza
* **Subway**: 2, 3 at Eastern Parkway–Brooklyn Museum
* **Bike**: There are bike paths on Eastern Parkway

82. Sunset Park Pond

Near the northern border of the **Sunset Park** neighborhood is the 24-acre hilltop park that gave the neighborhood its name. The park was acquired by the city of Brooklyn for $165,000 in 1891 with the goal of developing it into a southern version of Fort Greene Park, a hill with a view. At a height of nearly 200 feet, the summit afforded views of New York Harbor and the Atlantic Ocean.

Near the eastern side of the park was a man-made ice-skating pond ringed by a fence. It survived into the 1930s. By then, the city was building a dozen public pools across its park system, and Sunset Park's pond was filled to make way for a swimming pool. A Depression-period work of architecture, it opened on July 20, 1936. It was the sixth in a series of a dozen pools citywide that opened during that decade, with a total capacity for 360,000 swimmers within all the pools combined.

No trace of the pond remains today.

PLACES TO SEE:
+ **Sunset Park** Bound by Fifth Avenue, 41st Street, Seventh Avenue, and 44th Street   + www.nycgovparks.org/parks/sunset-park

GETTING THERE:
+ **Bus:** B63 at Fifth Avenue and 44th Street
+ **Subway:** R at 45th Street, walk east on 45th Street to Fifth Avenue, turn left and enter the park at 44th Street
+ **Bike:** There are bike lanes on Fifth Avenue and Seventh Avenue

BROOKLYN

Staten Island

➤ **The geology of Staten Island is the most complex of** the city's boroughs, containing the terminal moraine of the last ice age, a fault line from 470 million years ago, the southern tail of the Palisades formation, and sediments collected over the millennia. Across these formations, ponds occupy natural depressions, and brooks flow through valleys. As the last of the city's boroughs to experience urbanization, Staten Island has the largest number of waterways that are presently above the surface and the largest number of ponds that are enclosed within private properties.

On the borough's western side, Richmond Creek, Willow Brook, and Springville Creek merge into **Fresh Kills**, which runs past the world's largest former landfill—today being transformed into a park. On the southern shore, the surviving creeks have been adapted into the **Bluebelt**, a storm water management system that channels runoff from local streets into wetlands and creeks. Along the north shore, industrialization dammed and later filled some of the streams, but vestiges of them still appear within parks and in alleys between buildings.

83. Clifton Lake

Located in the **Shore Acres** neighborhood, this kettle pond is situated entirely within private land, divided between three properties. Its first mention as a named entity on a map appeared in J. W. Beers and Company's 1874 *Atlas of Staten Island*, where it was dubbed **Clifton Lake**. Shore Acres was named and developed in the 1930s by Cornelius G. Kolff; but prior to its development, the land around Clifton Lake was a single property, whose stone wall still lines Bay Street between Harborview Place and Sea Gate Road.

Tucked between the older Clifton neighborhood and the former military base at Fort Wadsworth, Shore Acres is a secluded enclave of mansions amid densely forested terrain, with spectacular views of the Verrazano-Narrows Bridge. The best place to catch sight of the fenced-off Clifton Lake is from its southern side on Sea Gate Road.

To the immediate south of Sea Gate Road, the 14-acre **Arthur Von Briesen Park** occupies the former estate of Arthur Von Briesen, a noted immigration advocate and founder of the Legal Aid Society. He lived on this property from 1901 until his death in 1920, and he called his home here "Gernda," a German term for "wishing to be there." In 1945, a quarter century after his death, Von Briesen's heirs donated his estate to the city.

Farther south, Bay Street enters **Fort Wadsworth**, a unit within Gateway National Recreation Area. The fort is one of nearly a dozen built around the city to protect it in the early 19th century against the British, should they ever wish to recapture the former colony.

PLACES TO SEE:

+ **Arthur Von Briesen Park** Bay Street at School Road ✦ www.nyc govparks.org/parks/von-briesen-park
+ **Fort Wadsworth** Bay Street at Wadsworth Avenue ✦ www.nps .gov/gate/historyculture/fort-wadsworth.htm

GETTING THERE:

+ **Bus**: S51 at Bay Street and Sea Gate Road
+ **Train**: Staten Island Railway to Clifton, transfer to S51
+ **Ferry**: Staten Island Ferry to Saint George, transfer to S51
+ **Bike**: There are bike lanes on Bay Street

84. Brady's Pond

Located in the Grasmere neighborhood, **Brady's Pond** has the distinction of being the only freshwater pond in the city that is deemed suitable for swimming. With the exception of the city-owned Brady's Pond

Park on the pond's northeast corner, the spring-fed pond is surrounded by residential properties that jointly contribute to the maintenance of the pond.

The history of development around Brady's Pond and its downstream counterpart, **Cameron Lake**, began in the mid-19th century, when shipping executive Sir Roderick Cameron purchased land around the two ponds. He named his estate **Grasmere**, after a village in the Lake District of England. In the 1880s, Cameron sold his land to Philip Brady, who placed a dam on the upper marshland to form Brady's Pond. A second, smaller pond downstream on the property became Cameron Lake, formed from the run-off of the dam. During Brady's administration of the ponds, they were used for ice harvesting and skating.

Following Brady's death, the property was subdivided and developed in pieces. In 1930, the **Cameron Lake Club** was founded by surrounding property owners to prevent further development and to ensure the good condition of the pond. Membership in the club is restricted to property owners within a certain distance of the pond. While the entire pond is zoned as a single private parcel, the tiny beach operated by the Cameron Lake Club can be found on a private road branching off from Lakeview Terrace on the western side of Brady's Pond.

When a lake is entirely enveloped by private property, the lake's water quality and appearance are entirely dependent on its neighboring owners. For Brady's Pond, two of the properties on its shore are public agencies: the city's Parks Department, which operates **Brady's Pond Park** as a nature reserve; and the state's Department of Transportation, which is responsible for the Staten Island Expressway. While Brady's Pond is entirely private, some of the water that enters it includes excess storm water runoff from the highway, which endangers the quality of this lake. Although such runoff is rare, it worries property owners, who have paid top prices to live by the lake.

Cameron Lake is connected to Brady's Pond by an underground channel. It does not have a beach and is subject to algae blooms that obscure its appearance. In times of excessive rain, the two ponds act as part of the 1,267-acre South Beach Watershed, a series of underground channels, wetlands, and ponds that transport storm runoff downstream toward Lower New York Bay.

✦ **Brady's Pond Park** Hylan Boulevard at Narrows Road South

✦ **The Cameron Club** www.cameronclub.net

✦ **Bus**: S79 at Steuben Street and Olga Place; S53, S78 at Clove Road and Grasmere Station**Subway**: R to Bay Ridge–95th Street, transfer to S53 or S79
✦ **Train**: Staten Island Railway to Grasmere
✦ **Ferry**: Staten Island Ferry to Saint George, transfer to S53 or S78
✦ **Bike**: There are currently no bike lanes near Brady's Pond

85. Eibs Pond

The neighborhood of **Park Hill** is located below Clifton on the slope of Grymes Hill. A 17-acre green space hemmed by apartments and tract housing, **Eibs Pond Park** contains three kettle ponds. Together, **North Pond, Hattie's Pond**, and **Eibs Pond** form a miniature watershed that collects runoff from the surrounding slopes.

Eibs Pond's namesake is a German immigrant family who owned a farm around the pond in the 19th century. Among the distinguished visitors was writer Henry David Thoreau in May 1843. "The whole island is like a garden," he wrote. In the 1870s, property owner Lewis Henry Meyer named his land Fox Hills, in a nod to its pastoral scenery that made for pleasant foxhunting.

In the following century, Fox Hills served a variety of diverse functions before its final role as the centerpiece of a park. In 1899, the 110-acre farmland was a cricket ground that failed to generate revenue, and a year later, **Fox Hills Golf Club** was founded on the property. Eibs Pond served as a water hazard for golfers in the summer and a curling competition site in winter.

During the vaudeville period in filmmaking, the golf course and its pond appeared in several episodes of *The Perils of Pauline*, starring Pearl White and Milton Berle, in 1914.

During the First World War, a section of the golf course was developed into a military hospital that housed 20,000 patients—at the time, a world record. With the Great Depression, the golf club filed for bankruptcy, and the site sat vacant. It was pressed into service again during the Second World War, when it served as a prisoner-of-war camp for Italian soldiers.

Following the war, the former military hospital was demolished, and land around the pond again became neglected. Illegal dumping greatly degraded the freshwater marsh. Change arrived in the late 1980s, when the Urban Investment Development Company planned the construction of an apartment building and multistory hotel overlooking the pond.

Amid concerns over the environmental impact of building around the pond, the state designated Eibs Pond and the surrounding area as a wetland in 1987, and the developer donated the designated portion of the land to the nonprofit Trust for Public Land. Two years later, it was transferred to the city as **Eibs Pond Park**. In the 1990s, 37 acres to the north and east of the pond were mapped out for **Celebration at Rainbow Hill**, a neo-urban private development of 586 townhouses.

In 1999, the Trust for Public Land donated an additional nine acres of land to the park. That year, the Fox Hills Tenants Association, led by Rev. Hattie Smith-Davis, teamed up with the Parks Council to restore the park. In tribute to the activist, one of the three ponds in Eibs Pond Park is called Hattie's Pond.

A pond that languished for a half century has become a focal point in the revival of older apartments, a selling point for new townhouses in Park Hills, and an outdoor science classroom for students of Public School 57.

PLACES TO SEE:

✦ **Eibs Pond Park** Palma Drive at Hanover Avenue ✦ www.nycgov parks.org/parks/eibs-pond-park

GETTING THERE:

✦ **Bus**: S74, S76 at Targee Street and Palma Drive, walk east on Palma Drive toward Eibs Pond Park
✦ **Ferry**: Staten Island Ferry to Saint George, transfer to S74 or S76
✦ **Bike**: There are currently no bike lanes near Eibs Pond

STATEN ISLAND

86. Silver Lake

One of the sources of Clove Brook was **Silver Lake**, a spring-fed waterway resting on the northern slope of Grymes Hill. Its first mention was in 1687, when it was referred to as Fresh Pond in the Palmer Patent, a document that awarded 5,100 acres of land on the island to Captain John Palmer.

In the second half of the 19th century, the pond was the site of a resort and ice-harvesting business, tucked inside a valley but close enough to the ferry landings to attract patrons from beyond Staten Island. In 1900, state lawmakers set aside the grounds around Silver Lake as a public park, with the intention of making it the island's equivalent to Central and Prospect Parks.

As happened throughout the city, functionality trumped all else. The lake was drained in 1913 and replaced in 1917 with a holding reservoir for Staten Island's water supply. Using pipes that were laid on the bottom of the Narrows—the channel that separates Staten Island from Brooklyn—water from the Catskill aqueduct system flowed from Brooklyn into Silver Lake and was then distributed throughout the island. The shape of the lake resembles an expanded number eight, with a dam across the lake's midpoint to separate its two basins.

While the lake was ringed with picnic pavilions, the surrounding hills formed a belt of small cemeteries: Silver Mount, Silver Lake, Woodland, and Marine Cemeteries. All but the last of these once had natural ponds inside them that enhanced the scenery at a time when cemeteries were known widely as "burial parks."

On September 15, 1878, Silver Lake revealed its own morbid tale when local boys tending cattle discovered a partially buried barrel with human remains. Investigators found that the woman had been bludgeoned to death and may have given birth while being killed. The body was identified as Stapleton resident Mary Ann Reinhardt, and her estranged husband Edward Reinhardt was charged and convicted for her murder. At the time of her death, he was also married to another woman, which made him a bigamist—highly unacceptable at the time.

Until his last breath, Reinhardt denied being the "Silver Lake Murderer." On January 14, 1881, taverns across Staten Island held celebrations, and crowds jostled to receive a ticket to see him executed. He was buried at **Silver Mount Cemetery**, within view of the lake. Two months following the execution, undertaker Daniel Dempsey swore that he saw

1917 Silver Lake reservoir in Staten Island

the ghost of Edward Reinhardt standing by a barrel on the Richmond Turnpike, the ancient road now known as Victory Boulevard.

The eastern edge of **Silver Lake Golf Course** used to be **Marine Cemetery**, which served as a repository for victims of various outbreaks who died at the Marine Hospital. Founded in 1799 in Tompkinsville, the hospital served as a prison of sorts for victims of smallpox, cholera, typhus, and yellow fever and was locally known as "the Quarantine."

In 1848, a yellow fever outbreak on the island was blamed on the hospital, despite its fortresslike walls. A decade later, on September 1, 1858, rioters torched the hospital and celebrated its destruction. Two of the riot's organizers, Ray Tompkins and John C. Thompson, were acquitted of all charges by Judge Henry B. Metcalfe, himself an outspoken opponent of the hospital.

As a result of the riots, the Quarantine was relocated off the coast of Staten Island onto two artificial landmasses, Swinburne and Hoffman Island. Marine Cemetery was acquired by Silver Lake Golf Course in 1924, and most of the bodies were relocated. Inevitably a few were left behind, and to this day they rest anonymously beneath the 18th fairway. In 2002, a memorial boulder with a plaque was installed at this location, describing the fairway as the "Forgotten Burial Ground." It reads: "Here lie the unmarked graves of Irish immigrants who fled the Great Famine in search of freedom. Those who are buried here died from disease, alone and isolated, in the Tompkinsville Quarantine before ever tasting freedom. The 7,000 dead, most of whom had no survivors who could afford markers, were buried anonymously. They will not be forgotten."

STATEN ISLAND

At **Silver Lake Cemetery**, the city's indigent Jewish immigrants were buried between 1892 and 1909 by the Hebrew Free Burial Association. Although the cemetery is locked, it hosts volunteer cleanups twice a year. After filling up with nearly 15,000 dead, the organization moved its operations to Mount Richmond Cemetery on the island's south, which remains in use.

With the completion of the 6,238-yard **Silver Lake Golf Course** in 1929, a brook that drained from Silver Lake, called **Clove Brook**, was covered, and a downstream millpond, **Valley Lake** (also known as Britton's Pond and Schoenian's Pond), was reduced in size. Prior to its role as a water hazard, Valley Lake was also an ice-harvesting site. From Valley Lake, the eastern branch of Clove Brook is channeled through an underground culvert into Clove Lakes Park, where it merges with the brook's southern branch at Clove Lake.

PLACES TO SEE:

+ **Silver Lake Golf Course** 915 Victory Boulevard ✦ 718-447-5686 ✦ www.silverlakegolf.com
+ **Silver Lake Park** Bound approximately by Victory Boulevard, Forest Avenue, and Silver Lake Park Road ✦ www.nycgovparks.org/parks/silver-lake-park
+ **Woodland Cemetery** 982 Victory Boulevard ✦ 888-761-9001 ✦ www.woodlandcemetery.net
+ **Silver Lake Cemetery** 926 Victory Boulevard ✦ 718-667-0915 ✦ www.hebrewfreeburial.org
+ **Silver Mount Cemetery** 918 Victory Boulevard ✦ 718-727-7020

GETTING THERE:

+ **Bus**: S61, S62, S66, S91, S92, X30 at Victory Boulevard and Eddy Street
+ **Ferry**: Staten Island Ferry to Saint George, transfer to S61, S62, S66, S91, and S92
+ **Bike**: There are bike paths within Silver Lake Park

87. Clove Brook

Separated from Silver Lake Park by Clove Road is the much larger **Clove Lakes Park**. A former estate of colonial governor Thomas Dongan, the valley around **Clove Brook** contains dense forest, hiding the Ordovician-era serpentine rock that forms Emerson and Grymes Hills on either side of the valley. The valley was acquired by the city for parkland in 1921 and 1923 following decades of impassioned advocacy by residents William T. Davis, Charles Leng, and Frederick Law Olmsted. Along with Silver Lake Park, they envisioned Clove Valley as the island's Central Park.

Clove Brook's name is an English corruption of the Dutch term *kloven*, meaning "cleft," in reference to the valley the brook ran through. The southern branch of Clove Brook originated at a spring near the present-day intersection of Little Clove Road and Logan Avenue in the Sunnyside neighborhood. The water collected in the spring from the slopes of **Todt Hill**, the island's highest point. A couple of blocks downhill from the corner where the brook originated is the **Marine Corps League**, a private club representing active and retired service members that uses its land for sports and barbecues.

On this property, between Logan and Ontario Avenues, is a concrete post with water flowing out of it. The fountain is a natural spring that was a popular source of water for local residents until the Marine Corps League cut off access in 2012 following too many fights and long lines among water collectors.

Clove Lakes Park

A block to the north of the Marine Corps League, the stream widens into **Clove Lake**, the largest of the park's three lakes. In the 19th century, the lake was used as an ice-harvesting and skating site. The lake was formed by a milldam constructed in 1825 by Abraham Britton. Farther downstream within the park is **Martling's Pond**, also formed by a mill; and **Brooks Pond**, formed in 1863 by property owner Erastus Brooks. The Staten Island Water Company, one of the local companies supplying water in the 19th and early 20th centuries, bought the rights to use the water from the Brooks Pond dam. An 1887 property map of the area shows four ice houses along both branches of Clove Brook. Prior to the invention of refrigerators, ice companies were present throughout the region's ponds and lakes.

Whimsically placed on an island in the middle of Clove Lake, **The Stone House** is a restaurant that also offers paddleboat and rowboat rentals. Another landmark farther downstream is **Saint Peter's Cemetery**, the island's oldest Catholic cemetery, which accepted its first burials in 1848. In its first century, most of its dead were Irish immigrants, including those fleeing the Irish Potato Famine in the first four years of the cemetery's existence.

Beneath the surface

At Forest Avenue, Clove Lakes Park comes to an end, and Clove Brook is abruptly channeled beneath the surface, passing under residential blocks that as recently as the early 1980s were undeveloped and saw the brook running through narrow channels. The former presence of the brook is evident in several dead-end streets that once terminated at the water's edge, such as Arcadia Place and Chrissy Court. One-block streets with elbow turns were also designed to avoid Clove Brook before it was covered with housing. These roads include Cornell Avenue and Brooks Place.

At Raymond Place and Disosway Place, Clove Brook split into two. The western fork continued north, where it merged with Palmer's Run, while an eastern fork drained into Factory Pond. The split in the stream was filled by the early 20th century, and within the next three decades, the sections running toward Post Avenue were also gradually filled. North of Post Avenue, the buried streambed of the western fork follows Driprock Street and Rector Street to **Levy Playground**, passing under the Castleton Bus Depot.

Located at the intersection of Castleton Avenue and Jewett Avenue, Levy Playground sits on the former confluence of Clove Brook and Palmer's Run. From this location, the stream continued as Palmer's Run toward its end at Kill Van Kull.

The most approximate path that one would take along the buried section would begin at Forest Avenue, turning on Raymond Place and walking north, turning left on Floyd Street, then right on Greenleaf Avenue, which continues north of Post Avenue as Driprock Street and Rector Street. At its intersection with Richmond Terrace, Clove Brook returns to the surface.

Eastern fork

No traces of the eastern fork remain except for two parks situated atop the former streambed. The smaller park is the **Joe Holzka Community Garden**, located at Castleton Avenue and Barker Street. The garden is named for a local activist who fought to preserve Snug Harbor and designate the Greenbelt as a park. Behind the park is Taylor Court, a one-block dead end that terminated at the former stream.

The eastern fork of Clove Brook ran in a northeast direction through the section of Port Richmond that was historically known as **Factory-ville**. The rural community was transformed in 1819 when Staten Island's first industrial enterprise, Barrett, Tileston & Company, opened its textile dyeing factory and printing works on a sixteen-acre tract near the present-day intersection of Broadway and Richmond Terrace. It was later renamed as the New York Dyeing and Printing Works. The factory expanded a small millpond for industrial use, which appeared on maps as **Factory Pond**. The company's founder, Col. Nathan Barrett, resided uphill of Broadway near Clove Lakes Park. His estate later became the site of the Staten Island Zoo.

PLACES TO SEE:

+ **Marine Corps League** 46 Ontario Avenue ✦ 718-447-2306 ✦ http://si-mcl.org/
+ **The Stone House at Clove Lakes** 1150 Clove Road (island in Clove Lake) ✦ 718-442-3600 ✦ www.thestonehousesi.com
+ **Saint Peter's Cemetery** 52 Tyler Avenue ✦ 718-442-2363
+ **Levy Playground** Castleton Avenue at Jewett Avenue
+ **Joe Holzka Community Garden** Castleton Avenue at Barker Street ✦ www.nycgovparks.org/about/history/historical-signs/listings?id=12140

GETTING THERE:

+ **Bus**: S53, X14 on Clove Road between Victory Boulevard and Broadway; S61, S62, S66, S91, S92, S93 at Victory Boulevard and Seneca Avenue
+ **Subway**: R to Bay Ridge–95th Street, transfer to S53 or S93
+ **Ferry**: Staten Island Ferry to Saint George, transfer to S61, S62, S66, S91, or S92
+ **Bike**: There are bike paths within Clove Lakes Park

88. Palmer's Run

A small section of **Palmer's Run** appears above the surface as an inlet of Kill Van Kull to the north of Richmond Terrace. Prior to the early 20th century, it was one of the longer streams of Staten Island, originating nearly three miles inland. Its longest branch emerged from a spring near present-day Bradley Avenue and the Staten Island Expressway in the

STATEN ISLAND

Castleton Corners neighborhood. Another branch originated near Todt Hill Road and Andes Place on the western slope of Todt Hill. A third unnamed branch flowed from the future site of the interchange where the Staten Island Expressway and Dr. Martin Luther King Jr. (formerly Willowbrook) Expressway meet.

As development encroached, each branch was channeled underground, leaving isolated portions above the surface. The farthest upstream surface location is on the southern side of Victory Boulevard between Perry and Wheeler Avenues, in front of an appropriately named Italian restaurant, **Waterfalls**. Here, the creek runs in a narrow stone channel for two blocks and again disappears beneath the landscape.

This neighborhood, Castleton Corners, was named after Castletown Kildrought, a town in County Kildare, Ireland, where Thomas Dongan, governor of New York from 1683 to 1688, was born. In the 19th century, Castleton was one of the six towns of Staten Island, and it had numerous villages inside it. The western boundary of the town to the north of Watchogue Road was Palmer's Run. The southern boundary was Richmond Turnpike, the present-day Victory Boulevard. During the Dongan administration, John Palmer was appointed as "ranger" for Staten Island in 1680 and set about building mills and forming ponds along the stream that would carry his name.

According to historian Ira K. Morris, it would be a mistake to presume that Watchogue is a native name. In his 1898 book *Morris's Memorial History of Staten Island*, the road's namesake was said to be Watch Oak, a farm owned by Isaac Merrill. Over the years, the name was corrupted into Watchogue. Palmer's Run appears in segments behind some backyards on the southern side of Watchogue Road, interrupting Marble Street, Frederick Street, and Iowa Place.

According to Morris, the stream's tributaries included the unattractively named Stinking Brook and Great Swamp Ditch. The former's name is blamed on the Four Corners brewery, which sent its runoff into the brook. The latter was a ditch that channeled some of the water from nearby Willow Brook to the Butcherville branch of Palmer's Run.

To the north of Watchogue Road, above-surface remnants of Palmer's Run appear as a drainage ditch at Columbus Place and Dickie Avenue. On the western edge of the Westerleigh neighborhood, interruptions in Leonard, Lathrop, Garrison, and Maine Avenues also hint to the stream's former path. At Forest Avenue, the stream is hidden beneath the parking lot of a strip mall. In the Port Richmond neighborhood, the following streets have dead ends that used to abut the streambed and property lines that follow the former stream's path: Catherine Street, Dryden Court, Bache Street, Mitchel Lane, and Wygant Street.

To the north of Post Avenue, the underground stream follows Jewett Avenue, passing beneath the Castleton Bus Depot and Levy Playground. The depot was a millpond in the 19th century, operated by the Bodine family. They emigrated from France, part of a larger influx of Huguenot refugees at the end of the 17th century.

At Richmond Terrace, the stream emerges to the surface at sea level as an inlet of Kill Van Kull. On its eastern side, the **Port Richmond Water Pollution Control Plant** absorbs much of the storm water from North Shore communities, filtering it before the water is discharged into Kill Van Kull.

Near its confluence with Kill Van Kull, Palmer's Run passes beneath the abandoned **North Shore Branch** of the Staten Island Railway. In 1953, the Baltimore & Ohio Railroad threatened to abandon all of its holdings on Staten Island. In a painful compromise, the city agreed to subsidize the Tottenville Branch while abandoning the North Shore and South Beach lines. The closing of the Arlington, Port Richmond, and West Brighton stations, among others, sent those communities into an economic decline for the next half century.

As the city's Department of Environmental Protection seeks to expand the Bluebelt program to Staten Island's north shore, Palmer's Run would likely become a major component of a Port Richmond Bluebelt. A Bluebelt system would transform undeveloped lots along the buried streambed back into wetlands that would collect storm runoff from surrounding streets.

The most visible street corners where Palmer's Run appears above the surface are Watchogue Road and Marble Street, Watchogue Road and Saint John Avenue, and Victory Boulevard and Wheeler Avenue.

PLACES TO SEE:
+ **Waterfalls Restaurant** 2012 Victory Boulevard + 718-815-7200 + www.waterfalls-restaurant.com

GETTING THERE:
+ **Bus:** S57 to Watchogue Road and Frederick Street; S62, S92, S93 to Victory Boulevard and Mann Avenue
+ **Train:** Staten Island Railway to New Dorp, transfer to S57

STATEN ISLAND

+ **Ferry**: Staten Island Ferry to Saint George, transfer to S62 or S92
+ **Bike**: There are currently no bike lanes near the former path of Palmer's Run

89. Harbor Brook

Harbor Brook originates in the neighborhood of Randall Manor, widening into **Goodhue Pond** and **Allison Pond** before disappearing beneath the ground. To the north of Henderson Avenue, this stream returns to the surface, running through one of the top tourism destinations on Staten Island: **Sailors' Snug Harbor**. The 83-acre campus has a proud history as a former community for retired seamen. It dates back to 1801, when Captain Robert Richard Randall stipulated in his will that his Manhattan estate should be left as an "asylum or marine hospital, to be called 'The Sailors' Snug Harbor,' for the purpose of maintaining and supporting aged, decrepit, and worn-out sailors."

Randall's heirs contested the will, and ultimately the institution's trustees built the facilities on Staten Island instead. It welcomed its first retirees in 1833. The neighborhood that later developed around Snug Harbor was named Randall Manor. Over the course of the following century, nearly 40,000 retired sailors called this campus home. Following the Second World War, the population of sailor retirees declined, and the trustees of Snug Harbor found the maintenance of the buildings to be too expensive.

Since its transfer to the city between 1972 and 1978, the site has become a cultural hub for the island. Its landmark Greek Revival and Italianate structures provide homes for the Snug Harbor Cultural Center, Staten Island Botanical Garden, Newhouse Center for Contemporary Art, artist John A. Noble's Maritime Collection of artworks, the Staten Island Children's Museum, the Art Lab school, and the Staten Island Museum Archives and History Center.

Although Snug Harbor has a fishpond near its northern entrance and another inside its renowned Chinese Scholar's Garden, they are not related to Harbor Brook, which has its own lake near the campus's western border. Hidden behind the baseball fields of the **Sailors' Snug Harbor Little League**, Harbor Brook blissfully descends northward. Along the way, it picks up a tributary brook that emerges behind Wales Place.

Harbor Brook drains into Kill Van Kull in a forest preserve to the north of Snug Harbor.

PLACES TO SEE:
✦ **Snug Harbor** 1000 Richmond Terrace ✦ 718-273-8200 ✦ www
.snug-harbor.org

90. Factory Pond

The neighborhood name Factoryville was practical for identifying industrial land, but for residents it was very unattractive. Toward the end of
the 19th century, the name West New Brighton was adopted in order to
associate the community with the upscale New Brighton neighborhood
to its east. The name was shortened to West Brighton by the time the
city's Housing Authority completed the **West Brighton Houses** in 1962.
This housing project and a portion of **Cpl. Lawrence Thompson Park**
stand on the site of **Factory Pond**.

At the northwestern corner of the pond was the **New York Dyeing
and Printing Works**, a major employer—and polluter—on the North
Shore. The pond was filled in the early 20th century, and in 1932, the
dyeing factory ceased operations. A portion of the former pond and
the factory later became a city park, renamed in 1972 for Cpl. Lawrence
Thompson, the first African American from Staten Island to be killed
in the Vietnam War. Refusing a medical discharge for a foot ailment,
Thompson reenlisted for a second tour of duty and was killed in action
in 1967.

At the northwestern corner of the former pond, overlooking the park's
football field, is a wooded patch of land pockmarked with tombstones.
The **Fountain Cemetery** and **Staten Island Cemetery** are believed to
be the oldest on the island, originally used as a burial ground by the
native Lenape residents. Under the leadership of Lynn Rogers, the
group Friends of Abandoned Cemeteries of Staten Island manages 11
cemeteries across the borough. Since 1998, the organization has restored
fallen headstones, provided tours, and assisted individuals in finding the
graves of their ancestors.

The eastern fork of Clove Brook flowed out of Factory Pond and disappeared underground beneath a shipbuilding yard, where it emptied
into Kill Van Kull. No trace of Factory Pond remains today.

STATEN ISLAND

PLACES TO SEE:
✦ **West Brighton Swimming Pool** 899 Henderson Avenue ✦ 718-816-5019
✦ **Cpl. Lawrence Thompson Park** Bound by Broadway, Henderson Avenue, and Chappell Street ✦ www.nycgovparks.org/parks/corporal-thompson-park

GETTING THERE:
✦ **Bus**: S54 at Broadway and Wayne Street; S40 at Richmond Terrace and Broadway, walk south on Broadway toward Wayne Street
✦ **Ferry**: Staten Island Ferry to Saint George, transfer to S40
✦ **Bike**: There are currently no bike lanes near the former site of Factory Pond

91. Richmond Creek (Fresh Kills)

The longest of Staten Island's inland waterways, **Richmond Creek** originates deep within the borough at **Ohrbach Lake**. The lake is man-made, a donation from Ohrbach's, a once-great department store empire that operated from 1923 to 1987. At this location, the stream rushes beneath dense foliage and between rocks through the **Egbertville Ravine**, a link in the Staten Island Greenbelt that can be explored using the Blue Trail, which is the longest of the hiking trails within this interconnected park system. In the ravine, Richmond Creek receives additional water from tributary brooks that originate in **Blood Root Valley** and the **Bucks Hollow** swamp. The neighborhoods of Egbertville and Lighthouse Hill surround the ravine, offering residents plenty of nature and land, with parkland as a buffer.

Overlooking the ravine, **Lighthouse Hill** is a community of upscale homes whose growth was stopped by the zoning of parcels for the Greenbelt and the Bluebelt. While many older maps show a neat street grid, in reality the stream cuts through Nugent Street, Saint George Road, and Saint Andrews Road.

Despite the neighborhood's isolation from public transit, it appears in tourist guidebooks thanks to its unique attractions, which are clustered close together. The **Jacques Marchais Museum of Tibetan Art** is the creation of art dealer Jacqueline Klauber, who professionally went by the name Jacques Marchais. Open to the public since 1947, it resembles a

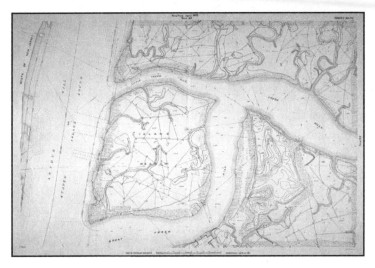

Topographical survey of Isle of Meadows, Fresh Kills, and Arthur Kill.

Himalayan monastery and was visited by the 14th Dalai Lama in 1991. One block uphill from this museum, the **Staten Island Lighthouse** is sandwiched on a parcel at 418 Edinboro Road, between two mansions. The 90-foot-high light tower has been active since 1912. Its original beacon extended for 21 miles. The tower stands 141 feet above sea level. One block to the west of the lighthouse is the third unique destination of the neighborhood, **Crimson Beech** at 48 Manor Court. Completed in 1959 for then owners Catherine and William Cass, it is the only residential structure in New York City designed by Frank Lloyd Wright.

Downhill from the upscale neighborhood is a collection of historic structures brought together in an arrangement comparable to Colonial Williamsburg in Virginia. As with many things on Staten Island relating to history and folklore, the creation of **Historic Richmond Town** also involved William T. Davis, along with official island historian Loring McMillen and banker David Decker. The 100-acre open-air museum is built around the former county seat of Staten Island and contains 46 historic structures and sites. With New York City's annexation of Staten Island in 1898, the island's administrative institutions shifted to Saint George in order to be closer to the Manhattan-bound ferry. In 1934, the Staten Island Historical Society transformed the former **County Clerk's and Surrogate's Office** into a museum, and it formed the nucleus of Historic Richmond Town, which was established in 1958.

On Richmond Creek, a reconstructed Dunn's Mill forms a pond and serves as a reminder of a gristmill that used the stream's water to grind grain. The pond was restored by the city's Department of Environmental

STATEN ISLAND

Protection as part of the Bluebelt program. Beyond the milldam is **Town Bridge**, a stone arch that carries Richmond Hill Road over the stream. Dating to 1845, it is the last arch bridge in the borough. Richmond Hill Road is among the oldest roads on Staten Island, and the first mention of a bridge at this location was in 1718. To the south of the bridge is the intersection of Richmond Hill Road, Richmond Road, and Arthur Kill Road, all predating the island's urbanization and designed to connect Richmond Town to the farthest ends of Staten Island. The bridge was financed by Rev. David Moore, rector of the **Church of Saint Andrew**, which stands on the north bank of the bridge. The congregation was granted its charter in 1713 by Queen Anne. Its current structure dates to 1872.

On the southern bank of the stream, across from the church cemetery, is the **Christopher House**. Constructed between 1720 and 1730 in the Willowbrook neighborhood, it served as a meeting place for the Committee of Safety during the American Revolution. In 1852, owner Thomas Standring enlarged the house and built a mill next to it to harness the water of Willow Brook. The structure was relocated to Richmond Town in 1974 and placed next to another stream to faithfully reconstruct its previous setting.

Beyond Richmond Town, the stream becomes navigable as it enters **LaTourette Park,** an 844-acre space that includes hiking trails and a golf course. The park's namesake was a Huguenot family who established a farm in the area in 1830 and kept the land until 1928, when it was sold to the city. Although the original farmhouse no longer exists, the family's 1870 mansion serves as the golf course's clubhouse.

The site was transferred to the Parks Department in 1955, and the mansion was designated a city landmark in 1973. In 1982, the mansion was added to the National Register of Historic Places.

Within the park, Richmond Creek widens and meanders through a freshwater marsh, where it becomes a navigable stream. As the proposed Willowbrook Parkway once threatened to destroy the unspoiled landscape of the Staten Island Greenbelt, the marshes of LaTourette Park were marked in the 1960s for the northern extension of the Richmond Parkway. As a result of public opposition, this highway ends abruptly at Arthur Kill Road, with two unused overpasses leading into the park as a reminder of what could have been built.

Richmond Avenue crosses Richmond Creek at the point where the stream leaves LaTourette Park and enters **Freshkills Park**, the former landfill. The first Richmond Avenue Bridge at this location was completed in 1931, a bascule drawbridge that anticipated a possible future for Richmond Creek as a seaport. The current bridge is a humble overpass. At its confluence with Main Creek, Richmond Creek takes on the name **Fresh Kills** and continues toward **Isle of Meadows**. This 87-acre island nearly became part of the Fresh Kills landfill but for protests led by the New York Audubon Society. Instead, it is a bird habitat primarily colonized by species of egret, heron, and ibis. Boats traveling into Fresh Kills enter and leave along the southern side of this island, where the channel is wider and deeper. Passing the island, Fresh Kills flows into Arthur Kill.

PLACES TO SEE:

+ **Egbertville Ravine** Rockland Avenue and Manor Road
+ **Blood Root Valley** Accessible by the Purple Trail within the Greenbelt
+ **Bucks Hollow** Accessible by the Red Trail within the Greenbelt
+ **Jacques Marchais Museum of Tibetan Art** 338 Lighthouse Avenue
  + 718-987-3500 + www.tibetanmuseum.org
+ **Staten Island Lighthouse (not open to the public)** 418 Edinboro Road
+ **Crimson Beech (not open to the public)** 48 Manor Road
+ **Historic Richmond Town** 441 Clarke Avenue + 718-351-1611 + www.historicrichmondtown.org
+ **Town Bridge** Richmond Hill Road between Richmond Road and Old Mill Road
+ **Church of Saint Andrew** 40 Old Mill Road at Richmond Hill Road + 718-351-0900 + www.churchofstandrew-si.com
+ **LaTourette Golf Course** 1001 Richmond Hill Road + 718-351-1889 + www.latourettegc.com
+ **LaTourette Park (southwest)** Accessible by the Purple Trail at Old Mill Road

GETTING THERE:

+ **Bus:** S54, S74, X15 at Richmond Road and Saint Patricks Place
+ **Ferry:** Staten Island Ferry to Saint George, transfer to S74
+ **Train:** Staten Island Railway to Great Kills, transfer to S54
+ **Bike:** There is a bike path within LaTourette Park

STATEN ISLAND

92. Clay Pit Ponds State Park Preserve

Throughout the state of New York, there are 180 parks managed by the New York State Office of Parks, Recreation, and Historic Preservation. These include beaches on Long Island and Lake Ontario, mountains in the Adirondacks and the Catskills, scenic waterfalls, and Revolutionary War battlefields—all far removed from the densely built city, which has its own municipal parks system.

But surprisingly, within the city's borders there are nine state parks, all located on or near streams, administered and financed by the state for the benefit of city residents. The lone state park on Staten Island is a densely wooded terrain in the southwest section of the borough between the neighborhoods of Rossville and Charleston. As with all state parks, the 260-acre **Clay Pit Ponds** has a rich natural and human history that merited its designation as a park. The landscape includes sand, pine barrens, freshwater wetlands, and streams. It can be accessed by walking or horseback along designated trails. For certain plant species within the park, it is the northernmost or southernmost location where they can be found.

Prior to European settlement, the future park was used by the Lenape for harvesting clay for pottery. The first European landowners in this area were the Androvette family, French Huguenot refugees who built a farmhouse in 1700 and later made their fortune in tugboats and marine towing on Arthur Kill. The businesses and homes that surrounded the family's property became known as **Androvetteville**. A reminder of this family is Androvette Street, which intersects with Kreischer Street, named after a subsequent developer of the neighborhood.

The rediscovery of Androvetteville's clay pits as an industrial material brought industrialist Balthazar Kreischer to the neighborhood. Following the opening of the B. Kreischer & Sons brickworks factory, Androvetteville was renamed **Kreischerville**, a company town that employed more than 300 workers who produced over three million bricks a year from local clay during the company's height in the 1890s. Anti-German sentiment during the First World War led residents to change the community's name to Charleston, after one of Balthazar's sons. Charles's mansion at Arthur Kill Road still stands and is a city landmark. The brickworks closed in 1927 during a slump in the building industry. The family's last holdings in Charleston were sold at auction in

Clay Pit Ponds

1931. The clay pits were left undeveloped, and nature has turned them into ponds.

For Charleston and Rossville residents, the forest around Clay Pit Ponds was an irreplaceable natural area with native and industrial history. In 1951, Parks Commissioner Robert Moses proposed filling in the freshwater wetlands with trash to prepare the land for development. The Federation of Sportsmen and Conservationists, the Staten Island Museum, and the Audubon Society teamed up to save the seven ponds in the preserve, home to herons, ducks, muskrats, and bitterns. "I can't imagine any park commissioner in the world permitting the dumping of garbage into such beautiful ponds," said W. Lynn McCracken, chairman of the Park Association of Staten Island. "Our counterproposal is to have garbage dumped in Babylon, Long Island"—the town where Moses lived. Each of the organizations wrote letters and mounted photography exhibits, and eventually they succeeded in defeating the landfill plan.

Although most of the preserve was spared from development, between 1967 and 1976 construction of the 8.3-mile **West Shore Expressway** chopped away at the forest's eastern edge. What remained of the forest and wetlands was designated a state park in 1980. The streams within **Clay Pit Ponds State Park Preserve** are Blue Factory Bog, Tappen's Pond, Clay Pit Pond, Ellis Swamp, Abraham's Pond, and Sharrott's Pond.

STATEN ISLAND

+ **Interpretive Center at Clay Pit Ponds** 2351 Veteran's Road + 718-605-3970 + www.nysparks.com/parks/166/details.aspx
+ **Sandy Ground Historical Society** 1538 Woodrow Road + 718-317-5796 + www.sandygroundmuseum.org

GETTING THERE:
+ **Bus**: S74, S84 at Arthur Kill Road and Clay Pit Road
+ **Ferry**: Staten Island Ferry to Saint George, transfer to S74 or S84
+ **Bike**: There are currently no bike paths within Clay Pit Ponds State Park Preserve

93. Willow Brook

Willow Brook lends its name to a neighborhood, park, highway, and a defunct mental hospital. According to the 1873 F. W. Beers *Atlas of Staten Island*, Willow Brook originated on the western slope of Todt Hill, near the present-day corner of Todt Hill Road and Manor Road, and flowed west toward Willowbrook Road. On the block bound by Westwood Avenue, Willowbrook Road, and Collfield Avenue, the stream appears in a ditch behind backyards, along the northern border of the CUNY College of Staten Island campus; and it reappears in Willowbrook Park, where the partially buried stream enters a pond.

Prior to the completion of the Verrazano Bridge in 1964, the landscape along Willow Brook was mostly rural. Following the opening of this bridge, tract housing was built atop the streambed. Along with Willowbrook Park, the College of Staten Island offers open space in an otherwise rapidly developing borough.

Completed in 1994, the 204-acre **College of Staten Island** is located on the former site of the **Willowbrook State School**, an asylum for mentally disabled children that operated between 1947 and 1987. It is the largest college campus within the City University of New York; before it acquired this space, the college had to be split across two campuses, in Sunnyside and Saint George. The neat neo-Georgian buildings were designed to give the campus a sense of history and order while distancing the college from the previous occupant of the site.

The asylum was designed for 4,200 children, but at its height in 1962, there were 6,200 patients crammed into its facilities, which became known for abusive practices. On a tour of Willowbrook in 1965, Senator Robert F. Kennedy spoke of its patients as "living in filth and dirt, their clothing in rags, in rooms less comfortable and cheerful than the cages in which we put animals in a zoo." Hepatitis outbreaks were common, and repeated exposés by investigative journalists put pressure on Willowbrook. The last patients were transferred from Willowbrook in 1987, putting an end to a shameful chapter in the state's treatment of the disabled.

To the west of the college is the densely forested **Willowbrook Park**, a 215-acre parcel that is connected to the borough's other large parks through the **Staten Island Greenbelt**, a 3,500-acre series of linear parks zoned on the right-of-way of two planned highways that were later cancelled. Willowbrook Park's story begins in 1909, when the city acquired the former site of a water pumping station for a park. In 1929, the property was declared a park. Inside the park is **Willowbrook Lake**, the largest man-made pond in the borough. The park's unique features include an archery course, tennis courts, a boathouse, and the **Carousel for All Children**, a 94-foot structure that is accessible to children and adults with disabilities.

Within the woods of Willowbrook Park used to be another hidden streambed, **Corson's Creek**. This tributary of Willow Brook originated in the woods to the south of the College of Staten Island, in a tract known as Corson's Brook Woods. In 1985, these woods were in danger of being felled—the Staten Island Developmental Center began removing trees for the expansion of its campus. But local activist Terence Benbow, a lawyer who had previously won numerous other legal battles to preserve Staten Island's natural features, fought successfully to save these trees. Following heavy rainfall, Corson's Creek reappears within Corson's Brook Woods as a seasonal stream. In some parts of the forest, the creek forms freshwater wetlands.

As early as 1930, Parks Commissioner Robert Moses proposed a system of arterial highways across Staten Island, lined with parks as buffers to shield neighborhoods from traffic. Named after the park, Willowbrook Parkway would have run from Bayonne Bridge on the North Shore to its destination at Great Kills Park. In November 1964, the section between Bayonne Bridge and Victory Boulevard opened to the public. However, this highway ends abruptly at the northern edge of Willowbrook Park, where it encountered determined public opposition.

STATEN ISLAND

The Willowbrook Parkway was never built, and the land that was set aside for this highway is now a linear park, the Staten Island Greenbelt, which runs across most of the borough.

Leaving Willowbrook Park, Willow Brook flowed beneath the **Bulls Head** intersection, where Victory Boulevard and Richmond Avenue cross paths. The neighborhood around the intersection is also called Bulls Head, named after a colonial-period tavern that was a hotbed of loyalist activity during the American Revolution. The tavern had a bull's head as its logo and served the farming communities of northern Staten Island.

Willow Brook flows beneath the **Hillside Swim Club** and Rustic Woods subdivision, both of which are bordered on the south by Signs Road. This two-lane street predates development, and on its opposite side is a forest and freshwater wetland where Willow Brook returns to the surface. This 428-acre preserve is the city's oldest, designated in 1928 and later renamed the **William T. Davis Wildlife Refuge** after its leading advocate.

Inside the preserve, the brook widens into a navigable channel and merges with Springville Creek, which originates in the neighborhood of New Springville. Beyond this confluence, the river carries the names Main Creek and Fresh Kills as it flows through the former Fresh Kills Landfill.

PLACES TO SEE:

+ **College of Staten Island** 2800 Victory Boulevard + 718-982-2000 + www.csi.cuny.edu
+ **Willowbrook Park** Bound approximately by Ashworth Avenue, Richmond Avenue, Victory Boulevard, and the College of Staten Island
+ **William T. Davis Wildlife Refuge** Bound by Park Drive North, Signs Road, Victory Boulevard, and Shelley Avenue + 212-639-9675 + www.nycgovparks.org/greening/nature-preserves/site?FWID=16

GETTING THERE:

+ **Bus**: S62, S92 at Victory Boulevard and Morani Street, walk into Willowbrook Park
+ **Ferry**: Staten Island Ferry to Saint George, transfer to S62 or S92
+ **Bike**: There is a bike path within Willowbrook Park

STATEN ISLAND

94. Old Place Creek

On the southern side of the Goethals Bridge approach is **Old Place Creek**. The stream had a number of forks from which it originated. The branch farthest inland emerges to the surface at Lisk Avenue and South Avenue in Graniteville. Another branch originates in **Staten Island Industrial Park** and a third at **Old Place Creek Park**. Both serve as nature preserves under the protection of the city's Parks Department.

Old Place
On the stretch of dry land between Old Place Creek and Bridge Creek were a few homes inhabited by fishermen. Among the names used to describe the settlement were Tunissen's Neck, Summerville, and Skunk Town. Its current name arose when a house in this community used for religious services was replaced by a new church; it was, however, inconvenient, so the worshipers repaired and returned to the "old place."

A local legend attributes the name Skunk Town to a slave named Fortune Crocheron who made money by extracting grease from skunks and marketing the substance as a cure for croup.

In the 1920s, the construction of the Goethals Bridge resulted in the demolition of Old Place's fishing shacks. In 1958, the approach to the bridge was widened and connected to the Staten Island Expressway.

Gulfport
On the southern side of the stream is a vast expanse of meadows and marshland punctured by a grid of unused streets. It has the desolate appearance of a last frontier on the city's southwestern edge. Yet for much of the 20th century, the marshland marked on maps as **Bloomfield** was also known as **Gulfport**, a massive fuel storage facility that operated between 1928 and 1998, with nearly 100 tanks sprawled across a 440-acre campus.

The Gulf Oil company put its name on the map with its facility, which generated more than 5,000 jobs. Its proximity to the Goethals Bridge, Arthur Kill, and the Staten Island Railway made it an ideal location for receiving and transporting oil to the metropolitan region.

On the southern edge of the tank farm, the Texas Eastern Transmission Corporation stored natural liquefied gas in the world's largest gas storage dome. Its tank had a 225-foot diameter and was as tall as an 11-story building; it had the capacity to hold 600,000 barrels of liq-

STATEN ISLAND

The Goethals Bridge stretches over Old Place Creek and Arthur Kill

uefied gas. On February 10, 1973, the tank was emptied for repairs, but a small amount of gas remained, causing a fire. The blaze and the resulting collapse of the dome room killed 40 workers at the site.

The disastrous explosion generated community opposition to an even larger proposed twin tank site in the Rossville neighborhood. Led by local residents Gene and Edwina Cosgriff, the group BLAST—Bring Legal Action to Stop the Tanks—succeeded in pressuring city and state lawmakers to ban future liquefied gas tanks within the city. For the next decade, the Bloomfield tank site stood empty as grass grew on its slopes. From above, it resembled a volcanic crater. The Rossville tanks were completed but never put to use. They stand abandoned, amid phragmites, as relics of industry.

The racetrack that never was

Following the gradual demolition of the oil tanks in the 1990s, the name Gulfport faded in favor of Bloomfield, though the company's name remains on the map in Gulf Avenue, a service road to the West Shore Expressway. While nature reappeared on the eerily abandoned mudflats, ambitious planners sought to bring automobile racing to the site in the form of a NASCAR racetrack.

To the tune of $100 million, the International Speedway Corporation, which owns NASCAR, purchased the 450-acre property in 2004. They quickly encountered opposition, however, from Staten Island residents, who feared traffic congestion from the sports venue. The racetrack would have been accompanied by a shopping center and accessible by two adjacent highways and a newly constructed ferry dock. A year later, International Speedway announced that it was giving up the planned racetrack.

In 2013, the site was sold for $80 million to Staten Island Marine Development, which plans to turn it into a seaport with warehouses and offices. In order to build on the site, 4.3 million cubic yards of earth will be needed to raise the property's elevation. The company will preserve 245 acres of the property as wetlands and develop the remaining 330 acres. The planned seaport will preserve the path of Old Place Creek, including the marshes on either of its banks.

Leaving Bloomfield, the stream flows beneath the Goethals Bridge and empties into Arthur Kill.

GETTING THERE:

Note: There are no paths or trails near this stream.

✦ **Bike**: There are currently no bike lanes near Old Place Creek, but one may use Gulf Avenue to pass near the stream

95. Bridge Creek and Goethals Pond

Historically, **Bridge Creek** did not have a pond. It was a brook that meandered through marshland, emptying into Arthur Kill near Howland Hook. Some local sources referred to it as Back Creek for its location and Lawrence Creek after a local property-owning family. An early mention of it as Bridge Creek appears in the 1874 Beers *Atlas of Staten Island*.

Its history being shaped by humans began in the 1880s, when the Travis railroad branch was constructed across the marshland. The earthen levee on which the tracks were laid divided the wetland, creating **Goethals Pond** on the eastern side of the tracks. The pond and the creek both became magnets for migratory birds as a result of their brackish water—not too fresh or too salty. Bridge Creek and Goethals Pond were officially adopted as the names for this mini-watershed in 1992. Between 1992 and 1996, the New York State Department of Environmental Conservation took possession of 67 acres, including the pond and some surrounding land, in order to create the Goethals Pond Complex.

Located on the southern side of the wetland, the **Goethals Bridge**

STATEN ISLAND

carries the Staten Island Expressway to New Jersey. The bridge was completed in 1928 and named after engineer George Washington Goethals, who died five months before the bridge opened to the public. Best known for his design work on the Panama Canal, he founded an engineering firm that assisted in the construction of the bridge that would carry his name. The original Goethals Bridge is currently in the process of being demolished, with a new cable-stayed Goethals Bridge to be completed in 2017. The new 21st-century design includes pedestrian access, linking the bike routes of Staten Island with New Jersey.

A quarter mile downstream on the southern side of the wetland is the **Goethals Community** at 2701 Goethals Road North, the only mobile home development in the city. Comprising 128 mobile homes on nine acres of land, the unique trailer neighborhood is hemmed in by the wetland to the north and the Goethals Bridge to the south. Its story began in 1969, when property owners Fred and Frank DeDomenico discovered that mobile homes were permitted on land zoned for manufacturing. Public opposition and the City Planning Commission rushed to close the legal loophole, but the DeDomenico brothers successfully took the city to court, which allowed the development to proceed. In the early 1980s, the first residents arrived.

Bridge Creek turns north at Western Avenue, passing underneath the North Shore Branch of the Staten Island Railway. The single-track line rises above the marshland toward the west, approaching the **Arthur Kill Lift Bridge**, which was built in 1959. It is the longest lift bridge in the world. Designed to allow for oceangoing ships to pass beneath it, the bridge rises from 31 feet to 135 feet above high water. The bridge replaced an earlier swing bridge dating from 1890 that was the source of maritime traffic congestion on Arthur Kill.

Bridge Creek flows through the grounds of the New York Container Terminal, running between massive truck parking lots. It reaches Arthur Kill only a few yards south of Howland Hook, where Arthur Kill, Newark Bay, and Kill Van Kull converge. At this location, Richmond Terrace also ends.

A ferry here used to connect Howland Hook with Elizabeth, New Jersey. Although the Goethals Bridge was designed to put the ferry out of business, it persisted for a few more years, offering a cheaper fare for motorists. In the long run, the ferries could not compete, since they were only able to accommodate eight or nine vehicles and three dozen passengers at a time. The ferry to Elizabethport ceased operation in 1961. In the following two years, the Port Richmond–Bergen Point and

Tottenville–Perth Amboy ferries also ended service. The only full-time ferry operating on Staten Island today is at Saint George, connecting to downtown Manhattan.

PLACES TO SEE:
✦ **Goethals Community** 2701 Goethals Road North

GETTING THERE:
Note: There are no paths or trails near this stream
✦ **Bus**: S40, S90 at Goethals Road North and Admin Parking Lot (near Western Avenue)
✦ **Ferry**: Staten Island Ferry to Saint George, transfer to S40 or S90
✦ **Bike**: There are currently no bike lanes near Bridge Creek

96. Mill Creek

Mill Creek is the southernmost stream flowing into Arthur Kill. It separates the neighborhoods of Tottenville and Charleston. The creek originates at **Long Pond Park,** a nature preserve mapped around its namesake glacial kettle pond. Within the park, a 1.5-mile hiking trail takes visitors past the park's ponds and wetlands. Beginning at Richard Avenue and Hylan Boulevard, the trail goes north past **Buegler Pond** and **Camden Pond**. Farther along, the trail passes **Pam's Pond** followed by **Pratt's Pond** before reaching the five-acre **Long Pond**. The park also contains two named wetlands, Cleaves Swamp and Thoreau Swamp.

When Long Pond overflows, the excess water flows through the forest toward the north. The creek reappears to the south of the **Richmond Valley station** on the Staten Island Railway, the fourth station from the Main Line's Tottenville terminus. Constructed in 1860, it never served a large clientele, and only the first three cars of a train open their doors at this station. In spring 2016, two similar stations to the west, **Nassau** and **Atlantic,** will be closed, and a new station will open between them. The new station, **Arthur Kill,** will be accessible to the disabled and will have a 150-car parking lot. Nassau's namesake was the former Nassau Smelting and Refining Plant, and Atlantic was named after the Atlantic Terra Cotta Company. Both of those industries closed by the mid-20th century, reducing the importance of the two stations.

To the north of the Richmond Valley station, a spur track branched off the Main Line, following Mill Creek toward Arthur Kill. This one-

STATEN ISLAND

track line was constructed in the 1920s to supply materials for the construction of the **Outerbridge Crossing**. The spur remained active into the 1990s. At present, the tracks are gone, but the roadbed remains visible, cutting through the marshes along the creek.

In 1712, the present-day marshland at Mill Creek was a pond, formed by a gristmill dam constructed by Cornelius Disosway. It was the earliest commercial establishment in southwestern Staten Island. The mill continued to function into the 1870s. Nearly 500 feet to the east of the flooded site of the milldam, Arthur Kill Road cuts across the stream.

PLACES TO SEE:

+ **Long Pond Park** Bound approximately by Page Avenue, Amboy Road, North Mount Loretto State Forest, and Hylan Boulevard + www.nycgovparks.org/parks/long-pond-park

GETTING THERE:

+ **Bus**: S59, S78 at Hylan Boulevard and Richard Avenue
+ **Train**: Staten Island Railway to Richmond Valley
+ **Ferry**: Staten Island Ferry to Saint George, transfer to Staten Island Railway or S78
+ **Bike**: There is a bike lane on Hylan Boulevard

97. Ohrbach Lake

The 17-acre **Ohrbach Lake** is the centerpiece of **Pouch Camp**, the only Boy Scout camp within New York City and a link in the Staten Island Greenbelt of parks, golf courses, and cemeteries. From 1897 until his death in 1920, noted Beaux-Arts architect Ernest Flagg purchased and developed properties throughout eastern Staten Island. He owned the property that became Pouch Camp, but it remained undeveloped, though the kettle pond within the property took on the name **Flagg Pond**. In 1949, the estate was sold to the Boy Scouts of America in a purchase that was partially backed by department store executive Nathan Ohrbach and Boy Scouts leader William H. Pouch, and their names, too, ended up on the site.

The Boy Scout camp dammed Flagg Pond, and it grew in size and was renamed Ohrbach Lake. The surrounding 140-acre camp was named after Pouch. In 1955, Robert Moses mapped out the route of Richmond Parkway to the south of Pouch Camp, nearly impacting Ohrbach Lake.

A coalition of civic activists under the name SIGNAL (Staten Island Greenbelt Natural Areas League) succeeded in having the highway plan withdrawn. The only element of the highway that was completed was an unused interchange in Sunnyside that branched off from the Staten Island Expressway, cutting into Todt Hill. Rubble from the interchange excavation was dumped in High Rock Park, and the 260-foot hill was informally named Moses Mountain. Mayor John Lindsay's cancellation of the highway in 1966 led to the creation of the Greenbelt Conservancy, the nonprofit partner of the city's Parks Department in managing the 2,800-acre chain of connected parks.

The biggest threat to the camp was in 2009, when the cash-strapped Boy Scouts of America proposed selling the property to pay off its $15 million debt. Rescue was provided by the Trust for Public Land, a non-profit that brokered an agreement between the scouting organization and the state. Through its Environmental Protection Fund, the state paid the organization $6 million to keep the camp undeveloped.

PLACES TO SEE:

✦ **Pouch Camp** 1465 Manor Road ✦ 718-351-1905 ✦ www.pouch camp.org

GETTING THERE:

✦ **Bus**: S54, S57 at Rockland Avenue and Manor Road, walk north on Manor Road toward Pouch Camp
✦ **Train**: Staten Island Railway to New Dorp, transfer to S57
✦ **Ferry**: Staten Island Ferry to Saint George, transfer to S40 and take it to Broadway, transfer to S54
✦ **Bike**: There are currently no bike lanes near Ohrbach Lake

98. High Rock Park

In a survey conducted in 2008 by the Parks Department's Natural Resources Group and the Greenbelt Conservancy, seven "aquatic features" were identified within **High Rock Park**. Three of them have names: **Pump House Pond**, **Loosestrife Swamp**, and **Walker Pond**. Adjacent to High Rock Park is the Richmond Parkway right-of-way, which is managed by the Greenbelt Conservancy and contains **Hourglass Pond** and **Stump Pond**.

Hourglass and Stump Ponds are accessible by hiking trails that circle

STATEN ISLAND

High Rock Park

behind Pouch Camp. The lengthy walk that is required to reach Hourglass Pond gives it the distinction of being the most secluded natural area in the city, according to Bruce Kershner, author of *Secret Places of Staten Island*.

High Rock Park had its origins as part of the Boy Scouts' Pouch Camp property, which was sold to the Girl Scouts Council of Greater New York in 1951. In 1964, the campsite was nearly developed into housing following its sale. The builder, New Dorp Gardens, faced opposition from scouting advocate Gretta Moulton. Seeking to preempt changes in zoning, the developer poured concrete foundations on the edge of the camp. But former parks commissioner Robert Moses backed Moulton up, supporting the city's acquisition of the camp to turn it into a park; and Laurance Rockefeller, chairman of the New York State Council of Parks, provided the money. On July 7, 1965, the ribbon was cut for High Rock Park, with speeches describing it as a future conservation center.

Although Robert Moses was involved in this parkland acquisition, its future as a recreational space was not a guarantee, as many of his previous parks have ended up as road shoulders or divided by highways. Even as the new park was celebrated, mapmakers put it near the convergence of Willowbrook and Richmond Parkways, and Moses had every intention to see these roads completed.

A visit to the area by Governor Nelson Rockefeller contributed to turning the tide against Moses, in favor of Moulton. Uncompromising in her vision for the park as a nature preserve, Moulton opposed plans by the Parks Department to cut down trees in favor of a lawn, among other proposals. She died in November 1971, a few months shy of the park's designation as a National Environmental Education Landmark.

PLACES TO SEE:

✦ **High Rock Park** 200 Nevada Avenue ✦ 718-667-2165 ✦ www .nycgovparks.org/parks/high-rock-park

GETTING THERE:

✦ **Bus**: S54, S57 at Rockland Avenue and Florida Terrace, walk one block south to Nevada Avenue, turn left on Nevada Avenue toward High Rock Park
✦ **Train**: Staten Island Railway to New Dorp, transfer to S57
✦ **Ferry**: Staten Island Ferry to Saint George, transfer to S40 and take it to Broadway, transfer to S54**Bike**: There are currently no bike lanes near High Rock Park

99. Blue Heron Park

Separating the neighborhoods of Huguenot and Eltingville, the 222-acre **Blue Heron Park** sits partially on land whose name was inspired by Shakespeare—**Woods of Arden**. The development was a successor to Arden Heights, the neighborhood to its north named by Canadian publisher Erastus Wiman, who purchased a farm in the area in 1886 and named it after the forest mentioned in the Bard's comedy *As You Like It*. Although Woods of Arden was never fully developed, there is a Woods of Arden Road to the east of the remaining forest. In the early 20th century, mapmakers marked a street grid across the forest, and developers built homes on the lots in piecemeal fashion. Examples of such properties can be found on Barclay and Poillon Avenues, which cut through the park.

Recognizing the unique natural qualities of the forest, the city acquired Blue Heron Park between 1974 and 2001, with the official dedication taking place in 1996. At the celebration, officials spoke about removing numerous abandoned cars and, in their place, constructing walking trails crossing over ponds, brooks, meadows, and woodlands.

The park contains six ponds, the largest being the 1.75-acre **Spring Pond** and the 1.4-acre **Blue Heron Pond**, both of which are kettle

STATEN ISLAND

ponds. The **Blue Heron Park Nature Center**, on Poillon Avenue inside the park, offers classrooms, a library, and observation decks for visitors. As with many of the borough's recent parks, tours of the park and much of the literature on it are provided by a community nonprofit—in this case, the Friends of Blue Heron Park.

PLACES TO SEE:
+ **Blue Heron Park Nature Center** 222 Poillon Avenue + 718-967-3542 + www.nycgovparks.org/parks/blue-heron-park

GETTING THERE:
+ **Bus**: S59 and S78 at Hylan Boulevard and Poillon Avenue, walk north on Poillon Avenue toward Blue Heron Park Nature Center
+ **Train**: Staten Island Railway to Annadale, walk south on Annadale Road toward Poillon Avenue and turn left, walk on Poillon Avenue toward Blue Heron Park Nature Center
+ **Ferry**: Staten Island Ferry to Saint George, transfer to S78
+ **Bike**: There is a bike lane on Hylan Boulevard to the southwest of Blue Heron Park Preserve

100. Mount Loretto Ponds

Separating the Prince's Bay and Tottenville neighborhoods on Staten Island's southwestern tip is a wide expanse of state-owned land, the **Mount Loretto Unique Area**. The property operated as an orphanage from 1882 to 1998 by the Roman Catholic Mission of the Immaculate Virgin for the Protection of Homeless and Destitute Children. On its 258 acres, the mission ran a farm.

In 1998, the Trust for Public Land negotiated a deal with the Archdiocese of New York to purchase the waterfront portion of the Mount Loretto property south of Hylan Boulevard. The agreement mandated that the state would purchase the land from the trust in three phases and would use the property for a public park.

On the grounds of Mount Loretto, the **Old Church of Saint Joachim and Saint Anne** is familiar to film buffs for its use as a wedding chapel in *The Godfather*. Facing the church is a sculpture of Rev. John C. Drumgoole accompanied by two orphans. The figures appear to be walking toward the church. Drumgoole was the founder of the Mission of the Immaculate Virgin at Mount Loretto.

In 2006, the state also purchased **Butler Manor Woods,** an 18-acre parcel adjacent to Mount Loretto, creating the largest state-owned preserve within the borough. In the northern parcel of Mount Loretto, a series of wetlands drain into Mill Creek, while ponds to the south of Hylan Boulevard drain into Raritan Bay.

Prince's Bay Lighthouse

The southern portion of Mount Loretto, bound by Hylan Boulevard and Raritan Bay, is the former girls' orphanage, and it contains three ponds. At the western border of the park, an unnamed pond is visible from Hylan Boulevard. The pond is separated from Raritan Bay by an 85-foot hill. The highest waterfront point on Staten Island's South Shore, this hill is part of the terminal moraine and is topped by the **Prince's Bay Lighthouse**. The first lighthouse at this site was approved by Congress in 1826 and activated two years later. In 1864, the present lighthouse tower was built, and three years later the keeper's house was completed. The lighthouse was deactivated in 1922 and replaced with a shorter-range light structure on the shoreline. The keeper's brownstone house initially served as the residence of Mount Loretto's director and later as the summer home of John Cardinal O'Connor. Following O'Connor's death in 2006, the tower was renamed the John Cardinal O'Connor Lighthouse. Although the Fresnel lens is gone, a smaller rotating beacon spins atop the flat-topped tower.

Mount Loretto Pond and Cunningham Pond

On the western border of Mount Loretto, on either side of Cunningham Road, are two ponds that are part of the Bluebelt: **Mount Loretto Pond** and **Cunningham Pond**. The ponds collect runoff from Hylan Boulevard, and excess water flows out of the ponds into Mount Loretto Stream, which takes the water to the sea. Water from Hylan Boulevard's sewer emerges to the surface on the southeastern corner of the intersection of Hylan Boulevard and Cunningham Road, entering Mount Loretto Pond. This pond is separated from Cunningham Pond by Cunningham Road, a lightly used roadway that extends south to the beach.

PLACES TO SEE:

✦ **John Cardinal O'Connor (Prince's Bay) Lighthouse** Monsignor Road (a continuation of Kenny Road)

✦ **Old Church of Saint Joachim and Saint Anne** Cunningham Road, north of Hylan Boulevard

STATEN ISLAND

+ **Butler Manor Woods** Hylan Boulevard between Richard Avenue and Page Avenue, bordering Raritan Bay ✦ www.dec.ny.gov/outdoor /44085.html
+ **Mount Loretto Unique Area** Hylan Boulevard between Richard Avenue and Sharrott Avenue, bordering Raritan Bay ✦ www.dec.ny .gov/outdoor/8291.html

LEARN MORE:

+ **Mission of the Immaculate Virgin** www.mountloretto.org

GETTING THERE:

+ **Bus**: S59, S78 at Hylan Boulevard and Richard Avenue, walk one block east to Cunningham Road, and the ponds are on the southern side of Hylan Boulevard
+ **Train**: Staten Island Railway to Arthur Kill, transfer to S59
+ **Ferry**: Staten Island Ferry to Saint George, transfer to S78
+ **Bike**: There are bike lanes on Hylan Boulevard near Mount Loretto Pond and Cunningham Pond

101. New Creek

It is fitting that the final waterway entry for this book originates at **Last Chance Pond** in the Dongan Hills neighborhood. The pond is the start-ing point for **New Creek**, an undeveloped block of freshwater wetland that was initially zoned for development but saved following a campaign by local residents to preserve the 50 built lots. In contrast to some of the other ponds on Staten Island's South Shore, this pond is almost entirely covered with vegetation and surrounded by a thick forest. An undevel-oped park, it has no trails or signs indicating the pond's presence. In the 1960s, Staten Island was undergoing massive residential development following the completion of the Verrazano-Narrows Bridge, and gradu-ally the lots surrounding the pond were cleared, filled in, and developed.

Led by local residents Louis Caravone and John P. Mouner, the Last Chance Pond and Wilderness Foundation fought to designate the pond as a park. The site was assigned to the Parks Department in 1999 and designated as part of the New Creek Bluebelt. The creek's name was given by 19th-century mapmakers who noticed how the stream's course fluctuated as a result of storms and currents.

The watershed of New Creek totals 2,249 acres and has three sources:

STATEN ISLAND

the West Branch, which originates in **Boundary Avenue Park**; Main Channel, originating at Last Chance Pond; and the East Branch, which originates at Dongan Hills Avenue. These are fed in turn by sources farther uphill—an upper watershed contains **Moravian Brook** and **Mersereau's Valley Brook**, both of which disappear into sewers before reappearing as the West Branch and Main Channel, respectively.

Moravian Brook

This tributary originates in the **Saint Francis Woodlands**, where **Priory Pond** marks the starting point of the stream at its highest location. The brook leaves the pond in a trickle, hiding beneath a thick forest cover and invisible at Helena Road, a curving dead end that extends for a half mile in Todt Hill to connect isolated mansions that were developed before most of the hilltop was zoned for parkland. Among the properties on Helena Road is **Theater in the Woods**, a professional acting school for teenagers, founded in 2004 by Jo Anna and Bill Petrouleas, who own the property.

Moravian Brook reappears behind the mansions on the southern side of Helena Road on the grounds of **Richmond County Country Club**. The last private golf club in New York City, its 135-acre Dongan Hills course has operated on this site since 1897. In its early years, the club also hosted the country's first lawn tennis tournaments and foxhunting. Somehow, as the city's other private golf clubs ceased operations or migrated to the suburbs, the RCCC lived on. In 1989, the state purchased the golf course as part of the Greenbelt expansion and offered the country club a 99-year lease at an annual rent of $1.

Leaving the golf course, Moravian Brook travels between neat rows of graves at **Moravian Cemetery**. Founded in 1740, it is the oldest active cemetery on Staten Island, established by the Moravian Church in order to discourage burials on farmland. In the mid-19th century, the Vanderbilt family of Staten Island accumulated wealth from railroads and steamships and hired top architects to redesign the cemetery into a "burial park." Under architect Richard Morris Hunt, the cemetery received the superintendent's house and a Romanesque crypt for the Vanderbilt family in an 8-acre cemetery within the cemetery. The cemetery grounds also host the **New Dorp Moravian Church**, a congregation founded in 1763. It is one of the oldest churches on Staten Island, second only to Saint Andrews Episcopal Church in Richmondtown. As part of the burial park design, Moravian Brook was expanded in the cemetery to form **Crystal Lake** and **Sylvan Lake**. It leaves the cemetery in a sewer beneath Richmond Road.

STATEN ISLAND

Moravian Brook flows beneath Locust and Bryant Avenues in the New Dorp neighborhood. In the northeast corner of **Miller Field**, the underground pipe turns east beneath Boundary Avenue. At Lincoln Avenue, it emerges to the surface in **Boundary Avenue Park**, undeveloped woodland in the Midland Beach neighborhood. Here it turns into the West Branch of New Creek and follows Hunter Avenue, widening into a freshwater wetland where it merges with the creek's other tributaries.

Mersereau's Valley Brook

This tributary originated on the eastern slope of Todt Hill at **Reed's Basket Willow Swamp**, a freshwater wetland designated as a preserve by the Parks Department. Although separated from nearby parks, it is part of the larger Greenbelt chain of parks that run atop the serpentine ridge.

The park's namesake was John Read, who owned this property in the first half of the 19th century. A basket weaver, he grew purple willow trees in the swamp and used their bark for basket material. The swamp was acquired by the city in the 1970s and later designated as a park. Within the swamp, Mersereau's Valley Brook begins near Wooddale Avenue and Woodhaven Avenue, flowing through the swamp before disappearing at the southern end of the park. A trail inside the park allows for views of the brook.

Mersereau's Valley Brook returns to the surface at Last Chance Pond, continuing toward the ocean as the Main Channel of New Creek. It merges with the western and eastern branches, flowing past dead-end streets that are part of an unfinished grid. Olympia, Slater, and Graham Boulevards traverse the meadows surrounding New Creek, where one may feel distant from the city while still passing by its standard street lights and signage.

The stream ends a few yards short of South Beach. Here, Father Capodanno Boulevard follows the shore for 2.6 miles between Fort Wadsworth and Miller Field. The road is a humble remnant of the planned Shore Front Drive that would have followed the beach. Originally named Seaside Boulevard, the road was renamed for a local chaplain killed in combat in the Vietnam War.

PLACES TO SEE:
+ **Saint Francis Woodlands** Todt Hill Road between Whitwell Place and Helena Road • www.dec.ny.gov/outdoor/45344.html
+ **Richmond County Country Club** 135 Flagg Place • 718-351-0600 • www.richmondcountycc.org

STATEN ISLAND

✦ **Reed's Basket Willow Swamp** Bound by Ocean Terrace, Emerson Court, Merrick Avenue, and Chapin Avenue ✦ www.nycgovparks .org/parks/reeds-basket-willow-swamp-park
✦ **Moravian Cemetery** 2205 Richmond Road ✦ 718-351-0136 ✦ www.moraviancemetery.com
✦ **Last Chance Pond Park** Naughton and Stobe Avenues between Zoe Street and Husson Street ✦ www.nycgovparks.org/parks/last -chance-pond-park

GETTING THERE:

✦ **Bus**: S78, X1, X2, X3, X9 at Hylan Boulevard and Seaver Avenue, walk east on Seaver Avenue or Slater Boulevard to follow New Creek; S51, S81 at Father Capodanno Boulevard and Slater Boulevard, walk north on Slater Boulevard to follow New Creek
✦ **Ferry**: Staten Island Ferry to Saint George, transfer to S51, S81, or S78
✦ **Bike**: South Beach Greenway runs in proximity to New Creek's wetlands near Father Capodanno Boulevard

STATEN ISLAND

➤ Bibliography

All Manhattan entries

Adams, John Wolcott, and I. N. Phelps Stokes. *Redraft of the Castello Plan New Amsterdam in 1660.* 1916.

Brown, Henry Collins. *Valentine's Manual of Old New York.* Vol. 7. 1923.

Dunshee, Kenneth Holcomb. *As You Pass By.* Hastings House, 1952.

Hill, George Everett, and George E. Waring Jr. "Old Wells and Water-Courses of the Island of Manhattan," in *Historic New York: the First Series of the Half Moon Papers.* 1899.

Moscow, Henry. *The Street Book: An Encyclopedia of Manhattan's Street Names and Their Origins.* New York: Macmillan Publishing Company, 1978.

Randel, John Jr. *The City of New York as Laid Out by the Commissioners with the Surrounding Country.* 1814.

Ratzer, Bernard. *Plan of the City of New York, in North America.* London: Faden and Jefferys, 1776.

Risse, Louis Aloys. *General Map of the City of New York.* New York City Board of Public Improvements Topographical Bureau, 1900.

Sanderson, Eric W. *Mannahatta: A Natural History of New York City.* New York: Harry N. Abrams, 2009.

Solis, Julia. *New York Underground: The Anatomy of a City.* London: Routledge, 2005.

Viele, Egbert Ludovicus. *Topographical Map of the City of New York.* 1865.

Wilson, Rufus Rockwell. *New York: Old and New: Its Story, Streets, and Landmarks.* Philadelphia: J. B. Lippincott, 1902.

Collect Pond

American Scenic and Historic Preservation Society. *Seventeenth Annual Report, 1912, of the American Scenic and Historic Preservation Society to the Legislature of the State of New York.* March 28, 1912.

Anbinder, Tyler. *Five Points: The 19th-Century New York City Neighborhood that Invented Tap Dance, Stole Elections, and Became the World's Most Notorious Slum.* New York: The Free Press, 2001.

Harris, Leslie M. *In the Shadow of Slavery: African Americans in New York City, 1626–1863.* Chicago: University of Chicago Press, 2003.

New York City Department of Parks and Recreation. "Collect Pond Park." www.nycgovparks.org /parks/M242/history.

New York Times. "New Five Points Mission: Work of Demolishing the Old Structure Begun." May 20, 1894.

Shapiro, Julie. "City Puts the Pond Back in Collect Pond Park." *DNAinfo New York*, July 22, 2011. www.dnainfo.com/new-york/20110722/downtown/city-puts-pond-back-collect-pond-park.

Canal Street

Chan, Sewell. "In TriBeCa, a New Park Called CaVaLa." *City Room* (blog), *New York Times*, September 18, 2008. cityroom.blogs.nytimes.com/2008/09/18/in-tribeca-a-new-park-called -cavala/?_php=true&_type=blogs&_r=0.

De Voe, Thomas Farrington. *The Market Book, Containing a Historical Account of the Public Markets in the Cities of New York, Boston, Philadelphia and Brooklyn.* New York, 1862.

New York City Department of Parks and Recreation. "Parks & Recreation Reopens a Long-Lost Haven." *The Daily Plant*, October 24, 2005. www.nycgovparks.org/news/daily-plant?id =19706.

Place Matters. "Canal Street Triangle/Canal Park." placematters.net/node/1076.

Rogers, Josh. "Trees Grow on Canal: Park to Reopen 85 Years Later." *Downtown Express*, June 17, 2005. www.downtownexpress.com/de_110/treesgrowoncanal.html.

Shapiro, Julie. "CaVaLa Park Renamed for Albert Capsouto, TriBeCa Leader and Restaurateur." *DNAinfo New York*, October 28, 2010. www.dnainfo.com/new-york/20101028/downtown/ cavala-park-renamed-for-albert-capsouto-tribeca-leader-restaurateur.

"The Canal Came Back." *Edison Monthly* 6 (March 1914): 390.

Watal, Divya. "New Conservancy Raises Big Funds for a Small Park at End of Canal St." *Villager*, December 8, 2004.

Williams, Timothy. "An Oasis Beckons in a Spot Once Used by Trash Trucks." *New York Times*, October 21, 2005.

Minetta Brook

Callahan, Jennifer. "Minetta Moments." City Lore, *New York Times*, January 30, 2005.

"Diggers at Jefferson Market Unearth Old Minetta Creek." *New York Times*, December 1, 1929.

Gray, Christopher. "Vestiges of a Developer's Greenwich Village Enclave." *New York Times*, August 29, 1999.

Harris, Luther S. *Around Washington Square: An Illustrated History of Greenwich Village.* Baltimore: Johns Hopkins University Press, 2003.

"Minetta Brook Out Again." *New York Times*, December 4, 1930.

New York City Department of Parks and Recreation. "Father Demo Square." www.nycgovparks .org/parks/M191/.

———. "Minetta Playground." www.nycgovparks.org/parks/M125B/history.

———. "Minetta Triangle." www.nycgovparks.org/parks/minettatriangle/history.

———. "Washington Square Park." www.nycgovparks.org/parks/washingtonsquarepark/history.

———. "Winston Churchill Square (Downing Street Playground)." www.nycgovparks.org/parks /M027/history.

"Sources of Great Danger: Underground Streams as Breeders of Contagion." *New York Times*, January 17, 1892.

Maiden Lane

Downtown Alliance. "Louise Nevelson Plaza." www.downtownny.com/louisenevelson.

Sill, Louise Morgan. *In Sun or Shade: Poems.* New York: Harper and Brothers, 1906.

Trapnell, Kelli. "History of Streets: Maiden Lane." *Untapped Cities* (blog), November 21, 2012. untappedcities.com/2012/11/21/history-of-streets-maiden-lane.

Wolf, Stephen. "Memories of Maiden Lane." *Villager*, February 10, 2010. thevillager.com /villager_354/memoriesofmaidenlane.html.

Murray Hill Reservoir

Barreneche, Raul A. "Davis Brody Bond Gives New Life to a Beaux-Arts Grande Dame, with the Modern New South Court of the New York Public Library." *Architectural Record* 190 (November 2002): 134.

Bryant Park Corporation. "Early History." www.bryantpark.org/about-us/history.html.

Fiske, Amos K. "Murray Hill and the Reservoir." *New York Times*, February 27, 1898.

McDowell, Edwin. "For Public Library, New Building within the Old One." *New York Times*, September 17, 2000.

"New York's Expensive Public Library." *New York Times*, April 28, 1907.

"New York's Great Public Library Nearing Completion." *New York Times*, October 1, 1905.

"Removal of the Reservoir: The Bill Signed That Gives Murray Hill a Larger Park." *New York Times*, June 8, 1881.

"The Crystal Palace: Opening of the Exhibition." *New York Times*, July 15, 1853.

"The Murray Hill Reservoir: Judge Davis Grants a Temporary Injunction Forbidding Its Removal."
New York Times, October 23, 1881.

All of Central Park
Blackman, Elizabeth, and Roy Rosenzweig. *The Park and the People: A History of Central Park*.
Ithaca, NY: Cornell University Press, 1992.
Miller, Sara Cedar. *Central Park, an American Masterpiece*. New York: H. N. Abrams, 2003.
Reiss, Marcia. *Central Park Then and Now*. San Diego, CA: Thunder Bay Press, 2010.
Viele, Egbert Ludovicus. *Plan of Drainage for the Grounds of the Central Park*. 1855.

Central Park Pond
Blau, Eleanor. "A New Ice Age Starts at Wollman Rink." *New York Times*, November 14, 1986.
Daley, Suzanne. "Trump to Rebuild Wollman Rink at the City's Expense by Dec. 15." *New York
Times*, June 7, 1986.
"Mayor Opens Ground for Wollman Center." *New York Times*, October 8, 1949.
"New Skating Rink in Central Park to Be Opened to Public Thursday." *New York Times*, December 18, 1950.
"New Structures for the City Parks." *New York Times*, September 27, 1896.

Central Park Lake
"A Row on the Lake at Central Park." *New York Times*, July 18, 1862.
"Cleaning the Lakes in Central Park." *New York Times*, July 17, 1910.
"Ramblings in the 'Ramble.'" *New York Times*, July 15, 1859.
"Restored Bow Bridge Reopens to Pedestrians." *New York Times*, September 24, 1974.
Santo, Ernest. "Ramble Reviving in Central Park." *New York Times*, December 28, 1956.
"The Bethesda Fountain." *New York Times*. June 1, 1873.

Conservatory Water
Beckett, Kathleen. "Jon Elmaleh: Model-Boat Designer." *New York Times*, October 13, 1991.
Kennedy, Shawn G. "17 Miniyacht 'Skippers' Set Sail in Park Regatta." *New York Times*, July 17,
1983.
"On Central Park Pond, Miniature Sails in the Sunset." *New York Times*, August 6, 1995.
"This Is for Children: Andersen Statue in Park to Be Dedicated on Tuesday." *New York Times*,
September 16, 1956.
"'Wonderland' to Be Dedicated." *New York Times*, May 6, 1959.

Turtle Pond
"25 in Park Shanties Politely Arrested." *New York Times*, September 22, 1932.
"Defends Memorial for Central Park: Architect Hastings Says Reservoir Site Would Be Lost If
Not Used for War Monument." *New York Times*, February 9, 1924.
Dunlap, David W. "Great Lawn: Saving Dragonflies in Belvedere Lake." *New York Times*, February 2, 1987.
"For an Esplanade in Central Park: John D. Crimmins Would Have Lower Reservoir Covered."
New York Times, January 25, 1904.
Hardwicke, Irene. "Put a Little Dragonfly in Your Life Today." *New York Times*, September 9,
1990.
"Lawn Plan Chosen for Park Reservoir." *New York Times*, March 4, 1931.
"Memorial Planned for War Dead, Converting Central Park Reservoir." *New York Times*, November 19, 1922.
"Pleading a Case to Save Love on the Wing." *New York Times*, February 1, 1987.
"To Enlarge Central Park." *New York Times*, February 8, 1903.

Jacqueline Kennedy Onassis Reservoir
Cardwell, Diane. "Central Park Reservoir Fountain Returns to Life." *City Room* (blog), *New York
Times*, July 30, 2007.
Fisher, Ian. "Central Park Reservoir to Stay As Is." *New York Times*, October 28, 1993.
Healy, Patrick. "Fountain Revived for Central Park's 150th." *New York Times*, July 19, 2003.
Martin, Douglas. "Diving in Central Park for Trash and Love." *New York Times*, October 1, 1996.
"Park Reservoir Called a Menace: Roulstone Says Dirt on Ice and Dead Fish Endanger the Public
Health." *New York Times*, March 20, 1926.

Purnick, Joyce. "Light at the End of the Reservoir: Replacing an Unloved Fence." *New York Times*, June 2, 2002.

Roberts, Sam. "1862 Central Park Reservoir Is Deemed Obsolete." *New York Times*, May 6, 1993.

Shapiro, Gary. "A Geyser-Like Fountain May Again Mark Park's Center." *New York Sun*, July 30, 2007.

Montayne's Rivulet (the Loch)

Collins, Glenn. "Bet You Didn't Know: Falls Are Everywhere." *New York Times*, June 29, 2008.

Harlem Meer

"Central Park to Get Swimming Pool and Ice Rink." *New York Times*, February 24, 1962.

Kennedy, Shawn G. "A Nature Center Blooms in Central Park Woodlands." *New York Times*, May 9, 1993.

"Lindsay and Hoving Give New Skating Rink a Whirl." *New York Times*, December 22, 1966.

Phillips, McCandlish. "Lake Bed Is Fun to Get Stuck In: Children Find Diversion in Drained Harlem Meer." *New York Times*, July 31, 1964.

"Tablet Is Unveiled at Old Fort Clinton: Children Whose Pennies Bought It Attend the Exercises." *New York Times*, November 25, 1906.

"Towers and Turrets at Harlem Meer." *New York Times*, January 18, 1990.

Morningside Pond

Dunlap, David W. "Pond Springs Where Gym Fouled Out." *New York Times*, June 5, 1989.

Gray, Christopher. "An Oasis of Green, Reclaimed by City and Community." *New York Times*, July 31, 2005.

Highbridge Reservoir

"2 Reservoir Sites to Serve As Parks; Abandoned Land in the Bronx and Upper Manhattan Is Offered by Davidson." *New York Times*, April 4, 1934.

Cunningham, Jennifer H. "Exclusive: Bad Weather, Additional Project Work Has Put High Bridge's Re-opening Off Schedule." *New York Daily News*, January 30, 2014.

Gray, Christopher. "Streetscapes: The High Bridge Water Tower; Fire-Damaged Landmark to Get $900,000 Repairs." *New York Times*, October 19, 1988.

Hu, Winnie. "Restoring a Bridge, and a Link Between Neighbors." *New York Times*, May 18, 2012.

Landmarks Preservation Commission. *High Bridge Water Tower*. No. 5. New York, July 12, 1967. LP-0319. www.neighborhoodpreservationcenter.org/db/bb_files/water-tower.pdf.

"Moses to Get Two Unneeded Reservoirs As Sites for Stadium and Swimming Pool." *New York Times*, April 5, 1934.

Scanlon, Breanne. "Highbridge Park, Pool & Water Tower." Place Matters. www.placematters.net/node/1235.

Sherman Creek

Black, Led. "Historic Inwood—The Dyckman Oval." *Uptown Collective* (blog), March 24, 2012. www.uptowncollective.com/2011/03/24/historic-inwood-%E2%80%93-the-dyckman-oval-2/.

"Dyckman Houses Open." *New York Times*, September 26, 1950.

"Harlem Rowing Club Regatta." *New York Times*, September 26, 1873.

Hellman, Peter. "On Harlem River, Hope Floats." *New York Times*, October 30, 2003.

Lee, Denny. "California, Here We Come: Scientists Warn of Earthquakes Here." Neighborhood Report: New York Up Close, *New York Times*, May 12, 2002.

"McKenzie, Old Rowing Enthusiast Himself, Cancels Evictions of Three Clubs on Harlem." *New York Times*, October 23, 1941.

New York City Economic Development Corporation. *Sherman Creek: Planning Workshop*. January 31, 2004. www.nyc.gov/html/dcp/pdf/sherman_creek/booklet.pdf.

"Rowing Clubs Parade." *New York Times*, May 12, 1902.

Zanoni, Carla. "Final Proposal Unveiled for Sherman Creek Waterfront." *DNAinfo New York*, July 14, 2011. www.dnainfo.com/new-york/20110714/washington-heights-inwood/final-proposal-unveiled-for-sherman-creek-waterfront.

Spuyten Duyvil Creek

"All Land Acquired for Harlem Canal." *New York Times*, October 1, 1933.

"Awards $3,275,000 in Ship Canal Case." *New York Times*, January 9, 1926.

"Harlem Canal Opening June 17." *New York Times*, June 2, 1895.
"Harlem Ship Canal Opening." *New York Times*, June 15, 1895.
"Opinion Is Divided on Bridge Project." *New York Times*, April 21, 1931.
Renner, James. *Washington Heights, Inwood, and Marble Hill.* Mount Pleasant, SC: Arcadia Publishing, 2007.
"Ship Canal to Be Finished." *New York Times*, August 4, 1935.
Slattery, Denis. "Bronx Residents Attempt to Claim Manhattan's Marble Hill As Part of Borough." *New York Daily News*, May 7, 2014.
"'Sudeten' Claimed by Bronx Fuehrer." *New York Times*, March 9, 1939.
Thompson, Cole. "Johnson Iron Works." *My Inwood* (blog). myinwood.net/johnson-iron-works/.
———. "The Harlem Ship Canal." *My Inwood* (blog). myinwood.net/the-harlem-ship-canal.
Walsh, Kevin. "Hi C, Spuyten Duyvil." *Forgotten New York* (blog), November 6, 2013. forgotten-ny.com/2013/11/hi-c-spuyten-duyvil.
———. "Spuyten Duyvil in the Details." *Forgotten New York* (blog), December 2012. forgotten-ny.com/2004/12/duyvilinthedetails.
"Widening Harlem Costs 1,000 Jobs." *New York Times*, July 1, 1923.

Little Hell Gate
"Against Filling Up Little Hell Gate." *New York Times*, February 27, 1877.
"Fill Project to Add to Randalls Island for New Play Fields." *New York Times*, August 18, 1962.
"Little Hell Gate to Be Filled Up." *New York Times*, February 20, 1877.
"Randalls Island Soon to Grow by 46 Acres in No-Cost Project Benefiting Everyone." *New York Times*, July 7, 1955.

All of the Bronx
Bien, Julius, and Cornelius C. Vermeule. *Long Island Sound, Westchester North to Mt. Vernon, Queens South to Jamaica.* 1890.
De Kadt, Maarten. *The Bronx River: An Environmental and Social History.* Charleston, SC: The History Press, 2011.
Goodman, Fred. *The Secret City: Woodlawn Cemetery and the Buried History of New York.* New York: Broadway Books, 2004.
McLaughlin, Robert, and Frank R. Adamo. *Freedomland.* Charleston, SC: Arcadia Publishing, 2010.
McNamara, John. *History in Asphalt: The Origin of Bronx Street and Place Names, Borough of the Bronx, New York City.* Harrison, NY: Harbor Hill Books. 1978.
Miller, Stuart, and Sharon Seitz. *The Other Islands of New York City.* Woodstock, VT: The Countryman Press, 2001.
Twomey, Bill. *The Bronx: In Bits and Pieces.* Bloomington, IN: Rooftop Publishing, 2007.
Twomey, Bill, and Thomas X. Casey. *Northwest Bronx.* Charleston, SC: Arcadia Publishing, 2011.
Twomey, Bill, and John McNamara. *Throggs Neck and Pelham Bay.* Charleston, SC: Arcadia Publishing, 1999.
Ultan, Lloyd, and Barbara Unger. *Bronx Accent: A Literary and Pictorial History of the Borough.* New Brunswick, NJ: Rutgers University Press, 2011.

Bronx River
Fowle, Farnsworth. "New City Market in Bronx Backed." *New York Times*, May 18, 1959.
Fowler, Glenn. "New Life for the Old Bronx River?" *New York Times*, February 1, 1979.
Kaufman, Michael T. "Bronx River Channel: An Urban Junkyard." *New York Times*, April 6, 1971.
"Snuff Mill Relic to Be De Luxe Cafe." *New York Times*, May 16, 1952.
Topping, Seymour. "City to Get Plan for Huge Market." *New York Times*, December 3, 1959.

Tibbetts Brook
Trangle, Sarina. "City Outlines First-Ever Master Plan for Vannie." *Riverdale Press*, October 31, 2013.
Wisnieski, Adam. "A River Runs through . . . Kingsbridge?" *Riverdale Press*, March 23, 2011.

Rattlesnake Brook
Cook, Harry T. *The Borough of the Bronx, 1639–1913: Its Marvelous Development and Historical Surroundings.* New York: printed by author, 1913.
McNamara, John. *McNamara's Old Bronx.* New York: Bronx County Historical Society, 1989.

New York City Department of Parks and Recreation. *Natural Area Mapping and Inventory of Givans Creek Woods 2007 Survey.* Prepared by the Natural Resources Group, January 8, 2008.

Twomey, Bill. *East Bronx: East of the Bronx River.* Charleston, SC: Arcadia Publishing, 1999.

Walsh, Kevin. "Rattlesnake Brook: Hidden Creek in the Bronx." *Forgotten New York* (blog), July 1999. forgotten-ny.com/1999/07/rattlesnake-brook.

Hutchinson River

Anderson, Steve. "Hutchinson Parkway: Historic Overview." NYC Roads. www.nycroads.com/roads/hutchinson.

Bronx Times Reporter. "Duck Boat Excursion to Goose Island." September 17, 2009.

Fowle, Farnsworth. "Big Exhibit Planned in Bronx." *New York Times*, May 26, 1959.

Gilbert, Morris. "Freedomland in the Bronx." *New York Times*, June 12, 1960.

"Planners Accept Bronx Co-op City; Reject Protests on Housing at Freedomland Site." *New York Times*, May 13, 1965.

Delafield Ponds

Barbanel, Josh. "Large Riverdale Estate Gets Fourth Chance." *Wall Street Journal*, November 9, 2011.

Walsh, Kevin. "Speed the Ploughman. Hidden lanes in Riverdale." *Forgotten New York* (blog), April 2001. www.forgotten-ny.com/2001/04/speed-the-ploughman-hidden-lanes-in-riverdale.

Wisnieski, Adam. "Delafield Lots Sold for over $6 Million." *Riverdale Press*, November 22, 2012.

Williamsbridge Reservoir

"19.7-Acre Play Area Completed in Bronx." *New York Times*, February 12, 1938.

Gray, Christopher. "For an 1890 Reservoir Keeper's House, a New Use." *New York Times*, December 20, 1998.

"Moses to Get Two Unneeded Reservoirs As Sites for Stadium and Swimming Pool." *New York Times*, April 5, 1934.

New York City Department of Parks and Recreation. "Williamsbridge Oval." www.nycgovparks.org/parks/williamsbridgeoval.

"Promenade to Cap Huge Play Centre." *New York Times*, May 9, 1935.

Cromwell's Creek

"City Must Restore Stream." *New York Times*, December 18, 1904.

New York City Department of Parks and Recreation. "Mullaly Park." www.nycgovparks.org/parks/mullalypark/.

"Plan Recreation Parks; Plot of Ground near Central Bridge for Outdoor Sports." *New York Times*, October 12, 1902.

Mott Haven Canal

"Big Trailer Depot Planned in Bronx." *New York Times*, April 15, 1963.

"Mott Haven Canal Case." *New York Times*, May 16, 1900.

"North Siders' Woes Aired." *New York Times*, November 21, 1896.

"The Mott Haven Canal." *New York Times*, July 16, 1890.

"To Close the Old Mott Haven Canal." *New York Times*, November 17, 1894.

All of Queens

Bien, Julius, and Cornelius C. Vermeule. *Long Island Sound, Westchester North to Mt. Vernon, Queens South to Jamaica.* 1890.

Greater Astoria Historical Society, Thomas Jackson, and Richard Melnick. *Long Island City.* Charleston, SC: Arcadia Publishing, 2004.

Seyfried, Vincent. *Corona: From Farmland to City Suburb (1650–1935).* New York: Edgian Press, 1986.

Ullitz, Hugo. *Atlas of the Borough of Queens. City of New York Complete in Three Volumes.* E. Belcher Hyde, 1907.

Wolverton, Chester. *Atlas of Queens Co., Long Island, New York.* New York: printed by the author, 1891.

Dutch Kills

Anderson, Steve. "Long Island Expressway." NYC Roads. www.nycroads.com/roads/long-island.

Angelos, James. "A Humble Bridge with One Fetching Feature." *New York Times*, January 18, 2009.

Evelly, Jeanmarie. "Community Garden Grows with New Expansion." *DNAinfo New York*, May

24, 2013. www.dnainfo.com/new-york/20130524/long-island-city/long-island-city-community-garden-grows-with-new-expansion#slideshow_modal_slot_1.

McDowell, Edwin. "Commercial Real Estate; Changing Designs, a Project Revives." *New York Times*, June 28, 2000.

New York City Bridge Centennial Commission. "Borden Avenue Bridge." www.nycbridges100.org/borden-ave.php.

New York City Economic Development Corporation. "Dutch Kills Green." www.nycedc.com/transition/dutch-kills-green.

"Ronzoni Pasta Plant in Queens Moving South." *New York Times*, January 6, 1993.

Anable Basin

Blumenthal, Ralph. "Letter by Letter, Pepsi Rejoins Skyline." *City Room* (blog), *New York Times*, February 25, 2009. cityroom.blogs.nytimes.com/2009/02/25/letter-by-letter-pepsi-rejoins-sky line.

Kern-Jedrychowska, Ewa. "'Floating Garden' Coming to Long Island City." *DNAinfo New York*, August 22, 2012. www.dnainfo.com/new-york/20120822/long-island-city/floating-garden-coming-long-island-city.

Lee, Jennifer 8. "Condos with Water Views, for the Birds." *City Room* (blog), *New York Times*, October 30, 2007. cityroom.blogs.nytimes.com/2007/10/30/condos-with-water-views-for-the-birds/.

MacMurtrie, Chico. "A Tree for Anable Basin." www.anabletree.com.

Waterpod. "A Floating Garden." afloatinggarden.blogspot.com.

Luyster Creek

Daily Mail. "Inside Astoria's Historic Steinway Mansion That Nobody Wants to Buy as Price Drops for Second Time in Three Years to $1.9m." April 24, 2013.

Green Shores NYC. "Waterfront Vision Plan." 2012. www.greenshoresnyc.org/waterfront-vision-plan.html.

Historical Guide to the City of New York. New York: F.A. Stokes Co, 1913.

Nutt, Edgar Alan. *The Rikers: Their Island, Homes, Cemetery and Early Genealogy in Queens County, NY.* 2004. Quoted in New York Correction History Society. "The Rikers." www.correctionhistory.org/html/chronicl/cw_units/html/rikersbook006.html.

Sunswick Creek

"2 Wheels of 1829 Mill Uncovered in Queens." *New York Times*, April 20, 1957.

Miss, Mary. "City As Living Laboratory." www.cityaslivinglab.org/ravenswood-r-call.

"Old Long Island Mansions." *New York Times*, March 18, 1894.

Flushing Creek

Anderson, Steve. "Grand Central Parkway." NYC Roads. www.nycroads.com/roads/grand-central.

———. "Van Wyck Expressway." NYC Roads. www.nycroads.com/roads/van-wyck.

Boorstin, Robert O. "Stern Calls Queens Grand Prix 'Dead.'" *New York Times*, March 24, 1986.

Carmody, Deirdre. "City Agency Agrees to Allow Auto Race in Flushing Meadow." *New York Times*, June 5, 1985.

———. "Plan for a Grand Prix in Park Raises Objections in Queens." *New York Times*, March 21, 1983.

Driscoll, James. *Flushing 1880–1935.* Charleston, SC: Arcadia Press, 2005.

Editorial. "A Not-So-Grand Prix." *New York Times*, June 9, 1985.

Lauinger, John. "Flushing River Wetlands Project May Be Soaked." *New York Daily News*, May 20, 2008.

Meislin, Richard J. "U.S. Is Said to Investigate Manes's Links to Grand Prix Effort." *New York Times*, January 31, 1986.

———. "Evicters' Big Day Ends in Waterloo." August 4, 1936.

———. "Great World Fair for City in 1939 on Site in Queens." *New York Times*, September 23, 1935.

———. "Long Island Ship Canal." February 5, 1895.

———. "New York May Get '83 Auto Grand Prix." October 28, 1982.

———. "Plan Golf Courses in Corona Meadows." July 22, 1929.

———. "Proposed Canal across the Island." May 31, 1908.

———. "To Open New Section of Nassau Boulevard: Five-Mile Link from Strong's Causeway to Rocky Hill Will Be Ready Tomorrow." August 13, 1928.

Pirmann, David. NYC Subway. www.nycsubway.org.

Purnick, Joyce. "Auto Race Plan for Queens Gets 2 New Setbacks." *New York Times*, June 11, 1985.

Shepard, Laura. "Haber Fights for Flushing Meadows." *Queens Chronicle*, March 21, 2013.
Stern, Robert A. M., Thomas Mellins, and David Fishman. *New York 1960: Architecture and Urbanism between the Second World War and the Bicentennial*. New York: Monacelli, 1997.
Van Dort, Paul M. "1939 World's Fair." www.pmphoto.to/WorldsFairTour/home.htm.
Young, Bill. "1964 World's Fair." www.nywf64.com.

Kissena Creek

Chiwaya, Nigel. "Queens Velodrome a Secret Oasis for Bikers." *DNAinfo New York*. www.dnainfo
   .com/new-york/20120806/flushing/kissena-velodrome-secret-oasis-for-cyclists.
Cutolo, Lou. "Forgotten Architects." Metropolitan Golf Association, January 22, 2012. www
   .mgagolf.org/news/2012/january/forgotten_architects.
Marzlock, Rom. "How Robert Moses Saved Utopia Playground." *Queens Chronicle*, November
   21, 2012.
Miller, Dan. "Greenest Building Opens." *Queens Gazette*, October 3, 2007.
New York City Department of Environmental Protection. *2009 Waterbody Watershed Facility Plan for Alley Creek and Little Neck Bay Appendices*. issuu.com/alleycreek/docs/2005_alley_creek_
   waterbody_watershed_facility_plan.
New York City Department of Parks and Recreation. "Captain Mario Fajardo Park." www.nyc
   govparks.org/parks/Q300/highlights/9779.
———. "Utopia Playground." www.nycgovparks.org/parks/Q294/history.
Pennington, Bill. "Forgotten Architects, Timeless Courses." *New York Times*, August 4, 2008.
Sherman, Diana. "If You're Thinking of Living In/Kissena Park, Queens." *New York Times*, March
   5, 2000.

Mill Creek

"4 Hurt in Queens in Airplane Crash." *New York Times*, June 3, 1934.
"Argues for Retaining Whitestone Branch." *New York Times*, November 25, 1931.
Brooklyn Daily Eagle. "Action by City on Whitestone Line Unlikely." February 24, 1932.
———. "Long Battle in Courts Marked Attempts to Halt Whitestone Abandonment." January
   5, 1932.
Buglione, Nick. "From Flying High to Sinking Deep: The Life & Death of an Airport." *Queens Tribune*. August 31, 2000.
"Contractor Buys Whitestone Spur." *New York Times*, April 26, 1932.
Fuchs, Chris. "Flushing Window Biz Makes Move to College Point." *Queens TimesLedger*, August
   9, 2001.
Habib, Philip, and Associates. *Police Academy–College Point, Queens: Final Environmental Impact Statement*. September 3, 2009. www.nyc.gov/html/nypd/html/reports/pa_college_point_eis
   .shtml.
Kaiser, Emily. "German Visionary the Father of College Point." *Queens Chronicle*, November 11,
   2010.
Lederer, Victor. *Images of America: College Point*. Charleston, SC: Arcadia Publishing, 2004.
Long Island Star-Journal. "Innerwyck is Landmark in Flushing." October 8, 1946.
New York City Department of Parks and Recreation. "George U. Harvey Playground." www
   .nycgovparks.org/parks/Q089B/history.
New York City Economic Development Corporation. "College Point Corporate Park." www
   .nycedc.com/project/college-point-corporate-park.
"Offers to Give City Whitestone Branch." *New York Times*, July 14, 1926.
Stern, Walter. "City to Study Flushing Airport as Site for an Industrial Park." *New York Times*,
   March 19, 1960.
"Two Hurt as Plane Crashes at Airport." *New York Times*, June 8, 1940.
Walsh, Kevin. "College Point, Queens." *Forgotten New York* (blog), May 2006. forgotten-ny.com
   /2006/05/college-point-queens/.
"Whitestone Fights as Last Train Runs." *New York Times*, February 16, 1932.

Horse Brook

"Alexander's Opens Store in Rego Park." *New York Times*, February 27, 1959.
Berkun, Todd. "The Sendek's and the Macy's." *Places That Are No More* (blog), August 5, 2012.
   placesnomore.wordpress.com/2012/08/05/sendeksandmacys.
Blumenthal, Ralph. "Phone Tower Plan Upsets Rego Park." *New York Times*, October 18, 1971.
Bolton, Reginald Pelham, and Edward Hagaman Hall. *Historical Guide to the City of New York*.
   New York: City History Club of New York, 1906.

Bradley, John A. "LeFrak Starts Queens Housing." *New York Times*, November 20, 1955.

Dickinson, Ernest. "Lefrak City Crucible of Racial Change." *New York Times*, February 1, 1976.

Dunlap, David W. "Philip Birnbaum, 89, Builder Celebrated for His Efficiency." *New York Times*, November 28, 1996.

"Expanded JCPenney, Macy's Highlight Queens Center." *Queens Gazette*, March 31, 2004.

Fairview at Forest Hills. thefairview.com.

"Fear in Forest Hills." *Time*, November 29, 1971.

Fried, Joseph P. "Alexander's Plans $150 Million Mall for Rego Park." *New York Times*, September 5, 1986.

Gustafson, Colin. "Rego Park Mall Slated for Alexander's Lot." *Queens Chronicle*, November 23, 2006.

"Highway is named for Horace Harding." *New York Times*, May 5, 1929.

"J. Horace Harding, Banker, Dies at 65." January 5, 1929.Onishi, Norimitsu. "Stabilizing Lefrak City: Jewish and Muslim Immigrants Help Revive Troubled Complex." *New York Times*, June 6, 1996.

Lipton, Eric. "Nothing Gaudy but Sales Figures; No-Frills Queens Center Outshines Most Luxury Malls." *New York Times*, February 2, 2002.

Maple Grove Cemetery. "Edward Mandel (1869–1942) Prospect 121A." www.maplegrove.biz /MGCHistoryArchive/edwardMandel.htm

Marzlock, Ron. "Rego Park and Its Superstitious Old Farmers." *Queens Chronicle*, December 3, 2009.

New York City Department of Education. "Modernism." schools.nyc.gov/community/facilities /PublicArt/Architecture/Modernism/default.htm.

New York City Department of Parks and Recreation. "Barrier Playground." www.nycgovparks .org/parks/barrierplayground.

———. "Horace Harding Playground." http://www.nycgovparks.org/parks/Q428/history.

———. "Lost Battalion Hall Recreation Center." http://www.nycgovparks.org/parks/Q401.

Pozarycki, Robert. "Ground Broken on Rego Park Center." *Ridgewood (NY) Times Newsweekly*, May 31, 2007.

Queens, Vol. 2, Double Page Plate No. 28; Part of Ward Two Newtown, Corona, Hopedale and Richmond Hill. The New York Public Library Digital Collections. 1901–1904.

Roberts, Sam. "Metro Matters; Forest Hills '72: Some Parallels to Queens Arson." *New York Times*, April 27, 1987.

Sciulli, Lorraine. "Return to Fairyland." Juniper Park Civic Association. November 27, 2009. www.junipercivic.com/latestNewsArticle.asp?nid=323.

Seyfried, Vincent. *Corona: From Farmland to City Suburb (1650–1935)*. New York: Edgian Press, 1986.

———. "Elmhurst: From Town Seat to Mega-Suburb. Queens Community Series. 1995.

Skillman, Francis. *The Skillmans of New York*. Whitefish, MT: Kessinger Publishing, 2009.

Sheftell, Jason. "LeFrak City in Queens Turns 50." *New York Daily News*, September 13, 2002.

Walsh, Kevin. "ForgottenTour 39, Newtown/Elmhurst, Queens." *Forgotten New York* (blog), April 18, 2010. forgotten-ny.com/2011/04/forgottentour-39-newtown-elmhurst-queens.

Strack Pond

Bendelow, Stuart W. "Biography of Tom Bendelow." The Cultural Landscape Foundation, May 15, 2007. tclf.org/pioneer/tom-bendelow/biography-tom-bendelow.

Colangelo, Lisa, and Tanay Warerkar. "Forest Park Carousel Gets Its Brass Ring—Landmark Status." *New York Daily News*, June 25, 2013.

Joiner, Bryan. "Strack Memorial Pond Unveiled after Two Years of Construction." *Queens Chronicle*, May 27, 2004.

New York City Department of Parks and Recreation. "Forest Park Highlights: George Seuffert, Sr. Bandshell." www.nycgovparks.org/parks/forestpark/highlights/12782.

———. "Parks and Recreation Celebrates Restoration of Strack Pond." May 19, 2004. www .nycgovparks.org/news/press-releases?id=18980.

Seyfried, Vincent. *Corona: From Farmland to City Suburb (1650–1935)*. New York: Edgian Press, 1986.

Jackson Pond

Ballenas, Carl, Nancy Cataldi, and Richmond Hill Historical Society. *Images of America: Richmond Hill*. Charleston, SC: Arcadia Publishing, 2002.

New York City Department of Parks and Recreation. "Jackson Pond Playground." www
    .nycgovparks.org/parks/forestpark/highlights/12235.
————. "Pine Grove." www.nycgovparks.org/parks/forestpark/highlights/19170.
Walsh, Kevin. "Myrtle Avenue Part 4, Glendale, Forest Park, Richmond Hill." *Forgotten New
    York* (blog), March 2010. forgotten-ny.com/2010/03/myrtle-avenue-glendalerichmond-hill-2.

Bowne Pond

Colangelo, Lisa L. "Vanishing Turtles and Fish at Bowne Park Pond Stir Up Poaching Fears
    among Residents." *New York Daily News*, August 17, 2001.
Koons, Cynthia. "Crackdown on Algae Clears Bowne Park Pond Waters." *Queens TimesLedger*,
    June 24, 2004.
New York City Department of Parks and Recreation. "Bowne Park." www.nycgovparks.org
    /parks/bownepark/history.
Rhoades, Liz. "Red Tide Algae a Problem at Bowne." *Queens Chronicle*, July 12, 2012.

Goose Pond

Ballenas, Carl. *Images of America: Jamaica*. Charleston, SC: Arcadia Publishing, 2011.
New York City Department of Parks and Recreation. "Captain Tilly Park." www.nycgovparks
    .org/parks/captaintillymemorialpark.
Reyes, Nina. "Winning a Round at Goose Pond, an Unlikely Battleground." Neighborhood
    Report: Jamaica Hills/Electchester, *New York Times*, November 14, 1993.
Shaman, Diana. "If You're Thinking of Living In/Jamaica Hills; Tranquil Haven for Many Ethnic
    Groups." *New York Times*, June 8, 2003.
Sheets, Connor Adams. "Community Fills Captain Tilly Park for Family Day in Jamaica." *New
    York Post*, October 4, 2006.
Weir, Richard. "A Pond by Any Other Name? Pea Soup." *New York Times*, July 25, 1999.

Crystal Lake

Kew Gardens Civic Association. "Crystal Lake." www.oldkewgardens.com/ss-beginning-0800.
    html.
Lewis, Barry. *Kew Gardens: Urban Village in the Big City*. New York: Kew Gardens Council for
    Recreation and the Arts, Inc., 1999.

Jackson's Mill Pond

"6,000 Old Cars to Be Sunk in East River Airport Fill." *New York Times*, June 29, 1929.
"E. H. Holmes Bankrupt." *New York Times*, February 3, 1940.
"Fight on Queens Airport Fails." *New York Times*, April 7, 1937.
First Presbyterian Church of Newtown. "William Leverich (1662–1677)." www.fpcn.org/history
    /pastors/10-history/26-leverich.
Helen Uffner Vintage Clothing. "Queens Scandal—La Guardia Airport's Rise from Infamous
    Gambling Den." uffnervintage.blogspot.com/2011/03/queens-scandal-la-guardia-airports-rise.
    html.
"New Holmes Airport Is Opened in Queens." *New York Times*, March 17, 1929.
"New Terminal and Tower at LaGuardia Airport to Be Dedicated Today." *New York Times*, April
    16, 1964.
Queens Cuisine. "Welcome to North Beach." www.queenscuisine.com/stories/NorthBeach.htm.
"Queens Plane Base Opened at Flushing." *New York Times*, June 16, 1929.
Rather, John. "Some Notable 'Firsts'; Firsts by Air." *New York Times*, November 15, 1998.

Linden Pond

Walsh, Kevin. "Corona, Crown of Queens." *Forgotten New York* (blog), December 24, 2005.
    forgotten-ny.com/2005/12/corona-crown-of-queens.

Shady Lake

Queens, Vol. 2, Part of Ward Two Corona Park. The New York Public Library Digital Collections.
    1901–1904.
New York City Department of Parks and Recreation. "William F. Moore Park." www.nyc
    govparks.org/parks/Q029/history.
Skillman, Francis. "The Skillmans of New York." Kessinger Publishing, 2009.

Alley Pond Park

"Alley Pond Park to Reopen Today." *New York Times*, September 2, 1940.

Ben-Yehuda, Ayala. "State Dredges Alley Pond for Highway Renovations." *Queens TimesLedger*, January 29, 2004.

Bockmann, Rich. "Alley Pond Environmental Center Saved Wetlands." *Queens TimesLedger*, November 19, 2011.

"Connolly Suggests Queens Park Site." *New York Times*, May 15, 1927.

Kilgannon, Corey. "In Obscurity, the Tallest and Oldest New Yorker." *New York Times*, March 27, 2004.

———. "Korean Word for Golf? Chances Are, You'll Hear It Here." *New York Times*, June 20, 2005.

"Mayor, Moses Open 2 Park Projects." *New York Times*, July 27, 1935.

McKay, Allison, and Bayside Historical Society. *Bayside*. Charleston, SC: Arcadia Publishing, 2008.

New York City Department of Parks and Recreation. "Alley Pond Park Adventure Course—Team Building Activities." www.nycgovparks.org/programs/rangers/adventure-course.

New York City Department of Parks and Recreation. *Natural Area Mapping and Inventory of Alley Pond Park 1987 Survey*. Prepared by the Natural Resources Group. www.nycgovparks.org/sub_about/parks_divisions/nrg/documents/Ecological_Assessment_Alley_Pond_Park.pdf.

New York State Department of Transportation. *Project Overview Long Island Expressway/Cross Island Parkway Interchange Improvement Project*. www.dot.ny.gov/regional-offices/region11/projects/project-repository/liecip/liecip.html.

Oakland Lake

Busch, Jennifer Thiele. "Without Prejudice: TEK Architects Designed the Kupferberg Holocaust Resource Center at Queensborough Community College." *Contract Design Magazine*, June 21, 2010. www.contractdesign.com/contract/design/features/Without-Prejudice-T-2319.shtml.

"College Site Weighed: Board of Estimate Inspects Golf Club in Queens." *New York Times*, October 8, 1959.

Duran, John. "Queensborough: A History of Pride." *Queensborough Communique*, December 2012.

Foley, Maurice. "$3,000,000 Is Paid for Queens Tract." *New York Times*, March 25, 1956.

"Girl Golf Caddies Agitate Bayside." *New York Times*, June 17, 1922.

Metcalf, Ronald Radoshfrank. "College Arrests." *New York Times*, May 14, 1969.

New York City Department of Environmental Protection. "DEP, Parks Department Complete Improvement Project for Oakland Lake Park." July 11, 2011. www.nyc.gov/html/dep/html/press_releases/11-55pr.shtml.

———. "Queens Adds Notch to 'Blue-Belt.'" May 29, 2012. www.nyc.gov/html/dep/html/news/dep_stories_p3-126.shtml.

New York City Department of Parks and Recreation. "Alley Pond Park Highlights: Oakland Lake." www.nycgovparks.org/parks/alleypondpark/highlights/12634.

"Oakland Golf Club Plans to Buy Links." *New York Times*, March 5, 1911.

"Oakland Golf Links Open." *New York Times*, April 11, 1897.

Golden Pond

Calta, Louis. "John Golden Left Estate as Park." *New York Times*, June 24, 1955.

"John Golden Park, Near Completion, Dedicated by City." *New York Times*, October 20, 1965.

Nagler, Barney. "Gentleman in the House on Corbett Road." *New York Times*, September 1, 1985.

"Philharmonic Draws 40,000 at Crocheron Park in Queens." *New York Times*, August 8, 1966.

"Queens Park Mapped: Street Chart Preliminary to John Golden Memorial." *New York Times*, December 25, 1955.

Gabler's Creek and Aurora Pond

Belluck, Pam. "Saving Salt Marsh of Remotest Queens." *New York Times*, August 8, 1995.

Douglaston and Little Neck Historical Society. "Bloodgood Cutter." www.dlnhs.org/neighborhoods/DouglastonHill/modules/residents/Cutter.cfm.

———. "Zion Church." www.dlnhs.org/neighborhoods/DouglastonHill/modules/highlights/ZionChurch.cfm.

Frank, Carol. "Shedding Light on a Forgotten Past and Protecting Sacred Ground." *Great Neck Record*, July 12, 2012.

Fried, Joseph P. "After Long Battle, Tract of Marshes in Queens Becomes a Park Preserve." *New York Times*, November 23, 1990.
Lauinger, John. "City Acquires 3 Acres of Udalls Cove." *New York Daily News*, October 23, 2007.
Mann, Joseph. "Prospects Good for a Marshland Park at Udalls Cove." *New York Times*, October 10, 1971.
———. "Udalls Cove Park Backed by Planners." *New York Times*, October 15, 1972.
New York City Department of Parks and Recreation. "Forever Wild: Udalls Cove Park Preserve." www.nycgovparks.org/greening/nature-preserves/site?FWID=33.
———. "Swamps in the City: Aurora Pond Restored." October 26, 2006. www.nycgovparks.org/parks/Q452/pressrelease/19822.
———. "Udall's Park Preserve: The Ravine and Aurora Pond." www.nycgovparks.org/parks/Q452/highlights/12027.
Webster, Bayard. "Neighborhoods: Marsh at Stake." *New York Times*, February 23, 1970.

Fort Totten Ponds
Bayside Historical Society. www.baysidehistorical.org.
FortTotten.org. "Historical Timeline." www.forttotten.org/Timeline.shtml.
Gaiter, Dorothy J. "U.S. Weighs Sale of Land at Fort Totten." *New York Times*, October 17, 1982.
McKay, Allison, and Bayside Historical Society. *Bayside*. Charleston, SC: Arcadia Publishing, 2008.
Stewart, Barbara. "From U.S. Fort to City Park." *New York Times*, February 21, 2000.

Potamogeton Pond
Berliner, David C. "State Joins Fight for a Pond." *New York Times*, January 25, 1976.
Montgomery, Paul L. "Conservationists Fight Desecration of Queens Pond." *New York Times*, November 2, 1970.
———. "Drive Is On to Save Northern Queens Woodlands." *New York Times*, March 21, 1971.
Walsh, Kevin. "Potamogeton Pond." *Forgotten New York* (blog), March 21, 2011. forgotten-ny.com/2011/03/5604.

Old Mill Creek
Bennett, Charles G. "Six New Sites Will Open Soon along Laurelton Parkway Stretch." *New York Times*, August 3, 1941.
Feller, Michael. "Idlewild Park HEP Priority Restoration Site." *Tidal Exchange Newsletter* (Summer 2005). www.harborestuary.org/news/TESummer05.pdf.
New York City Department of Environmental Protection. *Volume 1: Jamaica Bay Watershed Protection Plan*. October 1, 2007. www.nyc.gov/html/dep/pdf/jamaica_bay/vol-1-complete.pdf.
Walsh, Kevin. "Rosedale: The Beginning and the End." *Forgotten New York* (blog), October 29, 2005. forgotten-ny.com/2005/10/rosedale-queens.

Thurston Creek
Chinese, Vera. "City to Begin $70 Million Plan to Alleviate Flooding in Springfield Gardens," *New York Daily News*, August 21, 2012.
Feller, Michael. "Idlewild Park HEP Priority Restoration Site." *Tidal Exchange Newsletter* (Summer 2005). www.harborestuary.org/news/TESummer05.pdf.
New York City Department of Parks and Recreation. "Montbellier Park." www.nycgovparks.org/parks/Q396/.
———. "Springfield Park." www.nycgovparks.org/parks/Q107/history.
Walsh, Kevin. "Rosedale: The Beginning and the End" *Forgotten New York* (blog), October 29, 2005. forgotten-ny.com/2005/10/rosedale-queens.

Cornell Creek
"Ice Company's Nuisance." *New York Times*, April 26, 1906.
Marzlock, Ron. "Tragedy at Baisley Pond." *Queens Chronicle*, May 17, 2012.
Onderonk, Henry. *Queens County in Olden Times*. New York: Charles Welling, 1865.
Worth, Robert F. "At a Legendary Cemetery, a Rare Look behind the Gates." *New York Times*, May 22, 2004.

Hawtree Creek
"Bridge Load Lightened." *New York Times*, January 13, 1957.
LeDuff, Charlie. "Shaky House to 'Nut House' to Rebuilt Home: A Costly Trip." Neighborhood Report: Hamilton Beach, *New York Times*, October 12, 1997.

Lii, Jane H. "A Bridge Too Near, Too Narrow." Neighborhood Report: Hamilton Beach, *New York Times*, December 17, 1995.

———. "Evicted Again, and Angry." *New York Times*, June 30, 1996.

"Local Laws of the City of New York for the Year 1967." LaGuardia and Wagner Archives, CUNY LaGuardia Community College. www.steinway.lagcc.cuny.edu/FILES_DOC/Microfilms /05/023/0000/00001/052010/05.023.0000.00001.052010.11101967.PDF.

Rafter, Domenick. "Both 'Green' and 'Gray' Flood Barriers Explored." *Queens Chronicle*, October 31, 2013.

———. "New Ambulances for West Hamilton." *Queens Chronicle*, December 19, 2013.

Ridgewood (NY) Times Newsweekly. "Pol: Bergen Basin Must Be Cleaned." September 13, 2009.

Shellbank Basin

Benjamin, Andrew. "Goats Led to founding of Howard Beach." *Queens Chronicle*, November 11, 2010.

Cohen, Joyce. "An Urban Enclave with Prow to the Sea." *New York Times*, October 25, 1998.

Colangelo, Lisa L. "Howard Beach Relief: New Air Compressor in Shellbank Basin Will End Foul-Smelling Fish Kills." *New York Daily News*, February 6, 2012.

Marin, Matthew. "Renovations on First Phase of Frank M. Charles Park Begins." *Queens Chronicle*, July 11, 2011.

Marzlock, Ron. "Tragedy at Baisley Pond." *Queens Chronicle*, May 17, 2012.

Onderonk, Henry. *Queens County in Olden Times.* New York: Charles Welling, 1865.

Oser, Alan S. "Hot Dogs, Volleyball Courts and Waterfront Access." *New York Times*, March 19, 1995.

"Oyster and Clam Beds Halt Cross Bay Boulevard Work." *New York Times*, May 13, 1922.

"Plan to Build Boulevard across Jamaica Bay before Board of Estimate." *New York Times*, June 16, 1918.

Yurcan, Bryan. "Still Waiting after All These Years." *Queens Chronicle*, July 15, 2010.

East and West Ponds

"Blaze in Jamaica Bay Almost Daunts Firemen." *New York Times*, March 21, 1955.

Ferriss, John. "The Scene: The Raunt." *Life.* March 17, 1967.

Foderaro, Lisa W. "Environmental Group Proposes Options for Breached Pond at Jamaica Bay in Queens." *New York Times*, February 10, 2014.

Lucev, Emil. "A Further History of Broad Channel." *The Wave*, October 15, 2004.

Magoolaghan, Brian. "New Station Is Friend to Nature and Visitors." *The Wave*, June 15, 2007.

Prial, Frank J. "$300 Million Development Plan Offered for Gateway National Recreation Area." *New York Times*, September 23, 1976.

Rafter, Domenick. "Busted Pipe Ruining Broad Channel Lakes." *Queens Chronicle*, September 6, 2012.

———. "Jamaica Bay Walloped by Hurricane Sandy." *Queens Chronicle*, November 21, 2012.

All of Brooklyn

Armbruster, Eugene L. *The Eastern District of Brooklyn.* New York, 1912.

Bangs, Charlotte Rebecca. *Reminiscences of Old New Utrecht and Gowanus.* New York: Brooklyn Eagle Press, 1912.

Benardo, Leonard, and Jennifer Weiss. *Brooklyn by Name.* New York: New York University Press, 2006.

Newtown Creek

Armbruster, Eugene L. *The Eastern District of Brooklyn.* New York, 1912.

"Bridge Awaits a Name." *New York Times*, August 11, 1954.

Collum, Chase. "Newtown Creek Alliance Pushes to Cleanup Plank Road." *Greenpoint Star*, April 23, 2014. www.greenpointstar.com/view/full_story/24980803/article-Newtown-Creek -Alliance-pushes-to-cleanup-Plank-Road?instance=home_news_1st_left.

DeJohn, Irving. "State Seeking New Suitors to Build New Kosciuszko Bridge." *New York Daily News*, January 29, 2013.

Driscoll, James. "Garrit Furman." Juniper Park Civic Association, January 2014. www.junipercivic .com/historyArticle.asp?nid=71#.U3-PYXJdXEg.

Hamboussi, Anthony. *Newtown Creek: A Photographic Survey of New York's Industrial Waterway.* Princeton, NJ: Princeton Architectural Press, 2010.

Johnson, A. J. *Johnson's New Illustrated Family Atlas.* 1866.

"Mayor Opens Span with Peace Plea." *New York Times*, August 24, 1939.

Navarro, Mireya. "Newtown Creek Is Declared a Superfund Site." *New York Times*, September 28, 2010.

Newman, Andy. "A Tired Old Bridge Gets a New Look. No, Four of Them." *City Room* (blog), *New York Times*, February 18, 2010. cityroom.blogs.nytimes.com/2010/02/18/a-tired -old-bridge-gets-a-new-look-no-four-of-them/?_php=true&_type=blogs&_r=0.

"New Pulaski Span Will Open Friday." *New York Times*, September 7, 1954.

New York State Department of Transportation, and Federal Highway Administration. *Newtown Creek Navigation Analysis.* September 22, 2005. https://www.dot.ny.gov/content/delivery/ region11/projects/X72977-Home/X72977-Repository/appendix%20f.pdf?nd=nysdot.

Schneider, Daniel B. "F.Y.I. Mystery Island." *New York Times*, October 29, 2000.

"The Maspeth Improvement." *New York Times*, November 26, 1922.

Waxman, Mitch. "Approaching Locomotive." *Newtown Pentacle*, March 21, 2012. newtownpen tacle.com/2012/03/21/approaching-locomotive.

———. "DUMABO—Down under the Metropolitan Avenue Bridge Onramp." *Newtown Pentacle*, September 9, 2012. newtownpentacle.com/2009/09/09/dumabo-down-under-the -metropolitan-avenue-bridge-onramp.

Wilson, H. M. *State of New York—Represented by the Department of Public Works. Brooklyn Quad-rangle.* 1888.

Gowanus Canal

Bonislawski, Adam. "With Its Namesake Canal Finally Getting Clean, Gowanus Grows." *New York Post*, February 5, 2014.

Bridges of NYC. "Carroll Street Bridge." March 8, 2010. www.bridgesnyc.com/2010/03/ carroll-street-bridge.

Brooklyn Daily Eagle. "Work on the Carroll Street Bridge Completed." September 26, 1889.

"Celebrate Clean-up of Gowanus Canal." *New York Times*, June 22, 1911.

Chan, Sewell. "No Offense Intended, J. J. Byrne." *City Room* (blog), *New York Times*, December 3, 2008. cityroom.blogs.nytimes.com/2008/12/03/no-offense-intended-j-j-byrne/?_php=true &_type=blogs&_r=0.

Environmental Protection Administration. "Self-Guided Walking Tour of the Gowanus Canal." www.epa.gov/region2/superfund/npl/gowanus/pdf/tour_gowanuscanal.pdf.

Gray, Christopher. "Getting a Landmark in Shape for Its 100th Birthday." *New York Times*, May 21, 1989.

Higgins, Charles. "Brooklyn and Gowanus in History. The Battle of Long Island." *Kings County Historical Society Magazine*, August 1916.

Musumeci, Natalie. "Sneak Peek inside Gowanus Whole Foods, the Company's First Brooklyn Store." *New York Daily News*, December 15, 2013.

Newman, Andy. "The Hard Decision Not to Rescue an Ailing Dolphin." *City Room* (blog), *New York Times*, January 26, 2013. cityroom.blogs.nytimes.com/2013/01/26/the-hard -decision-not-to-rescue-an ailing dolphin/?smid-tw-share.

Bushwick Creek

Berger, Joseph. "Brooklyn Waterfront Plans Threaten Dream to Honor a Warship in Brooklyn." *New York Times*, March 30, 2013.

Brooklyn Daily Eagle. "A Fact a Day about Brooklyn." January 21, 1941.

———. "Greenpoint Growing." March 21, 1909.

New York Times. "Rum Runner Seized with $250,000 Load." August 17, 1924.

———. "Stampede of Texas Steers." September 27, 1893.

Wallabout Creek

Berner, Thomas F. *Brooklyn Navy Yard.* Charleston, SC: Arcadia Publishing, 1999.

Furman, Gabriel. "A History of the City of Brooklyn: Including the Old Town and Village of Brooklyn, the Town of Bushwick, and the Village and City of Williamsburgh." 1824.

———. "Hundreds Attend Ceremonies Marking End of Old Brooklyn Market Where 58,000-Ton Warships Will Be Constructed Soon." June 15, 1941.

"Schaefer to Close Its Brewery Here." *New York Times*, January 23, 1976.

"Seek Cob Dock Removal." *New York Times*, January 29, 1904.

"Wallabout Canal." *New York Times*, February 27, 1855.

All of southern Brooklyn
Hendrick, Daniel M. *Jamaica Bay*. Charleston, SC: Arcadia Publishing, 2006.

Coney Island Creek
Blau, Reuven. "City Seeks Experts to Study Flood Prevention Ideas in Spots near Coney Island Creek in Response to Hurricane Sandy." *New York Daily News*, May 19, 2014.
Duffy, Peter. "For a Beloved Old Enclave, the End of the Road." Neighborhood Report, White Sands, *New York Times*, April 9, 2000.
Moynihan, Colin "In Coney Island Creek, Hulk of a Yellow Submarine Sticks Out." *New York Times*, November 9, 2007.
New York City Economic Development Corporation. *Coney Island Creek Tidal Barrier and Wetlands Feasibility Study*. November 19, 2014. www.nycedc.com/project/coney-island-creek.
Walsh, Kevin. "The Yellow Submarine of Coney Island Creek." *Forgotten New York* (blog), September 2006. forgotten-ny.com/2006/09/the-yellow-submarine-of-coney-island-creek-part-1.
———. "White Sands, Brooklyn." *Forgotten New York* (blog), October 29, 2007. forgotten-ny.com/1999/10/white-sands-brooklyn.

Sheepshead Bay
"$1,618,114 Is Awarded for Condemned Land." *New York Times*, March 5, 1936.
"F.W.I.L. Lundy Brothers Restaurant Building." *NYC Landmarks Preservation Commission* (report). March 3, 1992. www.neighborhoodpreservationcenter.org/db/bb_files/92-LUNDY-BROS.pdf.
Merlis, Brian, Lee Rosenberg, and Stephen Miller. "Brooklyn's Gold Coast: The Sheepshead Bay Communities." Sheepshead Bay Historical Society, 1997.
Mindlin, Alex. "On the Waterfront, Locked Gates and Grumbling." *New York Times*, June 8, 2008.
"To Honor Anniversary: Old Timers' Dinner Tonight to Start Celebration at Varuna Boat Club." *New York Times*, July 27, 1926.
Walsh, Kevin. "Sheepshead Bay, Brooklyn, Part 2." *Forgotten New York* (blog), April 2006. forgotten-ny.com/2006/04/sheepshead-bay-brooklyn-part-2.
Williams, Keith. "Sheepshead Bay: Built on the Bay of Kings." *The Weekly Nabe* (blog), August 27, 2012. theweeklynabe.com/2012/08/27/sheepshead-bay-brooklyn-history.

Plumb Beach Channel
"1,000 with Shovels Win Feud with City." *New York Times*, December 4, 1933.
"Armed U.S. Troopers Take Plum Island." *New York Times*, May 17, 1909.
Brooklyn Daily Eagle. "Plum Island's History." June 28, 1891.
Cohen, Joyce. "If You're Thinking of Living In/Gerritsen Beach: Secluded Peninsula in South Brooklyn." *New York Times*, March 3, 2002.
"Ferry Trip to Plum Beach Shortest Five-Cent Ride." *New York Times*, October 12, 1924.
"Home Building in Gerritsen Beach." *New York Times*, April 3, 1927.
LeDuff, Charlie. "A Hop, and Another, and a Lucky Library Lands on Home." *New York Times*, May 25, 1997.
Lowenthal, Zvi. "Gerritsen Beach Volunteers Keep the Lid on Fires in Area." *New York Times*, October 15, 1972.
Rush, Alex. "Life's a Kiddie Beach." *New York Post*, June 11, 2011.

Gerritsen Inlet
Bankoff, Arthur H., Christopher Ricciardi, and Alyssa Loorya. *Gerritsen's Creek: 1997 Archaeological Field Excavations*. New York City Department of Parks and Recreation, Historic House Trust Division. January 1998.
Borders, William. "600-Acre Marine Park Expansion Awaits Funds." *New York Times*, December 28, 1964.
"City Wins Verdict in Land-Fill." *New York Times*, June 22, 1949.
"Flatbush Avenue Growth." *New York Times*, June 24, 1917.
"Indian Relics Found in Brooklyn." *New York Times*, July 9, 1979.
"New Yorker Wins Olympic Medal for Marine Park Landscape Plan." *New York Times*, August 1, 1936.
"Relief Is Promised Marine Park Area." *New York Times*, July 29, 1948.
"Walker Favors Lay as Park Designer." *New York Times*, May 13, 1931.

Weisman, Steven R. "Neighborhoods: Serenity of Marine Park Is Periled." *New York Times*, September 4, 1970.

Mill Basin
Behar, Ely Maxim. "The Oldest Dutch Farmhouse in New York City." *New York Times*, June 22, 1923.
Bennett, Charles G. "City Set to Pave Mill Basin Roads." *New York Times*, September 2, 1964.
Chaban, Matt. "Want to Buy the Top Mansion in Brooklyn? It's Just $30M." *New York Daily News*, October 27, 2013.
"City Planning Unit Bars Mill Basin Development." *New York Times*, September 24, 1970.
Cohen, Mark Francis. "Kings Plaza at the Crossroads." *New York Times*, December 1, 1996.
Hudson, Edward. "Residents Block Brooklyn Roads." *New York Times*, September 12, 1970.
Hughes, C. J. "Mill's Long Gone, but the Basin's Still Full." *New York Times*, May 3, 2009.
"Mill Basin Development: Great Tract Available for Factory and Home Improvement." *New York Times*, February 20, 1916.
"Mill Basin Tract to Be Home Site." *New York Times*, June 24, 1956.
Radomsky, Rosalie R. "If You're Thinking of Living In/Mill Basin." *New York Times*, March 17, 1991.
"Schenck House, Built in 1656, Is Offered to City for $10,000." *New York Times*, November 22, 1924.
"Shopping Plaza and Marina Are Dedicated in Brooklyn." *New York Times*, July 9, 1968.

Paerdegat Basin
"Brooklyn 'Forest' Is Site for Homes." *New York Times*, May 19, 1940.
Calder, Rich. "$15M Canarsie Wetlands Cleanup Plan on Track." *New York Post*, January 8, 2010.
Crowell, Paul. "A New Community Proposed by City." *New York Times*, June 4, 1962.
"Flatbush Schools Propose Stadium: Would Erect Community Center on Paerdegat Woods Tract Owned by Water Company." *New York Times*, June 22, 1947.
Furlong, James R. "Canarsie Corners the Canoe-Kayak Cult." *New York Times*, April 23, 1972.
"New-Fangled H2O Divides Flatbush Folks but Area Will Get City Water on June 30." *New York Times*, June 19, 1947.
New York City Department of Environmental Protection. *Paerdegat Basin CSO Facility*. www.nyc.gov/html/dep/html/press_releases/11-36pr.shtml.
"Pushes Port Plans for Jamaica Bay." *New York Times*, October 22, 1930.
Schultz, Paul. "Paddle Pushers: Kayaking in NYC an Easy Way to Float Your Boat." *New York Daily News*, July 10, 2010.
"Start Brooklyn Housing: Ground to Be Broken Tomorrow on Old Water Works Site." *New York Times*, January 11, 1949.
Walsh, Kevin. "Brooklyn's Last Frontier." *Forgotten New York* (blog), November 22, 2008. forgotten-ny.com/2008/11/bergen-beach-georgetown-brooklyn.
Williams, Keith. "'Aqua Flatbush': The Flatbush Water Works Company." *The Weekly Nabe* (blog), December 14, 2012. theweeklynabe.com/2012/12/14/aqua-flatbush-brooklyn-the-flatbush-water-works-company.

Fresh Creek
Fried, Joseph P. "Planners Preparing for Starrett City's Tenants." *New York Times*, October 13, 1974.
———. "People Move In, and Starrett City Is Homey at Last." *New York Times*, May 23, 1976.
"Youth Found Slain, Buried in Sand Pit." *New York Times*, July 20, 1934.

Hendrix Creek
Brustein, Joshua. "In City Waters, Beds (and a Job) for Oysters." *New York Times*, February 24, 2008.

Spring Creek (Old Mill Creek)
Brooklyn Daily Eagle. "A View of the Old Mill." August 15, 1886.
Chang, Kenneth. "A Wooded Prairie Springs from a Site Once Piled High with Garbage." *New York Times*, September 6, 2009.
Dillon, Nancy, and Adam Lisberg. "A Road Full of Bodies and Secrets." *New York Daily News*, March 2, 2006.
Farrell, Bill. "Landfill May Flower as a Nature Site." *New York Daily News*, July 30, 2003.

Kolbert, Elizabeth. "Key City Landfill Is Forced to Close, Adding Pressure to Find Alternatives." *New York Times*, December 26, 1985.

Kurutz, Steven. "Student Is the Latest Victim to End Up in Swampland." *New York Times*, March 12, 2006.

Walsh, Kevin. "Old Mill Road, New Lots." *Forgotten New York* (blog), November 7, 2014. forgot ten-ny.com/2014/11/old-mill-road-new-lots.

Wilner, Anne. "Weeds among the Graves, and Dismay among the Survivors." *New York Times*, August 15, 2008.

Prospect Park Waterways

Berenson, Richard J., and Neil DeMause. *Complete and Illustrated Guidebook to Prospect Park and the Brooklyn Botanic Garden*. New York: Silver Lining Books, 2001.

Blau, Reuven. "What a relief! Green Latrine Planned for Brooklyn's Prospect Park Will Convert Waste to Plant Fertilizer." *New York Daily News*, March 18, 2013.

Colley, Andrew. *Prospect Park: Olmsted and Vaux's Brooklyn Masterpiece*. Princeton, NJ: Princeton Architectural Press, 2013.

Hays, Elizabeth. "Prospect Park Boss Tupper Thomas Capping Career with $70 Million Lakeside Center with Music Island." *New York Daily News*, April 11, 2010.

Martin, Douglas. "Prospect Park's Ravine Inching Closer to Past." *New York Times*, September 14, 1998.

Newman, Andy. "Where Rink Now Stands an Isle Is Planned." *City Room* (blog), *New York Times*, December 10, 2009. cityroom.blogs.nytimes.com/2009/12/10/where-rink-now-stands-an-isle-is-planned/?_r=0.

Tolchin, Martin. "Boathouse Saved at Prospect Park." *New York Times*, December 11, 1964.

Walsh, Kevin. "The Bridges of Prospect Park." *Forgotten New York* (blog), August 16, 2001. forgotten-ny.com/2001/08/the-bridges-of-prospect-park.

Walsh, Kevin. "The Secrets of Prospect Park." *Forgotten New York* (blog), May 30, 2005. forgotten-ny .com/2005/05/secrets-of-prospect-park.

Green-Wood Cemetery

"Green Wood Cemetery." *New York Times*, June 7, 1868.

Ridgewood Reservoir

Brady, Emily. "Brooklyn-Queens Up Close: Amid the Willows and Chickadees, Bird-Watchers Spot a Red Flag." *New York Times*, November 25, 2007.

Colangelo, Lisa L. "Ridgewood Reservoir Could Keep Its Wild Appeal under New State Plan." *New York Daily News*, September 4, 2014.

Kilgannon, Corey. "As Old Reservoir Becomes a Park, a Camper Gets an Eviction Notice." *New York Times*, July 8, 2004.

Ridgewood (NY) Times Newsweekly. "Our Neighborhood the Way It Was." January 21, 2010.

Thompson, William C. Jr., and Robert F. Kennedy Jr. "A Wilderness, Lost in the City." *New York Times*, May 29, 2008.

"Wounded Near Her Husband's Grave." *New York Times*, March 21, 1884.

Dyker Beach Park

"An Ideal Spot for a Home." *Wall Street Journal*, October 24, 1899.

Japanese Hill-and-Pond Garden

The Architect's Newspaper. "Planting the Seeds." June 10, 2015.

Brooklyn Daily Eagle. "Replica of Japanese Garden a Feature of Brooklyn botanical display." July 10, 1915.

Brooklyn Life and Activities of Long Island Society. "The Japanese Garden at the Brooklyn Botanic Garden." July 26, 1930.

"Japanese Garden Open for Season." *Brooklyn Daily Eagle*, June 1, 1934.

"Japanese Garden Reopens at Botanic." *Brooklyn Daily Eagle*, June 7, 1931.

Raver, Anne. "Human Nature: Revealing a Japanese Garden As Serene Melting Pot." *New York Times*, May 18, 2000.

Mount Prospect Reservoir

Kingsley, Charles F. Letter to the editor. *New York Times*, May 7, 1934.

Kirkwood, James Pugh. *Brooklyn Water Works and Sewers: A Descriptive Memoir*, pp. 44–58. New York: D. Van Nostrand, 1867.

"Moses Studies Reservoir Site." *Brooklyn Daily Eagle*, March 30, 1934.

"Park Plan Site for Rear Area of New Library." *Brooklyn Daily Eagle*, February 25, 1938.

"Reservoir Site Now Likely from B'klyn College." *Brooklyn Daily Eagle*, July 5, 1931.

Sunset Park Pond

"Brooklyn's Sunset Park." *New York Times*, August 5, 1894.

"Mayor Opens Pool in Brooklyn Park." *New York Times*, July 21, 1936.

"Safe Places to Go Swimming." *Brooklyn Daily Eagle*, March 2, 1936.

"Work on Sunset Park Swimming Pool Will Begin Soon." *Brooklyn Daily Eagle*, October 10, 1934.

All of Staten Island

Atlas of Staten Island, Richmond County, New York, from Official Records and Surveys; Compiled and Drawn by F. W. Beers. New York: J. B. Beers & Co., 1874.

Beers' New Map of Staten Island from Careful Surveys. New York: J. B. Beers & Co., 1887.

Bromley, George W., and Walter S. Bromley. *Atlas of The City of New York—Borough of Richmond, Staten Island*. G. W. Bromley & Company, 1917.

Leng, Charles W., and William T. Davis. *Staten Island and Its People*. New York: Lewis Historical Publishing Company, 1930.

Morris, Ira K. *Morris's Memorial History of Staten Island*. Vol. 1. New York: Memorial Publishing Company, 1898. www.statenislandhistory.com/old-town-names.html.

———. *Morris's Memorial History of Staten Island*. Vol. 2. 1900.

New York City Board of Public Improvements, Topographical Bureau. *Proposed General Map of the Borough of Richmond (Staten Island) in the City of New York*. 1901.

Smith, Dorothy Valentine. "Ice Harvesting." *The Staten Island Historian*. Staten Island: Staten Island Historical Society, July 1938.

Soren, Julian. *Geologic and Geohydrologic Reconnaissance of Staten Island, New York*. New York: U.S. Geological Survey, 1988. pubs.usgs.gov/wri/1987/4048/report.pdf.

Walsh, Kevin. "Staten Island Streams." *Forgotten New York* (blog), September 13, 2009. forgotten-ny.com/2003/09/staten-islands-streams.

Clifton Lake

Peck, Richard. "A Touch of San Francisco on Staten Island's Shore." *New York Times*, February 10, 1974.

Brady's Pond

Beyer, Gregory. "Bucolic and Bustling, All at Once." *New York Times*, September 7, 2008.

Sherry, Virginia N. "Brady's Pond, Cousin Cameron's Pond, Dying Slow Death in Grasmere." *Staten Island Advance*, March 10, 2011.

———. "New Website Celebrates 'Best Kept Secret' on Staten Island." *Staten Island Advance*, June 5, 2014.

Eibs Pond

"Club Files Bankruptcy Petition." *New York Times*, November 14, 1935.

"Great Hospital Is Ready." *New York Times*, June 27, 1918.

Griswold, Mac. "Coaxing a Staten Island Walden Back to Idyllic Splendor." *New York Times*, September 3, 1998.

O'Grady, Jim. "Herons Replace Hoodlums at a Park with a Pond." *New York Times*, October 24, 1999.

Oser, Alan S. "Perspectives: Staten Island Development; Introducing a New Style in Tract Housing." *New York Times*, April 29, 1990.

Staten Island Advance. "Fox Hills Boasts World's Largest Army Hospital." March 6, 2011.

Silver Lake

"A Life Taken for a Life; Edward Reinhardt Hanged in Staten Island." *New York Times*, January 15, 1881.

"Apartment Planned on Staten Island." *New York Times*, February 3, 1940.

"Hebrew Free Burial Association Volunteers to Gather for Event at 10 a.m." *Staten Island Advance*, October 29, 2010.

New York City Department of Environmental Protection. "City Siphoned All its Engineering

Talent to Get Water to Staten Island." February 28, 2012. www.nyc.gov/html/dep/html/news/dep_stories_p3-113.shtml.
Salmon, Patricia M. *Murder and Mayhem on Staten Island.* Charleston, SC: The History Press, 2013.

Clove Brook
Bindley, Katherine. "The Secret Spring of Clove Lakes Park." *New York Times,* October 12, 2008.
Sherry, Virginia N. "10 Things to Know about Clove Lakes Park on Staten Island's North Shore." *Staten Island Advance,* September 14, 2014.
Silvestri, Pamela. "Staten Island's Natural Sunnyside Spring Closed Indefinitely." *Staten Island Advance,* August 15, 2012.

Harbor Brook
Barry, Gerald J. *The Sailors' Snug Harbor History.* New York: Fordham University Press, 2000.
Goldberger, Paul. "Architecture View; the Slow, Stylish Redesign of Snug Harbor." *New York Times,* July 5, 1987.
Sherry, Virginia N. "Staten Island's Allison Pond is Ecologically Sound, Parks Says." *Staten Island Advance,* August 23, 2013.
Slepian, Stephanie. "Staten Island's Goodhue Center: 100 Years of History and Service." *Staten Island Advance,* June 9, 2012.
Wrobleski, Tom. "Parks Finalizes Latest Purchase of Goodhue Property, Buying 11-Plus Acres of Bucolic Area." *Staten Island Advance,* July 28, 2014.

Factory Pond
Ishayik, Edna. "Uncovering Legacies in Staten Island's Neglected Graveyards." *New York Times,* February 21, 2002.
New York City Landmarks Preservation Commission. "John De Groot House." June 28, 2005. www.nyc.gov/html/lpc/downloads/pdf/reports/degroothouse.pdf.

Richmond Creek (Fresh Kills)
"Fresh Kills Bridge Open." *New York Times,* October 30, 1931.
"Fresh Kills Bridge Ready." *New York Times,* October 27, 1931.
Hack, Marjorie. "John Mitchell's Original History of the Greenbelt Has Been Expanded Upon in New Book." *Staten Island Advance,* January 25, 2012.
Newman, Andy. "From Landfill to Landscape, a Staten Island Cinderella Story Still Unfolding." *New York Times,* June 25, 2006.
O'Grady, Jim. "The Richmond Creek Bridge: Built, 1845; Future Uncertain." Neighborhood Report: Richmondtown, *New York Times,* September 17, 2000.
Wilson, Claire. "On an Island That's Worth Remembering." *New York Times,* August 17, 2001.

Clay Pit Ponds State Park Preserve
"Conservationists on Staten Island Score Plan to Fill In Wildlife Area." *New York Times,* November 14, 1951.
Fioravante, Janice. "A Staten Island State of Mind." *New York Times,* October 3, 1993.
———. "Neighborhood That Grew from a Clay Pit." *New York Times,* June 2, 2002.
SecretSI.com. "Kreischer Brick Works, 1874." March 16, 2012. www.secretsi.com/2012/03/16/kreischer-brick-works-1874.
Sherry, Virginia N. "10 Things to Know about Huguenot on Staten Island's South Shore." *Staten Island Advance* July 28, 2014. www.silive.com/southshore/index.ssf/2014/07/things_to_know_about_huguenot.html.
Stein, Mark D. "Sandy Ground's Place in History Secured." *Staten Island Advance,* February 10, 2001.
Walsh, Kevin. "Mr. Steinway, Meet Mr. Kreischer." *Forgotten New York* (blog), March 2, 2000. www.forgotten-ny.com/2000/03/mr-steinway-meet-mr-kreischer.
"West Shore Road on S.I. Is Approved." *New York Times,* February 22, 1967.
Wilson, Claire. "Small-Town Feeling and Coveted Schools." *New York Times,* May 4, 2003.
Wollney, Clay. "What Products Did Staten Island's Kreischer Brickworks Produce?" *Staten Island Advance,* December 30, 2014.

Willow Brook
Carroll, Maurice. "City Urges Preservation of Staten Island Greenbelt." *New York Times,* February 6, 1983.

Dugger, Celia W. "Big Day for Ex-residents of Center for the Retarded." *New York Times*, March 12, 1993.

Hack, Marjorie. "John Mitchell's Original History of the Greenbelt Has Been Expanded Upon in New Book." *Staten Island Advance*, January 25, 2012.

Newman, Maria. "Where Grim Willowbrook Stood, College Opens New Campus." *New York Times*, May 30, 1993.

New York City Department of Parks and Recreation. *Natural Area Mapping and Inventory of Willowbrook Park 2009–2011 Survey*. Greenbelt Natural Resources Team, July 2011. www.nycgov parks.org/sub_about/parks_divisions/nrg/documents/ecological_assessment_willowbrook .pdf.

Rohter, Larry. "On S.I., a Fight to Stay Green." *New York Times*, January 29, 1985.

Old Place Creek

Bagli, Charles V., and Eric Dash. "Staten Island, Start Your Engines: Nascar May Be on Its Way." *New York Times*, May 28, 2004.

Delaporte, Gus. "Proposed NASCAR Site on Staten Island Sells for $80M." *New York Observer*, August 6, 2013.

Kensinger, Nathan. "Bloomfield, Staten Island." *Nathan Kensinger Photography* (blog), December 31, 1011. kensinger.blogspot.com/2011/12/bloomfield.html.

McFadden, Robert D. "Buried in Huge Gas Tank after Staten Island Blast Dome Breaks Up." *New York Times*, February 11, 1973.

New York State Department of Environmental Conservation. "Old Place Creek." www.dec .ny.gov/outdoor/55210.html.

Satow, Julie. "Staten Island Property Puts a Nascar Failure Behind It." *New York Times*, October 29, 2013.

Shapiro, Rachel. "Contaminated Soil Not Coming to Staten Island Industrial Development Site in Bloomfield." *Staten Island Advance*, October 8, 2014.

———. "Staten Island Liquefied Natural Gas Explosion in 1973 Led to Decades-Long Ban in New York." *Staten Island Advance*, January 30, 2015.

"To Build Refinery on Staten Island." *New York Times*, June 13, 1928.

Bridge Creek and Goethals Pond

"3,692 Vehicles Use Arthur Kill Bridges." *New York Times*, July 1, 1928.

Bamberger, Werner. "New Bridge Opens over Arthur Kill." *New York Times*, August 26, 1959.

"Bridges to End Staten Island's Isolation." *New York Times*, September 12, 1926.

Cudahy, Brian J. *Over and Back: The History of Ferryboats in New York Harbor*, pp. 288–289. New York: Fordham University Press, 1990.

"Ferries Open Rate War." *New York Times*, October 27, 1931.

Fowle, Marcia T., and Paul P. Kerlinger. *The New York City Audubon Society Guide to Finding Birds in the Metropolitan Area*, pp. 123–126. Ithaca, NY: Cornell University Press, 2001.

Hutchinson, Bill. "New $1.5 Billion Goethals Bridge Will Provide Pedestrian, Bike Paths to N.J." *New York Daily News*, April 25, 2013.

"Name Bridge for Goethals." *New York Times*, March 28, 1928.

New York City Audubon. "Goethals Pond Complex." www.nycaudubon.org/staten-island-birding /goethals-pond-complex.

Oser, Alan S. "After a Rent Strike, Recovery at a Mobile-Home Park." *New York Times*, October 8, 1995.

Van de Walle, Mark. "Single-Wides in the City." *New York Times*, March 15, 2009.

Waldman, Amy. "On the Ground Floor of the American Dream." *New York Times*, January 31, 1999.

Mill Creek

Stein, Mark D. "It's Official: New Staten Island Railway Access for Tottenville." *Staten Island Advance*, September 27, 2012.

Tottenville Historical Society. "Richmond Valley." www.tottenvillehistory.com/History-Totten ville-Staten-Island-New-York/history-richmond-valley.html.

Yates, Maura. "Nassau S.I. Railway Station Platform Gets Shorter." *Staten Island Advance*, September 1, 2010.

Ohrbach Lake

Berger, Joseph. "A Celebrated Scout Camp on Staten Island Is in Jeopardy." *New York Times*, January 24, 2010.

Donnelly, Frank. "$6 Million Deal Will Help Save Most of Staten Island's Pouch Camp." *Staten Island Advance*, December 5, 2013.

Lee, Jamie. "A 17-Acre Secret." *Staten Island Advance*, July 10, 2008.

Sherry, Virginia N. "Noted Architect Ernest Flagg Left His Mark on the East Shore." *Staten Island Advance*, May 5, 2011.

High Rock Park

Dominowski, Michael W. "Unused Staten Island Overpasses Being Dismantled, and So Is an Era." *Staten Island Advance*, April 29, 2012.

Mitchell, John G. *High Rock and the Greenbelt: The Making of New York City's Largest Park*. Charlottesville, VA: University of Virginia Press, 2011.

Mount Loretto Ponds

Bachand, Robert. *Northeast Lights: Lighthouses and Lightships, Rhode Island to Cape May, New Jersey*. Norwalk, CT: Sea Sports Publications, 1989.

Lighthousefriends.com. "Princes Bay, NY." www.lighthousefriends.com/light.asp?ID=583.

New York City Department of Environmental Protection. *Minor Modification to the Final Environmental Impact Statement of the South Richmond Watershed Drainage Plans CEQR No. 01DEP004R*. April 17, 2012. www.nyc.gov/html/dep/pdf/reviews/south_richmond/minor_modification_mt_loretto.pdf.

New York State Department of Environmental Conservation. *Draft Unit Management Plan for Southern Staten Island: Mount Loretto Unique Area, Lemon Creek, Arden Heights Woods, Bloesser's Pond*. Prepared by Ecology and Environment, Inc., February 2009. www.dec.ny.gov/docs/lands_forests_pdf/ssiump.pdf.

Revkin, Andrew C. "Albany to Buy 145 Staten Island Acres." *New York Times*, October 1, 1998.

Walsh, Kevin. "Mount Loretto's Rock Sculptures." *Forgotten New York* (blog), September 15, 2007. www.forgotten-ny.com/2007/09/mt-lorettos-rock-sculptures.

New Creek

Benanti, Carol Ann. "Staten Island's Theater in the Woods Has Students 'In Tents.'" *Staten Island Advance*, May 20, 2012.

Brown, Dawn Louise, and Julie Abell Horn. *New Creek Watershed Phase IA Archaeological Documentary Study*. Prepared by Historical Perspectives, Inc., March 2011. http://s-media.nyc.gov/agencies/lpc/arch_reports/1328.pdf.

"Golf on Staten Island." *New York Times*, April 11, 1897.

New York City Department of Parks and Recreation, Greenbelt Natural Resources Team. *Natural Area Mapping and Inventory of Reed's Basket Willow Swamp 2011–2012 Survey*. www.nycgovparks.org/pagefiles/55/nrg-reeds-basket-willow-swamp-natural-area-mapping-and-inventory.pdf.

New York City Department of Environmental Protection. *Staten Island Bluebelt Drainage Plans for Mid-island Watersheds: Final Generic Environmental Impact Statement*. November 4, 2013. www.nyc.gov/html/dep/html/environmental_reviews/midisland_bluebelt_drainage_plan.shtml.New York City Department of Environmental Protection. *Staten Island Bluebelt, Mid-island of Staten Island's South Shore*. Prepared by Historical Perspectives, Inc., March 2011. http://s-media.nyc.gov/agencies/lpc/arch_reports/1327.pdf.

Ravo, Nick "New York State Buys 24 Acres for Preserve on Staten Island." *New York Times*, March 21, 1997.

⌐ *Acknowledgments*

Gratitude for information on the hidden waters of New York City goes to the many historians, journalists, and educators who have made it their business to tell their histories. In no particular order, the author has found inspiration in the works of Kevin Walsh, Steve Anderson, Carl Ballenas, Dan Hendrick, Eric Sanderson, Steven Duncan, Mitch Waxman, and Vincent Seyfried. I extend thanks to the editorial staff of W. W. Norton & Company for believing in this book. For articles and maps, the New York Public Library, Queens Borough Public Library, Brooklyn Public Library, New York City Municipal Archives, and *New York Times* archives have all been helpful.

The academic endeavors of Robert Buchanan at the New School, Tarry Hum at Queens College, Ted Steinberg at Case Western Reserve University, and Ron Brown at Touro College have also inspired me to pursue the subjects of urban history and geography in this book. Finally, my wife, Keren Iryna, and our daughter, Rachel Talia, who have patiently accompanied me on my travels throughout the city.

⤳ *Credits*

~ Index

Italics indicate illustrations.